THE FROZEN CHOSEN

The country around the Chosin Reservoir in winter was never intended for military operations. Even Genghis Khan wouldn't tackle it.

Major General Oliver P. Smith,
Commanding General, 1st Marine Division, 1950

THE
FROZEN
CHOSEN

THE 1ST MARINE DIVISION AND THE
BATTLE OF THE CHOSIN RESERVOIR

THOMAS McKELVEY CLEAVER

OSPREY PUBLISHING
Bloomsbury Publishing Plc

1385 Broadway, 5th Floor, New York, NY 10018, USA
Kemp House, Chawley Park, Cumnor Hill, Oxford OX2 9PH, UK
29 Earlsfort Terrace, Dublin 2, Ireland

Email: info@ospreypublishing.com

OSPREY is a trademark of Osprey Publishing, a division of Bloomsbury Publishing Plc.

First published in Great Britain in 2016.
This paperback edition was first published in Great Britain in 2017 by Osprey Publishing.

A CIP catalogue record for this book is available from the British Library.

Thomas McKelvey Cleaver has asserted his right under the Copyright, Designs and Patents Act, 1988, to be identified as the Author of this Work.

ISBN: PB: 978 1 4728 2488 2
       ePub: 978 1 4728 1438 8
       ePDF: 978 1 4728 1437 1
       XML: 978 1 4728 2099 0

21 22 23 24   12 11 10 9 8 7 6

Cartography by Bounford.com
Typeset in Adobe Garamond and Walbaum
Originated by PDQ Digital Media Solutions, Bungay, UK
Printed and bound in Great Britain by CPI (Group) UK Ltd, Croydon CR0 4YY

All images are from the United States National Archives and Records Administration and are in the public domain.

Front cover: (Top) Tanks of the 1st Marine Division, December 9; (Bottom) 1st Marine Division withdraws from Koto-ri, December 8.
Back cover: Marines move forward after a CAS attack, December 7.

Osprey Publishing supports the Woodland Trust, the UK's leading woodland conservation charity. Between 2014 and 2018 our donations were spent on their Centenary Woods project in the UK.

To find out more about our authors and books visit **www.ospreypublishing.com**. Here you will find extracts, author interviews, details of forthcoming events and the option to sign up for our newsletter.

CONTENTS

List of Maps	*6*
List of Illustrations	*7*
Prologue	*10*
Introduction	*18*
CHAPTER ONE: Brother's Keeper	24
CHAPTER TWO: Background to War in the Land of The Morning Calm	31
CHAPTER THREE: The Wages of Hubris	57
CHAPTER FOUR: The Fatal Decision	121
CHAPTER FIVE: First Contact	161
CHAPTER SIX: Where is the Enemy?	202
CHAPTER SEVEN: The Chinese Attack	231
CHAPTER EIGHT: Holding On	261
CHAPTER NINE: Breakout	292
CHAPTER TEN: "Retreat, Hell, We're Just Attacking in a New Direction!"	309
CHAPTER ELEVEN: Evacuation	333
CHAPTER TWELVE: Aftermath	344
Bibliography	*380*
Index	*384*

LIST OF MAPS

The North Korean Invasion, June 25, 1950   61
The Pusan Perimeter, August 5 to September 17, 1950   98
The Inchon Landing   101
The Drive to Seoul, September 15–27, 1950   136
The Chinese Attack, November 25, 1950   233
The Battle of the Chosin Reservoir,
    November 27–28, 1950   265

LIST OF ILLUSTRATIONS

Marines advance past a destroyed tank, September 3.

Marines of a forward element pursue the enemy, September 17.

Maj-Gen O. P. Smith and Vice Admiral J. H. Doyle.

PFC Thomas Martell looks at a dead North Korean soldier, October 13.

LCVPs, amtracs, and DUKWs at Wonsan.

Wonsan: Maj-Gen Wallace, Lt-Gen Shepherd, Maj-Gen Smith, Maj-Gen Almond, and Maj-Gen Harris.

F4U Corsairs at Wonsan Airfield, November 2.

Wonsan Airfield – F4U Corsairs, November 2.

Chinese Communists captured by 1st ROK Corps, November 3.

H Battery, 11th Marines, run their guns forward, November 5.

Captured SU-76 tanks, November 5.

A tank of B Company fords a stream, November 10.

Technical Sergeant Patrick J. Duggan of the 7th Marines, November 17.

1st Tank Battalion on the way to Chosin, November 19.

Crewmen aboard USS *Badoeng Straits* arming an F4U-4 Corsair, November 21.

Brig-Gen Kiefer, Brig-Gen Hodes, Maj-Gen Almond, Maj-Gen Barr, and Col Powell Look across the Yalu to

Manchuria, November 21.

Gen MacArthur and Gen Walker, November 24.

Marines of the 5th and 7th Regiments.

Marines at an observation point near the Chosin Reservoir.

1st Marine Regiment at Koto-ri, November 28.

21st Troop Carrier Squadron loading ammunition cases, November 29.

5th and 7th Marines reorganize at Yudam-ni.

Men of 1st Marine Division take a break, November 30.

1st Marine Division waits for mortar crews to destroy an enemy position, November 30.

Ammunition and supplies being dropped for the 1st Marine Division, November 30.

A tank offers support to Fox Company.

Fox Company, November 30.

PFC Ralph Stephens receives a blood transfusion, December 1.

Exhausted Marines resting, December 1.

A Marine F4U Corsair at Yonpo Airfield, December 2.

Crewmen rearming a Marine Corsair, early December.

A Marine Corsair drops napalm, December 6.

Marines move forward after a CAS attack, December 7.

Marines defensively arrange a tank and Russian-type tank destroyer, December 8.

Tanks on an icy road.

1st Marine Division withdraws from Koto-ri, December 8.

Bodies of US Marines, British Royal Marines and ROK soldiers, December 8.

Marine tanks at Majon-dong, December 9.

Grant J. Miller of 3rd Infantry Division, December 9.

Tanks on the road back from the Chosin Reservoir, December 9.

Marines in sub-zero weather, Koto-ri, December 9.

Marines march south from Koto-ri, December 9.

7th Marines arrive at a blown-out bridge near Koto-ri.

Chinese prisoners of Charley Company, 7th Marines, December 9.

Col Litzenberg with C Company, 7th Marines, repairs a bridge near Koto-ri, December 9.

Marines outflank a Chinese roadblock.

Marines of 7th Regiment leave Hungnam, December 11.

Leathernecks of the 7th Marines near Hagaru-ri, December 26.

1st Marine Division and fleeing Koreans, December 10.

1st Marine Division checks the baggage of refugees, December 10.

Men of the 5th Regiment, 1st Marine Division, board a transport, December 13.

Koreans await evacuation from Hungnam, December 19.

USS *Begor* at Hungnam, December 28.

PROLOGUE

United States Marines are special people.

As an Army soldier, I only suspected this for 27 years – and with occasionally a tinge of jealousy, I must admit. Then in 1993, a man I had come to know fairly well while I worked for General Colin Powell – General Chuck Krulak, then-Commandant of the US Marine Corps – asked me to go to Marine Corps Base Quantico, Virginia and take over as deputy director of the Marine Corps War College. I did. What happened there, in one sense immediately, taught me a great deal.

The immediate lesson came from my new boss, the College's director, Marine Colonel W. R. ("Rick") Donnelly. Rick called me into his office as soon as I arrived, shut the door, told me to sit down, and then told me he was dying. From that moment on, I began to realize I had probably never met a braver man. It's one thing to breast enemy fire – to go "Once more unto the breach…" – to overcome one's fear in a rush of adrenalin or in a deep and frenetic desire to help one's buddies; it's quite another to succumb to an ugly death in the middle of life, no combat, no sounds of the guns, just the creeping, inexorable death that comes from a virulent and incurable cancer. At the end, as Rick had wasted almost completely away before our incredulous eyes, he refused even to let his sixteen-year old son see him. He wanted his son, he said, to remember him as the strong, healthy, vibrant Marine he had been. I understood completely.

A week or so after Rick's funeral, I made a special trip, alone, to Arlington Cemetery, to kneel before his freshly-turned grave and thank him for the brief period he had let me know him. To this day, I still have his office nameplate, its brilliant red backdrop trimmed in bright yellow, secured in my home. He was a man I shall never forget.

The longer-term lesson was that I came to realize over time that part of this man's demeanor and its underlying character were a product of the US Marine Corps – its ethos, its history, and its incredible cohesiveness. The other Services in general have concluded that the Marines have the best uniforms; what most won't admit, though, is they have the best warriors.

In this book, Thomas McKelvey Cleaver tells a typical story about these warriors, this one in 1950 in the heady days of the massive incursion of China into North Korea at a place identified in the history books as the Chosin Reservoir. It is by no means "typical" in the sense that men throughout history have done similar deeds; they most certainly have not. Perhaps on a dozen or so occasions in the past 5,000 years have men performed in the manner of these Marines in North Korea. This story is "typical" of the United States Marine Corps because of those dozen or so stories, at least a quarter belong to them.

It is not a story of strategic and tactical genius such as that of Alexander; or of the harnessing of new concepts or brilliant maneuvers as did the best of the German commanders in World War II; or of subtlety, creativity and critical thinking such as I think we military professionals imagine in Sun Tzu's armies. Neither is it the fundamental determination of Wellington's men at Waterloo or of Mao Tse Tung's fighters on the Long March; nor Marlborough's brilliant ubiquity at Blenheim or Slim's artful craftiness in Burma.

It's in many ways indefinable; but the reader will recognize it instantly: like the old saw says about pornography, we cannot define it but we know it when we see it.

In this book the reader "sees" a Marine fighting in sock-clad feet in temperatures of twenty-below zero, with Siberian wind-chills pushing the cold far below even that, against seemingly insurmountable odds, all night long. Later, having miraculously survived the battle, he will lose all his toes to frostbite.

The reader sees a unit of 200 men dwindle to 150, then to 100, then to 85, then still lower, and yet maintain unit cohesion, unit integrity, sufficient to repulse a determined and out-numbering enemy again and again and again. All in weather so appallingly cold that even the imagination is incapable of conjuring it. Such actions give full confirmation to the Marines' iron-clad concept of "every man a rifleman." Cooks, supply men, truck drivers – it does not matter – every Marine is taught how to fight, how to use his weapons, and how to be the ultimate key to survival if necessary, or to be the last man standing or dead. Like the Spartans, they retire from the fray with their shield or on it.

The reader sees Marine pilots taking off from icy carrier decks pitching so violently in 30-knot winds and an abominable sea state that just getting off successfully is the severest challenge, only once off to penetrate fog and ice-filled cloud cover that restricts vision completely until one penetrates it on the way back down to deliver ordnance without which the Marines on the ground might not make it through another day (or night in some cases). I used to consider Army aviation as being close-knit with its infantry – as I was for over a decade an Army aviator, including in the Vietnam conflict, in addition to being an infantry officer – but Army aviation is not comparable to Marine aviation. Marine pilots live and die for their ground-pounding riflemen; they have no other mission, indeed in combat no other reason to exist. The Marine Corps instills this team-ethos deeply.

In this book, the reader sees so many acts of unparalleled courage that from time to time he or she has to unlimber the book, put it aside, and just stare into the near distance, contemplating what it must have been like, knowing full well that there is no way really to know.

Courage, tenacity, even audacity are all inadequate terms.

In contrasts as sharp as the weather around the Reservoir, the reader also comes to grasp just how different these Marines are from those surrounding them – soldiers of the Eighth Army and X Corps, both US and South Korean, and the enemy, in the opening stages of the Korean War mostly North Korean, but, later and predominantly, Chinese "volunteers."

Similarly sharp contrasts exist among US and allied commanders, from the very top where an almost God-like figure named Douglas MacArthur reigned in utter disregard of the facts – surrounded by sycophants who kept him well-oiled in that regard – to the bottom where task force, battalion, and company commanders and platoon leaders of all stripes and complexions saved the day.

I had had some experience, vicariously, of one commander of the former category.

X Corps commander, General "Ned" Almond, had come to my somewhat intimate knowledge through the many interviews of African-American soldiers I had conducted during the four years in which General Colin Powell had inspired me to investigate how consistently African-Americans had answered the nation's call to arms, when Powell was the first African-American chairman of the US Joint Chiefs of Staff and I was his speech writer. The purpose of these interviews was to help chronicle the many contributions African-American servicemen had made to the defense of the nation while at the same time being treated as second-class citizens, or worse. "Or worse" included, for example, coming home from World War I battlefields and having their uniforms ripped off their bodies by white men and, as they kicked and fought back against the mob, being summarily hanged from trees, their necks breaking and their life ceasing in the southern-style "I'll-teach-you-boy," lynching.

To a man these soldiers and Marines whom I interviewed detested Almond, either from direct contact with him or from word-of-mouth criticism of him that passed through their ranks. Almond had commanded the almost exclusively African-American 92nd Infantry Division in Italy during World War II. From Luray, Virginia, a graduate of VMI and like most such men at the time a racist, Almond claimed his division's poor performance in Italy was due to its being composed of African-American troops who, in his view, would never make good soldiers and should not be called upon to serve in this way again.

In North Korea at the head of X Corps, Almond proved the opposite: that the poor quality of his leadership was the problem. Cleaver gives ample evidence to this effect. For glaring example, as the Marines at the reservoir are being virtually surrounded by tens of thousands of Chinese soldiers, Almond is still demanding that they continue their attack to the Yalu River. He admonishes them not to be afraid of "Chinese laundry men."

Almond makes cameo battlefield appearances several times during the ensuing battles, arriving from his heated airplane or car, pontificating for a few moments, and then retreating to his heated airplane or car and ultimately to his quintessentially safe headquarters. Once he even brings several Silver Stars with him and asks that men be quickly selected upon whose tunics he can pin these high awards for heroism. Two of the men, officers who must listen to their commanding general and obey, are so pinned. When Almond is gone, they pluck off the medals and toss them in the snow in utter disgust.

Poor leadership and an uncanny ability to underestimate the enemy's capabilities are not limited to Almond either. Many readers will already be aware of Douglas MacArthur's grave lack of military leadership in occupied Japan. While concentrating on his role as potentate-in-chief of Japan, he completely neglected his troops. Easy sex, lax work schedules, and almost no training at all characterized post-war service in Japan. Most soldiers could not even shoot well with their basic weapon. When war broke out on the Korean Peninsula in June 1950, the US Army in Japan was as unprepared as any Army in US history, and that is saying a great deal.

MacArthur's negligence did not stop there. Most readers will be familiar with the five-star general's bellicose and even insubordinate language – language that finally got him relieved by President Truman – but his fundamental failings in understanding his enemies, interpreting his intelligence, and calculating the proper strategy, despite his brilliant counter-stroke at Inchon, sort of beggar the imagination. One has to assume, I feel, that senility was beginning to affect the 70-year old general; certainly an unbridled arrogance and proud nature were. Having reached my own three score and ten years, I can attest personally to the diminution in powers old age often brings.

Truman and Marshall bear some of the blame here, of course, because they tolerated the self-loving and increasingly politically motivated MacArthur for far too long. And despite his Hollywood-like reprisal after World War II, the chairman of the Joint Chiefs of Staff, General Omar Bradley, was not noted for his great battlefield talents either. Bradley was the Army general sitting in Spa, Belgium, 200 miles from his forward units, playing a game of bridge when the Germans counterattacked in the Ardennes Forest in December 1944, perpetrating the worst defeat and more casualties on American forces than in any other single World War II battle – and this after Bradley and others had been warned by frontline intelligence about clear signs of a German attack but, in their comfortable ignorance, chose to ignore the intelligence.

The mission creep, as we might say today, that in 1950 infected both Washington and Tokyo, however, stands out as the cruelest blow to the Marines and others on the ground in North Korea who had to endure the numerically astounding Chinese intervention in the war.

Washington's calculations were as lopsidedly wrong in late 1950 with regard to China's understandable fears as they are today with regard to Russia's concerns in Georgia and Ukraine. From 1993 to the present day, the US pushed itself and the NATO alliance closer and closer to Russia's boundaries as if nothing would happen in response. Then, when Moscow did respond, in Georgia, in the Crimea, and then in Ukraine proper, US leaders acted as if they were gravely surprised. Perhaps they – and the leaders in 1950 – were in fact surprised. That would be a strong indictment of their leadership. They should not have been surprised, not at all, and in 1950 many men paid the ultimate price for this negligence.

No, Truman and his secretary of state, Dean Acheson, his secretary of defense, George Marshall, and the Joint Chiefs of Staff do not fare well in this recounting of the Marines' story, if only by indirection. Unlike the deeply pragmatic President George H.W. Bush who in 1991 wisely decided not to "go to Baghdad", Truman and his advisors are eager to "go to the Yalu". And the fledgling United Nations is eager to exceed its own implicit mandate and bless such an enterprise. Thousands of men, on both sides of the conflict, paid with their lives for this hubris; so did thousands of women and children. The strategic result was of course a dividing line between the two Koreas at about the same location as when the rush to the Yalu began. If so many had not paid the bloodprice, the failure would be risible.

In this debacle of American and allied arms – for that is surely what it was (in fact, following the Chinese intervention leaders of all the allied forces were seriously considering abandoning the Peninsula altogether) – the performance of the US Marines around the Chosin Reservoir stands out like a towering volcano rising from a flat desert. This incredible performance, by America's most valiant warriors, is far and away the main story of this book. It is well-told, as such a story should be.

Lawrence B. Wilkerson Col. USA (Ret)
College of William and Mary
December, 2015

INTRODUCTION

I well remember the first time I heard the words "Chosin Reservoir." It was the summer of 1951, the Sunday after my birthday. The occasion was the visit to our home in Denver, Colorado, of Cousin David, who was someone in the wider family of Cleavers, Thomases, McKelveys and Weists I had not heard of before. My father told me Cousin David was "home from Korea." That was a word I had learned over the previous year, having been confused in the summer of 1950 as to whether we were fighting with North Korea against South Korea, as I had declared mistakenly to my best friend, to his laughter before he straightened me out. Then my father said that Cousin David had "been at the Chosin Reservoir." What was that? I wondered.

Cousin David, when he arrived in our living room later that afternoon with his parents, turned out to be not much older than the students at South High School who passed in front of our house during the school year, walking down Louisiana Avenue to the school with the tall bell tower five blocks west, as my friends and I made our way over to Washington Park Elementary, two blocks north of the high school. But there was something about Cousin David (who I would learn in later years was all of 19 at the time) that was different from those teenagers. He seemed somehow older than he looked. At one point in the gathering, I found myself alone with him and I asked, "What's the Chosin Reservoir?" I remember he looked startled for an instant, before he laughed and replied, "Kid, you don't want to know." An aunt came over at that moment and he was gone. But my desire to know "What's the Chosin Reservoir?" has remained with me for all the years since. I was never able to ask Cousin David any more questions, since he was one of the 33,686 Americans who died on the battlefields of Korea. I have taken every opportunity in the years since to ask anyone I met who was there the answer to my question.

My interest in the Korean War was enhanced by my good fortune in meeting ex-President Truman during the summer of my 14th birthday. I had traveled from Denver to Independence, Missouri, to visit my grand-uncle, Jim McKelvey, who had served with Captain Truman in the battery of Missouri National Guard field artillery he had commanded during the Meuse-Argonne Offensive in 1918, and who had spent the next 30 years as a political operative for Mr. Truman in Missouri and later in Washington. The second morning I was there, we went out for an early morning walk, and soon came across Mr. Truman on his traditional "morning constitutional." I was introduced, and President Truman asked us to join him. We ended our walk (and I had to work to keep up with him) at his home, where he invited us in for breakfast. I think I am likely the only member of my generation who can say he once ate a breakfast personally cooked for him by a former President of the United States. (For the record, it was fried eggs up, sausage and bacon, and toast with orange marmalade, still my favorite way to start the day.) While he performed the duty of chef, Mr. Truman closely questioned me regarding my knowledge of history, and I was impressed by both the breadth and the depth of his historical grasp. (For the record, I passed the examination.)

I have always considered Harry Truman to be America's last republican (small "r" intentional) president, and I freely admit that my account of the events of 1950 takes his side of the argument. I believe any investigator cannot do otherwise when they review the facts.

Historian Marc Bloch wrote, "Misunderstanding of the present is the inevitable consequence of ignorance of the past." In studying the experience of the United States in the Korean War, the truth of that statement becomes terribly obvious. One can see that the road to involvement in Korea was the direct result of complete ignorance of the history of Korea, combined with a total misunderstanding of the nature of the Communist countries, leading to a failure to understand that they would act in defense of their perceived national interests as would any other country. This failure of understanding is a feature of the policy decisions and strategic choices made by the United States throughout the Cold War and in the years since. The failure to learn the lessons of the Korean War led inevitably to the Vietnam War, which was also the result of failing to understand the history of Southeast Asia and thus have an accurate understanding of the real nature of the war we so blithely entered, the war I would serve in.

The United States has not won a war since World War II, primarily due to this failure to understand the true nature of the perceived enemy; indeed it can still be seen today in the so-called "War on Terror" that has involved the United States in endless conflict throughout the Middle East, in wars that were and are incapable of being won, at least in ways that Americans understand the word "win."

Americans pride themselves on being people who show their best selves in the worst of circumstances. Thus, the battle of the Chosin Reservoir in 1950 has assumed mythological status in the national memory, given it is the one military event of the past 70 years that wholly and completely fulfills this national mythology. It is my hope that the reader will come to the end of this book with an understanding of how the Chosin Reservoir campaign, which really does fit all the requirements for being considered a mythic event, was the direct result of American failure to understand the past in Korea, which led to misunderstanding of the present in 1950, with all the danger such failure and resultant misunderstanding involved.

The United States Marine Corps, in its official history *The Chosin Campaign*, states:

> Not a mile was easy. The road was narrow and winding. Of dirt and gravel, ox carts had a hard time passing, let alone tanks, trucks and artillery. At times, it seemed to go straight up; at others, straight down. And always around a hairpin curve where a roadblock could be waiting. Breaking out from Yudam-ni to Hungnam cost the United States Marines two hundred men per mile. It was The Corps' finest hour.

Former Marine Private Ernie Gonzales, who at 17 was the youngest Marine in Fox Company in the battle at Toktong Pass, was one of the 240 men who held the pass against the assault of five Chinese battalions to insure escape of the 2nd and 5th Marine Regiments from the reservoir. Twelve years after the battle, he wrote, in an unpublished manuscript that he entrusted to me 25 years ago:

> The fire of patriotism dies quickly. It is cold by the time the band stops playing and the flags are furled and the voices of the cheering multitudes are faint in the distance. By the time the rifleman gets to the battlefield, all the fanfare and cheering is forgotten. All that remains is a suspicion that the hysteria of the send-off was manufactured so that the stay-at-homes would buy another bond or give another pint of blood. The men of Fox Company were not kept in

the line of fire by patriotism. The men of my company fought and died at Toktong Pass because we were Marines. We did it for each other.

It is that element of sacrifice that elevates Chosin to the level of myth.

Twenty-five years ago, I first thought to tell this story as a motion picture. I began the research to write the screenplay, and had the incredible good fortune to discover that the late Ed McMahon of *The Tonight Show* was a veteran. Ed gave me his support enthusiastically from my first call to his office, most importantly taking me to the Reunion Convention of "The Frozen Chosen," as the survivors call themselves, which was held in 1989 at the Century City Plaza Hotel in Los Angeles. With Ed's enthusiastic introduction, I was able over the next year to interview several of the leading survivors, all of whom are now gone.

While there was initial interest in my screenplay about "the Marines' finest hour," that interest quickly waned when I mentioned that a major character in the story was the worst blizzard to come out of Siberia in a century, and that the best place to shoot the movie would be the mountains of the eastern Sierra Nevada, in the dead of winter. Enthusiasm for the project died like a balloon slashed with a Bowie knife.

Everything was reluctantly filed away, but the interview notes and the script itself stayed there in my files, reminding me over the years that there was a story I yearned to tell. Fortunately, during these intervening years, there has been much research published about the Chosin campaign, and the events that led to the outbreak of war in Korea. The US Marine Corps Historical Division has now published online its complete Korean War Project, allowing a researcher to access all reports by all Marine units involved in the entire war from the comfort of one's own office, rather than making a laborious slog through the national archives in Washington, poking through unidentified boxes. Full reports of the actions of Army units involved are also available in similar Army files, as well as the complete combat reports of the carriers and air units of Task Force 77 that supported the battle. The Chinese and Russian governments have now released documentation on cooperation between the Soviet Union, the People's Republic of China and the Democratic People's Republic of Korea regarding the outbreak of war and the Sino-Soviet intervention in the fall of 1950, also online.

It is thus now possible to take my collection of first-person interviews about the battle, and put these stories into a much wider, more complex, and more complete "big picture" of the events of 1950 than previous efforts to tell the story have done. Placing the events at the Chosin Reservoir in this wider context only makes clearer the greatness of this incredible event. This book is that story. The heroism is theirs. Any mistakes are mine.

Thomas McKelvey Cleaver
Los Angeles, California, 2015

CHAPTER ONE

BROTHER'S KEEPER

Snow squalls fell from the dark sky, covering the heaving whitecaps of the slate-gray Sea of Japan. The mountains of North Korea came into view in the distance as the six dark-blue F4U-4 Corsairs of VF-32's Iroquois Flight went "feet dry" north of the port of Hungnam. The rugged pine-covered mountains below were smoothed by snow drifts that might be ten feet deep. The six Corsairs made their way through a line of valleys, looking up at the cloud-shrouded peaks from their altitude of 500 feet over the rugged terrain. As they swept out of the last valley, the clouds broke to show the flat, windswept expanse of the desolate frozen Chosin Reservoir. It was Monday, December 4, 1950.

Iroquois Flight leader Lieutenant Commander Dick Cevoli banked north as they passed the ruined village of Yudam-ni, site of a deadly battle between the 5th and 7th Marine Regiments, 1st Marine Division and the Chinese "volunteers" led by Marshal Peng Dehuai that had only ended that morning as the 5th and 7th Marines successfully made their way through the 11 miles of Toktong Pass to the relative safety of the village of Hagaru-ri, site of division headquarters, a 96-hour battle that had cost the Marines 100 men per mile.

The Navy fliers' job that day was reconnaissance, to locate any of the Chinese forces that had ambushed the Marines at every strongpoint they had held in the reservoir the previous Monday night, November 27.

Cevoli glanced over at his wingman, Lieutenant George Hudson. Beyond were the two Corsairs of the second element, Lieutenant (jg) Bill Koenig and Ensign Ralph McQueen. The third element, composed of element leader Ensign Jesse Brown and his wingman, Lieutenant (jg) Tom Hudner, were slightly to the rear. As the Corsairs winged their way over another mountain valley on the far side of the reservoir in the Tae Baek Mountains, Bill Koenig dropped beneath Brown's Corsair. Suddenly his voice came over the radio: "Jess, check your fuel status."

Brown glanced down at the gauges to see the fuel needle dropping alarmingly. Ahead, the ridgeline rose above his flight altitude. As he pulled back on the stick and soared over the ridge, he felt the engine stutter, and the rpms dropped sharply. "This is Iroquois One-Three. I'm losing power. I have to put it down. Mayday. Mayday."

As Brown went through the drill of dropping his belly tanks and under-wing ordnance, wingman Tom Hudner pulled close alongside. "Okay, Jesse, I'll walk you through the list. Lock your harness. Open your canopy and lock it." Hudner saw the big bubble canopy on Brown's Corsair slide back. As Brown's nose dropped, Hudner warned, "Watch your airspeed."

The other members of the flight could only watch helplessly as the Corsair dropped toward a bowl-shaped clearing on the side of a mountain. Brown lowered his flaps and set up to crash land. On the mountainside, the shadows of the trees were growing longer in the late afternoon sun.

Hudner winced as he watched the Corsair touch down in a cloud of snow and plow across the field, throwing up a rooster tail of snow behind until it came to an abrupt stop, nearly into the line of trees that bordered the clearing.

The five surviving Corsairs circled as their pilots anxiously watched for a sign of movement from their comrade. Hudner circled lower and spotted smoke wafting from beneath the broken cowling. "Get out, Jesse! Come on!" There was still no movement below. Hudner later recalled, "Somebody was going to have to go down and help. Since nobody else was volunteering, I decided it would have to be me."

Hudner ditched his ordnance and tanks and throttled back. "I'm going in."

"Roger," flight leader Cevoli responded.

All was silent while Hudner set up for a carrier approach at minimum speed, flaps down. Lower... lower... lower...

As he saw the ground coming up fast, Hudner told himself: "This is really stupid, you know?"

"The ground seemed to rush at me as I hit, and then I was out of control, snowplowing across the field and hoping I was going to end up somewhere close to Jesse." With a lurch, the Corsair slammed around 90 degrees and slewed to a stop. As the cloud of snow settled, Hudner could see he was about 80 yards from Brown's smoking airplane.

Tom Hudner and Jesse Brown couldn't have been more different. Hudner was a graduate of the US Naval Academy, class of 1947, which graduated in 1946 due to World War II. A graduate of Phillips Andover Academy, he had spent the war years at Annapolis, where a fellow midshipman was future President Jimmy Carter. At almost 26 in 1950, he was the oldest of five children of a successful Irish businessman who ran a grocery chain, Hudner's Markets, in Boston. After two years' sea duty, Hudner had entered flight training in 1948 and become a naval aviator a year previously, in late 1949.

Jesse L. Brown Jr., born a sharecropper's son in Hattiesburg, Mississippi, in 1926, had traveled a more difficult route into the ranks of naval aviators. Enrolled in the Navy's Aviation Midshipman program after graduating with an NROTC scholarship from Ohio State in 1946, Brown became the first African-American ever to wear the Wings of Gold when he graduated from flight school at Pensacola in 1948. The Navy was at that time perhaps the least socially progressive of all the American armed services, with a career officer corps that was primarily southern in origin. Brown had his job cut out for him to gain acceptance.

Hudner and Brown met when they were assigned to VF-32 in early 1950. The squadron was then flying Grumman F8F-1 Bearcats off the USS *Leyte* (CV-32). Brown was recognized as the best pilot in the squadron, whether all his squadron mates wanted to admit it or not, when he took a wave-off at the last moment, added throttle too rapidly – easy to do in the Bearcat – and survived a torque roll less than 100 feet above the carrier deck. He recovered in full view of everyone and then made a textbook landing, cool as could be.

When war broke out in Korea in June 1950, *Leyte* was in the Mediterranean. When she returned to the United States for further deployment to Korea, VF-32 traded in its beloved Bearcats for the F4U-4 Corsair, a far more capable fighter-bomber.

Leyte returned to the Mediterranean, transited the Suez Canal, and crossed the Indian Ocean to join the Seventh Fleet in Japan. She arrived just in time to take part in the invasion of Inchon on September 15, 1950. From mid-October, the carrier operated with Task Force 77, providing close air support for the 1st Marine Division during its push up the east coast of the Korean peninsula after United Nations Supreme Commander Douglas MacArthur made the fateful decision to cross the 38th Parallel and "roll back" the Communist North Koreans. By mid-November, *Leyte* had been on station in the Sea of

Japan for five weeks, in what would be a record-breaking tour of 92 days before she returned to Japan on January 19, 1951. Her fliers were among the first to discover that the Chinese warnings about military intervention if UN forces approached the Yalu River, which formed the Chinese–Korean border, were not mere bluster. The airmen had seen the evidence: numerous large units crossing the now-frozen river in late October.

The Marines had arrived at the Chosin Reservoir, in the high country of the Taebek Plateau, during the second week of November. By then, they had encountered fresh enemy troops they were able to definitely identify as Chinese. Despite warnings from both the Marines on the east coast of Korea and the Eighth Army troops on the western side of the peninsula that they were encountering the Chinese Army in combat, Douglas MacArthur not only discounted the reports but stated for the record in a press conference at his Tokyo headquarters that Chinese threats to enter the war were not to be taken seriously, since the Chinese leadership knew that Chinese troops had never been able to stand up against well-trained Western armies. He went further, promising America that "the boys will be home by Christmas," with Korea fully liberated from the Communists.

On Thanksgiving, November 24, 1950 the Marines at Hagaru-ri, Koto-ri, and Yudam-ni, near the Chosin Reservoir, looked forward to MacArthur's promised "hot turkey dinner for every man in Korea." They were disappointed to be served hacked-apart frozen turkeys boiled but still half-frozen in the bitter North Korean cold.

During the early morning hours of November 25, the worst Siberian blizzard in a century swept over the Korean peninsula, dropping to temperatures lower than minus 30 degrees Fahrenheit and covering everything with heavy snow. The storm finally ended at dusk on November 27.

At 2200 hours, bugles blared out of the frozen darkness throughout the Chosin Reservoir as the Chinese Ninth

Army Group of the Chinese People's Volunteer Army (PVA), under the command of Long March veteran General Song Shilun, struck every Marine position from Yudam-ni, on the western shore of the reservoir, south to Koto-ri, near the top of Funchilin Pass. The Ninth Army Group was composed of the 20th, 26th, 27th and 30th Armies: 120,000 hardened veterans of the Chinese civil war organized into 13 divisions. Their orders were: "Wipe out the Marines to the last man."

Aboard *Leyte,* the dawn of November 28 had found the flight deck and aircraft coated with snow. For the next seven days, the pilots of all four squadrons in Air Group 3 flew multiple sorties in bad sea conditions with blowing snowstorms as they gave close air support to the Marines.

And then there was the recon mission of December 4.

Badly shaken from his crash landing, Hudner climbed out of his Corsair. As he recalled, "The snow was waist-deep, it was colder than I have ever experienced anywhere else, and at first I couldn't move. It took me over thirty minutes to cover the distance to Jesse's airplane, and I was damn near frozen stiff by the time I got there."

Reaching Brown's Corsair, Hudner discovered his friend's legs had been crushed in the crash and it was impossible to pull him out of the cockpit because the fuselage had broken in such a way that he was jammed in the cockpit. The Corsair was still smoking. Hudner piled snow on the cowling to try and stop the flames. Brown slipped in and out of consciousness from loss of blood as Hudner fought to free him.

The sun was going down and it was even colder in the shadows. Hudner ripped at the instrument panel in an unsuccessful attempt to pry Brown loose. Finally, a Marine HO3S-1 helicopter from VMO-6 arrived. Hudner and the pilot, First Lieutenant Ward (a World War II Corsair ace and Navy Cross recipient) tried to break the plane open with a fire axe. In the last light of day, when he had to go or die of frostbite himself, Hudner realized his friend had frozen to death in the cockpit. The helicopter lifted off in a cloud of snow and disappeared over the peaks to the east, leaving Jesse Brown and his Corsair in the frozen stillness.

In March 1952, Lieutenant (jg) Thomas J. Hudner Jr. became the only member of the United States Navy to be awarded the Medal of Honor during the Korean War, for his willingness to risk his life above and beyond the call of duty in deliberately crash landing to save his friend. His award was one of 14 Medals of Honor awarded for heroism during the Chosin campaign, more than have been awarded for any other American battle.

CHAPTER TWO

BACKGROUND TO WAR IN THE LAND OF THE MORNING CALM

The Korean War was entirely accidental on the part of everyone other than Kim Il-Sung, leader of the Democratic People's Republic of Korea. So far as the United States was concerned, it was the wrong war, in the wrong place, at the wrong time, against the wrong enemy. What began as a civil war between the two major political factions of Korea rapidly changed to an international war fought directly by the United States and by proxy on the part of what was seen as the real opponent, the Soviet Union, which supplied both North Korea and the People's Republic of China with the means to fight, limiting its direct involvement to the provision of air defense in the form of Soviet aircrew "volunteers." Korea was the last international war fought by large military formations on both sides, maneuvering and fighting in the classic manner used by armies for hundreds of years, ending in a stalemate reminiscent of the worst trench warfare of World War I. At the same time, it was the first "limited war," fought under the threat of an ultimate nuclear apocalypse, with both sides convincing themselves that their participation in this war would head off such a confrontation. The result was the spread of the Cold War from Europe to Asia, which would ultimately result in the American war in Vietnam in the following decade.

More importantly for the United States, the Korean War happened as the result of a faulty analysis of the enemy, one that would affect US decision-making and policies throughout the Cold War. That faulty analysis was the belief that Communism was monolithic and centrally controlled, and all Communist-ruled countries were puppets of the Soviet Union, unable to act without Soviet direction and approval. That individual states ruled by Communists might also have their own national policies and strategies that were the result of national experience, in which traditional national interests would be controlling factors, was declared impossible under the Communist system according to American policymakers from the outset of what became the Cold War. To an extent, this was based on knowledge of the operation of the Comintern before World War II, where Communist parties outside the Soviet Union were subject to political domination and control by the USSR, with dissidents expelled for failure to conform to the USSR party line, regardless of the negative influence of the pro-USSR party line on the national fortunes of any member party. It was thus a given for US analysts and policymakers that such control would continue when any of these Communist parties took power in their respective countries. Thus, the very idea that North Korean objectives might be the result of a 100-year struggle for national independence, separate to and even in opposition to decisions and policies of the USSR, was considered impossible.

This view of Communism as a monolithic enemy would be responsible for every mistake made by US decision-makers throughout the 44 years of the Cold War. The American failure to understand the true situation, i.e., that "Communism" as practiced in the Soviet Union, the People's Republic of China, the Democratic People's Republic of Korea, or any other nation ruled by a Communist party, was in practice no different from traditional national politics, so far as perceived national interests were concerned, put blinders on American decision-makers which resulted in political and military interventions around the world that did not in the long run serve the national interests of the United States. As with the Soviets, "dissidents" to this worldview were sidelined and marginalized by those who believed the "common wisdom," despite these dissident views being demonstrated by events over time to be more realistic. It is said that, in war, what you don't know can kill you. This was certainly true of the United States in 1950, when what was not known or understood about the enemy created the greatest military reverse suffered by American forces in the history of the country. From the outset of American involvement with Korea, the failure to understand Korean history and the influence of that history on contemporary events led inexorably to the events of 1950.

In truth, from the time of the Russian Revolution, there were always two "Communisms" at work in international politics. The first was "Communism" as defined by the Soviet Union following the success of the revolution. Through the design of Lenin in creating a system of "democratic centralism" in which a policy would be the result of internal debate and would be unquestioned once decided, and under the rule of Josef Stalin, which led to the totalitarian system known as "Stalinism," the Communist Party in the Soviet Union, and in the countries of Eastern Europe following the end of World War II were highly centralized, disciplined organizations in which the views and interests of the Soviet

Union were paramount and controlling. This was the "Communism" the United States opposed in Europe after the war as what became known as the Cold War took hold of international relations in postwar Europe.

The other "Communism" had more to do with anti-colonialism, and it was here that countries which became "Communist" were more likely to follow their ancient national interests as they became independent of the Western imperial powers. Many of the leaders of these movements embraced "Communism" because of the anti-colonial policies of the Soviet Union, and their own inability to convince any of the Western imperial powers to voluntarily give up their empires and grant national independence to their colonies. The leaders of these movements gravitated toward the Soviet Union for political and material support of their struggles, and in the process adopted the ideology of Communism, though it was a Communism that was in accord with their national struggle. Two good examples of this are seen in the careers of Mao Zedong and Ho Chi Minh. Both were essentially nationalists. Ho Chi Minh had attended the Paris Peace Conference at Versailles in 1919, in hopes of obtaining support from President Woodrow Wilson to prevail on France to grant independence to Vietnam in accordance with Wilson's Fourteen Points. When he was ignored by the West, he turned to the one political power that would provide any support, the Soviet Union. His adoption of Communism came through his involvement with the French Communist Party that had grown out of the French Socialist Party with which he had been associated when he emigrated to France as a young man. The Communism that would arise in Indochina was an expression of Vietnamese nationalism. Mao Zedong was born the son of a wealthy farmer in Shaoshan, Hunan, who adopted a Chinese nationalist and anti-imperialist outlook in early life which was particularly influenced by the events of the revolution of 1911 that led to the fall of the

Manchu Dynasty, and his experience as a university student in the May Fourth Movement of 1919, which was a nationalist movement that developed in opposition to increasing Japanese influence in China after the Japanese took over the former German-dominated territories of China during World War I. Mao converted to Marxism-Leninism while in university following the Russian Revolution. Throughout his career, however, he always perceived "Communism" through the prism of Chinese nationalism, which became most notable following the split with the Soviet Union over the leadership of the anti-imperialist struggle in 1959.

This was a "Communism" that American authorities did not recognize or understand. This lack of understanding that Communism in the colonized countries was not the kind of Soviet-style Communism that had been externally imposed as the result of Soviet victory in eastern Europe, and was not monolithically subservient to Soviet political control because these were genuinely independent countries founded by genuinely independent movements and not Soviet satellites completely dependent on Soviet support for their existence, would have profound influence on the events of 1950.

As will be seen, Kim Il-Sung, leader of the Democratic People's Republic of Korea, was more in the mold of the Eastern European Communist leaders, installed in power by the occupation authority of the Red Army in the postwar period. Yet, when it came to the national aspirations of post-colonial Korea, even this hardline Stalinist saw himself as a nationalist first and a "Communist" second.

Korea had been ruled by the Joseon Dynasty from 1392 until 1910. After two Japanese invasions during the first half of the 16th century, internal power struggles within the dynasty and peasant rebellions began in the late 16th century. The Korean monarchy sought military support from China, which became increasingly important in maintaining rule. Because of this, the dynasty developed and maintained a strict isolationist policy to all countries except China, which resulted in it being known as The Hermit Kingdom. By the mid-19th century, China was in no position to protect Korea, being unable to protect itself from foreign intervention.

American involvement with Korean affairs began in 1866, when the American merchantman *General Sherman* was destroyed in the Taedong River below Pyongyang and its crew massacred. Report of this tragedy resulted in the dispatch of a ship of the Asiatic Squadron, the USS *Wachusett*, under Commander Robert W. Shufeldt. Shufeldt's mission proved fruitless, but the incident led ultimately to a proposal in 1871 by Rear Admiral John Rodgers, commander of the Asiatic Squadron, that a naval expedition, modeled on that of Commodore Perry that had "opened Japan," be turned loose on Korea. The American minister to China was ordered to carry out the negotiation in cooperation with Admiral Rodgers. A force was assembled at Nagasaki with the objective of obtaining a treaty of commerce with the Korean government, and on May 30, 1871 five United States ships of war dropped anchor off the mouth of the Han River. Receiving no communication from the Koreans, the port of Inchon was invaded on June 10, with landing parties of US Marines and sailors from the ships overrunning the initial objectives without difficulty. The Koreans in the forts defending the port fought back, and the landing force was unable to advance toward the capital of Seoul, which was beyond the range of supporting naval gunfire. Though Rodgers had the power to capture the forts, it was obvious that doing so would not result in the Koreans acknowledging the American desire for a treaty. On June 3, 1871, honor having been satisfied, the Americans returned to their ships and the fleet returned to Japan without achieving its objective.

With the dynasty unwilling to modernize on terms the country could control, Korea was forcibly opened to international relations by a Japanese military force sent to "establish a treaty of friendship and commerce," which the defeated Koreans signed on February 26, 1876, opening their ports and granting Japanese citizens extraterritorial status. The Chinese advised the Koreans to establish relations with a Western power to balance the Japanese and suggested the United States, which alone among Western powers had shown no territorial desires in Asia. In 1880 now-Commodore Shufeldt returned aboard the USS *Ticonderoga* with authority to negotiate a treaty, though communication with the Koreans was unproductive. In July 1880 an offer of assistance was received from the Chinese viceroy Li Hung-Chang. With China and Japan currently at odds, Li wanted American aid in developing his navy. In exchange for such technical assistance, he promised to forward negotiations with Korea. Shufeldt proceeded to China, where advice and advisors were provided by the Chinese, and talks with Li commenced. A treaty of "amity and commerce" was finally signed between Korea and the United States on May 22, 1882.

The Japanese, enraged by this "American interference," took even greater interest in internal Korean politics, while Great Britain became interested in Korean politics out of a desire to limit Russian influence in the region, while the Russians countered the rise of Japan by further developing their Pacific port at Vladivostok. This opening of Korea also saw the arrival of American Presbyterian and Methodist missionaries, who were the first direct involvement of the United States with the country. By 1893, Korea had signed treaties with every major European power.

Japan destroyed the last influence of China over Korea through their victory in the First Sino-Japanese War of 1893–94. Following that Chinese defeat, an internal coup within the Korean monarchy led to a brief period of independence and reform known as the Korean Empire, which lasted from 1897 until 1910. Russia and Japan competed intensively during this period for influence in the country.

Following the Russian defeat in the Russo-Japanese War, Japan made Korea a protectorate through the Eulsa Treaty in 1905. Armed resistance to Japan came from an alliance of Confucian scholars and government leaders, Christians, traditional bandits and peasants, with the guerrilla army reaching a peak of 70,000 in 1908. The Japanese occupiers broke this resistance through full-on repression, with thousands of executions and imprisonments. Full annexation came on August 22, 1910 with the Japan–Korea Annexation Treaty in which the Korean emperor signed away his sovereignty. For the next 35 years, Japan pursued a policy of dominating Korea, which was considered part of the Japanese Empire as an industrialized colony along with Taiwan, in what eventually became the Greater East Asia Co-Prosperity Sphere.

In 1937, a deliberate policy of Japanese cultural assimilation was adopted by the Governor-General, General Jiro Minami. Use of the Korean language and study of Korean history, language, literature and culture was banned and replaced by the mandatory use and study of their Japanese counterparts. In 1939, the 23.5 million Koreans were required to adopt Japanese names under the "So-shi-kaimei" policy.

Many Korean nationalists fled the country after 1910. Korean resistance to Japanese domination became open in the widespread nonviolent March 1st Movement of 1919, which saw the foundation of the Provisional Government of the Republic of Korea that year with the support of the nationalist Kuomintang Party in China. Exiled Korean nationalists became active in Manchuria, China and Siberia, in a struggle that would see the leading figures from these exiled organizations become important political players in Korea following World War II.

The Provisional Government failed to achieve international recognition and failed to unite Korean nationalist groups, as the political struggle divided between the Provisional Government's American-based founding President Syngman

Rhee, and his followers, and Koreans still resident in Korea or in exile outside the United States.

Korean nationalists took part in the founding of the Chinese Communist Party in 1919, which led to the founding of the Korean Communist Party in the early 1920s. Domestically, Korean Communists with the support of the Comintern and the Chinese Communists became the primary agents of domestic opposition to Japanese rule for the next twenty years.

In 1939, Koreans were conscripted for work in Japanese war industries in Japan, and for service in the Imperial Japanese Army, with some 2.3 million Koreans serving in the Army and over 750,000 being sent to Japan for war work. During World War II, Koreans fought on both sides, with Koreans in the Imperial Japanese Army holding low-level positions, while a Korean army backed by Chiang Kai-Shek's Kuomintang and led by Yi Pom-Sok fought in the Burma campaign. A Korean Communist guerrilla movement fought the Japanese in Korea and Manchuria, while a substantial number of Korean Communists fought as soldiers in Mao Zedong's Red Army in Northern China.

All of this history and political activity was largely unknown in the United States, particularly at the higher levels of government. In November 1943, the Republic of China, Great Britain and the United States declared at the Cairo Conference that "in due course Korea shall become free and independent." The Tehran Conference saw Soviet leader Josef Stalin commit the USSR to enter the Pacific War after the successful conclusion of the war in Europe. At the Yalta Conference in February 1945, the Soviets committed to an invasion of Manchuria 90 days after the surrender of Germany. The agreement at Yalta foresaw a "government of national unity" being formed to control the whole peninsula, with both Soviet and United States occupation forces leaving afterwards. This initially was in line with the policy advocated before his death by President Franklin Roosevelt, who wished to see an end to empires in Asia, with a committee of Great Powers – the United States, China and the Soviet Union – awarded "trusteeship" over the former Asian empires of Japan, Great Britain, France and the Netherlands. During the "trusteeship" the dependent people of these countries would be "prepared and educated" for self-government. This concept found no support from the other Allies, including China and the Soviet Union, all of whom were following their own national interests.

As early as 1943, Far Eastern analysts in the State Department had expressed fear over Soviet objectives in the Far East once they entered the Pacific War, writing that:

> Korea may appear to offer a tempting opportunity to apply the Soviet conception of the proper treatment of colonial peoples, to strengthen enormously the economic resources of the Soviet Far East, to acquire ice-free ports, and to occupy a dominating strategic position both to China and Japan... A Soviet occupation of Korea would create an entirely new strategic situation in the Far East, and its repercussions within China and Japan might be far reaching.

In 1945, State Department employee Tyler Dennett laid out a particularly clear-eyed analysis of the future:

> Many of the international factors which led to the fall of Korea are either unchanged from what they were half a century ago, or are likely to recur the moment peace is restored in the East. Japan's hunger for power will have been extinguished for a period, but not forever. In another generation, Japan probably will again be a very important influence in the Pacific. Meanwhile, the Russian interest in the peninsula is likely to remain what it was forty years ago.

Quite possibly that factor will be more important than ever before. The Chinese also may be expected to continue their traditional concern in the affairs of that area.

Unfortunately, little attention was paid at the time to this most prescient analysis, since the American military was preoccupied with planning the coming invasion of Japan and was more than happy to let the Soviets deal with Japanese forces in Manchuria and Korea, which the Pentagon did not see as being of importance to American interests.

In the aftermath of the rapid Japanese surrender following the atomic bombing of Hiroshima and Nagasaki, with the Soviet Red Army moving rapidly through Manchuria against little Japanese opposition, the United States military suddenly became interested in the Korean peninsula, since they did not wish to see Soviet forces occupying the southern region opposite Japan. A unilateral decision was reached on August 10, 1945, immediately after the bombing of Nagasaki, that United States forces would participate in the postwar occupation of Korea. Future Secretary of State Dean Rusk proposed dividing the occupation at the 38th Parallel (the horizontal line of latitude at 38 degrees north), which conveniently bisected the country with the capital city Seoul south of the line and the best agricultural land and the majority of the population in the southern part of the peninsula. To the relief of the Americans, the Soviets readily acceded to the adoption of the 38th Parallel as a border.

The US XXIV Corps, veterans of the Okinawa campaign and led by Lieutenant General John R. Hodge, were alerted they would transfer to Korea on August 14. Hodge was informed the occupation would be "semi-friendly," that he need only worry about the small group of Japanese collaborators. General MacArthur proclaimed that the Koreans should be treated as "liberated people." Fourteen Americans arrived in Inchon on September 11, 1945, a month after the Red Army had halted its advance. Part of Operation *Black List Forty*, they were met by a delegation of Japanese colonial officials in top hats and tails. After taking a train from the shuttered city of Inchon to Seoul, they found Koreans waving little Korean flags at every village they passed along the way. In Seoul, they were surrounded by a vast throng of exultant Koreans. They were the first Americans to experience the nationwide Korean desire for independence. Unfortunately, those who followed these pioneers into the country struggled to find any Koreans able to maintain orderly control other than former Japanese colonial officials and their Korean collaborators. The Americans came to view the Japanese as cooperative, orderly and docile, while the Koreans who were competing to establish control of their country were seen as "headstrong, unruly and obstreperous," in the words of one report signed by Hodge. Hodge and many of his officers were strongly anti-Communist, which came to color their views of the Korean nationalists. Hodge's State Department advisor, H. Merrell Beninghoff, wrote a report on September 15 stating:

> South Korea can best be described as a powder keg waiting to explode at the application of a spark. There is great disappointment that immediate independence and sweeping out of the Japanese did not eventuate. Although the hatred of the Koreans for the Japanese is unbelievably bitter, it is not thought they will resort to violence as long as American troops are in surveillance... There are no qualified Koreans for other than the low-ranking positions, either in government or in public utilities and communications.

Over the following year, Korea came to be dominated by the political struggle between two men, Syngman Rhee and Kim Il-Sung.

Born April 18, 1875, Syngman Rhee was the only son of a rural family of modest means that traced its lineage to King Taejong of Joseon as descendants of Grand Prince

Yangnyeong. Rhee and his family moved to Seoul in 1877, where he received a traditional Confucian education in preparation to join the Korean civil service, which was abolished in the reforms of 1894. Thereafter, he attended a Methodist school where he studied English and liberal arts. He became a journalist in Seoul and supported himself by teaching Korean to Methodist missionaries. In 1896, Rhee was accused of involvement in the plot to assassinate Empress Myeongseong, but the charges were dropped. As the reforms of the new Korean Empire began to take effect over the next several years, he worked to create Korea's grassroots independence movement and organized several protests against corruption and the influences of Japan and Russia in Korean affairs. In November 1898, he joined the government as a low-level bureaucrat. In 1899, he was implicated in a plot to remove King Gojong and was imprisoned until 1904, when he was released and went into exile in the United States through the intercession of his Methodist missionary friends.

In August 1905, Rhee and Yun Bung Gu met with Secretary of State John Hay and President Theodore Roosevelt during the peace talks in Portsmouth, New Hampshire, held to end the Russo-Japanese War. Despite their efforts, the two Koreans failed to convince Roosevelt to help preserve independence for Korea. Rhee remained in exile until 1910, in the meantime obtaining a Bachelor of Arts from George Washington University in 1907, a Master of Arts from Harvard University in 1908, and a PhD from Princeton University in 1910. He returned to Korea in 1910 as a Methodist missionary. In 1912, he was implicated in the "105 Man Incident" and arrested by the Japanese. Released to attend a Methodist conference in Minnesota, he returned to the United States where he settled in Honolulu and published the *Tae Pyoung Yang* Magazine. In 1918, he was chosen as a delegate to the Versailles peace conference by the

Korean National Association but was not allowed to travel to Paris, though he was able to meet with President Woodrow Wilson in an attempt to gain American support for Korean independence.

With the outbreak of the March 1st Movement in 1919, Rhee was appointed President of the Provisional Government. That summer, he notified the leaders of the Versailles peace conference of the declaration of Korean independence, which was ignored. He moved to Shanghai in 1920 to act as president of the government-in-exile, but returned to the United States the following year. In 1925, the Koreans in exile in China removed him as president of the provisional government. From then on, he was involved in Korean exile politics in the United States, where he strengthened his ties with conservative American religious leaders.

In November 1939, Rhee and his wife left Hawaii and moved to Washington. Following the outbreak of the Pacific War, he used his position as Chairman of the Foreign Relations Department of the Provisional Government of Korea in Chongqing to lobby President Franklin D. Roosevelt and the United States Department of State to recognize the Korean Provisional Government. As part of this campaign to gain American support, he cooperated with the Office of Strategic Services in attempting to insert agents inside Korea. In 1945, he attended the United Nations Conference on International Organization in San Francisco as the leader of the Korean representatives to request the participation of the Korean Provisional Government in the organization.

While Syngman Rhee was settling in Honolulu as a political refugee in 1912, Kim Il-Sung, whose name was originally Kim Song-Ju, was born in a village outside of Pyongyang to a poor family who had been the beneficiaries of Presbyterian education from American missionaries. His father had become an opponent of the Japanese out of religious conviction as a Christian. The family fled Korea to avoid Japanese repression in 1920 and settled in Manchuria with other Korean exiles. Kim was sent to the Whasung Military Academy in Manchuria at age 14 in 1926, but left the following year. In 1929, at age 17, he became the youngest member of an obscure underground Marxist organization with fewer than 20 members, led by Ho So, a member of the South Manchurian Communist Youth Association. The group was discovered by the police three weeks after it was formed, and Kim was jailed for several months. While the Communist Party of Korea had been founded in 1925, it was expelled from the Comintern in 1930 for being "too nationalist." In 1931, Kim joined the Chinese Communist Party and became involved with guerrilla groups in Manchuria following the Japanese invasion in late 1931.

In 1935, Kim joined the Northeast Anti-Japanese United Army, a guerrilla group led by the Chinese Communist Party and took the name Kim Il-Sung, meaning "become the sun." Later that year he was appointed political commissar for the Third Detachment of the Second Division, leading 160 soldiers. At this time, he met the man who would become his mentor as a Communist, Wei Zhengmin, who was chairman of the Political Committee of the Northeast Anti-Japanese United Army and a confidante of Kang Sun, who was close to Mao Zedong. Kim was appointed commander of the Sixth Division in 1937, at the age of 24. On June 4, 1935, he led a raid on Poch'onbo, Korea. Although Kim's division only captured the small Japanese-held town just across the Yalu River border for a few hours, it was nonetheless claimed as a military success, since it came at a time when the guerrilla units had experienced difficulty in capturing any enemy territory. This event gave Kim a measure of fame among Korean guerrillas operating with the Chinese. For their part, the Japanese considered him one of the most effective and popular Korean guerrilla leaders and hunted him as such, which added to his fame.

By the end of 1940, Kim was the only Korean Communist army leader still alive. He and what remained of his army escaped their Japanese pursuers by crossing the Amur River into the Soviet Union, where he was sent to a camp at Vyatskoye near Khabarovsk. After thorough vetting by the People's Commissariat for Internal Affairs (NKVD), Kim was commissioned a major in the Soviet Red Army and served until the end of the war, participating in the Soviet invasion of Manchuria in August 1945.

The Soviet Red Army entered Pyongyang, North Korea, with almost no resistance on August 15, 1945. Stalin instructed NKVD Commissar Lavrenti Beria to recommend a Communist leader for the Soviet-occupied territories. After meeting Kim several times, Beria recommended him to Stalin. Kim arrived in the Korean port of Wonsan on September 19, 1945, where the Soviets installed him as Chairman of the North Korean branch of the Korean Communist Party in December 1945. With the support of the Soviets, he was elected chairman of the Interim People's Committee on February 8, 1946.

Following the surrender of Japan on September 2, 1945, Syngman Rhee was flown to Tokyo from Washington aboard a US military aircraft. Following a secret meeting with Supreme Allied Commander Douglas MacArthur, Rhee was flown to Seoul in mid-October 1945 aboard MacArthur's personal transport *Bataan*, where he convinced the local Korean nationalists that he had the backing of the Americans. He assumed the posts of president of the Independence Promotion Central Committee, chairman of the Korean People's Representative Democratic Legislature, and president of the Headquarters for Unification. Though he had the support of the most important American in the Far East, Rhee and his followers were not yet supported by the Americans in charge of the occupation in Korea.

Korea in the fall of 1945 was a place of intrigue and political struggle. Koreans who had collaborated with the

Japanese Empire worked to ingratiate themselves with the Americans, who were happy to find people who wanted to work with them and who knew how things such as municipal government waterworks were supposed to run. While the Americans had taken a dislike to the domestic Korean nationalists, Rhee and his fellow Americanized exiles were able to exploit the fact they could communicate with the Americans in English, which the native nationalists could not. Staunchly anti-Communist, they also played into the anti-Communism of General Hodge and his staff. As Koreans increasingly saw what appeared to be American support for Rhee, he was accorded leadership by other Korean factions. On October 20, 1945, he gave a rousing anti-Soviet speech at the first public meeting of the Korean Democratic Party (in reality, a conservative party as opposed to actual democracy as was the Japanese Liberal Democratic Party which was founded in roughly the same time period and represented the same Japanese imperial militarists who had fought the Pacific War). Rhee's domestic career as South Korea's most celebrated politician was launched.

There was, however, one American on the scene who looked at Rhee and didn't like what he saw. General Hodge told military historian Clay Blair that Rhee was "devious, emotionally unstable, brutal, corrupt, and wildly unpredictable."

At the same time, the United States, which had become the most powerful nation on earth as a result of the war, was quickly returning to its traditional isolationism. Americans wanted the troops home now, which resulted in a massive draw-down of the US presence in the Far East. Little attention was paid in Washington to events in Korea, with American policymakers increasingly involved in what appeared to be a new struggle with the Soviet Union in Europe. Assistant Secretary of War John J. McCloy advocated for the first time in November 1945 that the United States provide support to those anti-Communist forces they could work with in countries such as Korea. As the Truman administration became progressively antagonistic to Soviet moves in Eastern Europe in the years immediately following the end of the war, it became an idealistic fantasy that the United States would allow Communists and anti-Communists to compete without restraint to work out their own destiny. Just as the Soviets were working to build up the power of Kim Il-Sung in the north, the Americans decided to support the anti-Communists led by Rhee and his allies.

The Three-Power Foreign Ministers Conference was held in Moscow in December 1945. The Soviets accepted the American proposal that Korea become an "international trustee" under the trusteeship of the US, the USSR, China and Great Britain, for a period of five years, to end in the establishment of a unified state. The Moscow Accords reflected the low priority Stalin gave Korea. He was willing to appease Western fears in the Far East in the expectation Washington would oppose less vigorously his takeover of Eastern Europe. Additionally, the Soviets saw the power of the Left in Korea as a whole, both Communist and non-Communist, as likely strong enough to carry the day when the time came to hold the promised elections.

All sides in the domestic Korean political scene not only distrusted but largely hated each other. There were the hard-line Communists supported in the north by the Soviets, the hard-line anti-Communists who were generally supported by the Americans, and the domestic nationalists who wanted independence, who were seen as the enemy by both Communists and anti-Communists. Eventually, Rhee and his supporters were able to portray the domestic nationalists as either Communist dupes or actual Communist agents for their support of a national government that would include all parties, and to exclude them as what became the government of South Korea was organized.

When the first US–Soviet Cooperation Committee meeting concluded without result in June 1946, Rhee argued that the government of Korea must be established as an independent entity. He returned to Washington DC from December 1946 to April 1947 to lobby for support of his plan. While he was there, President Harry S. Truman proclaimed the Truman Doctrine in March 1947, calling for the containment of Soviet Communism in Europe. Rhee returned to Korea the next month with tacit support among leading members of the Truman administration to proceed with the establishment of the anti-Communist Republic of Korea.

Throughout this period, Korea remained a very low priority with the senior American in Asia. Between 1945 and 1950, Douglas MacArthur was deeply involved in the reformation of Japan, which in retrospect is likely his greatest achievement. For such an instinctive autocrat as MacArthur was, a deeply conservative man with strong ties to the domestic American conservative movement, an avowed anti-New Dealer who held Franklin D. Roosevelt in personal contempt, MacArthur's achievement in bringing truly democratic political reform, land reform, labor unions and rights for women to a society which had none of that and was still basically feudal in 1945 is nothing short of astounding, viewed from 70 years on. However, all this effort completely absorbed his attention. When he received pleas from General Hodge for his personal involvement in American decision-making in the re-making of Korea, his response was to tell Hodge to use his own judgment, as he did in one reply, "I am not sufficiently familiar with the local situation to advise you intelligently, but I will support whatever decision you make in this matter." Hodge even traveled to Tokyo to meet with MacArthur personally, only to be kept waiting for hours and then told to take care of things himself. After the meeting, MacArthur told his principal aide, Fabion Bowers, "I wouldn't put my foot in Korea. It belongs to the State Department.

They wanted it and got it. They have jurisdiction. I don't. I wouldn't touch it with a ten-foot barge pole. The damn diplomats make the wars and we win them. Why should I save their skin? I won't help Hodge. Let them help themselves."

MacArthur himself was nearing 70 and suffered from Parkinson's disease to the extent that the shaking of his hands during the surrender ceremony aboard the battleship *Missouri* in 1945 was commented on by General Joseph Stilwell. His hearing was gone and his attention span got shorter and shorter over the years, which was why his meetings were more monologues than meetings. Still, in both Asia and the United States he was considered an American icon with a vast store of political capital.

MacArthur was not alone in his indifference to Korea. While China had long fascinated and interested many powerful Americans, very few knew anything about the former Japanese colony. None had the knowledge and insight of American missionary Homer Hulbert, who had written of Korea in 1906:

> Koreans have been frequently maligned and seldom appreciated. They are overshadowed by China on the one hand in respect to numbers, and Japan on the other hand in respect to wit. They are neither good merchants like the one, nor good fighters like the other. And yet they are by far the pleasantest people in the East to live amongst. Their failings are such as flow in the wake of ignorance everywhere, and the bettering of their opportunities would bring swift betterment to their condition.

In November 1947, the United Nations General Assembly recognized Korean independence and established the United Nations Temporary Commission on Korea (UNTCOK) through Resolution 112, with the goal of creating a unified national government. In May 1948, the South

Korean Constitutional Assembly election was held under the supervision of UNTCOK. Rhee was elected to the National Assembly and was consequently selected speaker of the House, where he passed a law that the president of Korea had to be elected by the National Assembly. The Constitution of the Republic of Korea was adopted on July 17, 1948. By this time, the Communists had ceased participation, and the domestic nationalists had been either driven into exile in the north or arrested. On July 20, Syngman Rhee was elected President of the Republic of Korea with 92.3 percent of the vote, a margin usually associated with the politics of a one-party state – which South Korea was rapidly becoming, or had already become. On August 15, 1948, the Republic of Korea was formally established in Seoul, with Rhee inaugurated as the first President. Soon after, laws were enacted that severely curtailed political dissent. Many leftists were arrested, with some being killed. Rhee allowed the internal security force, headed by his long-time collaborator Kim Chang-Ryong, to detain and torture suspected Communists and North Korean agents.

To solidify his control in the north, Kim Il-Sung established the Korean People's Army (KPA) in December 1947. Aligned with the Communist Party, a cadre of guerrillas and former soldiers who had gained combat experience in battles against the Japanese and later against Nationalist Chinese troops as part of Mao Zedong's People's Liberation Army were recruited to lead the new force. Following the proclamation of the Republic of Korea in August, the Democratic People's Republic of Korea (DPRK) was proclaimed on September 9, 1948, with Kim as the Soviet-designated premier. On October 12, the Soviet Union recognized the DPRK as the government of the entire peninsula. The Communist Party merged with the New People's Party to form the Workers Party of North Korea. In 1949, the Workers Party of North Korea merged with its southern counterpart to become the

Workers Party of Korea (WPK) with Kim as party chairman. Kim and the Communists consolidated totalitarian rule in North Korea and all parties and mass organizations were either eliminated or consolidated into the Democratic Front for the Reunification of the Fatherland, a popular front in which the Workers Party predominated. At this time, the "cult of personality" was promoted by the Communists with the appearance of the first statues of Kim, and he began calling himself "Great Leader."

Both United States and Soviet forces withdrew from Korea in the summer of 1948, leaving two nationalist police states that each saw the other as the personification of evil, both committed to the imposition of their respective rule throughout the Korean peninsula.

Using Soviet advisers and equipment, a large army skilled in infiltration tactics and guerrilla warfare was created in North Korea. The USSR equipped the Korean People's Army with Soviet-built T-34 medium tanks, trucks, artillery, and small arms. An air force was also formed, initially equipped with Soviet Yak-9 fighters and Ilyushin Il-10 attack aircraft. By the spring of 1950, North Korean forces numbered between 150,000 and 200,000 troops, organized into ten infantry divisions, one tank division with 280 tanks, and one air force division with 210 aircraft. The army was well motivated and saw itself as the leader of the fight for a unified independent Korea.

The Army of the Republic of Korea in the South was not so well equipped. The United States refused to provide any heavy weapons, to ensure that the army could only be used for preserving internal order and self-defense since there was a well-founded fear that, if his army were properly equipped, Rhee would start a war with the north. In the spring of 1950, the ROK Army had 65,000 combat troops, 33,000 support personnel, no tanks, and a 22-plane air force with 12 L-4 and L-5 liaison aircraft and ten AT-6 trainers. The ROK Army was composed of reluctant conscripts, many of whom did not support the government.

The United States viewed the Republic of Korea as one of several developing democratic nations that could serve as counterbalances to Communist expansion. In March 1949, President Truman approved National Security Council Memorandum 8/2, which warned that the Soviets intended to dominate all of Korea, and that this would be a threat to US interests in the Far East. In June 1949, Truman sent a special message to Congress citing Korea as an area where "the principles of democracy were being matched against those of Communism." He stated the United States "will not fail to provide the aid which is so essential to Korea at this critical time."

On August 29, 1949, the Soviet Union detonated an atomic bomb, becoming the second nation to possess a nuclear weapon. On October 10, 1949, Mao Zedong proclaimed the People's Republic of China in the Great Hall of the People in Beijing, ending the Chinese civil war. On December 7, 1949, Kuomintang troops loyal to Chiang Kai-Shek completed their withdrawal from the Chinese mainland to the island of Taiwan.

In January 1950, Secretary of State Dean Acheson publicly declared that the US defensive containment line against the Communist menace in Asia ran from Japan through the Philippines. Significantly, though unnoted at the time in the West, the Korean peninsula was outside that line.

Following the withdrawal of US forces from Korea, MacArthur instructed his long-time intelligence chief, General Charles A. Willoughby, a member of what was known throughout the rest of the Army as "MacArthur's Bataan gang," to establish a secret intelligence office in Seoul. Called the Korean Liaison Office (KLO), it was responsible for monitoring troop movements in North Korea and the activities of Communist guerrillas operating in South Korea.

In late 1949, the KLO reported that the Communist guerrillas represented a serious threat to the government in the South, noting that many of the guerrillas were originally from the South, and thus were able to slip back into their villages to hide from local security forces.

In the meantime, the newly formed Central Intelligence Agency (CIA) claimed there was clear evidence that the North Korean government and military was completely controlled by the Soviet Union, and that North Korea was a "Soviet puppet." While the CIA believed the North would have the necessary military capacity to attack the South in 1949, they officially stated that such an attack was considered unlikely due to the Soviet domination of decision-making in Pyongyang. The focus on the Soviet Union as "the" Communist state had become the dominant perception within the US Government's political and military leadership circles. Any questioning of the absolute authority of Moscow over other Communist states or noting that cultural, historic, or nationalistic factors in each country might come into play, fell victim to the political atmosphere in Washington as an anti-Communist movement whipped up domestic political fear of Communism over Russian "theft" of atomic secrets and the "loss" of China to Communism. In March 1950, Joseph McCarthy, an obscure Republican senator from Wisconsin, stated his belief that the State Department was infiltrated by Communists who were responsible for all these perceived American "reversals of fortune." McCarthyism was born and in the coming years the American government would answer to it.

In the meantime, Kim Il-Sung traveled to Moscow in January 1950 for a meeting with Stalin where he presented his plan to invade the South and unify the country, and asked what Soviet support could be expected. Stalin advised him to discuss the plan with Mao Zedong, who was also in Moscow for the signing of a Sino-Soviet Mutual Defense agreement. Mao agreed that the South was weak enough to be conquered; Stalin also approved the invasion, taking note of Acheson's declaration that the Korean peninsula was outside the United States' line of defense for its sphere of influence in Asia. Within a matter of months, North Korea's preparation for war was readily recognized. CIA reports for April and May 1950 described the buildup of DPRK military forces, though they also discounted the possibility of an actual invasion, referring to the belief that the Soviet Union understood President Truman's June 1949 statement of US interests in the Korean peninsula. US intelligence analysts believed that North Korean forces could not mount a successful attack without Soviet assistance, and that such assistance would indicate a worldwide Communist offensive. Since there were no indications in Europe that such an offensive was in preparation, the Korean preparations were dismissed as an attempt to bring political pressure on the South Korean government.

On May 10, 1950, the South Korean Defense Ministry warned at a press conference that North Korean troops were massing at the border and there was danger of an invasion. No attention was paid to this warning in Washington.

The United States was caught by surprise due to the fact that within the political and military leadership circles in Washington, it was believed that only the Soviets could order an invasion by a "client state," and that such an act would be a prelude to World War III. The American government was confident that the Soviets were not ready to take such a step and that therefore no invasion would occur. This belief, and its broad acceptance within the US policy community, was clearly stated in a June 19, 1950 CIA paper on DPRK military capabilities, which stated that "The DPRK is a firmly controlled Soviet satellite that exercises no independent initiative and depends entirely on the support of the USSR for existence." While noting that the DPRK could take control of parts of the South, the report stated it did not have the capability to destroy the South Korean government without Soviet or Chinese assistance, which would not be forthcoming because the Soviets did not want general war. The Department of State and the military intelligence organizations of the Army, Navy, and Air Force concurred.

This position was maintained despite reports from South Korea throughout June that provided clear descriptions of North Korean preparations for war, including the removal of civilians from the border area, the restriction of transport capabilities for military use only, and movement of infantry and armor units to the border area. A CIA report issued on June 6 noted that all East Asian senior Soviet diplomats had been recalled to Moscow for consultations. The CIA believed the purpose of this was to develop a new plan to counter Western anti-Communist efforts in the region.

On June 20, a report based primarily on intelligence from human assets in the north concluded that the North Koreans had the capability to invade the South at any time. President Truman, Secretary of State Acheson, and Secretary of Defense Johnson all received copies of this report.

Five days later, on June 25, 1950, at 0400 hours local time, North Korea invaded the South. Both Washington and the Far East Command in Tokyo were surprised and unprepared. On June 30, 1950, President Truman authorized the use of US ground forces in Korea.

The intelligence failure that led to the outbreak of the Korean War was years in the making, the result of hubris founded in ignorance. As a result, the United States was completely unprepared militarily to undertake such a war at this time, and certainly not in this place.

CHAPTER THREE

THE WAGES OF HUBRIS

S everal years after the war, former Secretary of State Dean Acheson wrote in his memoirs, "If the best minds in the world had set out to find us the worst possible location to fight this damnable war politically and militarily, the unanimous choice would have been Korea."

The United States was caught as unprepared by the events of Sunday, June 25, 1950 as it had been by the events of Sunday, December 7, 1941. Most American military leaders in Japan were away from their commands on weekend leave with their families. The commander of all Far Eastern Air Force units was airborne from Hawaii on a return flight to Japan from a conference in Washington. With a forecast for a weather front heading east across the Sea of Japan with low clouds and heavy rain, air defense units were not on alert. The first report of war, sent by the Duty Officer of the Office of Special Investigations in Seoul, did not reach MacArthur's Tokyo Headquarters until 0945 hours. Other than flashing the news to the operational commands in the Far East, there was not a great deal that could be done. The Fifth Air Force commander, General Earl "Pat" Partridge, did not receive notification until 1130 hours.

North Korean infantry units attacked out of the dawn at 0400 hours, the four infantry divisions spearheaded by T-34 tanks and supported by a massive artillery barrage that devastated ROK Army positions. Taken completely by surprise, the ROK forces broke and ran. The T-34s headed for their first objectives at Kaesong and Chunchon as North Korean infantry and marines came ashore from an armada of small craft near Kangnung. Kaesong fell by 0900 hours. It was clear this was a far larger operation than the numerous skirmishes both sides had instigated along the 38th Parallel over the previous months.

In Washington, it was the middle of a summer Saturday, June 24. President Truman was visiting his family in Missouri. Only duty personnel were present in the State Department and the Pentagon. At 2126 hours that evening, a dispatch reporting the invasion was received from Ambassador Muccio in Seoul. Telephones began to ring. By midnight, Secretary of State Dean Acheson had reached President Truman by telephone, and Trygve Lie, the Secretary General of the United Nations, had been notified.

American forces in the Far East were at a low ebb. Army troops in Japan were engaged in occupation duty only, and had not engaged in serious military training for over a year, due in part to budgetary restraints in addition to the widespread official belief that there was no prospect of the Soviet Union starting a war in the region in the foreseeable future.

The newly independent United States Air Force constituted the military force most able to conduct operations, and also the service most prepared to do so among the occupation forces. The US Fifth Air Force was headquartered on the Japanese home islands, with bases spread from Kyushu in the south to Hokkaido in the north. The Air Force was tasked with the defense of Japan against an anticipated Soviet attack originating from Siberia. While the Fifth Air Force was the largest of the air force commands in the Far East, there was also the Twentieth Air Force based on Okinawa and Guam, and the Thirteenth Air Force in the Philippines. American air power was a shadow of what it had been five years earlier. Postwar budget constraints had reduced the service to the minimum necessary to conduct a policy of nuclear deterrence and if necessary to fight an offensive nuclear war with a limited delivery system of a few hundred B-50 and B-36 bombers based in the United States. There were five fighter wings in the Far East equipped with the Lockheed F-80C Shooting Star. These were the Fifth Air Force's 35th Fighter-Interceptor Wing at Yokota Air Force base (AFB) outside Tokyo, the 8th Fighter Bomber Wing at Itazuke AFB on Kyushu, and the 49th Fighter Bomber Wing at Misawa AFB in northern Honshu, the Thirteenth Air Force's 18th Fighter Bomber Wing at Clark AFB in the Philippines, and the Twentieth Air Force's 51st Fighter Interceptor Wing at Kadena AFB on Okinawa. These jet fighter units were backed by three fighter (all-weather) squadrons equipped with the piston-engine F-82G Twin Mustang: the 68th at Itazuke, the 339th at Yokota, and the 4th at Kadena, Okinawa. The F-80s were really not suited for the war they would soon find themselves fighting. They were unable to use the primitive airfields in Korea for forward deployment, but operating from Japan meant that their range was too limited to provide effective loiter time over the battlefield, essential for successful fighter-bomber operations. The F-82s, which had the range and the loiter capability, were not suited for close air support. Additionally, there were insufficient numbers of both types to undertake such operations. Backing the fighters were two squadrons of the 3rd Bombardment Wing at Yokota AFB, equipped with the B-26 Invader light bomber, and two squadrons of the 19th Bombardment Wing flying B-29 Superfortress medium bombers from Andersen AFB on Guam.

The Fifth Air Force's only assigned mission in the event of an outbreak of hostilities in Korea was the evacuation of American nationals, which could only begin at the request of the American ambassador. While this was the immediate situation, the Fifth Air Force had already made operational plans for action in such an event. F-80 and F-82 fighters were prepared at Itazuke for use in covering the evacuation of Seoul when ordered. By the end of the afternoon of June 25, a force of 12 C-54s and three C-47s had been assembled at Itazuke, where the commander of the 8th Fighter-Bomber Wing, Colonel John M. Price, was placed in charge of operations. The transports were ready to depart at 0330 hours on June 26.

Confusion continued to reign in Tokyo. According to reports coming from the front, the North Korean drive appeared exhausted, while American advisors with the ROK forces reported several units were holding their positions and there was a chance the line could be stabilized. This changed that afternoon, when the North Korean Air Force appeared over Seoul. The South Koreans had nothing in their air force to oppose the four fighters, which disappeared after 20 minutes. At 1500 hours, two other Yak-9s appeared over Kimpo airfield outside Seoul, where they strafed the control tower and set fire to a fuel dump that exploded. They also damaged an American C-54 on the ground. At 1900 hours, a second attack was made on Kimpo, during which the C-54 was attacked and set afire. By midnight, North Korean tanks were reported to be only 17 miles north of Seoul.

Shortly after midnight, June 26, Ambassador Muccio ordered the evacuation of American women and children from Seoul and Inchon. The seaborne evacuation would be made from Inchon, where several freighters were standing by. At 0100 hours, General MacArthur ordered General Partridge to provide air cover for the evacuation. The fighters were not to enter Korean air space and were to engage in

The North Korean Invasion, June 25, 1950

1. 17th ROK Regt. evacuates by sea.
2. June 28: Amphibious movements by Regt. from 6th NK Div.
3. North Korean amphibious outflanking movements.
4. 7th ROK Div. virtually annihilated along with 2nd ROK Div. (not shown).

combat only if the freighters were directly threatened. The only fighters capable of making the 500-mile trip from Japan and remaining overhead for any length of time were the F-82s. The 68th Squadron had only 12 F-82s available at Itazuke, so the 12 F-82s of the 339th Squadron were transferred there from Yokota and prepared for the mission.

In Washington, Sunday June 25 (a day behind events in Korea) was a day of frenzied activity, with decision-makers meeting as early as 0200 hours when Secretary Acheson telephoned President Truman and the two decided to seek action by the UN Security Council, which was scheduled to meet in New York that afternoon at 1500 hours. By now, a report of the invasion had been received from UNCOK, and a US resolution calling on the North Koreans to cease aggression was presented. In a 9-0 vote, with Yugoslavia abstaining, the resolution was approved, made possible by the fact the Soviet delegation was not present, since they had been boycotting the UN since January over issues involving Germany. In the meantime, Washington was in crisis mode. The Secretary of State, the Secretary of Defense, the Secretary of the Army, and the Joint Chiefs were in conference at the Pentagon all day. In response to another call from Secretary Acheson, President Truman flew back from Missouri and met with his advisers at Blair House until midnight, a meeting where the first decisions leading to American commitment in Korea were taken.

By 1950, President Harry S. Truman was no longer a man who felt he was living in the shadow of Franklin D. Roosevelt, whom he had succeeded in the presidency following Roosevelt's death in 1945. He was by now the man who had faced down Stalin internationally over the Berlin blockade, defeating the Soviet leader with the Berlin Airlift, and the Republican Party domestically in the election of 1948, in an upset campaign in which he had "given them hell" and defeated Governor Thomas E. Dewey when the

Republicans had believed they would win without difficulty. He was no longer in awe of such men as former Army Chief of Staff, Secretary of State and soon-to-be Secretary of Defense George C. Marshall, "the architect of victory" in World War II, Joint Chiefs Chairman General of the Army Omar Bradley who had led the American Army in the field in Europe, or Secretary of State Dean Acheson. He considered these giants to be his colleagues. When he walked into Blair House, the critical decisions had been made when he received Acheson's first phone call. To a man, the president and his advisers considered the attack a violation of the UN Charter and an act of Communist aggression against the West. There was no consideration in their minds of the fight in Korea being any sort of a civil war. For these men, the North Korean action, coming on top of all the other developments between the West and the Soviet Union following the end of World War II, reminded them too much of events in Europe 15 years earlier, when the Western democracies had failed to stop the rise of Hitler and the Nazis. For them, opposing the invasion was the only way they could see of convincing the Communists that they must avoid provoking World War III.

From the Soviet perspective, Stalin's most important mistake was his failure to see that the North Korean action would be seen in Washington through the prism of Munich. In his memoirs, Truman later wrote of his thoughts while flying back to Washington from Missouri, of how the democracies had failed to stop Mussolini in Ethiopia, the Japanese in Manchuria, of how easily the British and French could have stopped Hitler at Munich with a display of determination. It was clear in the president's mind that this action had been taken with the approval of Stalin. For Truman and his counselors, the invasion of South Korea had instantly placed America's prestige at stake, prestige that Acheson described as "the shadow cast by power, which is a very important deterrent."

To the decision-makers in Washington, the previous five years had been difficult, as two formidable and anxious new world powers – each governed by a political and economic system that saw the other as its sworn enemy, each seeing the other through an apocalyptic lens as being sworn to its destruction, and both fearful and anxious in the new and terrifying atomic age – groped to understand each other. After getting Stalin wrong at their first meeting at Potsdam in 1945, when he thought the Soviet leader was a man who would appreciate Midwestern forthrightness, Truman had come to see the Soviet leader as the personification of evil. Stalin, too, had gotten Truman wrong, underestimating him as an "accidental" president who did not have the intellectual or personal capability to hold the office, one who would soon be gone. In June 1950, the Cold War was entering its coldest period, with NATO having been formed the previous year and the Marshall Plan for the rebuilding of Europe well underway. As President Truman put it at the conclusion of the Blair House meeting, "Korea is the Greece of the Far East. If we stand up to them there, like we did in Greece, they won't take any next steps. But if we just stand by, they'll move into Iran and they'll take over the whole Middle East. There's no telling what they'll do if we don't put up a fight now."

George Kennan, the director of the State Department's Policy Planning staff, had been the man who first described the Soviet policy of postwar expansion and named the strategy for opposing it, "containment." By the summer of 1950 he had been eased out at State and was preparing to move to Princeton as an academic. Acheson, however, valued Kennan's views and advice. In the days following the decision to enter the Korean War, still fearing that Korea was a Communist feint, he closely questioned Kennan about what he thought the Russians were up to. Kennan did not see the attack as part of something larger, telling Acheson he believed the Soviets did not seek a larger war with the United States and the

West, though they would be happy to see either the United States tied up in a "profitless and endless war" or reviled internationally for doing nothing. For Kennan, the great danger was not in Europe, but rather in Asia. He pointed out China's traditional interests in the Korean peninsula, which the Russians might use with effect in goading China into intervening in the war should the United States take any action that could be seen as a "provocation." Kennan's final advice was that the war would not become larger if it was limited politically and geographically, and that limitation was made known publicly.

Following the president's decision regarding US action in Korea, the first step was the complete evacuation of American diplomatic and civilian personnel, which began at first light on Monday, June 26, 1950. The refugees made their way aboard ship under the watchful eye of eight F-82s. At 1330 hours, a North Korean La-7 dove out of the low clouds straight through the American formation, cannons blazing. The F-82s took evasive action as the North Korean fighter disappeared back into the clouds. Shortly thereafter, US fighters were cleared to enter Korean airspace to cover refugee convoys on their way from Seoul. The fighters continued to escort the freighter carrying the refugees when it left Inchon at last light, remaining overhead until the destroyers USS *Mansfield* and *DeHaven* arrived to provide escort to Japan.

The airlift of Americans from Korea finally got underway on June 27. A group of six hastily assembled C-47s and two C-54s had departed Itazuke before dawn, escorted by F-82s. The transports arrived at Kimpo and Suwon airfields outside Seoul at dawn. The F-82s remained overhead at low altitude, while four F-80s of the 8th Fighter Bomber Wing orbited at 25,000 feet over the Han River. Shortly after 1200 hours, five North Korean Yak-9s were spotted inbound to Kimpo. They were intercepted by five F-82s of the 68th and 339th Squadrons. In a one-sided five-minute dogfight, three of the Yaks were shot down in flames, with First Lieutenant William G. Hudson of the 68th Squadron becoming the first American pilot to down an enemy fighter in the Korean War. An hour later, eight Il-10 Shturmovik attack aircraft were spotted over Seoul by the pilots of the four F-80s. Two of the Il-10s were shot down by First Lieutenant Robert E. Wayne, while Captain Raymond E. Schillereff and First Lieutenant Robert H. Dewald scored one each. The other four Il-10s turned tail and ran. With no orders to pursue, the F-80 pilots resumed their patrol.

In Washington, there were further high-level meetings that Monday, June 26. Generalissimo Chiang Kai-Shek's ambassador had already contacted both Secretary of State Acheson and Defense Secretary Johnson with an offer to provide his best troops to strengthen the ROK forces. Initially, Truman was intrigued by the idea and was inclined to accept it. Acheson, who had discussed the question of possible Red Chinese intervention with Kennan that morning before the meeting, had expected such an offer since he understood Chiang sought a widening war that would in some way lead to Red Chinese involvement and the likelihood of American support for a possible return to the mainland by the Guomintang to contest the result of the Chinese civil war, making his interests and those of the United States in no way parallel. Acheson was certain he was right and immediately laid out his opposition to the idea, pointing out that the record of the Guomintang armies in China in the four-year civil war had been poor. Marshall, who had direct experience with Chiang and his forces from his time as Secretary of State when he attempted to negotiate an end to the Chinese civil war three years earlier, echoed Acheson's argument about the political ramifications of such a move, which he strongly believed would bring the Red Chinese into the war as a "natural reaction," while Joint Chiefs Chairman General Bradley supported the Secretary of State's points regarding the combat efficiency of Chiang's troops.

Truman had to deal with his domestic political opponents in making a decision on the matter. The China Lobby, a movement closely associated with the Republican Party, was already in full cry over "who lost China?" and the Republicans already saw the outbreak of war as a way of striking at the administration in the run-up to the mid-term elections, where they saw a fair chance of regaining the Congressional majorities they had lost in 1948. Only a few hours earlier, Senator Styles Bridges of New Hampshire rose in the Senate to ask "Will we continue appeasement? Now is the time to draw the line!" Bridges was a leader of the China Lobby and an early defender of the charges made the previous February 9 by an obscure Senator Joseph McCarthy from Wisconsin, who had ended three undistinguished years in the Senate since his election in 1946 by electrifying a Republican audience in Wheeling, West Virginia, with the claim he had "a list of 205 members of the Communist Party" who were employed in the State Department. Bridges had been followed by California Senator William F. Knowland, known as "the senator from Formosa" for his close association with the Guomintang and leadership of the China Lobby, who added, "If this nation is allowed to succumb to an overt invasion of this kind, there is little chance of stopping Communism anywhere on the continent of Asia." Nevada Senator George Malone, another McCarthy supporter, tied the outbreak of war to the case of Alger Hiss, a State Department employee who had just been convicted of spying for the Soviets, stating that what had happened in China the year before and in Korea now had been brought on by "left-wingers" in the State Department.

Truman's first response to word of the North Korean invasion had been instinctual and almost apolitical, but he knew that he would have to deal with the Republican opposition. Bringing in Chiang's army could defuse that, but he had to weigh the cost in terms of international relations and the ultimate involvement of the US in a war on the Asian mainland. While Acheson considered Chiang a lost cause and was supported in that belief by Marshall, Secretary of Defense Louis Johnson, who had been Truman's strong ally in the recent political fights over the size of the defense budget and service integration, was strongly and publicly pro-Chiang. He was also the only major Democratic politician who had forthrightly endorsed and supported Truman in 1948, and had stood by the president when other members of the party tried to get him to step aside as a candidate, obtaining the finances for Truman's "whistle stop" train campaign in September and October 1948 that had turned the election around. Truman owed him a political debt of deep gratitude. Johnson was described by other Washington Democrats as "a wheeler-dealer, a self-made man with an inflated sense of his political abilities and possibilities." His political base was the conservative American Legion, of which he had been president, and he reflected that organization's views on foreign policy, which were isolationist and anti-Communist. Johnson hoped to replace Truman as the Democratic nominee for the presidency in 1952. To Acheson, Johnson was a member of the opposition and most certainly a personal political opponent. In fact, Johnson – who hated Acheson – had privately promised Wellington Koo, Chiang's Washington ambassador, that he would drive Acheson out of office for his opposition to Chiang. These battle lines made for a difficult in-house political struggle. Johnson stated that American security was more affected by events in Taiwan than Korea, and that bringing Chiang's troops into the war would signal to the Red Chinese that there was American support for the continued "independence" of the island under Chiang's control and prevent what was believed to be the coming Red Chinese invasion. Acheson tried to bring the discussion back to Korea, but Johnson continued, pointing out the value of such a decision with regard to domestic politics. Truman finally ended things by announcing dinner.

After dinner, Johnson again tried to bring up the topic, but Truman cut him off. The discussion turned to the situation in Korea, with further reports of the collapse of the ROK Army, which seemed to require a decision about committing troops. Even during World War II, it had been US policy to avoid putting American combat troops on the mainland of Asia. Bradley suggested putting the decision off for a few days. Truman looked around at his advisors. "I don't want to go to war," the president stated.

While Truman and his advisors met in Washington, in New York City the Security Council adopted a resolution to supply such aid as necessary to the Republic of Korea to repel the North Korean attack. This vote was the only time in its history that the Security Council would be able to take such action until the Iraqi invasion of Kuwait in 1991, after the end of the Cold War. The fact that the Soviets were absent and taken by surprise in this manner has long been pointed to as evidence that Stalin was not aware of the North Korean decision to attack when they did. In the wake of the Security Council vote, President Truman immediately authorized General MacArthur to employ United States air and naval forces in support of South Korea, and named MacArthur the Supreme Allied Commander of United Nations Forces in the conflict.

Truman's decision caught the US Navy even more unprepared for combat in the Far East than the other services. In the years following the end of World War II, the Navy and Marine Corps had been drastically reduced. In the aftermath of the creation of the Air Force as an independent co-equal service, and the creation of the Department of Defense to unify the armed forces, there had been a series of political battles over the dominance of the Air Force as the prime delivery force of the US nuclear arsenal. Following the cancellation of the new aircraft carrier USS *United States* in 1949, there had been a real fear that naval aviation would be transferred to the Air Force, while the Marine Corps was inducted into the Army.

An example of how bad things were for the Marine Corps during this period was the experience of VMF-451 fighter pilot First Lieutenant Reed King in late 1948. "I had flown a Corsair from our base at Cherry Point to New Orleans. When it came time to return, the right gear wouldn't retract after take-off. After sitting there in New Orleans for almost a week, the powers that be ordered me to fly it back to Cherry Point with the gear extended. A Corsair flies at about 100 mph in that configuration." A series of events King could only describe as "continued pilot error" found him over the dark countryside of South Carolina at 2300 hours when he ran out of gas. Unable to glide as far as the nearest civilian airfield, he was forced to bail out. "They had me on three strikes: flying a damaged airplane at night, running out of gas, and losing the airplane." When he got back to Cherry Point, he was told he had just assisted the Corps' job of reducing the number of Marine Aviators by 35 in the face of budget reductions. "Nobody could save me. They had to make the reductions and I'd made it easy in my case." As a regular Marine officer, King became a "mud Marine" in a rifle company, where he would later participate in the 1950 Korean campaign.

These inter-service battles had led to some remarkable events in late 1949. An anonymous document produced in the Navy Department alleged Air Force procurement policies were dominated by the financial interests of those in authority. In a speech at the National War College, Louis A. Johnson, newly appointed Secretary of Defense following the suicide of James Forrestal, accused the Navy of being engaged in a "campaign of terror" against unification. The press reported naval officers being shadowed by detectives hired by the Air Force. In September, Admiral Radford declared the Navy was being purposely eliminated as a factor in the defense establishment. A copy of a letter in which a prominent flag officer expressed to the Secretary of the Navy his fear that the country's security was being jeopardized by acceptance of the theory of quick victory through strategic bombing forced a congressional investigation into the fundamentals of national security. The public hearings began in October 1949, in an atmosphere sobered by the report of an atomic explosion within the Soviet Union. The hearings became known as "the Revolt of the Admirals." Secretary of Defense Johnson was hostile to the Navy, having been appointed by Truman with the task of reducing naval expenditures to pre-World War II levels, a duty he undertook with relish. The focus was on the B-36 intercontinental bomber, seen as the symbol of a strategy of nuclear deterrence which was as much for domestic propaganda as it was for any actual operational capability. Clarification of the current implications of such a strategy for naval and amphibious capabilities was undermined by the general acceptance of the idea that the Soviet Union was the only possible enemy and Europe the only possible theater, with nuclear war the only outcome. Testimony by three major fleet commanders, the commandant of the Marine Corps, and the chief of Naval Operations forcefully developed the fact that the type of armed force embodied in the Navy and the Marine Corps was being whittled down to a dangerously low level.

The problem of funding was confronted by all three armed services. President Truman had unilaterally imposed a limit of $13 billion on defense spending for fiscal year 1949, a level unseen since before World War II. This was seen by all three services as too low to sustain the level of force needed to back up the administration's new commitments in the building confrontation with the Soviet Union in Europe. Despite the arguments made by the services, the president remained adamant in his decision. This would be the major reason for the lack of US preparedness in the events of the coming year. In addition, the hearings fully revealed to the Soviets the United States' view of the Soviet Union as the only enemy and Europe as the only theater of operations, which bolstered the belief held by Stalin and Mao Zedong that there would be no American response to an attempt to unify Korea under Communist rule.

The Navy was so reduced by budget constraints that before January 1950, no US aircraft carrier had operated west of Hawaii since 1947. USS *Boxer* (CV-21) had deployed to the Far East on January 11, returning to the United States on June 13 when she was relieved by USS *Valley Forge* (CV-47). Additionally, since there were no major operating facilities for naval ships in Japan, the Seventh Fleet was based at Subic Bay in the Philippines, distant from Korea. USS *Valley Forge* carried 86 aircraft of Carrier Air Group 5, the first air group to operate two fighter squadrons equipped with the new jet-powered Grumman F9F-2 Panther, along with two fighter-bomber squadrons of F4U-4 Corsairs, and an attack squadron of AD-4 Skyraiders, with 14 other Skyraiders from photographic, night attack, and radar early warning units rounding out the complement. Fortunately, Air Group 5 had conducted several close support training missions with the Marines at Camp Pendleton, California, prior to their deployment to the western Pacific. In addition to *Valley Forge*, the Seventh Fleet Striking Force included the heavy cruiser USS *Rochester* (CA-124), Destroyer Division 31 consisting of USS *Shelton, Eversole, Radford*, and *Fletcher*, and Destroyer Division 32, composed of USS *Maddox, Samuel L. Moore, Brush*, and *Taussig*. US forces in Japanese waters consisted of Task Force 95, with the light cruiser USS *Juneau* (CL-119) and four destroyers of Destroyer Division 91: USS *Mansfield, DeHaven, Collett*, and *Lyman K. Swenson*, operating from the old Imperial Japanese Navy base at Sasebo.

At 0515 hours on June 27, the Seventh Fleet Striking Force sortied from Subic Bay. Acting on his own on June 26, Rear Admiral Sir William G. Andrewes, RN, commander of the Royal Navy's Far Eastern Fleet, departed Hong Kong at 0130 hours, directing his ships to concentrate in Southern Japanese ports. The light fleet carrier HMS *Triumph*, with Carrier Air Wing 13 aboard, consisting of 800 Squadron with 12 obsolescent Seafire FR 47 fighters and 827 Squadron equipped with 12 obsolete Firefly FR I attack aircraft, was nearing Hong Kong after departing Japan for its voyage home. The light carrier had been in the Far East since the previous December, and had flown air support missions as part of Operation *Firedog*, the British campaign against Communist guerrillas in Malaya. *Triumph* joined the heavy cruisers HMS *Jamaica* and Admiral Andrewes' flagship HMS *Belfast*, destroyers *Cossack* and *Consort*, and frigates *Black Swan, Alacrity, Hart*, and *Shoalhaven*, with the Australian HMAS *Bataan*. The Commonwealth fleet arrived at the Royal Australian Navy base in Kure, Japan, on June 28. By June 29, all Commonwealth forces in the Far East as well as Canada had been ordered to participate in the UN force. Task Force 77 (the official designation of the Seventh Fleet Striking Force) arrived at Buckner Bay, Okinawa, on June 30 and was joined there the next day by the Commonwealth fleet. The combined fleet sortied from Okinawa on July 1, with the British cruisers and frigates, now designated Task Group 96.8, the West Korean Support Group, departing to reinforce the American fire support group off the coast of South Korea. HMS *Triumph* and its escorting destroyers were designated Task Force 77.5.

The issue of exactly what the American military commitment to Korea would be was still unresolved. Following the meeting of June 26 where no decision had been made, the president had met the next morning with congressional leaders to discuss what had happened. Republican Senator Alexander Smith of New Jersey, who was supportive of what had been done, asked Truman if he planned to request a joint resolution from Congress on military action. In truth, Truman and his advisors hadn't thought about this, and he responded he would get back to the congressional leaders in the next few days. Later that day, the president met with Acheson and Averill Harriman, a high-level special aide whose views were respected due to his shrewd understanding of domestic politics. Acheson advised the president not to seek congressional approval, pointing out the UN Resolution gave him the authority he needed to commit the country to military action, citing the United Nations Participation Act which stated:

> The President shall not be deemed to require the authorization of the Congress to make available to the Security Council on its call in order to take action under article 42 of said Charter and pursuant to such special agreement or agreements the armed forces, facilities, or assistance provided for therein: Provided, That ... nothing herein contained shall be construed as an authorization to the President by the Congress to make available to the Security Council for such purpose armed forces, facilities, or assistance in addition to the forces, facilities, and assistance provided for in such special agreement or agreements.

Acheson also reminded Truman of his continuing difficulties with the Republican leadership, who would certainly take the opportunity to "raise trouble" which would slow any action at a moment when "speed is of the essence." Harriman advised the opposite, pointing out that if Truman himself were still in the Senate, he would be outraged by any president's attempt to go over the head of "the people's representatives" on the issue of war and peace.

The morning of June 29, four days after the outbreak of war, Senator Robert Taft of Ohio, leader of the conservative, Midwestern, isolationist wing of the Republican party, rose in the Senate and attacked the president for not seeking congressional approval to go to war, stating further that the North Korean invasion revealed the flaws of the Acheson foreign policy that had led to a policy that was "soft on Communism" and called for Acheson's resignation. Later that afternoon, President Truman met reporters at Blair House and attempted to downplay events in Korea because he was intent on limiting any sense that there was a growing confrontation with the Soviet Union, as Republicans had been claiming. One reporter asked if the United States was actually at war, to which Truman replied it was not. A second reporter asked "Would it be possible to call this a police action under the United Nations?" "Yes," the president answered. "That is exactly what it amounts to." Out of a question casually asked and answered would a war and its policies be defined. Following the press conference, Truman learned that North Korean forces were close to Seoul. General MacArthur called shortly thereafter and stated his belief that the situation could not be stabilized without the introduction of American ground combat forces.

This was the moment for Truman to seek Congressional support through a joint resolution. Instead, the president took his answer to the reporter's question, that what was happening was a "police action," and decided to follow Acheson's advice over Harriman's. Because he did not try for Congressional support, the Republicans were off the political hook for any responsibility regarding American actions. Army Secretary Frank Pace was astounded to learn the president's decision to commit ground troops without political approval. To Truman's statement "Frank, it isn't necessary. They're all with me," Pace responded, "But we can't be sure they'll be with you over the long term." When the news reached the House of Representatives, where any such resolution would be initiated, that the president had decided to send arms to Korea, virtually the entire body stood to cheer.

At 0130 hours on the morning of June 30, Ambassador Muccio notified Acheson that "things were desperate on the peninsula," and that MacArthur was going to formally request the authority to commit ground troops. The general's cable to the Joint Chiefs arrived 90 minutes later. His words were fateful:

> The only assurance for holding of the present line, and the ability to regain the lost ground, is through the introduction of US ground forces into the Korean battle area. To continue to utilize the forces of our Air and Navy without an effective ground element cannot be decisive.

His initial intention would be to send a regimental combat team, to be followed by up to two divisions of his forces in Japan to undertake a counteroffensive. He concluded that unless this was done, "our mission will at best be needlessly costly in life, money and prestige. At worst, it might be doomed to failure." At 0430 hours, MacArthur confirmed his request to Army Chief of Staff General J. Lawton Collins, who informed Army Secretary Pace, who in turn called the president. At 0500 hours on Friday, June 30, 1950, President Truman approved the commitment of ground troops to the war in Korea. Three hours later, the news came that Seoul had fallen.

Later that day, Truman met again with his advisors. In light of the worsened conditions in Korea, the president mused, perhaps they should take a second look at Chiang's offer of troops. Acheson jumped to his feet, arguing that would be the one action the president could take that would guarantee the entry of Red China into the war, which would make the situation immeasurably worse. Truman nodded his agreement with his Secretary of State. Defense Secretary Johnson left the room in dismay.

That same day, the *New York Times* published its first editorial on Korea, telling its readers and the nation how fortunate they were to have MacArthur in charge. "Fate could not have chosen a man better qualified to command the unreserved confidence of the people of this country. Here is a superb strategist and an inspired leader; a man of infinite patience and quiet stability under adverse pressures, a man equally capable of bold and decisive action."

With the president's approval, the 24th Infantry Division was ordered to establish a regimental combat team for transfer to Korea. On July 1, the two squadrons of B-29s flew from Guam to Kadena AFB on Okinawa, where they prepared to commence bombing operations in North Korea as soon as possible.

Of the four divisions assigned to occupation duty in Japan, the 24th Infantry Division was generally acknowledged to be the weakest and least prepared. The troops were primarily African-American, with white officers leading them, despite Truman's executive order desegregating the armed forces issued two years earlier. Stationed on Kyushu, the southernmost of the Japanese Home Islands and far from Tokyo, the 24th Infantry Division received the last pick of everything that came into Japan, from officers and men to equipment. The regimental and battalion officers were generally considered third-rate, with many sent there as their final assignment before leaving the Army. The regimental S-1 of the 34th Infantry Regiment had written a report calling his unit's equipment "a national disgrace." Mortar ammunition was faulty, the .30-caliber machine guns were worn and inaccurate. They only had the old 2.36-inch bazookas, known to be useless against tanks like the T-34. One of the unit's officers later wrote that "it was rather sad, almost criminal, that such understrength, ill-equipped and poorly trained units were committed."

By 1950, the World War II veterans were largely gone from the Army, including most of the NCOs, replaced by men who would be fighting a war they didn't understand, since they had no knowledge of either their ally or their enemy, and hated the country they were fighting in. The men who volunteered for the Army in the period immediately following World War II were, in the words of company commander T. R. Fehrenbach, "men who enlisted for every reason known to man except to fight." MacArthur's chief of staff, General Edward Almond, thought the Army that was sent to Korea was "about 40 percent combat-effective." Like the rest of the occupation army, postwar budget cuts had degraded operational capability, with the division having only two infantry battalions per regiment rather than the standard three. Making matters worse, when ordered to create a regimental combat team, the division commander initially sent only two of his three regiments, both badly understrength. Once in Korea, they were badly placed, broken down into three smaller units that would find themselves badly outnumbered, easily encircled, and incapable of holding off the North Korean assault.

That the troops were not battle ready was no secret in the Army. General Anthony McAuliffe, the Bastogne commander renowned for replying "Nuts!" to a German surrender demand, commanded the troops in southern Japan in 1948. When Keyes Beech of the *New York Times* visited him and asked if he liked his duty, McAuliffe replied that he liked it fine but,

> ... the troops don't like me. In fact, I'm just about the biggest sonofabitch in these parts. The only excuse for an army in peace or war is that it be ready to fight. This army here is no damn good. I'm turning the place upside down and seeing that all the men get out in the field on maneuvers. I want them to sleep on the ground and get their feet wet.

McAuliffe's tour did not last long.

For the Eighth Army in Japan during 1945–50, duty in Tokyo was a very good deal, with all the pleasures that accrued to a victor living exceptionally well in a very poor country, and little in the way of military responsibility. In impoverished and desperate postwar Japan, privates could hire houseboys who pressed their uniforms, shined their boots and made up their beds. The imbalance of personal power, with an American private or corporal who was momentarily "rich," living among Japanese who were now all supplicants, had only reinforced innate American racism toward Asians in general. For the African-American troops of the 24th Infantry Division, duty in Japan was far superior to anything they could find in Jim Crow America, even with the lack of opportunities available to them in a still-segregated army. In an army of easy occupation, men did not show up for roll call and it was often the responsibility of creative company clerks to work wonders with paperwork to show a unit that appeared combat effective. When they received their orders to Korea, the men of the 24th Infantry Division expected that their mere appearance on the battlefield as Americans would be sufficient to make the "gooks" think twice about continuing the war. In October, Colonel John Michaelis, the first 24th Infantry Division regimental commander to lead his troops well in Korea, told Robert Martin of the *Saturday Evening Post*:

> When they started out, they couldn't shoot. They didn't know their weapons. They had not had enough training in plain old-fashioned musketry. They'd spent a lot of time listening to lectures on the differences between Communism and Americanism and not enough time crawling on their bellies on maneuvers with live ammunition singing over them. They'd been nursed and coddled, told to drive safely, to buy War Bonds, to give to the Red Cross, to avoid VD, to write home to mother – when someone ought to have been telling them how to clean a machine gun when it jams. They were so roadbound they almost lost use of their legs. Send out a patrol on a scouting mission and they load up in a three quarter ton truck and start riding down the highway.

If the Americans were a reflection of postwar American society, uninterested in the outside world unless pushed, the North Korean troops these men were sent to fight were a reflection of their country, moving from oppressed, colonized backwardness to instant modernity using a crude replica of Stalin's original model. Nearly one third of the North Korean People's Army (NKPA) had fought in the Chinese Communist People's Liberation Army during the Chinese civil war and were tough, battle-hardened, elite troops. They were in better physical condition than their American opponents, and better able to live off the land. Their motivation was strong, believing this war was a continuation of the war they had fought in China against the Guomintang and the war they had fought against the Japanese. When captured, they were so well indoctrinated that there was almost a robotic certainty to the way they expressed their political beliefs. They believed the Americans and their proxies in Seoul were agents of the past and the same as the Japanese oppressors and Korean turncoats they had fought against before, seeing the ROK leaders as the traitors who had fought for the Japanese, which in fact was frequently the case. The North Korean troops believed they were fighting white foreigners, imperialists and capitalists, and they were certain they would win. Their American opponents on the other hand, had no idea why they were where they were, other than they had been ordered to go there by men they largely disrespected.

The first American Army unit to arrive in South Korea was "Task Force Smith," named for its commander, Lieutenant Colonel Brad Smith of the 21st Infantry Regiment. They were transported to Pusan by air on the morning of July 2. That evening, they boarded a train and arrived at Taejon, which was halfway between Pusan and what was believed to be the front, the next morning. There, General John Church, who had been sent to Korea as head of a survey team by MacArthur, informed Smith that all he would need were a few GIs who would not fear tanks, to make a stand, which would "stiffen the spine of the ROKs." He told Smith to make his stand near Osan, just south of Suwon. Task Force Smith headed north by train to Ansong, where they were cheered by Koreans who were more likely cheering the arrival of a train on which they could escape the onrushing North Koreans.

While this was going on, the 34th Infantry Regiment arrived in Pusan on July 3, where they were directed to take position at Pyongtaek, southeast of Osan on the Seoul–Pusan highway. Major General William Dean, 24th Infantry Division commander, was advised to concentrate the two regiments and take position 40 miles south, on the natural barrier of the Kum River. Dean disregarded this advice, in the belief that the mission was going to be "short and easy." In fact, the men of the 34th Infantry Regiment had been ordered to pack their summer dress uniforms before they left Japan, for the victory parade that would shortly be held in Seoul once the "gooks" had been driven out. Lieutenant Colonel Harold Ayres, commander of the 1st Battalion, 34th Infantry Regiment, told his men, "There are supposed to be North Koreans north of us. These men are poorly trained. Only about half of them have weapons and we'll have no difficulty stopping them." Captain Fred Ladd, then an aide to General Almond, later wrote that "there was a deep and pervasive racism that ran through the American Army – a belief that gooks could not stand up to Americans. It was hard to tell whether it ran from top to bottom, or bottom to top, or both." As the men of the 34th Infantry Regiment moved north, they came across some ROK engineers about to blow bridges. The Americans scolded them for their lack of spirit and threw away the explosives.

On July 4, Lieutenant Colonel Smith led 540 men, two reinforced companies, a few miles north of Osan. Their supporting artillery was still back in Pusan. They reached their positions at 0300 hours on July 5 in a rainstorm that chilled them. At dawn, Sergeant Loren Chambers spotted eight T-34 tanks moving down the road from Suwon, followed by a long line of infantrymen, and then another 25 T-34s moved into view. When the North Korean column got within a mile of Task Force Smith, the Americans opened up with mortars. There were a few hits and many duds, but the enemy kept coming. As the tanks closed in, the Americans took them on with their 57mm recoilless rifles. Despite several hits, the North Koreans kept advancing and the Americans ran out of ammunition. When the Americans fired bazookas at the tanks, the 2.36-in rounds bounced off. There was no artillery available past the 60mm mortars the Americans carried with them, which were useless against the tanks. As the North Koreans pressed the attack, Task Force Smith began withdrawing. It quickly turned into a rout, with many men dropping their weapons and even taking off their boots so they could move more quickly through the rice paddies.

Within an hour, the North Koreans came upon the 34th Infantry Regiment at Pyongtaek. Australian war correspondent Dennis Warner, who decided to stick around for the fight, moved forward to see what was happening. Peasants fleeing south filled the roads, outnumbered by fleeing ROK troops. A Korean officer warned him about oncoming tanks. When he saw the first T-34s, he retreated and reported the tanks to Colonel Ayres, who responded "We don't have any tanks," and refused to believe Warner when told they were North Korean. Shortly thereafter, survivors of the routed Task Force Smith began to straggle in. When the T-34s showed up, attempts to stop them with bazooka teams failed. Ayres ordered a withdrawal, which became a precipitous retreat through the afternoon and night. By dawn of July 6, the North Koreans were in Pyongtaek. Before the day was over they had advanced 36 miles to Chonan.

In the first week of combat for US forces, the North Koreans had virtually destroyed two American regiments. 3,000 men were killed, wounded, or missing in action and enough equipment had been left behind to outfit a North Korean regiment.

By dawn on July 3, Task Force 77 had reached the middle of the Yellow Sea, 150 miles from their North Korean targets, but only 100 miles from Chinese airfields on the Shantung peninsula and less than 200 miles from the Soviet air base at Port Arthur. At 0500 hours, USS *Valley Forge* launched combat air and anti-submarine patrols. At 0545 hours, HMS *Triumph* launched 12 Seafires and nine Fireflies to attack the airfield at Haeju. At 0600 hours, *Valley Forge* launched 16 Corsairs from VF-53 and VF-54, and 12 Skyraiders from VA-55 against Pyongyang airfield. When the propeller planes had gained a suitable head start, *Valley Forge* catapulted eight F9F-2 Panthers of VF-51 that would be the first aircraft over the target. When the American jets swept over the North Korean capital, two airborne Yak-9s were spotted and destroyed, with another damaged, while nine aircraft were reported destroyed on the ground by strafing attacks. The Corsairs and Skyraiders followed the Panthers, bombing hangars and fuel storage at Pyongyang airfield while the British strike force hit the North Korean airfield at nearby Haeju with a rocket attack which destroyed hangars and buildings but unfortunately no aircraft were present. The only British casualty from the attack was a Seafire that returned with serious damage to its engine caused by debris thrown up by its own rockets. Antiaircraft opposition at both targets was negligible, and the attackers suffered no flak damage or loss. That afternoon, aircraft from *Triumph* flew a second strike against railroad lines, while *Valley Forge* launched a second strike against the rail marshaling yards in Pyongyang and the bridges over the Taedong River. Considerable damage was inflicted on locomotives and rolling stock, but the bridges survived.

In view of the "rapidly deteriorating Korean situation," as General MacArthur reported it, additional strikes were flown on July 4. The British strike force included 12 Fireflies and seven Seafires, which made rocket and cannon attacks on army barracks, bridges, gun positions, and vehicles, including two dangerous flak lorries. One Firefly received flak damage in the fuselage, while a Seafire had one of its wing-mounted combat fuel tanks holed by flak. Another Firefly had to make a forced landing aboard *Triumph* with only one wheel when the other failed to lower. Aircraft from the USS *Valley Forge* destroyed two gunboats, and attacked railway bridges, locomotives, and tunnels, while one bridge over the Taedong was knocked down. Four Skyraiders were damaged in these final strikes, but nine aircraft aboard *Valley Forge* were lost when a flak-damaged Skyraider failed to catch an arresting wire on landing and bounced over the barrier, careering into the deck park. The ship's Sikorsky HO3S-1 rescue helicopter was also forced to ditch after engine failure, leaving the fleet with only the obsolete Supermarine Sea Otter amphibian seaplane aboard *Triumph* for the rescue of downed pilots.

The sudden appearance of US and British aircraft more than 400 miles from the nearest American airfield was a rude awakening for the North Koreans. Indeed, the attacks may have deterred a sizable commitment of Russian aircraft to North Korean bases that week, for which the North Koreans had been negotiating since the outbreak of war. In addition to deterring immediate Soviet participation in the war, the value of carrier striking forces had been proven once again and would never again be seriously questioned. The US Navy had won the political argument over service integration; there would never again be any proposals to abolish naval aviation.

During the Pyongyang strikes, it had become obvious that the longer-ranged aircraft aboard *Valley Forge* were better for attacks against targets ashore, since otherwise the carriers were forced to move closer to the coast to use the shorter-ranged British aircraft. It was agreed that the Fireflies and Seafires would provide defensive cover for the fleet while the Americans mounted operations over Korea. The Seafires were by far the best defensive fighters in either fleet, with a greater rate of climb than the F9F Panthers. The Seafires thus flew combat air patrols while the Fireflies flew anti-submarine patrols. These missions were vital, since the North Korean Navy possessed a credible submarine threat and their small air force was still active offensively.

In the wake of the disaster to American arms in the initial contact with the North Korean People's Army, the mood in

Tokyo and Washington became grim. There was growing fear that American troops in a limited war might not be able to hold the enemy and that pressure could rise for use of the atomic bomb. A *New York Times* editorial of July 16 caught the mood:

> Our emotions, as we watch our outnumbered, out-weaponed soldiers in Korea, must be a mingling of pity, sorrow and admiration. This is the sacrifice we asked of them, justified only by the hope that what they are now doing will keep this war a small war, and that the death of a small number will prevent the slaughter of millions. The choice has been a terrible one. We cannot be cheerful about it, or even serene. But we need not be hysterical. We need not accept a greater war and the collapse of civilization.

The popularity of both the war and the Truman administration began a steady decline that would not be halted over the next two years.

The carriers continued strikes against North Korean targets over the rest of the month. On July 19, Lieutenant Commander Peter Cane with his crewman Chief Petty Officer Aircrewman G. O'Nion, performed the last operational rescue by a Sea Otter when they rescued the pilot of an F4U-4 Corsair from *Valley Forge* that had been shot down by antiaircraft fire and forced to ditch in very rough seas. The Sea Otter landed despite these adverse conditions, though it lost one stabilizing float on touchdown. The pilot was quickly rescued, and Cane managed to take off despite the rough sea, then returned to *Triumph*. Cane was awarded the US Air Medal for his actions.

The British aircraft maintained their combat air patrols and anti-submarine patrols in all weather around the clock. Through July and early August, HMS *Triumph* averaged 27 CAP sorties and ten anti-submarine sorties per day.

With such intensive flight operations, it was not long before accidents started to happen, with four Seafires being written off from heavy landings. The lightweight Seafire was particularly prone to damage to the rear fuselage in such a landing, which wrinkled the fuselage skin. A special micrometer gauge was used to determine whether the wrinkles were sufficient to ground an aircraft or for it to continue flying. Upon reaching a certain level, the "wrinkled" Seafires were to be grounded on the spot and returned to Britain to be re-jigged, which was impossible in the current situation. The engineering officer and his team stretched the rules under wartime conditions and managed to keep many flying. By the time HMS *Triumph* was relieved of its operational duties off Korea following the Inchon invasion and peacetime rules returned, all the surviving Seafires were grounded on the spot due to excessive wrinkling.

On July 28, a tragic event occurred when a flight of four Seafires on combat air patrol were vectored to investigate possible enemy air activity and found a flight of American B-29 bombers. Visually, the Seafire resembled the Yak-9, with its in-line engine and bubble canopy and one of the bombers opened fire and hit a Seafire in its rear fuel tank, which burst into flames. The pilot immediately rolled, inverted and bailed out, but not before suffering burns to his face, arms and shoulders. He landed in appalling sea conditions that made rescue by Sea Otter impossible, and was forced to wait about an hour in his raft until he was rescued by the American destroyer USS *Eversole*.

Over the course of July 1950, United Nations forces in Korea would be savagely mauled when they came up against North Korean People's Army forces. The American Army units lacked training and equipment, and much of their initial leadership was not up to the requirements of combat. The 24th Infantry Division never really recovered from its initial blood-letting. Despite the commitment of the 25th Infantry

Division and 1st Cavalry Division in mid-July, UN forces fell back until July 26, when they were able to stabilize a position that came to be known as "The Pusan Perimeter," a defensive line around the last deep-water port on the southeastern corner of the Korean peninsula, while North Korean troops occupied the rest of the country. For most of July and August there was good reason to believe the North Koreans might defeat the UN forces before further reinforcements could arrive.

On July 29, MacArthur led a major contingent of his staff and reporters to Taiwan, where he met with Chiang Kai-Shek. While the administration in Washington believed that the issue of Chinese troops in Korea had been settled a month before, that was not MacArthur's view. He ran the visit as though he was a head of state, publicly calling Chiang "my old comrade-in-arms" and kissing Madame Chiang's hand. Chiang said that the United States and China were going to make "common cause" against their enemies. While there was no change in policy, MacArthur's visit gave the appearance of a change in policy. As Bradley observed, "The net effect of the Nationalist propaganda was to give the impression that the United States was, or was going to be, far more closely allied with Chiang militarily in the struggle against Communism in the Far East, that we might even arm him for a 'return to the mainland.'" In Beijing, the result of MacArthur's visit was to reinforce in the minds of Mao Zedong and Zhou En-Lai that serious thought must be given to the possibility of war with the United States in Korea.

There was at this time a strong feeling in both Washington and Tokyo that Eighth Army commander Lieutenant General Walton Walker was not up to the task. An effective divisional and corps commander under Patton during World War II, Walton did not cut a commanding figure, overweight and only 5 feet 4 inches tall. When his size had been commented on to Patton, the legendary general had replied, "Yeah, but he's a fighting little sonofabitch." When he arrived to take command of Eighth Army in 1949, MacArthur had seen him as an enemy not to be trusted, due to his association with the war in Europe which the "Bataan Gang" believed had been waged at their expense in the Pacific. On August 8, a week after MacArthur's return from his visit with Chiang, presidential advisor Harriman, accompanied by Army Major General Matthew B. Ridgway and Air Force Major General Lauris Norstad, arrived in Tokyo to assess both the situation and the commanders. Harriman was tasked with trying to understand what was up with MacArthur. In fact, as Harriman had flown to Tokyo, an obviously leaked story came from MacArthur's headquarters that he was going to tell Harriman that "the war in Korea would prove useless unless the United States fought Communism everywhere it showed its head in Asia."

Ridgway, who had commanded the 101st Airborne Division at Normandy, was considered the best high-level combat commander in the US Army, and many thought he should command the Eighth Army. Though he was appalled at the situation he found in Korea, Ridgway himself was reluctant to have his criticism of the way Walker was running the battle be seen as an attempt on his part to take the command away for himself. MacArthur, who also wanted to replace Walker and thought Ridgway was the man for the job, said nothing, and the three left Tokyo under the impression MacArthur supported Walker and would react negatively to their advice he be sacked. Back in Washington, Harriman recommended to Truman that the president suggest this move to MacArthur, but when Ridgway expressed a fear that replacing the commander at such a difficult moment might affect morale in the Eighth Army, Truman deferred. Ridgway would eventually take command of Eighth Army in the wake of the coming disaster – a disaster he might have been able to avoid had he taken command in August 1950 rather than December.

During the meeting, MacArthur first presented his proposal for an amphibious operation at Inchon, utilizing the

1st Marine Division and Army 7th Division. Old paratrooper Ridgway's reaction was that it was a highly original strategy and he enthusiastically supported it, becoming the first Washington insider to step onto the Inchon bandwagon. He particularly agreed with MacArthur's belief that they must strike as soon as possible in order to end the fighting before the onset of the Korean winter, since a winter campaign would be so bitter and harsh that non-combat casualties might exceed battlefield casualties. Because of this, Ridgway would later find it highly ironic that MacArthur would insist on launching his final offensive into the teeth of the Korean winter. For Harriman, the originality of the proposal illuminated the basic problem of dealing with MacArthur: he was militarily brilliant, but he was not to be trusted politically. Harriman's trip perfectly summed up the problem, with the brilliance of Inchon counterposed to the political mess created with Chiang.

Harriman also reported to Truman that MacArthur viewed any form of accommodation with the Communist Chinese as a policy of appeasement, and that he had told Harriman that Chiang should be treated better. "For reasons that are rather difficult to explain," Harriman reported,

> I did not feel that we came to a full agreement on the way we believed things should be handled in Formosa and with the Generalissimo. He accepted the president's position and will act accordingly, but without full conviction. He has the strange idea that we should back anybody who will fight communism, even though he could not give me an argument why the Generalissimo's fighting communists would be a contribution towards an effective dealing with the communists in China.

MacArthur further contributed to the frustrations felt in Washington a few weeks later, when a speech he had written to be read in his name at the national convention of the Veterans of Foreign Wars was leaked. In it, the general stated his belief in the value of Taiwan in extending American domination over east Asia. This – that Taiwan was a great military base for the United States – was exactly the argument made by the Soviets on the part of their Chinese allies at the UN and the point the administration wanted to minimize in order to limit the scope of the war. The speech's conclusion was,

> Nothing could be more fallacious than the threadbare argument by those who advocate appeasement and defeatism in the Pacific that if we defend Formosa we alienate continental Asia. Those who speak thus do not understand the Orient. They do not grant that it is in the pattern of Oriental psychology to respect and follow aggressive, resolute and dynamic leadership.

Though released, the speech had not officially yet been given. A furious Truman called Johnson to his office and gave him a direct order to give MacArthur a direct order that the speech not be made and to inform the general that it was an order from the commander-in-chief. Johnson returned to his office and wavered because he did not want to cross MacArthur. He called Acheson and asked if there was not a way to change the decision, arguing that it was one man's opinion and everyone had a right to their beliefs. Acheson reminded him it was a presidential order and proceeded to inform Truman of Johnson's betrayal. In the end, Truman dictated a cable ordering MacArthur to withdraw the speech. MacArthur, furious, obeyed. The VFW speech was the end of the line for Defense Secretary Johnson. Harriman had been in the room on June 29, when Johnson had taken a call from Senator Taft following Taft's speech calling for the resignation of Acheson, in which he had congratulated the Republican for "saying the exact right thing." After he had hung up, Johnson had crudely solicited Harriman's support for his 1952 presidential candidacy, promising to make Harriman his Secretary of State. When this act of disloyalty was reported to Truman, it changed his mind about his 1948 supporter. Now that Johnson had revealed his disloyalty again, Truman decided it was time for him to go, political debt or no and he was forced to resign two weeks later. He had been Truman's worst political appointment, and the president gained stature with the military leaders who had been united in their opposition to Johnson over the previous 18 months. Marshall was asked to return as Defense Secretary and accepted. At the time Johnson left in early September, a joke was making its way around the Pentagon that the Joint Chiefs had informed the Defense Secretary he could finally call off his relentless troop reduction demands, since enough men were being killed in Korea every day to bring the Army's strength down to the desired level. In the wake of all of this, the president and his commanding general were even more distrustful of each other.

The only thing that saved UN forces during this dark period was control of the air. After early July, the North Korean Air Force made no appearance over the battlefield. At the same time, the Air Force and Navy kept up their attacks on North Korean supply lines. The B-29s were not ideal for battlefield interdiction, since there were no strategic targets in North Korea other than the attacking army and its supplies. The B-29s did attack Pyongyang and the few rail lines that supported the invading forces.

The crucial need was to expand the available force. The Pacific Fleet had two fleet carriers, USS *Boxer* (CV-21) and USS *Philippine Sea* (CV-47), and two *Commencement Bay*-class escort carriers, USS *Sicily* (CVE-118) and USS *Badoeng Strait* (CVE-116), at San Diego. *Boxer* was preparing to depart for overhaul at the Bremerton Naval Yard. *Philippine Sea*, the final *Essex*-class carrier to join the fleet, had arrived in San Diego from the east coast the previous May. *Philippine Sea's* Air Group 11 was equipped similarly to *Valley Forge's* Air Group 5, though its squadrons were not up to the same level of training, since the F9F-2 Panthers had only arrived in June. Nevertheless, *Philippine Sea* departed San Diego on July 6 and arrived in Pearl Harbor on July 11 to undergo two weeks of accelerated training before heading on to the Far East.

In the meantime, it had become obvious that the F-80 was not suitable for providing battlefield air support, due to its inability to use Korean airfields. The Air Force decided to re-convert the two fighter-bomber wings back to the F-51 Mustang, which could operate in Korea. F-51s were stripped from Air National Guard units throughout the continental United States and flown to the Alameda Naval Air Station in San Francisco Bay. Diverted from its voyage to Bremerton, USS *Boxer* docked at the base on June 8 and 145 F-51s, hurriedly treated for trans-ocean shipment, were loaded aboard. *Boxer* departed for Japan on July 14, arriving in Yokosuka on July 23 after a record trans-Pacific crossing of eight days and 16 hours. The two CVEs were primarily tasked for anti-submarine warfare, though they had also been used to provide refresher carrier training to Marine fighter squadrons on the west coast. *Sicily* departed San Diego for Guam on July 2 to provide anti-submarine defense. *Badoeng Strait* had only just arrived in Pearl Harbor on a summer midshipmen's cruise. The midshipmen were deposited in Hawaii while the ship hurriedly returned to San Diego. Two heavy cruisers based at Long Beach, USS *Helena* (CA-75) and USS *Toledo* (CA-133), which had only returned from the Far East the month before, departed on July 6, headed for Japan with their escorting destroyers.

By July 8, 1950, the Pacific Fleet had deployed all the ships it had that were immediately available. That day, Chief of Naval Operations Admiral Forrest Sherman authorized reactivation of ships in the mothball fleet. The days of budgetary restrictions were over.

On June 25, 1950, the total active strength of the Marine Corps was 28,000 men, with 12,000 assigned to the 1st Marine Division at Camp Pendleton, California, and its attached First Marine Air Wing at nearby MCAS El Toro. Budgetary constraints had hit the Marines, too. The 1st Marine Division was operating with two platoons to a company, two companies to a battalion, and two battalions to a regiment, rather than the standard three, three, and three. All units were undermanned. Second Lieutenant Joseph R. Owen, who was with the 2nd Marine Division in Camp Lejeune, North Carolina, when the war broke out, recalled that:

> Although budget cuts had left us short of both people and ammunition for training purposes, we took to the swamps and woods and beaches with half platoons and shrunken rifle companies. We didn't realize its value then, but we were learning how to make skeleton formations cover large pieces of terrain. It proved to be good experience for the fighting we would do when we were spread perilously thin at the Chosin Reservoir.

At the time, the Marines were considered to have more experience in amphibious warfare than any other military force in the world, so the fact that Korea was a peninsula with miles of shoreline made their commitment obvious. Apart from their amphibious expertise, there were other advantages. Rapid reinforcement was required, and the Marine Corps has historically lived with its proverbial bags packed. The Marines were mobile and the requirements of seaborne assault had led to the development of an extremely powerful force package. Man for man, unit for unit, there was likely no stronger combat force in existence. The ground combat elements were made up of heavily armed and highly professional units in which every man from cook and clerk to commanding officer could handle a rifle. The air support team had become a fact by the end of the Pacific War. Marines had no need to beg for support from a separate force with separate responsibilities and objectives.

All Marine aviators had infantry training and all were carrier qualified, able to operate from ships offshore until shore-based airstrips were available. As Joe Owen recalled, "By 1950, every infantry leader knew how to summon and direct our flying artillery against enemy positions, often bringing it in only a few hundred yards from our force." The Marines really were capable of fighting anyone, anywhere. Between December 1949 and June 1950, the units of Fleet Marine Force Pacific had participated in two field exercises of regimental size or larger, an amphibious demonstration, and various lesser exercises involving submarines, helicopters, and the seizure of San Nicholas Island by a battalion airlifted by helicopter, so they were operationally prepared. Plans had been in place since 1948 for the rapid movement of a regimental combat team and a supporting Marine air group from the west coast to any point in the Pacific. The Navy Department was on ten-day notice to provide the necessary mounting-out equipment. While they had narrowly escaped induction into the Army following service unification in 1948, and while many thought that amphibious warfare was a relic of the past, the Marines were exactly what the war in Korea needed.

On June 28, the commandant of the Corps, General Clifton B. Cates, recommended employment of the Fleet Marine Force in Korea to the chief of Naval Operations. On July 1, Chief of Naval Operations Admiral Sherman asked Admiral Radford, commander of the Pacific Fleet, how long it would take to move out a battalion landing team or a regimental combat team. Radford's reply on Sunday July 2 stated that a battalion landing team could be loaded in four days and sailed in six, and a regimental combat team loaded in six and sailed in ten. The Seventh Fleet commander Admiral Turner Joy was notified that a Marine regimental combat team could be made available if desired, an offer General MacArthur accepted with enthusiasm. Before that Sunday was out, the 1st Marine Division had been alerted and orders had been given to the Pacific Fleet to move a regimental combat team with appropriate attached air strength to the Far East.

It took some doing for the Marines to provide a division of more than 20,000 men, not to mention the 4,000 or so additional personnel of the 1st Marine Aircraft Wing, and to do so without completely disorganizing the Fleet Marine Force Atlantic, as well as the supporting establishment. Only the president's decision of July 19 to call up the reserve allowed the creation of the division. One third of the troops assigned were taken from the 2nd Marine Division based in North Carolina, one third was made up of Marine reservists summoned to active duty, while the remainder was provided by reassigning a battalion of the 6th Marines, then in the Mediterranean, and by taking personnel from miscellaneous posts throughout the United States.

The general attitude of the Marine reservists called to active duty was not one of enthusiasm. Many had served during the war and some had fought in the Pacific and all felt they had done their bit for the country; none of the World War II Marines in the reserves had voluntarily joined, being assigned so they would fulfill their overall obligation from their original enlistment. Moreover, many World War II reservists in all the services felt that they were being called on to fight in a way others were not. This was particularly the case with the men who were in the "unorganized reserve," individuals not attached to a particular unit, while those in the organized reserves who did form units and underwent regular training, were not immediately called to active duty. This would be a general complaint throughout the Korean War.

On July 5, 1950, orders arrived to create the First Provisional Marine Brigade (Reinforced), built around the 5th Marine Regiment at Camp Pendleton and Marine Air Group 33 at nearby El Toro Marine Air Station. Command was given to Brigadier General Edward A. Craig, the

1st Marine Division assistant commander, while Brigadier General Thomas J. Cushman, deputy commander of the First Marine Aircraft Wing, was appointed both deputy brigade commander and commanding general of the air wing's forward echelon. This flexibility was unmatched by any other ground force in any country; that appointing an aviator second-in-command of an infantry brigade was considered routine demonstrated the promise of close ground-air teamwork.

From the time they received the warning order, division and wing staffs had been hard at work. The task of bringing the various units of the brigade up to authorized war strength was complicated. A directive of July 3 from the commandant of the Corps had required all sergeants and below whose enlistments would expire before March 1951 be transferred and left behind; however, this cut too deeply into the need for experienced NCOs and was soon reversed. Sergeant Paul Ritter, a ground crewman with VMF-214, had expected to leave the Marines in September, having joined in 1947. "I can tell you, there was a lot of grousing among the men. But with Marines, if you're not upset about something, it's because you haven't been paying attention. Everyone's life was turned upside down; I didn't finally leave the Corps until 1955, after spending all three years in Korea and not getting home until just before Thanksgiving in 1953. But orders were orders and if you're a Marine, you follow them." Leaves were canceled and transfers stopped. By the time the brigade was formally activated on July 7, personnel shortages were being filled from the Marine barracks at Camp Pendleton and other west coast stations. Supplies and gear were moving from Camp Pendleton to ships in San Diego, while weapons were transferred from the storage center at Barstow in the Mojave Desert. The speed with which the brigade moved out owed much to earlier planning, as well as the ten-day readiness stocks which had been maintained for both ground and air forces. When the first ships became available in San

Diego on July 9, embarkation plans were complete and loading could begin.

The Provisional Marine Brigade was built around the three infantry rifle companies of the 5th Marines, composed of 132 officers and 2,452 enlisted men. Artillery came from the 1st Battalion, 11th Marines. Motor transport, medical, shore party, engineer, tank, and amphibious tractor companies were assigned along with detachments of signal, ordnance, service, reconnaissance, and military police units. The air component was composed of an observation squadron, VMO-6, with eight Stinson OY-2 "Sentinel" observation planes and four Sikorsky H03S-1 helicopters. Marine Air Group 33's two day fighter-bomber squadrons, VMF-323 and VMF-214 with 48 F4U-4 Corsair aircraft, and a night fighter unit, VMF(AW)-513 with 24 F4U-5Ns, composed the forward air echelon of the First Marine Air Wing. The aircraft and aircrews went aboard USS *Badoeng Strait* on July 10.

On July 11 and 12, the brigade's ground forces embarked in three attack transports of Task Group 53.7: USS *George Clymer* (APA-27), *Henrico* (APA-45), and *Pickaway* (APA-222); the attack cargo ships USS *Whiteside* (AKA-90) and *Alshain* (AKA-55); and the Landing Ship Docks USS *Gunston Hall* (LSD-44) and *Fort Marion* (LSD-22). Air group personnel and equipment boarded the Military Sea Transportation System (MSTS) transport *General A. E. Anderson* and the attack cargo ship USS *Achernar* (AKA-53) at Terminal Island in Long Beach.

On July 12, exactly ten days after the receipt of the warning order, the two LSDs sailed from San Diego carrying the tank and amphibious tractor companies. The rest of the convoy followed on July 14. The Marines had justified their existence as the most combat-ready fighting force the United States possessed.

By July 15, the leading elements of the North Korean forces were halfway between the 38th Parallel and the port of Pusan, on the southeastern tip of the Korean peninsula. Unless Pusan

The Pusan Perimeter, August 5 to September 17, 1950

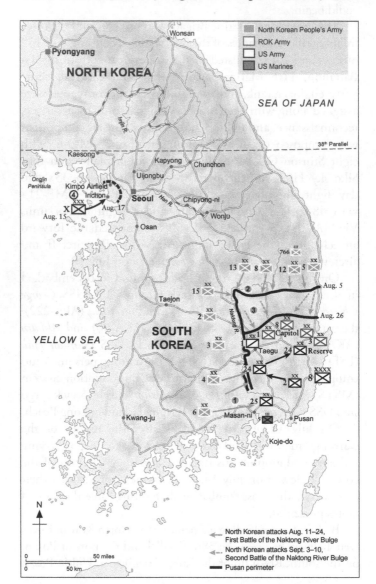

could be held, UN forces would be forced out of the battlefield. The 25th Infantry Division was hurriedly transferred to Korea from Japan during the first week of July, moving north to connect with the 24th Infantry Division that had been first to meet the North Koreans. On July 18 the elite 1st Cavalry Division was landed at Pohang, and relieved the battered 24th Division at Taejon on July 20. After covering the landing of 1st Cavalry, Task Force 77 entered the Sea of Japan. *Valley Forge* and *Triumph* launched strikes against railroad facilities, industrial plants, and airfields from Pyongyang and Wonsan north through Hungnam and Hamhung on the east coast of the peninsula on July 18–19. These strikes saw the destruction of the last North Korean Air Force aircraft when airfields were targeted. From this point on, the North Korean army in the south would have no air support. Fighting intensified as UN forces took up defensive positions along the line of the Naktong River just north of Pusan.

The convoy carrying the Provisional Marine Brigade arrived in Kobe, Japan, on July 31, 1950. USS *Sicily* had arrived in Kobe the day before from Guam and had sent its anti-submarine squadron ashore. On August 1, ground support personnel from VMF-214 left *Badoeng Strait* and went aboard *Sicily*, which departed for Korea that evening. The "Black Sheep Squadron" pilots flew their Corsairs aboard on August 2. At the same time, *Badoeng Strait* got underway from Kobe, spending two days of refresher air training with VMF-323. The Marine aviators were fully engaged in combat operations within 96 hours of their arrival in Japan.

The week from July 29 to August 5 saw American and ROK forces retreating on all fronts. In the northwestern sector of the front, the North Korean armies advanced 35 miles through the mountain passes into the Naktong Valley, where they stopped opposite Waegwan. To the east, in the northern hill sector, the NKPA pushed forward to Andong on the upper Naktong. In the south, at Hadong, American and ROK troops were overrun. While 100 survivors were evacuated by ROK small craft from the Chinhae Naval Base and others escaped overland, total casualties exceeded 50 percent. So confident were the North Koreans, now that their forces were through the mountains and able to maneuver in the open region of the Naktong, that a NKPA I Corps operation order made on August 3 called for the capture of Taegu and Pusan by the 6th. The one bright spot in all this came on July 27, when the newly arrived heavy cruiser USS *Toledo* brought its 8-inch guns to bear for the first time against the invading army north of Pohang. Through careful conservation of ammunition, the cruiser and its escorting destroyers fired on troop concentrations, supplies, and revetments by day and illuminated the battle line with star shells at night for 11 days. So effective was this operation, which was assisted by a 24th Division fire control party and by air spotting from L-4 and L-5 light aircraft, that the battle line remained stable.

In the midst of this, the transports carrying the ground units of the Marine Brigade arrived in Pusan on August 2, 1950. By August 3, the 5th Marines had moved into position at the village of Changwon, 30 miles north of Pusan. On August 6, the two escort carriers took up station offshore to provide air support. The Marine squadrons on these two small carriers were all the immediate air support available: Task Force 77 had retired to Buckner Bay, Okinawa, to resupply at the end of July, since the Navy did not at the time have the necessary support vessels on hand to perform underway replenishment. In Buckner Bay, USS *Philippine Sea* joined the fleet, doubling the Task Force 77 strength. With the arrival of a second American carrier, HMS *Triumph* was detached from Task Force 77 and joined the Commonwealth Task Force which had the responsibility of blockading enemy ports and attacking supply lines on the west coast of Korea. The Seafires and Fireflies went back to offensive operations, with their main role being flying armed reconnaissance sorties

The Inchon Landing

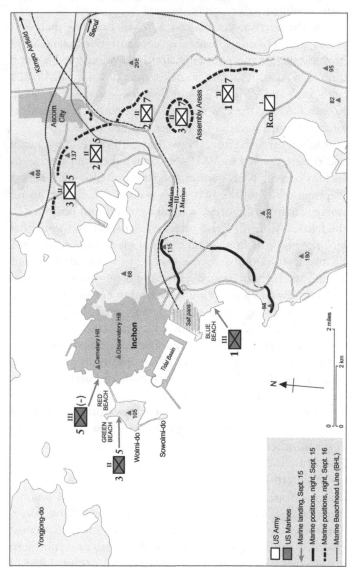

over ports and searching for camouflaged shipping within the many confined waterways in the area.

On the afternoon of August 3, VMF-214 flew their first strikes against North Korean troop concentrations near Chinju in the south of the perimeter and on the central Naktong front. On August 4, further strikes were flown by VMF-214 from *Sicily* and VMF-323 from *Badoeng Strait* against North Korean forces in the Chinju area. That evening, *Sicily* and its escorts steamed into the Yellow Sea, headed north.

On August 5, the Royal Navy heavy cruisers HMS *Jamaica* and *Belfast*, covered by VMF-214, entered the approaches to Inchon harbor. With gunfire spotting provided by a P2V-5 Neptune of VP-6, the two ships poured 8-inch fire on oil storage facilities, factories, warehouses, and gun positions in the harbor. VMF-214 also attacked transport and industrial facilities in the Inchon–Seoul region. One Marine aviator had his suspicions aroused by the multiple antiaircraft positions around an Inchon factory. He made a low pass at 50 feet and saw several pieces of military equipment inside. Pulling around and diving on the target, he put a napalm bomb into the building, which resulted in a very satisfactory secondary explosion and fire. The next day, *Sicily*'s Corsairs struck targets at Kunsan and Mokpo and NKPA troops on the south coast. As dusk fell, the little carrier arrived back off Pusan where she rendezvoused with *Badoeng Strait*.

Task Force 77 returned from Okinawa during the night of August 4. The next morning both *Philippine Sea* and *Valley Forge* launched strikes from a position south of the Korean peninsula. The *Philippine Sea* air group was assigned targets in southwestern Korea, with emphasis on the rail and highway bridges at Iri, east of Kunsan, where cuts would hamper movement of supplies to the enemy's southern flank. *Valley Forge* sent its aircraft off on close support missions against troops, supplies, and bridges in the dangerous northern sector. Two Corsairs attacked North Korean troops west of

Taegu, while five Skyraiders inflicted heavy casualties on troops behind the central front.

While the support missions flown on August 6 were valuable, the Navy did not provide the same level of "close support" the Marines could. It was thus decided that the Navy would concentrate on attacks against enemy supply lines and troop concentrations behind the front, while the Marines operating from the escort carriers would take responsibility for battlefield close air support. The Marines and Navy were far better situated to provide this sort of cover and support than was the Air Force since they were operating close to the battlefield, while the Air Force bases were no closer than Kyushu. F-80 jet fighters could only remain over the perimeter for 10 minutes, while the F-51s could remain up to 45 minutes, at the cost of a reduced ordnance load. There were no operational airfields inside the perimeter at this time other than the one at Pohang, where F-51s would land to operate during the day, returning at night to Japan.

On August 7, the first battle of the Naktong broke out as the North Koreans were able to ford the river due to lower water levels in the summer heat. MacArthur ordered both the Navy and Marines to provide close air support, which held all five carriers off Pusan from August 8–17.

On August 7, 1950, the eighth anniversary of the landing by the 1st Marine Division at Guadalcanal, the Provisional Marine Brigade entered combat in Korea. Eighth Army commander General Walton Walker ordered an attack westward from Masan toward Chinju, to contain the enemy's south coast advance. While Army forces moved west along the main highway, the Marines were responsible for cleaning out the left flank along the coastal road through Kosong and Sachon. As at Guadalcanal, the weather was hot, humid, and exhausting. The 5th Marines engaged in heavy and confused fighting for three days until the hills controlling the road junction at Chindong-ni were cleared on August 10. The coordinated use of brigade artillery and Marine aircraft from the escort carriers broke up enemy counterattacks. In the early morning of August 10, the Marines captured Paedun-ni.

That afternoon, leading elements of the 5th Marines were ambushed at Taedabok Pass. M-26 Pershing heavy tanks were brought forward while Corsairs attacked the North Koreans in the pass with napalm. By nightfall, the Marines were through the pass and two-thirds of the way to Kosong.

While the Marines experienced success in these fights, things were looking ominous elsewhere in the perimeter. During fighting at Chindong-ni on August 8, the North Koreans expanded their Naktong River bridgehead to regimental strength. By August 10, NKPA 4th Division was on the south side of the river in force.

On August 11, the Marines resumed their advance on Kosong. Shelling the town that morning resulted in an estimated 100 North Korean vehicles heading west out of the town. VMF-323 pilots from *Badoeng Strait* observed trucks retreating so fast that some missed turns and rolled down embankments. Taking advantage of this opportunity, the aviators finished off the enemy. By 1000 hours Kosong had been taken, and the Marines headed onward toward Sachon. Enemy roadblocks were broken and momentum was gained, while enemy casualties were estimated at nearly 2,000. The North Koreans appeared increasingly disorganized. However, in other sectors of the perimeter, the situation was deteriorating. US Army counterattacks failed to eliminate the Naktong bulge. North Korean forces re-emerged from the hills around Chindong-ni behind the Marines, and cut the main supply route for Army troops advancing on Chinju, which forced the Marines to return one battalion and a battery of artillery to clean this up just as they were closing in on Changchon.

On August 12, the 1st and 2nd Battalions encountered another ambush at Changchon, which was beaten off with heavy North Korean casualties. While this fight was going on, the 3rd Battalion arrived back at Chindong-ni. Before dark the battalion won its first objective, a hill ridge commanding the main supply route.

Due to the deteriorating situation elsewhere, the Brigade was ordered to withdraw on August 13, with the 1st and 2nd Battalions disengaging and joining the 3rd Battalion to clean up Chindong-ni. While the Marines had advanced 26 miles in four days, inflicting heavy damage on superior forces, the situation in the Naktong bulge was very nearly out of control. The ROK 3rd Division at Pohang was under heavy attack and the Navy was evacuating Air Force personnel from Pohang airfield. While surface ships attempted to provide fire support to cover this evacuation, the North Koreans surrounded the ROK 3rd Division north of the port.

On August 15, a seaborne evacuation was ordered. USS *Helena* and its accompanying destroyers were tasked with providing fire support. Medical supplies were flown in from the ships by helicopter, while further support was provided by Task Force 77 which had arrived from Sasebo. After further air strikes on August 16 stopped North Korean attacks on the ROKs, four LSTs were brought up from Pusan and the division was successfully evacuated overnight.

HMS *Triumph* flew the first sorties in its new role on August 13 when two Seafires photographed the ports of Mokpo and Kunsan and shot up two small ships with a second sortie flown later to photograph Inchon. The next day the main North Korean naval base at Chinnampo was photographed, with three ships found moored in the estuary. Even though the base had heavy flak defenses, six Seafires and six Fireflies armed with 60lb rockets took off in the afternoon to attack what turned out to be a camouflaged minesweeper, a 2,000-ton freighter and an 800-ton coaster, with all three substantially damaged. On August 15 a naval gunfire support spotting sortie was flown in conjunction with an attack by HMS *Jamaica* against shipping at Inchon. This would become a major role for the air wing. On August 19, a particularly successful patrol of two Fireflies discovered a camouflaged 150-ton motor junk armed with heavy antiaircraft guns which they set ablaze after firing 16 60lb rockets on it. They then proceeded inland and attacked railway wagons, oil storage tanks and small coastal junks using their cannon. Four Seafires made an armed reconnaissance to Chinnampo, then followed the river as far as Pyongyang where heavy antiaircraft fire was encountered, but found no worthwhile targets. Another long-range reconnaissance flight went as far as the Manchurian border.

While these events were playing out, the Marine Brigade moved north to Miryang and then west to Yongsan, to confront the crisis in the Naktong bulge. Having first crossed the river on August 6, the NKPA 4th Division was in position south of the river by August 12. Counterattacks on August 11 and on August 14–15 failed to dislodge the three North Korean infantry regiments which now held the eastern ridges with artillery and tank support, and were moving onto the Yongsan road. The danger was great.

If the North Korean forces could not be contained, the lowland river valley route to Pusan would lie open. Three Army regiments, all at less than half-strength at the time the enemy crossed the river, had been heavily engaged for ten days. The Marines' situation was not much better. No replacements had reached the brigade since its arrival in Korea and losses suffered in the Kosong offensive had not been made good, while each of the battalions still lacked their third company. To confront the crisis and restore the balance, these three under-strength battalions were to be committed against a force nearly twice their number.

Upon their arrival at 0800 hours on August 17, the Marines were ordered to attack westward along the road, with Obong-ni Ridge, which ran northwest–southeast across the entrance to the bulge, their first objective. Shortage of transport had delayed the arrival of the brigade and adversely affected the artillery preparation, while a misunderstanding with the Army unit on the right led to a lack of flank support. An air strike from the escort carriers was 15 minutes late, which meant that the 18 Corsairs had only half their planned time to hit the enemy positions. The uphill advance against a numerically superior entrenched enemy was carried out with great bravery but at heavy cost: the 2nd Battalion, which led the attack with 240 men, suffered 142 casualties by midday. The 1st Battalion was committed at 1300 hours. By 1800 hours, the northern end of the ridge had been taken and a counterattacking tank force destroyed by artillery and air strikes. To the north of the road, Army troops had moved up to parallel the brigade's position, and troops of the 24th Division had reached their objectives in the northern hills.

The North Koreans made strong counterattacks during the night along Obong-ni Ridge, but proved unable to exploit their gains. On the morning of August 18 the Marines' advance resumed. Held up by a heavy machine-gun nest less than 100 yards ahead of the troops, close air support was called in. Under ground control the Corsair pilots executed a dummy run, a target-marking run, and a strike within nine minutes. A 500lb bomb was dropped squarely on the position, which eliminated the machine gun and panicked enemy troops. By 0830 hours, the ridge had been cleared and the crisis was past.

Even before the ridgeline had been taken, the enemy commander had ordered withdrawal across the river after the failure of his night counterattack. This decision was expedited by the Marines' seizure of their second objective, a commanding elevation half a mile to the west, which was taken shortly after 1300 hours. With the North Koreans now in disorganized retreat, artillery fire was directed at the river crossings, while Corsairs strafed troops on the banks and in the water, turning the muddy Naktong red.

While this slaughter was in progress, the 3rd Battalion advanced toward the final objective, the dominating height within the bulge. The hill was taken by 0645 hours on August 19 and the bulge was secured. West of the Naktong, North Korean confusion radiated outward, expanded as the result of attacks by strike groups from *Philippine Sea* against North Korean troop concentrations and supply dumps between Hyopchon and the Naktong.

With its task completed, the Marine Brigade was detached on August 20 and assigned to Eighth Army reserve, moving back to the Masan area. There the infantry bivouacked in a bean patch, while the artillery was sent back to work at Chindong-ni, where enemy pressure had again mounted. During the three days of fighting in the bulge, the Marines had captured 22 pieces of artillery and large amounts of other materiel. Enemy loss estimates varied between 2,500 and 4,500 killed. For the North Koreans, the elimination of the Naktong bulge and the destruction inflicted on the 4th Division was their greatest defeat thus far. In contrast, Marine casualties totaled 345, with 66 KIA, an extraordinarily disproportionate result that testified to the professionalism of the Marines and to what command of the air can accomplish when it is exploited by a unitary air-ground force.

For the UN forces, the time gained by the Marine action was beyond all price. There would be a ten-day respite before the North Koreans would succeed in reestablishing their bridgehead across the Naktong.

Back at Camp Pendleton, the complete activation of the 1st Marine Division was moving as rapidly as possible. Raymond G. Davis, commander of the 1st Battalion, 7th Marines, remembered the summer of 1950 as one of frenetic activity:

First, I lost nearly every officer and NCO in the battalion with combat experience to the 5th Marines when they established the Provisional Marine Brigade in early July. I was fortunate in being able to corral several very promising young Lieutenants from the Second Marine Division when they arrived in mid-July. These young officers had to hit the deck running, take control of their units and institute effective training programs for Marines who had no experience with the weapons they would use, and even less experience in tactical maneuvering. This was particularly true with regard to the reservists, but many of the regulars were also without experience, having joined since the war. Eighteen-hour days became the norm, seven days a week. Within a few weeks, these young Marines were responding to the situation with outstanding effort. By the time we were ordered to move out, most of them still lacked the ability to look like Marines, but they all possessed the knowledge necessary to act like Marines. Every one of them was qualified on his weapon, including the clerks and other support personnel, and I believed they would acquit themselves in accordance with the best traditions of the Corps when they met the enemy. In retrospect, they all more than lived up to my expectations.

The division was fortunate that its leaders were among the most outstanding officers to ever wear the Marine uniform. The commander of 1/7, Davis would be remembered as the outstanding battalion commander. A Marine since graduation from the Georgia Institute of Technology in June 1938, he was in the first wave of the landing on Guadalcanal in August 1942, commanding the 1st Antiaircraft Machine Gun Battery. Promoted to major in February 1943, he served as commanding officer of the 1st Special Weapons Battalion, 1st Marine Division. In April 1944, while on Cape Gloucester, he took command of the 1st Battalion, 1st Marine Regiment. His extraordinary heroism in combat on Peleliu in September 1944 earned him the Navy Cross and

Purple Heart. Wounded during the first hour of the landing, he refused evacuation. When at one point the Japanese broke through the lines, he personally rallied and led his men to re-establish the defensive positions. He had been a lieutenant colonel since October 1944. As with the other leaders of the division, Davis was an officer who led from the front.

The commander of the 7th Marine Regiment, Colonel Homer L. Litzenberg, had enlisted in the Marines in 1922. Following a tour in Haiti, he was commissioned a second lieutenant in 1925. In 1943 he organized and commanded the 3rd Battalion, 24th Marines, 4th Marine Division and served as regimental executive officer during the assault on Roi-Namur in Kwajalein Atoll, where he earned his first Silver Star. As assistant operations officer in the Fifth Amphibious Corps, he had participated in the battle of Saipan and battle of Tinian. Since the war, Litzenberg had served in China and had seen the Chinese Communist military forces in action.

The commander of the 1st Marine Regiment was the legendary Lieutenant Colonel Lewis B. "Chesty" Puller, the only Marine ever awarded five Navy Crosses for bravery in combat. He had enlisted in 1918, just too late to see combat in World War I. A veteran of guerrilla warfare in Haiti and Nicaragua in the 1920s, he was awarded his first Navy Cross for actions from February 16 to August 19, 1930, when he led "five successive engagements against superior numbers of armed bandit forces." Puller had served as a "China Marine" in Beijing at the time of the Japanese invasion of Manchuria, later serving as a battalion commander in the 4th Marines in Shanghai just before the Pacific War. He first took command of the 1st Battalion, 7th Marines, in 1942, leading the battalion in combat on Guadalcanal, where he earned his second and third Navy Crosses. As executive officer of the 7th Marines at Cape Gloucester, he was awarded a fourth Navy Cross for his combat leadership, and commanded the 1st Regiment at Peleliu, where he was awarded the Legion of Merit. Puller had specifically requested assignment back to the 1st Marines for their deployment to Korea.

Raymond L. Murray, commander of the 5th Marine Regiment, was awarded his first Navy Cross for extraordinary heroism under fire on June 15, 1944, during the invasion of Saipan, when he was a lieutenant colonel commanding the 2nd Battalion, 6th Marines, 2nd Marine Division. Murray had joined the Marines in 1935 after graduating from Texas A&M, and served as a junior officer in China from 1937 to 1940, where he had gotten a good look at both the Japanese Army and the Red Chinese guerrilla forces. He was awarded his first Silver Star in January 1943 while leading the 2nd Battalion, 6th Marines on Guadalcanal and a second one while leading the unit in the bloody invasion of Tarawa that November. As commander of the 5th Marine Regiment in the Provisional Marine Brigade, he was awarded a fourth and fifth Silver Star and the Legion of Merit for actions during the fighting in the Pusan Perimeter in August and September 1950.

The 1st Marine Division was so severely understaffed that the decision had been quickly made when the Marines were activated to "raid" the 2nd Marine Division at Camp Lejeune, North Carolina, to provide experienced officers and NCOs. Getting volunteers from Camp Lejeune was the least of the problems faced in getting the division ready to go to war. Calling up the Marine Reserves was unlike what that decision would later mean, since the Marine Reserves called to active duty in 1950 included men who had not even attended training meetings, let alone gone through boot camp, and were basically untrained. Second Lieutenant Owen, who had seen combat at Iwo Jima as an enlisted Marine and later rejoined the service in 1949 after graduating from college on the postwar GI Bill, was among the Marine junior infantry officers who volunteered to make the trip west from Camp Lejeune. He remembered that when he finally landed a position as commander of the mortar platoon for

Baker Company, 1/7 Marines, there were only four men with any combat experience in the platoon of 40, two of whom were former World War II sailors who had joined the Marine Reserves after the war for the additional pay. Far from the mythology that the 1st Marine Division was filled with Pacific War veterans, Owen's platoon sergeant had never served in an infantry unit in his eight years in the Corps. The two ex-sailors, who had seen combat aboard ship, were quickly promoted as squad leaders. There were in addition five other Regular Marines, privates and lance corporals, who became squad and team leaders regardless of their lack of experience. No one in the platoon other than Owen had any experience at all with the 60mm mortars they were to use in combat. "I had three weeks to give my men what would normally have been three or four months of training, and that only after they had completed boot camp," Owen remembered. Fifteen-hour training days became the norm at Camp Pendleton throughout the division.

There was one Marine officer unlike every other officer who reported to Camp Pendleton at this time. First Lieutenant Kurt Chew-Een Lee was the first Asian-American commissioned as a Marine officer. Inducted into the Marines in 1944, he was assigned to learn Japanese after boot camp, then retained as an instructor at the Marine Corps Japanese Language School following graduation, an assignment that included accelerated promotion to sergeant, though he resisted the assignment at first in hopes of being sent into combat. At the end of the war, Lee had been accepted for officer training, and was commissioned in 1946. Having been raised in his family with books that told the story of ancient Chinese military commanders and Chinese military success, he took it as his personal mission to consciously demolish the belief that the Chinese, as a race, were too meek, obsequious and subservient to make good soldiers. When he took command of the heavy weapons platoon in Baker 1/7, Lee encountered some friction with his new recruits in the platoon, many of whom had never seen or spoken to any Chinese person and saw Asians as the enemy. Joe Owen remembered that Lee was also resented for his strict and intense training regimen. "He was absolutely a by-the-book officer," Owen later wrote. When two Marines came to Owen to request transfer to the mortar platoon and stated as their reason their resistance to taking orders from "a Chinaman," Owen informed them that Marine officers were Marines, period, and sent them back. Lee had one of the toughest training schedules in the company, since he only had three men with experience, and had to train machine-gun teams in the intricate work of operating their weapons in combat.

Among the other Marine reservists reporting for duty at Camp Pendleton that summer was Marine Aviator Ed McMahon, who had wanted to be a Marine fighter pilot when he joined during World War II. However, he had excelled so well in his training as a fighter pilot that he found himself assigned as an instructor in Training Command once he won his Wings of Gold in early 1944. His wish to see combat seemed to be granted when he was assigned to a Marine fighter squadron in June 1945 that was set to go aboard a carrier for the invasion of Japan. However, while the ship crossed the Pacific in August 1945, the war came to an end before he could put himself to that ultimate test. "I got out in early 1946 and went back to finish my education. I stayed in the Marine Reserves since it gave me some additional income to what I was getting with the GI Bill, which was a help since I was married, and once a month I had the opportunity to fly something a little more peppy than a Piper Cub." Graduating from the Catholic University of America in 1949, McMahon had just gotten his first job in broadcasting when he received his call-up for active duty in early July 1950. "I figured that since I had all that experience in the Corsair back during the war that I'd finally get my chance to see combat on a carrier."

Instead, when he arrived at MCAS El Toro, he found himself assigned to VMO-6, the division battlefield observation squadron, flying the Stinson OY-2 "Sentinel":

> It was exactly what I didn't want, but it was no time to protest and try to change things. I stayed behind when they sent the first planes of the squadron over with the Provisional Brigade, since I wasn't trained in artillery spotting. I went through a fast course in that and by the time we were ready to deploy I was pretty good at spotting fire. As it turned out, the job I did when we got to the Reservoir – evacuating casualties – was the best job I could have had.

On August 8, 1950, the day after the Provisional Marine Brigade entered combat, loading of the 1st Marine Division for deployment to Korea began. Originally, following the deployment of the Provisional Marine Brigade, a further regimental combat team based on the 1st Marine Regiment had been promised for deployment in September, with the entire division attaining combat capability in November. In the face of the emergency in South Korea, MacArthur had been able to convince Washington to deploy the entire division to Korea by early September, to lead the invasion of Inchon his staff had been planning since early July. In the end, the 7th Marine Regiment was only able to achieve full combat capability when it was decided to strip a battalion from the 6th Marine Regiment, then currently serving in the Mediterranean, to become the 7th Marines' 3rd Battalion. This unit shipped from the Mediterranean on August 8, through the Suez Canal, then across the Indian Ocean and South China Sea to meet their fellow Marines in Korea just before the Inchon invasion. The 1st Marine Division commander, General Oliver P. Smith, and his staff arrived in Tokyo by air on August 30, 1950.

On the night of August 31, 1950, the worst crisis of the Pusan Perimeter began when the North Koreans launched their greatest effort, which became known as the second battle of the Naktong. Heavy attacks began around the entire perimeter from Pohang to Haman, with heavy forces committed to the Naktong River front. It was obvious that a major emergency was at hand. All troops were ordered out of reserve and all available air support was urgently called for. At 0800 hours on September 1 the Marine Brigade was alerted to move north to Miryang and then to the Naktong bulge.

The brigade arrived in Miryang a few hours later, then moved west to Yongsan on September 2. The situation was even worse than it had been the month before. Most of two Communist divisions were across the river, and the North Koreans had broken out of the bulge, advancing 4 miles east along the Yongsan road. Local Army commanders wanted the Marines to attack immediately, but General Craig did not wish to commit his force until the troops had reached their assembly points and his air control personnel had arrived.

Both *Sicily* and *Badoeng Strait* were in Sasebo replenishing. VMF-214 and VMF-323 were ashore at Ashiya AFB in Kyushu. Typhoon Jane was approaching southern Japan and the weather was deteriorating.

The North Koreans struck Yongsan at dawn on September 3. A heavy attack penetrated the Marines' intended line of departure, a ridge occupied by the Army's 9th Infantry Regiment half a mile west of the town. As the Marines dismounted their trucks and moved forward, the North Koreans had made it through the American lines. Snipers were encountered as the Marines marched through Yongsan. When they emerged west of the town, they came under moderate enemy fire. While the Army troops pulled back, the Marines opened up with heavy fire by artillery, tanks, and automatic weapons, which halted the North Korean advance. The Marines then headed west from Yongsan, with the goal of clearing the hills that controlled the road junction and the road leading on to Obong-ni Ridge. The terrain was difficult and fighting was hard, but by noon the initial objectives had been achieved. However, with Typhoon Jane now centered over southern Honshu, there was no possibility of close air support missions being flown from Ashiya. Task Force 77 had been refueling in the Sea of Japan that morning when the Marines' cry for help was received. The first Navy mission arrived overhead at 1747 hours.

With guidance from the ground forces, 22 Corsairs from *Philippine Sea* attacked North Korean positions in the Masan area, in close proximity to American positions. *Valley Forge* sent in 24 Corsairs and Skyraiders, which attacked Kwangju and Samchonpo. Despite the bad weather, three flights of Corsairs from *Valley Forge* found success under Marine control near Masan, with six Corsairs destroying two tanks and 15 field artillery pieces, damaging two other tanks, and strafing North Korean troops.

Despite the lack of air support, the Marines continued their advance toward Yongsan during the afternoon of September 3. By nightfall they had passed the originally scheduled line of departure. The enemy, disorganized by the shock of the unexpected engagement, was retiring. However, the front was a long one, and the night was miserable with cold, driving rain. Fortunately, the tide had been turned west of Yongsan. The NKPA 9th Division, which led the advance, was fresh from garrison duty and deficient in training as compared with the original front-line units and thus was unable to stand up to the Marines. Early morning attacks on September 4 along the road to the bulge moved forward rapidly with light resistance. Groups of fleeing North Korean soldiers were cut down by artillery and Marine air, which was finally able to make an appearance as the weather had cleared over Japan sufficiently to fly missions. By midday, the Marines had advanced a mile and a half, with the enemy abandoning equipment, while much US gear was recaptured. A further advance was authorized that gained another mile in the course of the afternoon. By evening, the Marines were dug in on the hill from where, 18 days previously, they had launched their first attack in the first battle of the Naktong.

Action on September 5 began with a North Korean counterattack against Army troops north of the road, which was broken by heavy machine-gun fire. During the morning, despite heavy rain and fog which hampered the Marine Corsairs, the Marine infantry moved into position for an attack on Obong-ni Ridge. At 1200 hours this attack was canceled. While the Naktong Bulge had not been cleared, the situation was vastly improved. The Marine Brigade was now needed for a battle far more important. They took up defensive positions on the ridges south of the road. During the night they were relieved by troops of the 2nd Infantry Division. Shortly after midnight, the brigade marched back in the rain to load into trucks and move on to the Pusan staging area.

The Provisional Marine Brigade had saved not only the UN position in Korea, but the Marine Corps itself. No other American combat service was as ready to deploy as the Marines. Within days of their arrival on the battlefield, they had been deeply engaged with the enemy. The previously victorious North Koreans, who had almost effortlessly pushed aside the unready Army units sent to stop them had come up against an opponent for which they were unprepared. The Marines had proven their worth. For those still unconvinced, the next months would be conclusive.

By the end of August, the 13th Air Wing aboard HMS *Triumph* was nearly used up. Due to a succession of heavy landings caused by bad weather and pilot exhaustion some of the fuselage wrinkles on the Seafires were too large for comfort. The worst-affected aircraft were withdrawn and used for spares leaving only nine Seafires available for operations, while the repair carrier HMS *Unicorn* was down to its last six replacements. The situation with the Fireflies was not much better; many of the replacements which had been scraped together from all over the Far East were found to be unserviceable since the rubber seals in their engines and hydraulics had rotted away while they were in storage in tropical conditions. Some had not been flown since the end of World War II.

On August 29, Lieutenant Commander MacLachlen, commanding officer of 800 Squadron, became the only aircrew fatality of the entire Korean tour when he was mortally injured in a freak accident. While he was standing inside the operations room in the carrier's island, a Firefly crashed into the barrier on the deck; fragments of its wooden propeller detached and flew through an open porthole, hitting MacLachlen as he stood inside. His position as squadron commander was taken by the senior pilot, Lieutenant Commander Handley.

On August 30, HMS *Triumph* returned to Sasebo to replenish stores and receive the last six Seafires and eight Fireflies, which as the least serviceable of all the replacements had been held back until now. There were no other spares available in the entire Far East, as the Seafire FR 47 and Firefly FR 1 had been retired from every front-line squadron in the Fleet Air Arm apart from the two which were fighting a war. When she departed Sasebo, *Triumph* escorted HMS *Unicorn*, which carried the men of the 27th Commonwealth Infantry Brigade to join the fighting in the Pusan Perimeter. The Commonwealth Brigade was composed of the 1st Battalion, Middlesex Regiment; 1st Battalion, Argyle and Sutherland Highlanders; and the 3rd Battalion, Royal Australian Regiment. With the British Army heavily committed in Malaya, West Germany and the Middle East, these would be the only British troops to serve in Korea until more units could be brought up to strength to help form a British Commonwealth Division, which would enter combat in 1951.

By now the situation in Korea was critical following the second battle of the Naktong. HMS *Triumph* returned to Korea on September 3 and commenced operations straight away. The Fireflies flew armed reconnaissance sorties and sank several small junks, pontoon bridges, sampans and motor cruisers. The North Koreans were now savvy to the need of camouflage; a patrol of two Fireflies found three strange-looking heavily vegetated "islands" that turned out to be camouflaged North Korean gunboats, which were attacked and left heavily damaged. More naval gunfire spotting sorties were flown over the next few days by HMS *Jamaica* and HMS *Charity* against targets in Inchon and Kunsan but on September 6 *Triumph* sailed for the east coast to take over the vital job of supporting the UN forces from the US carriers USS *Valley Forge* and USS *Philippine Sea* which sailed for Okinawa to replenish.

The constant strain of operations aboard *Triumph* was seriously affecting aircraft serviceability. The increased tempo of operations over the Pusan perimeter resulted in a further four Seafires grounded due to skin wrinkling, leaving only five available. Most of those grounded came from the batch of replacement aircraft recently received from HMS *Unicorn*. These Seafires had not been subjected to excessive treatment since they were taken aboard, which highlights the fact they were in a poor state to begin with. Adding to the problem of aircraft availability, one of the serviceable Seafires was lost when the pilot was forced to bail out after his hook failed to lower for landing and another was written off when it crashed on deck, landing with only one of its undercarriage legs down when the other failed to lower. To add to these problems, a Firefly was badly damaged when it made a heavy landing and bounced off the deck, only to be held dangling over the side of the ship after its hook engaged an arrester wire. A successful strike was flown in bad weather by two Seafires and two Fireflies against Koryu airfield on September 9 that caused considerable damage but by now this was a maximum-effort operation with only a handful of aircraft still operational. On September 10, USS *Philippine Sea* arrived to take over and HMS *Triumph* was able to return to Sasebo to prepare for a vitally important operation in support of the UN campaign in Korea.

In nine weeks of warfare during the summer of 1950, the United States paid the wages of hubris, with the United States Army paying a terrible price for sending untrained and inexperienced troops against a better-trained foe in the mistaken belief that an Asian army could not stand against Western troops. Several hundred American soldiers died as a result, with hundreds more made prisoner, most of whom would not survive three years of callous treatment in North Korean prison camps. Once again, the military was given the lesson that no matter how the technology developed, warfare still comes down to men occupying ground and denying that ground to the enemy. The concentration on nuclear warfare in the years after Hiroshima and Nagasaki had come at the expense of the very forces that were needed in the war no American had expected to fight.

CHAPTER FOUR

THE FATAL DECISION

The successful invasion of Inchon marked the high point of General Douglas MacArthur's remarkable military career. It also set the stage for his greatest disaster.

Douglas MacArthur had been a general longer than most of the men in charge of the American military in 1950 had worn the uniform, having been promoted to brigadier general in 1917. At West Point, he had been the most outstanding cadet since Robert E. Lee. He had held every major Army command, including superintendent of West Point and Army chief of staff. By 1950 he was the senior serving officer and America's most famous general, with popular support among Americans, and was as much a political figure as a military icon. Considered "the Greatest" by the populace due to his campaigns in the Southwest Pacific, those in the military who had dealt with him over the years considered him a charlatan. General Dwight Eisenhower had served as an aide in Washington and later in the Philippines before the war. When once asked if he knew General MacArthur,

Eisenhower replied, "Not only have I met him, I studied dramatics under him for five years in Washington and four in the Philippines." Writing of MacArthur in his memoirs, Eisenhower said that there was a clear line between military and political affairs, which nearly all American senior officers scrupulously observed, "but if General MacArthur recognized the existence of that line, he usually chose to ignore it." It was generally believed in the Democratic Party that MacArthur would be a leading candidate for the Republican nomination for President in 1952, that his attempted run in 1948 had not quenched his political ambition. Truman's close advisors saw MacArthur as a threat rather than a general they could trust. Truman termed the general a "bunko man" not to be trusted, when he took office in 1945. There were two times between 1945 and 1947 when the president had considered recalling his Asian commander, but had recoiled at the last moment due to the political difficulties such a move could involve.

By 1950, after five years as the American emperor of Japan, MacArthur was so grand that everyone else had to play by his rules. He had his own army within the army, with a staff that had been with him from his time in the Philippines before World War II, known derisively throughout the Army as "the Bataan Gang." Journalist John Gunther wrote, "None of those around him can afford to be first rate." Unlike Eisenhower, under whose command many younger officers made public names for themselves and built sterling careers, no officer under MacArthur ever received credit for success gained, which was always ascribed to the general's leadership. Orders and instructions from Washington were ignored more often than not, even though from his nominal superiors, most of whom he did not consider his superiors, and who therefore had no right to question him or give him orders. His staff knew the general did not like to receive news that did not comport with his views and expectations, and acted accordingly; those not in awe did not last long. Visitors to the Dai Ichi Building got "The Performance," which he practiced in the morning in front of a mirror. During The Performance, he spoke with great confidence and certainty of future events which most men approached with a degree of caution. The Performance was frequently dazzling, the more so because while it was well-rehearsed, it was delivered as though impromptu. Given the unofficial rule – "he talked, you listened" – no one dared challenge his grandiosity. When George Kennan visited in 1948, he noted MacArthur was "distant and full of mistrust" toward the Truman administration. This feeling was no different from his attitude toward Franklin Roosevelt, a man he both loathed and believed he had faced down in 1944 when his threat to come home and campaign for the Republican presidential nomination had bent FDR to accept his plan to "return" to the Philippines, despite such an invasion being a strategic diversion. Roosevelt had from the beginning seen MacArthur as a man to be used but never trusted, once telling an associate that the general was "the most dangerous man in America, after Huey Long." He decided in favor of MacArthur's strategy on the purely political calculus that the invasion of the Philippines would happen just before the coming presidential elections, which would guarantee his re-election. MacArthur's late realization of what Roosevelt had done only added to his seething hatred of civilian authority.

While many military officers chafed under orders they received from civilians they believed were ignorant of the true facts, the American tradition of civilian control of the military was such that, however reluctantly, the superior position of the civilian leaders always prevailed. This was not so with MacArthur, who came to his hatred of his civilian superiors from his father, Arthur MacArthur, who had ended his stellar career as commander of American forces during the Philippine Insurrection with an ignominious dismissal and recall in 1901, due to his inability to work with William Howard Taft, who had been appointed civilian governor of the Philippines, and his open contempt for civilian leadership. In 1906, when the position of Army chief of staff was open, then Secretary of War Taft passed him over for the position despite MacArthur then being the highest-ranking general in the army, and he was unceremoniously retired in 1909. By 1950, MacArthur's attitude was even more combative and poisonous than had been his father's.

Shortly after the outbreak of the Korean War, Truman sent Republican power operative and future Secretary of State, John Foster Dulles, then a State Department advisor, to Tokyo to assess MacArthur's performance. On his return, Dulles had recommended a change of commanders, stating that MacArthur seemed too old, and that he was bothered by the way the general's attention span wavered. Truman responded that his hands were tied, because the general had such a strong political constituency. The president of the United States, the commander-in-chief, was waging a war led by a general he not only disliked but distrusted, but did not feel strong enough politically to replace.

July and August were bad politically in Washington, as every week brought news of a new defeat or withdrawal in the face of an enemy most Americans believed was an inconsequential satellite of the Soviets. The public still thought of the American military as the force that defeated Germany and Japan, and could not understand how such events could happen in Korea. The Republicans, who had gleefully supported the president's desire to decrease military spending, now turned on the administration, implying if not saying outright that the "Communists" Senator McCarthy had identified in the State Department were more widespread, that it was their insidious influence that had depleted the country's strength just when it was most needed.

From the first weeks, as the North Koreans took Seoul and continued their drive, MacArthur hoped to deliver a counterstroke at the Inchon–Seoul region, the strategic center of Korea. His chief of staff, General Edward Almond, was involved in the planning and was an enthusiastic advocate. The operation, code-named Operation *Bluehearts*, was set for July 22, with the 1st Cavalry Division landing at Inchon. However, by July 10 the operation was abandoned as it was clear the 1st Cavalry Division would be needed in the Pusan Perimeter, and it landed unopposed at Pohang on July 18. The planners realized that any invasion at Inchon would require troops experienced in amphibious operations. On July 10, MacArthur made his first request for an entire Marine division. The request was repeated twice, bearing fruit on July 20, when the Joint Chiefs approved movement of the 1st Marine Division, with arrival scheduled for November or December. By July 21, in the face of further UN reversals which called into doubt the ability of UN forces to remain on the peninsula at all, MacArthur requested reconsideration of this decision, stating that the arrival of the Marines by September 10 was "absolutely vital to accomplish a decisive stroke." On July 23, a new plan was formulated, Operation *Chromite*, which involved an amphibious assault by the Army 2nd Infantry Division and 5th Marine Regiment, to occur in mid-September. This, too, fell by the wayside as both units were deployed to the Pusan Perimeter. On July 25, MacArthur was informed that the 1st Marine Division had been ordered to depart for Korea between August 10 and 15. As it was, the division would only finally come together when the Provisional Marine Brigade was reunited with the 1st Regiment, while the 7th Regiment was brought up to strength by the arrival of a battalion of the 6th Marines from the Mediterranean.

Historically, Inchon is the most spectacularly difficult and successful amphibious operation ever attempted, other than Normandy. The tides and geography of the harbor made the landing appear impossible. The only approaches were two restricted passages, which could be easily blocked by naval mines. The current in the channels was 3–8 knots. Additionally, the anchorage was small with the harbor surrounded by tall sea walls due to the extreme tidal conditions, the tides having an average range of 29 feet and a maximum observed range of 36 feet, making the tidal range the largest in Asia. Because of these tides, extensive areas of muddy harbor bottom were exposed at low tide, leaving landing craft beached and immovable until the next high tide. Navy Commander Arlie Capps noted that the harbor had "every natural and geographic handicap." Every military leader with any knowledge of amphibious warfare opposed MacArthur's plan.

The Navy favored a landing at Kunsan, where conditions were more favorable. On August 23, Army Chief of Staff General J. Lawton Collins, Chief of Naval Operations Admiral Forrest Sherman, and Air Force operations deputy Lieutenant General Idwal Edward flew from Washington to hear MacArthur's briefing. During the briefing, nine members of the staff of the Seventh Fleet amphibious force commander Admiral James H. Doyle spoke for nearly 90 minutes on every aspect of the landing to demonstrate why Kunsan was a better choice. MacArthur replied that though a Kunsan landing would bring about an easy linkup with Eighth Army, a landing there "would be an attempted envelopment that would not envelop" and would place more troops in a vulnerable pocket of the Pusan Perimeter.

No final decision was made, though MacArthur's staff continued planning the Inchon operation. Admiral Sherman departed in agreement that the invasion should be attempted if a way could be shown that the invaders could cope with the tidal problem.

The final showdown meeting came in Tokyo on September 2. Admiral Sherman and General J. Lawton Collins returned. The commander-in-chief Pacific Command was represented by Admiral Arthur W. Radford and Fleet Marine Force Pacific commander General Lemuel Shepherd. The Seventh Fleet commander Admiral Turner Joy and Admiral Doyle were present. It rapidly became clear that the amphibious techniques the Navy and Marines had brought to high perfection, which Washington considered obsolete, were held in great esteem in Tokyo. Without denying the strategic importance of Seoul and the desirability of its capture, Navy and Marine planners could not ignore the tides and currents of the Yellow Sea, the absence of suitable landing beaches at the objective, the extensive mud banks which restricted movement once ashore, and the islands which covered the long approach from the Yellow Sea to Inchon. While the rules say that what is tactically impossible can never be strategically desirable, in the end the doubts of the experts were to no avail.

MacArthur had been reading the diary of British Brigadier General James Wolfe, and was particularly influenced by a passage in which the victor of Quebec described how he became more and more determined to carry out his dangerous assault plan after each of his advisors announced their disapproval, his conclusion being that if his advisors believed the attack so improbable, the opposing general would never expect it. MacArthur argued that "The very arguments you have made as to the impracticalities involved will tend to ensure for me the element of surprise." Yet even after that, the best Admiral Doyle could say about Inchon was that it was "not impossible." After two days of debate, Admiral Sherman agreed to support the plan and returned to Washington to put the decision to the Joint Chiefs, who concurred with Sherman shortly thereafter. It was formally agreed that the invasion would be conducted by two divisions, the 1st Marine Division and the Army's 7th Infantry Division, which had been the first division to be stripped during July to fill the ranks of units committed to Korea, then strengthened in August by the integration of 8,600 South Korean recruits, most barely trained and unable to communicate in English with their American counterparts, none of whom spoke Korean. Marines who had dealings with the 7th Infantry Division during the preparations were astonished such an organization could be considered combat-capable.

General Oliver P. Smith, commanding general of the 1st Marine Division, and his staff arrived in Tokyo at the end of August to prepare for the invasion. A World War I veteran who had not seen combat in France, he was frequently confused with the other Marine Generals Smith: Holland McTyeire "Howlin' Mad" Smith, or Julian C. Smith, who had commanded at Tarawa. O. P. Smith was "Howlin' Mad" Smith's polar opposite: a Marine who had seldom been heard to exclaim even so much as a "gosh" or a "darn," he was also known by his initials as the "Old Professor," for being the first Marine officer to graduate from the French *École Supérieure de Guerre*, which he accomplished in 1936 after serving during the 1920s with the Haitian Gendarmerie. He was considered an intellectual in an organization not noted for such a distinction. The two Generals Smith were considered the leading experts in amphibious warfare, with "Howlin' Mad" Smith known as "the father of amphibious warfare" and Oliver O. P. Smith as the staff officer who formalized much of the other General Smith's original vision. During World War II, O. P. Smith had risen from commanding officer of the 5th Marines during the fighting on Cape Gloucester, to assistant division commander of the 1st Marine Division at Peleliu in September and October 1944. Promoted afterwards to Marine deputy chief of staff of the Tenth Army, he had participated in the battle of Okinawa. He became commander of the 1st Marine Division in June 1950, after serving as commandant of the Marine Corps Schools at Quantico, assistant commandant of the Marine Corps and chief of staff. The Marines considered Smith the best general they could provide for the coming battle.

Shortly after arrival in Tokyo, General Smith met Lieutenant General Edward "Ned" Almond, who was now not only MacArthur's chief of staff, but was also commanding general of X Corps, commanding the coming invasion. He quickly earned the scorn of Smith's staff during an early meeting when Almond, who had no experience with amphibious warfare, spoke about how easy such an operation would be. Later, aboard the command ship USS *Mount McKinley* on the day of the invasion, Almond watched Marine LVT amphibious tractors exit their LSD mother ship. He turned to Colonel Victor Krulak and asked if they could float. Krulak later related "I immediately went and told ten people, because I didn't want it forgotten. Here was the man commanding the landing force at Inchon, asking 'Can these things float?'" The relationship between Almond and the Marines was rocky at the beginning and went steadily downhill throughout the campaign, with Almond "at the very top of the Marines' always-lengthy shitlist," according to Marine and later historian Martin Russ.

A graduate of Virginia Military Institute and a combat veteran during World War I, "Ned," as he was known to his friends, had been highly regarded in 1942 by General George C. Marshall, also a VMI graduate. The result was Almond's promotion to major general ahead of his peers and command of the 92nd Infantry Division, a difficult assignment Marshall believed Almond would excel at, which he held from October 1942 until August 1945. Known among its Army opponents as "Eleanor Roosevelt's Running Riflemen" due to the First Lady's public involvement with the campaign to recruit African-Americans for combat roles, the soldiers were led almost exclusively by Southern white officers, because they were believed to know how to "handle the blacks." The 92nd Infantry Division had served in the Italian campaign of 1944–45, where it performed poorly. Almond, a Southerner born in 1892 with all the traditional prejudice of the region and era, ended the war more racist than he began, blaming the division's poor performance on the troops, and believing their poor performance had robbed him of the higher command he felt he deserved. After the war, Almond advised against using African-Americans as combat troops, a position that put him at odds with the changes that came with the desegregation of the armed forces in 1948. In Korea, his racism would lead to constant underestimation of his Chinese opponents – he was the first American officer to call them "laundrymen."

In 1946, Almond was transferred to Tokyo as chief of personnel at MacArthur's headquarters. Normally, such an assignment was a dead-end job held prior to early retirement. However, Almond successfully handled the difficult challenge of staffing the occupation forces in Japan while the American military rapidly demobilized. As a result, he became a stand-out among MacArthur's otherwise lackluster staff, a surprising event since most newcomers to "the Bataan Gang" didn't stick around long, particularly if they were any sort of achiever. Even though he arrived with two strikes against him, as both a "Marshall Man" and a "European War man," he won MacArthur's confidence as a loyal and capable staff officer who was happy to allow MacArthur to take credit for any success, and was promoted to chief of staff in January 1949. Almond became so loyal to his boss that he even changed his opinion of Chief of Intelligence General Willoughby, whom he had castigated as an incompetent directly to Marshall before the war for Willoughby's failure as a military attaché in South America; he now lauded Willoughby for his perspicacity about Asia and Asians. He acquired several nicknames, including "Ned the Dread," and – far more important in the political hothouse of cronyism and sycophancy that was MacArthur's headquarters – "Ned the Anointed." Historian J. D. Coleman, who served under Almond in Italy wrote that, "He had an instinctive knack of ingratiation." When MacArthur split X Corps from Eighth Army, Almond asked to be named commander, based on his enthusiasm for the Inchon operation and his participation in planning the event.

The Marines' administrative commander, Lieutenant General Lemuel C. Shepherd, Jr., commanding general of Fleet Marine Force, Pacific, was not in the operational chain of command, but was responsible for support of the 1st Marine Division, which allowed him to make frequent visits during the campaign. Shepherd and Almond got along well, both being Virginians and graduates of Virginia Military Institute, Almond being class of 1915 and Shepherd class of 1917. Questioned regarding his memory of Almond at the institute, Shepherd said, "I liked him, but I really can't say he was one of my closer friends."

When X Corps was created, Shepherd had reason to expect he would be put in command since he was the senior Marine commander in the Pacific. When MacArthur gave command to Almond, Shepherd gave no sign of holding a grudge. In turn, Almond always made Shepherd welcome when he visited Korea, and he often stayed with Almond in his mess. In return, Shepherd was the only Marine who considered Almond a competent corps commander. Years later, Shepherd said of Almond:

> He was energetic, forceful, brave, and in many ways did a good job under most difficult conditions... He and O. P. just didn't get along. They're two entirely different personalities. O. P.'s a cautious individual, a fine staff officer who considered every contingency before taking action. On the other hand, Almond was aggressive and anxious for the X Corps to push ahead faster than Smith thought his division should. Smith wisely took every precaution to protect his flanks during his division's advance into North Korea, which slowed him down considerably. I'm sure Almond got into Smith's hair – just like I'm sure that I did too.

From their first meeting the Marines recognized Almond for the sycophant and glory-seeker he was. A close associate, Maury Holden, G-3 of the 2nd Division, described him thus: "When it paid to be aggressive, Ned was aggressive. When it paid to be cautious, Ned was aggressive." Almond's loyalty to MacArthur as the man who had given him his long-denied higher command, and his belief that reality should be interpreted in light of what his commander believed, regardless of actual facts, would come dangerously close to creating complete disaster during the coming campaign. There was an additional reason for the disdain the Marines felt toward Almond. For Marine officers, it is a traditional point of honor that officers share as much as they can of the hardships of the men in the field, that there not be better food and greater warmth for the leaders. Throughout the campaign, Almond's personal trailer was filled with comforts and amenities, most importantly heat in a time when everyone else was cold. Creature comforts were important to him. The trailer even had a bathtub with hot water, and a separate tent with a heater for his toilet. He always ate well, with steaks flown in from Tokyo alongside fresh vegetables and fine wines, served by enlisted men in white uniforms. These facts were widely known to the men who served under him and resented the situation. A contemporary related that he was reminded of British generals of World War I. Chesty Puller estimated there were 3,000 men in Almond's headquarters, "enough to form an additional regiment." After the war, when General Smith was asked his view of Almond, he replied, "He was a MacArthur man, and anything MacArthur said, nothing could change it. MacArthur was God."

Surprise was of the essence for success, and to many in Japan it seemed such surprise had been completely compromised. The Japanese press mentioned the code-name, Operation *Chromite*, and termed it "Operation Common Knowledge." When a North Korean spy ring was apprehended in Tokyo just before the invasion, the leader had a copy of the operation order. No one knew if he had communicated any of this to the North Koreans. The UN forces created an elaborate deception operation to take enemy attention away from Inchon by taking steps to make it seem that the landing would happen at Kunsan, the beaches everyone considered far more favorable. On September 5, Air Force B-26 Invaders of the 3rd Bomb Wing made attacks on roads and bridges in the area around Kunsan – missions typical of attacks expected prior to an invasion. A naval bombardment followed on September 6. The B-29s joined the campaign on September 11, bombing installations in the area. Additionally, Marine officers of the Provisional Marine Brigade made public briefings on an upcoming landing at Kunsan as they loaded aboard ships in Pusan, within hearing of Korean dock workers. On the night of September 12/13, Army Rangers and Royal Marines from 41 Commando landed at Kunsan from the frigate HMS *Whitesand Bay* and conducted a reconnaissance, being sure the North Koreans were aware of their visit.

On September 10, the 1st and 7th Regiments and their combat support units departed Sasebo, Japan, to rendezvous with ships carrying the Provisional Marine Brigade from Pusan, along with the ship carrying the 6th Marines battalion that arrived from the Mediterranean. The 1st and 5th Marines were the main landing force, to be followed a few days later by the 7th Marines. The convoy narrowly missed a typhoon that turned north and hit Honshu rather than Kyushu after the ships had put to sea.

HMS *Triumph*, its air wing brought back up to 12 Spitfires and 12 Fireflies by dint of repairing as many of the dud aircraft as possible while in port following its early September deployment, escorted the troop convoy. By now, the air wing was in such straits that a newly arrived group of inexperienced replacement pilots were not allowed to be put onto the flying rotation in case they "bent" an aircraft;

the importance of every sortie had to be carefully considered before any aircraft took off.

Naval gunfire preparation commenced on September 13, when the first Canadian forces to enter the war, HMCS *Cayuga*, HMCS *Athabaskan*, and HMCS *Sioux* bombarded the harbor entrance. Shortly thereafter USS *Mansfield* led Destroyer Squadron 9 into Inchon harbor, where they opened fire on Wolmi-do island. North Korean artillery returned fire, lightly damaging several ships. Between them, the Canadian and American destroyers fired over 1,000 5-inch shells, inflicting severe damage on the island's fortifications. The US destroyers withdrew after an hour and the heavy cruiser USS *Toledo*, in company with the British cruisers HMS *Jamaica* and HMS *Kenya*, bombarded the island for three hours. Further naval gunfire preparation resumed at first light on September 14. HMS *Triumph* launched Fireflies carrying a 45-gallon drop tank under each wing to extend their time on station to serve as artillery spotters, which greatly improved the accuracy of the cruisers' salvos.

The Soviet Union had supplied North Korea with naval mines, the existence of which UN forces had only discovered in early September. Fortunately, only a relative few, unsophisticated mines were laid at Inchon, which were spotted and exploded.

At 0630 hours on September 15, the 3rd Battalion, 5th Marines, landed on Wolmi-do, supported by nine M-26 Pershing tanks brought in on an LST. The island was neutralized by noon at a cost of 14 casualties while North Korean casualties were 200 dead and 136 captured. The North Koreans had been completely taken in by the deception efforts and had sent their forces to Kunsan. Thus, they were outnumbered at Inchon.

Due to the tides, the main landing in the harbor could not take place until 1730 hours. As the LSTs carrying the 1st and 2nd Battalions, 5th Marines, and the 3rd Battalion, ROK

Marines, headed in to Red Beach, they came under heavy fire from defenders on Cemetery Hill. The LSTs made it to the muddy beach, where the Marines had to use ladders to scale the sea walls. Three of the LSTs took hits, and all remained overnight as the tide went out, being refloated on September 16. That night, the Marines secured the causeway to Wolmi-do, allowing the 3rd Battalion and the tanks to join up.

Further south, the 1st Marines landed on Blue Beach to take the road to Seoul. One LST was sunk on the way in, but by the time the regiment was ashore, the North Korean forces in Inchon had surrendered so they faced only a few holdouts. The 1st and 5th Marines headed toward Seoul on September 16.

Later that morning, six columns of T-34s were spotted near Kansong-ni, east of Inchon, by two flights of F4U-4 Corsairs from VMF-214. They had no infantry support. The Corsairs inflicted extensive damage while losing one F4U. M26 tanks moved in and destroyed the remainder, which cleared the way for the complete capture of Inchon.

At 0550 hours on September 17, a Yak-9 and an Il-10 *Shturmovik* attacked USS *Rochester*, anchored off Wolmi-do. Initially the two were assumed friendly until they dropped four bombs, one of which hit the ship but failed to detonate. *Rochester* and HMS *Jamaica* opened fire with their AA batteries. The Il-10 strafed HMS *Kenya*, killing one and wounding two. As the bomber pulled away, it was hit by fire from *Jamaica* and crashed. The Yak-9 escaped.

Later that morning, the 2nd Battalion, 5th Marines, took Kimpo airfield outside Seoul. The defenders were disorganized and many fled across the Han River to Seoul. With the capture of Kimpo, Marine Corsairs came ashore, while USAF units could also support the attack on Seoul. The Australian 77 Squadron was first to land their F-51s.

By September 19, after five days of constant armed reconnaissance and gunfire support missions, HMS *Triumph*'s air wing was reduced to three Seafires and eight Fireflies.

The Drive to Seoul, September 15–27, 1950

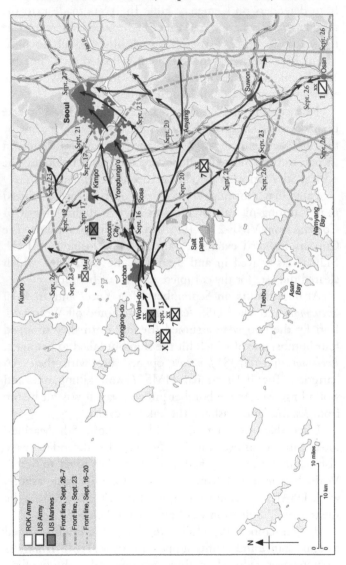

On September 21, the ship received orders to disengage and set sail to Hong Kong for eventual return to Britain. HMS *Triumph*, with a small air wing of obsolete aircraft, had contributed greatly to the ability of the UN forces to hold the line in the opening months of the Korean War. Truly, a ship had never been better named. The fact that *Triumph* and its aircrews had been called unexpectedly into action just when they expected to return home at the end of a long deployment made the contribution doubly outstanding. HMS *Theseus*, with a more modern air wing of Sea Fury FB 11 and Firefly AS 5 aircraft, arrived in Sasebo five days after *Triumph*'s departure to maintain the Fleet Air Arm's presence in the Korean conflict.

In contrast to the quick victory at Inchon, taking Seoul was slow and bloody. On September 18 the North Koreans launched another T-34 attack, which was trapped and destroyed, while a pair of Yak-9s made a bombing run in Inchon harbor, which did little damage. The North Koreans attempted to stall the Marines in order to allow time to reinforce Seoul and withdraw troops from the south. The 7th Division came ashore at Inchon on September 17, and entered the fight on September 19. On September 22, the Marines entered Seoul. Casualties were heavy in house-to-house fighting. On September 26, the Hotel Bando that had served as the US Embassy, was cleared by Easy Company, 2/1 Battalion. General Almond declared the city liberated on September 25, marking 90 days since the North Korean invasion, even though the Marines were still engaged in combat.

Inchon was MacArthur at his best, a brilliant, daring gamble that saved thousands of American lives. As biographer Geoffrey Perret wrote, "There was one day in MacArthur's life when he was a military genius: September 15, 1950. In the life of every great Commander there is one battle that stands out above all the rest, the supreme test of generalship that places him among the other military immortals. For MacArthur, that battle was Inchon." It was the culmination of his strategy from the Pacific War, to employ superior technology so that his under-strength troops would not be ground up in traditional infantry warfare against a numerically superior enemy. Had Inchon been the final battle of the Korean War, as it could have been, both the war and its general would be remembered far differently.

Much political history written in the past 65 years has laid responsibility for the decision to "liberate" North Korea on MacArthur. The facts do not support this. Long before the success at Inchon, Pentagon and State Department leaders had supported an invasion of North Korea. On August 17, American UN Ambassador Warren R. Austin called on the UN to support "establishing democratic government in the reunited Korea." In a radio broadcast on September 1, President Truman stated his support for a "free, independent, and united Korea." Secretary of State Acheson endorsed reunification, if necessary by force. In August and September, several influential members of the British Parliament publicly stated their support for unification after North Korea was "liberated."

Chinese involvement with the Korean War began in a piecemeal manner following the June 25 invasion. President Truman's June 27 statement, declaring that "the occupation of Formosa by Communist forces would be a direct threat to the security of the Pacific area and to US forces performing their lawful and necessary functions in that area," created almost casually an entirely new and firm commitment to supporting the forces led by Chiang Kai-Shek, which had retreated to the island following their defeat in the Chinese civil war. Truman's statement heightened fears of Western encirclement. As a result, the United States was now seen by the Communists as their main enemy. This was reinforced by the publicity of MacArthur's July 29 visit to Taiwan, and by publication of the speech he had intended to give to the Veterans of

Foreign Wars. Writing in the official *People's Daily* newspaper in mid-August, Politburo member Kuo Mo-Jo stated, "The American imperialists fondly hope that their armed aggression against Taiwan will prevent us from liberating it. Around China in particular, their designs for a blockade are taking shape in the pattern of a stretched-out snake. Starting from South Korea, it stretches to Japan, the Ryukyu Islands, Taiwan and the Philippines and then turns up at Vietnam." While the United States persistently sought throughout the war to understand the Communist logic behind Chinese actions, this statement is a clear indication the Chinese saw the war through historic perceptions of national interest. Korea had been the springboard for the Japanese invasion of Manchuria less than 20 years earlier, and the prospect of an American army on the Yalu was seen as the same kind of threat. The Chinese would likely have been even more disturbed had they known how close MacArthur came to accepting Chiang Kai-Shek's offer to provide 33,000 troops for combat in Korea, which had been made during MacArthur's visit.

There had been a moment in early July when things might have been different. On July 10, the Indian ambassador informed Acheson that the Indian government had a peace proposal for Korea in which the Chinese government appeared interested. This would have involved a ceasefire, with both sides returning to their respective positions on the 38th Parallel, while Communist China would take the Chinese seat at the United Nations. Kennan had advised Acheson this would be an initiative worth pursuing, since the Chinese Communists occupying the seat would make no strategic changes since the USSR already held a Security Council veto, while the proposal might have the effect of splitting the Chinese from the Russians. John Foster Dulles, who would have been Secretary of State had Thomas E. Dewey won the election of 1948, had joined the State Department in April as an advisor on negotiations regarding the Japanese peace treaty; when he heard of the Indian proposal, he shouted down Kennan, stating the proposal would "reward aggression," and would give the China Lobby the ammunition they needed to attack the administration. On July 17, Kennan recorded in his diary, "I hope that some day history will record this as an instance of the damage done to the conduct of our foreign policy by the irresponsible and bigoted influence of the China Lobby and its friends in Congress."

On August 20, Chinese Communist Premier Zhou En-Lai had informed the United Nations that "Korea is China's neighbor. The Chinese people cannot but be concerned about a solution of the Korean question." This had been the first intimation that China might intervene in Korea. President Truman interpreted the communication as "a bald attempt to blackmail the UN," and dismissed it.

On August 23, the same day MacArthur wrested initial approval for Inchon from Admiral Sherman, Mao Zedong met with his political and military leaders in Beijing. Up to this point, Mao's political position had been that the liberation of Taiwan and final defeat of Chiang Kai-Shek's forces must have priority over the unification of Korea. He had reluctantly given approval to Kim's plan in June, but had cautioned the Korean leader on the strong possibility of American intervention in support of South Korea. At the time of the invasion, the Chinese had almost no regular troops stationed in northeast China. Mao promised Kim he would move troops into Manchuria, but they would not intervene unless American forces crossed the 38th Parallel.

Even before the outbreak of war, following the Communist success in 1949, Mao Zedong had released four well-trained, experienced divisions of the People's Liberation Army composed of ethnic Koreans to return to Korea, where they had formed the core of the North Korean People's Army. After the invasion, acting on requests from North Korea, the Chinese government implemented the return of ethnic Koreans from China to

North Korea during the summer and fall of 1950. While their numbers were limited, once they had returned these Koreans became immediately involved in the war, serving as doctors, nurses, technicians, and drivers, among other critical positions. The Chinese did not begin concentrating armed forces along the Yalu until mid-July, when the Northeast China Border Defense Force was created with about 260,000 troops, but this changed after the Chinese became aware of MacArthur's VFW speech. The Ninth Army Group, which had been positioned near Shanghai for the invasion of Taiwan, was one of the major units ordered to move north as a result of this decision. Mao had become certain in late July that UN forces would attempt a major military move to change the situation in Korea. Lei Yingfu, one of the ablest members of the PLA General Staff, was assigned to study the situation and attempt to divine what might come next. Japan was a sieve of espionage; Japanese dockworkers were largely Communist, and evidence quickly came that the Americans were bringing in supplies that implied an amphibious operation, which matched with MacArthur's amphibious operations in World War II. Lei determined the Americans planned to land behind the lines, with the intent of capturing most of the North Korean army. Of six possible sites for such an operation, Lei decided Inchon was most likely because it was both strategically the best site and so operationally difficult that no one would expect it, which also comported with MacArthur's history of landing where least expected in his New Guinea campaign. On August 23, Mao called a meeting of the Politburo at which Lei gave a formidable briefing which carried the day. At its conclusion, Mao ordered the People's Liberation Army to complete all preparations for war in the event the UN forces did not stop at the 38th Parallel. When Mao passed on this estimate to Kim Il-Sung, his military advisors assured him such an operation was impossible.

Mao had also questioned Lei closely about the personality of MacArthur. Lei replied that MacArthur was "famous for his arrogance and his stubbornness." Mao replied, "Fine! Fine! The more arrogant and stubborn he is, the better. An arrogant enemy is easy to defeat."

The possibility of success at Inchon brought up the question of what the UN forces should do when they arrived at the 38th Parallel. Back in July, when the main question facing American officials in Washington was the very real possibility of the North Koreans throwing UN forces into the sea, John Allison, a hard-line member of the State Department, had written a memorandum on July 1 after returning from Tokyo, in which he stated that American forces should not only cross the 38th Parallel, but "continue right up to the Manchurian and Siberian border, and having done so, call for a UN-supervised election for all Korea." Both Dulles and Dean Rusk followed up with memos agreeing with Allison's position. On July 14, Dulles wrote an even stronger memo, stating that the 38th Parallel "was never intended to be, and never ought to be, a political line." Honoring it now, he said, "would provide asylum to the aggressor and was bound to perpetuate friction and the ever present danger of a new war." If it could be obliterated altogether, all the better "in the interest of peace and security in the region." On July 15, Allison echoed Dulles' argument about the parallel being an "arbitrary line" which had only been sustained by Soviet intransigence before the war. Allison argued the United States should adopt,

> ... a determination that the aggressors should not go unpunished and vigorous, courageous United States leadership to that end should have a salutary effect upon other areas of tension in the world. Notice would be served on the aggressor elsewhere, who is the same as the covert aggressor in Korea, that he cannot embark on acts of aggression with the assurance that he takes only a limited risk – that of being driven back only to the line from which the attack commenced.

On July 24, Allison followed up with a memo speaking of the shame the United States would incur if UN forces stopped at the 38th Parallel, of the loss of American stature in the eyes of the Korean people should the United States accept the prewar status as a postwar division. "If that happened, the people of Korea would lose all faith in the courage, intelligence, and morality of the United States. And I for one would not blame them." Allison then used the word most likely to have a seismic effect in domestic politics, arguing that those who opposed advancing north,

> ... assume we can buy more time by a policy of appeasement ... a timid half-hearted policy not to provoke the Soviets to war. We should recognize that there is grave danger of conflict with the USSR and the Chinese Communists whatever we do from now on – but I fail to see any advantage we gain by a compromise with clear moral principles and a shirking of our duty to make clear once and for all that aggression does not pay – that he who violates the decent opinions of mankind must take the consequences and that he who takes the sword will perish by the sword. That this may mean war on a global scale is true – the American people should be told and told why and what it will mean to them. When all legal and moral right is on our side, why should we hesitate?

Written for an audience of men who had lived through a political period defined by the word "Munich," these were strong words. At the end of July, Acheson said for the first time publicly that "The troops could not be expected to march up to a surveyor's line and stop." During the first week in August, California Senator William Knowland, a leader of the domestic far right and the China Lobby, called any failure to "liberate" North Korea "an act of appeasement of international communism." The week after Inchon,

Representative Hugh Scott of Pennsylvania rose in the House to say "The Hiss survivors association down at the State Department who wear on their breast the cross of Yalta are waiting for Congress to go home before they lift the curtain on the next act in the tragedy of Red appeasement."

Even as planning continued for the Inchon invasion, President Truman approved National Security Council Memorandum NSC 81/1 on September 11, which stated that UN forces would be authorized to cross the 38th Parallel for the purpose of either making the North Korean Army withdraw from South Korea or inflicting a decisive defeat on that force. In addition, MacArthur was authorized to prepare contingency plans for the occupation of North Korea. Giving such authority to a general as willful as MacArthur was tantamount to ordering that such events would indeed happen.

The aftermath of Inchon irrevocably reversed the fortunes of the UN forces. Having come close to triumph, the North Koreans now faced irredeemable disaster. The day the Marines went ashore on September 15, MacArthur received the basic provisions of NSC 81/1 from the Joint Chiefs; on September 27, with Seoul liberated and the North Korean retreat at the Pusan Perimeter now a rout, he received the crucial directive authorizing an offensive into North Korea. That directive included many phrases taken directly from NSC 81/1, and had solid support from President Truman, Secretary of State Acheson, and the new Secretary of Defense, George C. Marshall. It stated: "Your military objective is the destruction of the North Korean Armed Forces." He was told he would receive surrender terms to broadcast to North Korea and was instructed to submit plans for operations above the 38th Parallel and for the occupation of North Korea, which he did the next day. Following what was described as "some amount of inter-allied consultation," the United Kingdom, France, and some of the British Commonwealth nations backed the advance into North Korea.

The success at Inchon and the rapid North Korean collapse gave further urgency to Chinese preparations to intervene. Two days after the landing, a PLA liaison party went to Pyongyang. Kim Il-Sung requested assistance from Stalin, including a request that he pressure Mao to send troops. The decisions made in China over the next two weeks would be those of one man: Mao Zedong. He decided that it was right for the new China to take such a step and necessary for the future of the revolution. He also feared that not to intervene would mean the new China was seen as being the same as the old, a powerless giant when facing the West. Speaking at a private meeting of the Politburo in early September, Mao had said the United States would turn out to be weaker than anyone expected, since it would be waging an unjust war of aggression that would work against the morale of their troops and affect their battlefield performance. Mao saw America through his own revolutionary glasses, believing that American troops had fought badly in the opening months of the war not because the United States had let its military readiness fall dangerously low, but rather because the troops were from the working class, fighting for capitalist aims in which they did not believe, thus making them less pure of heart and motivation than the soldiers of the PLA. He also pointed out that Korean geography favored China, since as the Americans moved north they would move further and further from their bases of supply and become strung out in difficult country where they would have to cling to the primitive roads because of their mechanized military power, making them an easy target for the kind of warfare the PLA had employed successfully in the Chinese civil war. He finished by saying he did not fear the atomic bomb because the nature of Chinese society was rural, so there was no place the Americans could bomb that could be decisive in stopping anything. In the weeks after this speech, events continued to demonstrate to the Chinese leader the correctness of his decision.

On September 29, Marshall sent MacArthur a supportive message that included the following words: "We want you to feel unhampered strategically and tactically to proceed north of the 38th Parallel." Thirty years of Army history in which Marshall had been personally a participant should have made him wary of saying such a thing to a general as willing to create his own reality as MacArthur, who replied with confidence: "I regard all of Korea open for our military operations unless and until the enemy capitulates."

The spectacular Inchon success both fueled MacArthur's arrogance toward his superiors and further intimidated the Joint Chiefs. Matthew Ridgway later wrote,

> Complete victory now seemed in view – a golden apple that would handsomely symbolize the crowning effort of a brilliant military career. Once in reach of this prize, MacArthur would not allow himself to be delayed or admonished. Instead, he plunged northward in pursuit of a vanishing enemy, and changed his plans from week to week to accelerate this advance without regard to dark hints of possible disaster.

Looking at the decision to cross the parallel, there is no question MacArthur disobeyed the Chiefs, who had authorized him to go north with the proviso that no major Soviet or Chinese forces should have entered North Korea, or have announced their intention of doing so, or have threatened military action. UN forces were under no circumstances to violate the Manchurian or Russian borders, while none but ROK ground forces were to be employed in the border region. The unvarnished fact of the matter is that in the act of invading North Korea, MacArthur was implementing a policy that originated in Washington, not in his headquarters in Tokyo, though it was a policy with which he was finally in complete agreement with his civilian commanders.

The specific provision regarding a Russian or Chinese announcement of entering North Korea would shortly become of considerable importance. MacArthur had been authorized to call upon the enemy for surrender. The message was broadcast on October 1, with no response.

On September 30, Zhou En-Lai observed during an interview that the Chinese government would not tolerate UN forces crossing the 38th Parallel, and "would not stand aside" if North Korea were invaded. On October 2, Zhou pressed the Chinese position more forcefully during a meeting with the Indian ambassador, K. M. Panikkar, stating that if non-Korean forces crossed the 38th Parallel, China would send troops into Korea. Panikkar asked Zhou if he already had news of such a crossing, and Zhou indicated he did.

Tokyo and Washington paid no attention to the Chinese warning. Unfortunately, Panikkar was not the kind of diplomat Washington was used to dealing with. He was seen as a man of the left, a representative of a country that was a leader of the anti-colonialist forces internationally. It was easy to dismiss his attempt to communicate Zhou's warning as the words of a "pro-Communist," though Panikkar himself was well-known in diplomatic circles as a non-Communist who deplored Mao's callousness about loss of life. The CIA stated their belief that Panikkar was an "innocent instrument" being used by the Chinese, but that the Chinese were not serious in their threats. Besides, a Gallup poll taken the last week of September revealed 64 percent of the American public supported pursuit of the North Koreans across the parallel. At the General Assembly in New York on October 4, a debate on Korean policy ended with a vote on a resolution stating that since "unification has not yet been achieved" all appropriate steps should "be taken to ensure conditions of stability throughout Korea." While the language was vague, this resolution was of great importance. It signaled a change in the mission of the UN forces from repelling aggression and destroying enemy forces, to one of uniting Korea by force and ensuring stability by territorial occupation. MacArthur emphasized this with a statement in Tokyo on October 5 that if North Korean cooperation in establishing a unified Korea was not forthcoming, military action would be taken "to enforce the decrees of the United Nations." On October 9, the Joint Chiefs qualified their earlier caution concerning threatened Soviet or Chinese intervention. While the threat had now been made, the message rephrased the Chiefs' previous instructions concerning possible contact with the Chinese: should such forces now be met "anywhere in Korea," MacArthur was to continue action "so long as success seems probable."

The plan MacArthur submitted in response to this authorization had a restraining line drawn below the 40th Parallel, from Chongju in the west to Hungnam in the east, beyond which no non-Korean forces would advance. While Eighth Army would advance into North Korea on the western side of the peninsula, X Corps would invade the port of Wonsan on the east coast and proceed up the east side of the peninsula toward the Yalu. The Departments of State and Defense agreed that if North Korea collapsed and its Russian and Chinese neighbors kept hands off, MacArthur should occupy North Korea under the auspices of the United Nations. Some officials favored a unilateral occupation by the United States if the United Nations took no new steps authorizing occupation, "even at the expense of some disagreement with friendly United Nations nations," but this was a minority view.

Secretary of Defense Marshall also wanted United States troops to stay out of the picture during any occupation of North Korea. On October 3, Marshall told Acheson that "I wish to state that the Department of Defense continues to believe that as few United States troops as possible should engage in the physical occupation and pacification of areas north of the 38th Parallel, once organized military hostilities have ended. It remains important, therefore, to increase the number of other United Nations troops sent to Korea, particularly from countries in Asia."

The State Department had previously drawn up a resolution for the UN, which supported the political objectives of the UN in Korea, including the means for carrying them out through occupation if necessary. Since the Soviet delegation had returned in August, it was considered probable the Soviets would exercise their veto in the Security Council against any American-inspired resolution. Thus, the US delegation moved the Korean question before the General Assembly, where the USSR had no veto power and where US influence greatly outweighed that of the Soviets.

The resolution was passed by the General Assembly on October 7. It did not clearly call for the conquest and occupation of North Korea, but gave implicit approval, recommending that "(a) All appropriate steps be taken to ensure conditions of stability throughout Korea; and, (b) All constituent acts be taken, including the holding of elections, under the auspices of the United Nations, for the establishment of a unified, independent and democratic Korea."

While this was going on at the UN and in Washington and Tokyo, the two major Communist powers were also engaged in decisions about their involvement. In early October, General Nieh Jung-Chen, the acting chief of staff of the PLA, told Ambassador Panikkar that "... the People's Republic does not intend to sit back with folded hands and let the Americans come to their border... We know what we are in for, but at all costs American aggression has got to be stopped."

In Washington, the State Department's John Paton Davies and Edmund O. Clubb, the "old China hands" who would soon be excoriated by the right-wing China Lobby and the newly energized McCarthyites as the traitors who "lost China" and be run out of their careers, took heed of these Chinese statements and urged caution. Davies wrote that "A combination of irredentism, expansionism, Soviet pressure and inducements, strategic anxieties, ideological zeal, domestic pressures and emotional anti-Americanism..." might lead to Chinese intervention in the war. Clubb, director of the State Department's Office of Chinese Affairs, bluntly stated his belief that China would fight if the UN forces crossed into North Korea. Unfortunately, the "China Hands" were already on the way out at State, since Acheson had decided he did not need the further grief of trying to explain that there was a difference between Russian and Chinese interpretations of Communism. Dean Rusk, who would occupy Acheson's position at the time of the next major United States blunder in Asia, the decision to go to war in Vietnam, had replaced Kennan and was now brought in as Assistant Secretary for Far Eastern Affairs. For Rusk, the "fall" of China to Communism represented a historic change, "a shift in the balance of power in favor of Soviet Russia and to the disfavor of the United States." Under Rusk, there would be no questions raised regarding the taking of a hard line against Communism in Asia.

The "common wisdom" in Washington was expressed by the CIA, which reported on October 12 – four days after Mao had given the order for the People's Volunteer Army to enter North Korea – that "...despite statements by Chou En-Lai, troop movements to Manchuria, and propaganda charges of atrocities and border violations, there are no convincing indications of an actual Chinese Communist intention to resort to full-scale intervention in Korea." Acheson found the arguments that the Chinese would not risk losing all hope of obtaining their UN seat, that they would not want to become clients of the Russians in order to wage war, and that the army was too poorly equipped to face MacArthur's armies "irresistible," as he said to President Truman. Because the United States did not see its actions in Korea presenting any threat to legitimate Chinese interests, the Truman administration convinced itself that the Chinese government would reach the same conclusion.

Following Inchon, the Chinese government advised the North Koreans to implement a strategy of "protracted war," turning the North Korean People's Army into a guerrilla force operating throughout the peninsula to tie down the superior UN forces, pointing out the experience of the former Korean PLA troops in such warfare.

Both the North Korean and Chinese governments actively solicited the Soviet Union to become involved by providing air support for the invasion after the outbreak of war. This had almost become a reality by early July, but had been stopped by the appearance of American naval and air forces in the Yellow Sea and the strikes against Pyongyang on July 3–4.

On October 1, 1950, the day UN troops crossed the 38th Parallel, the Soviet ambassador to China forwarded a telegram from Stalin to Mao Zedong and Zhou En-Lai, requesting China send five to six divisions into Korea. Stalin considered that the most acceptable assistance by the Chinese armed forces would be in the form of "people's volunteers." In the telegram, Stalin advised: "The Chinese soldiers may be considered as volunteers and of course will be commanded by the Chinese." Mao responded the next day that such plans had already been made. Kim Il-Sung had also sent frantic appeals to Mao for Chinese intervention. At the same time, Stalin made it clear Soviet forces would not directly intervene, though he agreed to provide "unofficial" air support. Soviet aviation units would be transferred to airfields in Manchuria near the Yalu border with North Korea and undertake defensive actions against UN aircraft over North Korea, but the aircraft would carry North Korean markings and the pilots and other aircrews would wear North Korean uniforms and there would be no use of the Russian language over the radio.

Chinese Communist leaders met in a series of emergency meetings between October 2 and 5, where they debated whether to intervene. Many, including senior military leaders such as Marshal Lin Biao, resisted the idea of confronting the United States, though Mao strongly supported intervention and was supported by Zhou. When Lin Biao politely refused Mao's offer to command Chinese forces sent into Korea, citing upcoming medical treatment, Mao then appointed Long March veteran Marshal Peng Dehuai, commander of the North East Frontier Force of the PLA, after Peng stated that if US troops conquered Korea and reached the Yalu, they might invade China. On October 5, 1950 the Politburo agreed to intervene in Korea and on October 8 Mao redesignated the North East Frontier Force as the Chinese People's Volunteer Army. This was done to prevent a direct confrontation between the official PLA and the American army, since it was believed such a confrontation would lead directly to open war between China and the United States.

Zhou and a Chinese delegation left for Moscow on October 8 to enlist Stalin's support, arriving on October 10, after which they flew to Stalin's dacha on the Black Sea where they conferred with Stalin, Foreign Minister Vyacheslav Molotov, NKVD head Lavrenti Beria, and party leader Georgi Malenkov. Stalin initially agreed to send military equipment and ammunition, but would only provide China with equipment on a credit basis. In the end, Soviet supply shipments, when they did arrive, were limited to small quantities of trucks, grenades, machine guns, and such. On October 14, Zhou requested the Soviets also provide bombers in the Soviet "volunteer" air force and additionally requested that the Soviets provide air defense for major Chinese cities, since he foresaw the possibility of American attacks against China proper once the intervention was underway. Finally, he requested provision of modern jet fighters for the People's Liberation Army Air Force, which would allow the PLAAF to directly support Chinese forces in North Korea, as well as other military equipment for the PLA.

The Soviets provided units from both Frontal Aviation and the PVO-Strany air defense force of the Red Air Force. The Soviet units participating in the war were never large. The first unit to deploy to Manchuria in early November, the 64th Fighter Aviation Corps, included the 29th Fighter Regiment of the Frontal Aviation and the 151st Fighter Regiment of the PVO, which were each approximately the same strength as a US Air Force fighter wing with around 50 aircraft each. The Soviets, however, were equipped with the new MiG-15, a second-generation jet fighter with swept wings, which was superior to the F-80 Shooting Star and the F9F-2 Panther, which were first-generation jets. Only the superior training of USAF and Navy pilots and their combat experience in the months since the outbreak of war would allow the F-80-equipped 51st Fighter Interceptor Wing and the Panther-equipped squadrons of Task force 77 to hold their own when they became involved with MiG-15s in November. The fact that the Soviet units were still "finding their way" during most of the fighting in November–December 1950 was an additional reason why the UN aircraft did not suffer heavier losses.

Immediately on his return to Beijing on October 18, 1950, Zhou met with Mao, Peng Dehuai, and Gao Gang, and the group ordered 200,000 Chinese troops to enter North Korea.

The People's Volunteer Army that began entering North Korea in early October was an Asian army unlike any the West had before confronted. The army was made up of combat veterans of the Chinese civil war, many with more than ten years' service. As individuals, they had known war since their teenage years and were committed to the ideals of the Chinese Revolution. They saw their fight in Korea as a defense of their nation against the same Western forces that had done such harm to China over the previous 150 years.

Domestically, the United States was involved in a mid-term election in the fall of 1950, with President Truman and the Democrats attempting to hold the congressional majorities they had regained in 1948 against the Republicans. The Republican Party had determined to use the charges Senator McCarthy had made regarding Communist infiltration of the American government, as well as to continue the "who lost China?" campaign. With anti-Communism permeating domestic politics, there was no reason for any politician to be seen as "soft on Communism," a charge the Republicans were making against the administration. President Truman took the opportunity to meet with General MacArthur at Wake Island on October 15 to discuss the war to date and the campaign MacArthur had announced. MacArthur viewed the summons to meet as an attempt by the president to improve the electoral chances of the Democratic Party. What actually happened there set the stage for the coming conflict between the president and his unruly general. MacArthur had arrived the night before aboard his C-69 Constellation "Bataan," and provided further disrespect of his civilian superiors when he failed to salute President Truman when the president stepped off his airplane, "the Independence," and compounded the act with his failure to greet Frank Pace, the Secretary of the Army. Neither Truman nor MacArthur said anything publicly about any of this, and indeed they made certain the press reported their unanimity in deciding the future course of the war MacArthur proclaimed would "be over by Christmas." Writing in his memoirs, MacArthur stated that the possibility of Chinese intervention came up almost casually in their conversation, and that President Truman agreed the general consensus was that China had no intention of intervening. Writing in his memoirs, Truman said the threatened Chinese intervention in Korea was a prime reason for the meeting and that he had wanted MacArthur's "firsthand information and judgment." Truman stated further that what he took away from Wake Island was that the war in Korea was won and that the Chinese Communists would not attack, and that furthermore when he asked about the chances of Chinese intervention, MacArthur assured him there was very little chance the Chinese would come in, that "at the most they might be able to get fifty or sixty thousand men into Korea, but since they had no air force, if they tried to get down to Pyongyang, there would be the greatest slaughter." The general even went so far as to state that Army divisions in Korea could soon be reassigned elsewhere, and suggested that the 2nd Division, which had seen hard fighting in the Pusan Perimeter, could be transferred to Europe shortly after the new year.

MacArthur's memory of the conversation was very different, stating that it was a "prevarication" that he had predicted to the president "that under no circumstances would Chinese Communists enter the war," and he characterized his view on the possibility of Chinese intervention as "speculative." He said further that his own local intelligence was that large numbers of Chinese troops were massed across the Yalu, but that his estimate of possible enemy action was that the virtually unopposed air power available to UN forces "would make large-scale intervention impossible." Truman left the Wake Island meeting with a very different view of MacArthur than he had entertained before the meeting, having never before met his commanding general. The results of this meeting would greatly influence presidential decision-making in the events to come.

Four days after the Truman–MacArthur meeting, between October 18 and 25, a force of 130,000 troops and support units crossed the Yalu into eastern North Korea, moving into the Taebaek Mountains north and west of what UN maps called the Chosin Reservoir, its Japanese name, and the Chinese called the Chanjin Reservoir, its Korean name. Additionally, a force of approximately equal size entered western North Korea north of the Chongchon River, all without MacArthur's intelligence staff discerning the slightest evidence of the movement. The Chinese forces combined excellent fieldcraft and camouflage with a lack of radio communication, mechanized activity, or the creation of supply dumps – all the conventional means of detecting modern military movement. The Americans were not looking for anything of this sort, since MacArthur was thinking in terms of the Japanese army he had beaten in the Pacific, a traditional military force fighting a conventional war. China, on the other hand, was the least modern major nation and the Chinese leadership understood their vulnerabilities and adjusted their tactics accordingly. Chinese units could move 15 miles in one night without a single cigarette being smoked, carrying all supplies on the backs of individual soldiers, then burrow into caves during the day. The Americans were aware of none of this since they had persuaded themselves the war was all but over. Not seeing anything was almost a requirement to be taken seriously in the upper circles of both Washington and Tokyo.

Major General Charles Willoughby, MacArthur's chief of intelligence, had a crucial role in what would happen in Korea in November and December 1950. Willoughby was known by lower-ranking members of MacArthur's staff who were not members of "the Bataan Gang" as "Sir Charles," "Lord Willoughby," "Baron von Willoughby" (for his Prussian ethnic background) and "Bonnie Prince Charles." MacArthur once referred to him as "My lovable fascist." Because of MacArthur's habit of limiting and controlling the sources of intelligence so as to have no dissenting or alternative voices with which to contend, Willoughby became not just "an" intelligence officer but "the" intelligence officer, the only one whose words mattered to his commander. The result was that the intelligence provided to MacArthur was almost always deliberately fabricated. During World War II,

Willoughby openly stated his belief that "we should have given England to the Germans." Other than MacArthur, his other hero was "the second-greatest military commander in the world" as he put it, General Franciso Franco. He was writing a laudatory biography of the Spanish fascist dictator at the time of the outbreak of war in Korea. The higher he rose in the headquarters, the more "Prussian" he became, going so far as to wear a monocle, though, as one officer put it, "He was more Erich von Stroheim than Gerd von Rundstedt." His claim in *Who's Who In America* of having a German nobleman for a father and an American mother: "son of Freiherr (Baron) von Tscheppe-Weidenbach and Emma von Tscheppe-Weidenbach (nee Emma Willoughby of Baltimore)" was generally considered false, with many believing he was a self-invented nobleman. A search of the Heidelberg records by an opponent revealed that for his claimed birth date of March 8, 1892, there was only the birth of one Adolf August Weidenbach, son of August Weidenbach, a rope maker, and Emma Langhauser. The name "Willoughby" was a rough translation from "Weidenbach," which means "willow brook" in German. He had joined the Army in 1910 as Adolf Charles Weidenbach; after a term as an enlisted man, he had gone to college and rejoined the Army in 1916, commissioned as "Charles A. Willoughby" and serving on the Mexican border and later in France, where he did not see combat. After serving as a military intelligence attaché in South America, where he impressed then-Major Edward Almond as an incompetent, he had connected with MacArthur while he was teaching at the Command and General Staff College at Fort Leavenworth, and joined MacArthur's staff in the Philippines in 1940. From then on, his real job was amplifier of the MacArthur myth. In 1947, he wrote MacArthur:

There is no contemporary figure comparable to yours... Ultimately [people] have been attached to a great leader, to a man and not an idea, to a Malbrough {sic}, to a Napoleon, to a Robert E. Lee. Underneath it all, these are age old dynastic alliances... A gentleman can serve a grand-siegneur. That will be a good ending to my career... and as I scan the world, the grand-siegneurs are leaving the arena, fighting a bitter rearguard action against the underman, the faceless mob driven by Russian knouts.

The intensity of his far right political biases made even other members of MacArthur's staff, on which there were no liberals, uneasy. As with most political extremists, Willoughby was a believer in conspiracies. For him, what had happened in China was not an epochal event in which a long-suppressed nation found a way to express itself, but the work of plotters. In a letter to the House Un-American Activities Committee written in May 1950, he stated that "American Communist brains plotted the communization of China." He viewed reporters or government people who didn't hew the MacArthur line in Tokyo as likely Communists and even had his staff follow several of them to prove such, frequently passing on the information they concocted to HUAC investigators, and finally worked closely with McCarthy himself. After MacArthur was relieved, Willoughby surfaced in extreme right-wing organizations in the United States and was the author of racist and anti-Semitic material that appeared in the publication of organizations like the John Birch Society. This was thus the ideological prism through which all critical intelligence passed in Tokyo. The key was not Willoughby's own inadequacies, but that he represented the weakness of the man he served, the need to have someone who agreed with him all the time. Bill McCaffrey remembered, "MacArthur did not want the Chinese to enter the war in Korea. Anything MacArthur wanted, Willoughby produced. In this case, he falsified the intelligence reports." Bill Train, a low-level G-3 officer who fought against the upper-level certitude in these crucial weeks would remember "... in the end what he produced was absolutely worthless, there was nothing there at all. Nothing. He got everything wrong! *Everything!* What he was doing in those days was fighting against the truth, trying to keep it from going from lower levels to higher ones where it would have to be acted on." Great intelligence officers must be capable to telling their superiors that their beliefs and expectations may be wrong, no matter how much they want to believe otherwise, and to lay out the facts that prove the case. He knows he must challenge his own value system in order to understand the other side. Charles A. Willoughby was capable of none of this.

Throughout October 1950, as more and more reliable reports made their way to headquarters confirming the arrival of Chinese troops on the battlefield in North Korea, Willoughby set out to prove they either were not there, or, if they were, that they were present only in small numbers as volunteers. Many Army veterans of the period came to believe that his failure to admit the accuracy of the evidence and move quickly to get the high command to re-orient itself on the new enemy was directly responsible for the disastrous events that followed.

In the end, domestic political considerations, especially the imperative of winning a looming mid-term election in a hostile domestic political climate, played the dominant role in the US decision to invade North Korea. Presidential decision-making was formed out of the shared assumptions of Cold War Washington held by both political parties, which reinforced the fantasies under which the military headquarters in Tokyo was operating. Ultimately, the fatal decision was more influenced by considerations of domestic politics than by any diplomatic or strategic military logic.

On October 8, when he heard a radio report that the UN had authorized MacArthur to go north, Ambassador Panikkar wrote in his diary,

So America has knowingly elected for war, with Britain following. It is indeed a tragic decision, for the Americans and British are well aware that a military settlement of the Korean issue will be resisted by the Chinese and that the armies now concentrated on the Yalu will intervene decisively in the fight. Probably that is what the Americans, at least some of them, want. They probably feel that this is an opportunity to have a showdown with China. In any case, MacArthur's dream has come true. I only hope that it does not turn out to be a nightmare.

CHAPTER FIVE

FIRST CONTACT

The 1st Marine Division saw combat as a complete unit during the invasion of Inchon. When the division was first broken up to create the Provisional Marine Brigade in July, it had been determined that the three regiments would be organized as regimental combat teams, organizations capable of independent action, each with a separate artillery battalion from the 11th Marines and detached armor units from the 1st Tank Battalion, making them something more than a standard infantry regiment. This was how the division was organized and operated from the Inchon invasion on.

All the units of Marine Air Group-33 assigned to support the 1st Marine Division were also finally operating together. While VMF-214 and VMF-323 continued to operate their F4U-4 Corsairs from CVEs *Sicily* and *Badoeng Strait*, the rest of the air group was shore based. VMF-212 and VMF-312 were also equipped with F4U-4 fighter-bombers, while VMF(N)-513 operated the F4U-5N Corsair specially equipped for night fighting, and VMF(AW)-542 flew the twin-engine radar-equipped F7F-3N Tigercat. Both units were considered "all weather" squadrons and were not confined strictly to night operations. VMO-6's Stinson OY-2 Sentinel and Sikorsky HO3S-1 helicopters provided battlefield observation and reconnaissance and could airlift casualties from forward locations. VMR-152 flew Douglas R4D transports (the Navy designation for the C-47) for battlefield supply and transport.

The 7th Marines, now at full strength, had finally landed on September 20 and entered combat. While the 1st and 5th Marines engaged in house-to-house fighting until resistance ended on September 28, the 7th Marines fought from hilltop to hilltop north of Seoul to clear NKPA forces out of the territory between Seoul and the village of Uijongbu that commanded the pass the North Koreans needed for their retreat from Seoul, which was taken on October 3. The division was now combat-tested and experienced.

At the Pusan Perimeter, Inchon changed everything. The NKPA faced disaster when Eighth Army went on the offensive on September 16. By September 20, NKPA II Corps retreated from the Naktong; on September 25 a general withdrawal from South Korea was ordered. Eighth Army surged north in pursuit, with leading units reaching the 38th Parallel by the end of September.

Korean geography determined the manner in which the UN forces would enter North Korea. Lieutenant Colonel George Russell of the Army's 2nd Infantry Division wrote that "The worst aspect of the Korean War was Korea itself... in Korea, on the other side of every mountain was another mountain." The Taebeck Mountains roughly divided North Korea in half. Eighth Army would move up the western side of the peninsula, taking the North Korean capital of Pyongyang. X Corps would shift from Seoul on the western side of the peninsula to the eastern side, where the 1st Marine Division would enter North Korea with an invasion of the port of

Wonsan on October 20, thereafter driving west across the peninsula to link up with Eighth Army north of Pyongyang. The Marines were withdrawn from combat on October 7, with the first units boarding ships in Inchon on October 8. The Army's 7th Infantry Division was set to follow within a week of the invasion, once shipping became available.

The decision to keep X Corps separate from Eighth Army, with MacArthur's chief of staff in command while also maintaining his staff position at headquarters, created an impossible command situation, with Eighth Army commander Lieutenant General Walker reporting to MacArthur through corps commander and chief of staff Major General Almond. Of all the sacrosanct rules of the US Army, the most sacrosanct was not splitting command. When American generals thought of splitting command, they thought of Custer's force at the Little Bighorn. The split in command doubled the vulnerability of both parts of the UN force. Jack Murphy, at the time a young lieutenant in Korea and later a serious historian of the war termed it "perhaps the greatest conflict of interest at a high level in the American army that I know of." MacArthur was splitting his force and sending two under-strength columns into a region that called for maximum caution. It was part of his creation of a personal army within the Army. Such a move would decrease the role and independence of Walker, who he still saw as "Marshall's man," while creating a competition for who would be first to the Yalu that would limit Walker's ability to question decisions. Almond, on the other hand, would carry out the orders he had yet to receive without being asked, regardless of their effect. Thus, MacArthur had far more control while the Joint Chiefs in Washington had far less. General Ridgway warned against approving this decision, but after Inchon MacArthur's political position was so strong the chiefs felt they could not oppose him. In August and September, he had presented Inchon as the opportunity to end the war before the troops were forced to face the Siberian winter, yet now he was preparing to send them north to the Yalu in the very face of that winter, as if nothing said before had ever been said. Writing 40 years later, Ridgway said, "One of the things I found hardest to understand – and to forgive as a commander – was how completely oblivious the Tokyo command was to the conditions under which our men would have to fight."

The Marines' time aboard the ships was reckoned to be a matter of days as they loaded troop and cargo ships, LSDs and Japanese-manned LSTs. Joe Owen, whose mortar platoon had proven its worth in the Uijongbu campaign, and the rest of Baker 1/7 loaded aboard the transport MSTS *Okanogan*. The men crammed into whatever space was available, assured they were only putting up with the tight quarters for the few days it would take to steam around Korea to Wonsan.

Among the ships supporting the operation was the carrier USS *Leyte* (CV-32), which had been hurriedly recalled from the Mediterranean and sent through the Panama Canal direct to Japan, arriving in Sasebo on October 8 to become the first Atlantic Fleet carrier diverted to Korea.

Air Group 3 included VF-32 "Swordsmen," equipped with F4U-4 Corsairs. Among the squadron pilots were Lieutenant (jg) Thomas J. Hudner, Jr., Annapolis '46, who had joined the squadron the previous year after gaining his wings of gold, and Ensign Jesse L. Brown, Jr., who held the distinction of being the first African-American to become a naval aviator. None aboard *Leyte* could know that when they left Sasebo on October 9 to join the fleet, they would not set foot on land again until January 19, 1951, by which time they would have set a Navy record of 92 continuous days at sea, flying 3,933 sorties in 11,000 flying hours to provide air support through the Marines' darkest hour.

The plans for Operation *Tailboard* began to crumble when the naval bombardment force arrived offshore on October 10. The North Koreans had been supplied by the Soviet Union and

China with several different kinds of sea mines, both acoustic and magnetic, which they had laid in the harbor at the end of September under the guidance of Soviet naval advisors. This was a formidable defense, particularly since the Navy did not have sufficient minesweepers to clear the harbor quickly. Sweeping began on October 10, but two days later, while under accurate fire from shore batteries, the minesweepers USS *Pledge* (AM-277) and USS *Pirate* (AM-275) were sunk by mines, with 12 killed and dozens wounded.

General Almond railed at the Navy for the slowness of the sweeping operations following the loss of the two ships, insisting that the planned date for D-Day, October 20, must be met. For the men of Baker 1/7 and the rest of the division, the extended time at sea, in what they called "Operation Yo-Yo" for the way the fleet steamed north then south, became a crisis. Owen recorded that "Our three-night voyage became a three-week ordeal of misery and sickness." Many aboard *Okanogan* came down with a low-grade flu, for which medical personnel had no remedy, while the limited toilet facilities for men afflicted with dysentery created horrible conditions aboard the ship. In addition, rations were cut to extend the limited food supply and there was no space for men to exercise. The situation was the same throughout the invasion fleet.

The Marines finally landed on October 26, a week after the ROK 3rd Division had taken Wonsan, several days after Bob Hope and his USO troupe had given a show for the men of MAG-33 who were already ashore at Kunsan. "The troops came running off the amtracs whooping the war yells they had learned at Uijongbu," Owen remembered. "Almost to a man, they staggered and fell to the ground. Under heavy combat loads and softened by three weeks of inactivity, accustomed to hard steel decks, their legs wobbled against the soft earth."

By the time the Marines landed, the ROK 1st and 6th Infantry Divisions of ROK II Corps were advancing through the mountains of northern North Korea, while the

Capital Division and 3rd Division had taken Hamhung and Hungnam. The two divisions of ROK I Corps could best be described as light infantry, lacking any armored units, while their only artillery was obsolescent 75mm pack howitzers. Almond optimistically assessed the ROK's fighting capabilities as "they were a good deal better than the people they were chasing, the disorganized, disabled North Korean force." With the UN front now 50 miles north of Wonsan, the original plan of an offensive to the west to link up with Eighth Army was changed. The Marines would now advance north in support of the ROK forces, linking up with the 7th Infantry Division which finally came ashore at Iwon on October 29.

Following his meeting with President Truman, MacArthur stated at a press conference in Tokyo that the war would be over by Thanksgiving. Eighth Army would return to Japan in December while X Corps would remain in Korea an additional month or two while elections to unify Korea were organized and held. Questioned about the recent statements by the Chinese government about possible intervention, MacArthur replied that if the Chinese did intervene, it would be with small forces only. "If they were to attempt to move on Pyongyang, the slaughter would be tremendous," he concluded. He also pointed out that Chinese armies had historically never been able to stand against Western armies. Major General David Barr, commander of the 7th Infantry Division, had been the last commander of the Army military assistance advisory group in China, and had witnessed the fighting ability of the Red Chinese at the end of the civil war. As such, he had first-hand knowledge of the enemy the American forces would soon come up against. When reports came in of Chinese troops being discovered in North Korea, Barr personally contacted General Willoughby with an offer to brief the headquarters staff about what he knew, and write something that could be given out to American commanders in Korea to guide them in their planning. Willoughby did not even deign to reply, since the offer implied his intelligence section might not know everything there was to be known, most particularly because what Barr would say would dissent from MacArthur's viewpoint.

Throughout Eighth Army during late October, front-line units actually began removing combat equipment to clean and prepare them for return to Japan. Officers in some units discarded their field uniforms in favor of retaining the dress uniforms they would wear in the coming victory parade in Tokyo. In the 1st Cavalry Division, the word was the division would lead the parade; the men would wear their yellow cavalry scarves and had better look parade-ground sharp, not battlefield-grizzled. In Pyongyang, which had been liberated on October 20, the mood among American troops was a combination of exhaustion and optimism, emotional as well as physical. Syngman Rhee was proclaimed President of Korea in the city on October 21. MacArthur himself showed up for the event, asking "where is Kim Buck Tooth?" in mocking reference to the apparently defeated North Korean leader. He asked that anyone in the division who had been there since the beginning step forward. Of the 200 troopers assembled, four took the step. Replacements who had heard the stories about how hard the fighting had been at the Pusan Perimeter were relieved to learn the worst was over. Men set up betting pools about when they would ship out. On one of the last days they spent in the North Korean capital, 1st Cavalry was treated to a Bob Hope USO show. The next morning, they set out for a place called Unsan.

Eighth Army units crossed the Chongchon River north of Pyongyang on October 24, while units of ROK II Corps arrived at the Yalu on October 26, where many urinated in the river to confirm their victory. The Seventh Fleet planners issued Operation Plan 114-50 on October 19, listing naval missions in support of the pacification of North Korea, complete with an annex on the homeward movement of forces. Plans for the redeployment of the Marines reached General Smith before he arrived at Wonsan. Offshore, where the carriers *Boxer, Philippine Sea, Valley Forge* and *Leyte* cruised the Sea of Japan, sortie rates lowered as pilots found fewer targets. By the time the Marines went ashore, *Philippine Sea* and *Boxer* had departed for Yokosuka on October 22, with *Boxer* ordered to depart for the United States following arrival in Japan. On October 30, *Valley Forge* retired to Sasebo with *Leyte* expected to follow later in November. Plans had been made to withdraw the escort carriers *Sicily* and *Badoeng Strait* from Korean waters, with VMF-214 and VMF-323 departing the ships to operate from Kunsan.

South Korean General Paek Sun Yup, commanding the ROK 1st Division and considered by the Americans to be the best Korean officer, marveled at the lack of resistance his force encountered as they moved north while he became increasingly uneasy. He finally realized his sense of unease came from the almost total isolation his troops advanced in. There was overwhelming silence in the hills beyond the road, and no refugees streaming south as there had been. And every day it got a few degrees colder.

Efforts were made to "winterize" the UN forces, as the chilly North Korean fall rapidly replaced the warmer days of early fall with snowstorms blowing out of Siberia across the peninsula, but re-equipment was slow, and by the end of November, many soldiers in the Eighth Army were still wearing summer-weight uniforms, while the Marines had only just equipped their last units in the week before the battle began. The Yalu was covered with ice by mid-October, which was soon thick enough that Chinese units were able to cross without using the bridges. VF-32's pilots patrolling just south of the Yalu reported spotting signs in the snow-covered ice on the river of major personnel movements across the river and into the southern hills. They were not the only ones reporting the presence of a new enemy. Army I Corps G-2 Colonel Percy Thompson was sure from the reports he had from leading units that the Chinese were present, directly warning Colonel Hal Edson, commander of the 8th Cavalry Regiment, that there was a formidable Chinese presence around Unsan, but Edson met the warning "with disbelief and indifference." Thompson noted in his diary that "a sense of euphoria permeated the upper ranks of the Cav." These reports were discounted by General Willoughby, who declared the Chinese did not have the transport capability to move a large force of men into Korea.

MacArthur abandoned the "line of restraint" approved by the Joint Chiefs in late September on October 24 and declared that non-Korean forces would move on to the Yalu. While the mountains in central Korea between Wonsan and Pyongyang, which would have been the original "line of restraint," rose only some 3,000 feet, the mountains to the north in the watershed of the Yalu rose above 8,000 feet. The northern country was sparsely populated and rugged, with few roads of any sort and those that did exist being little more than oxcart paths. While lightly armed forces could maneuver in these conditions with ease, it was another matter for motorized armies using roads that climbed ever-higher into the crags through twisting, narrow defiles. Mutual support in these conditions was nearly impossible, since radio communication broke down due to the intervening mountains and batteries drained quickly as cold weather became the norm.

Though he had not set foot on the Asian mainland since 1905, MacArthur claimed to understand "Oriental psychology," or as he put it to the press, "the Oriental mind." In MacArthur's view, "the Asiatic respects powerful men who were strong and unshakeable in their vision." Pilot Mike Lynch, who flew both Generals Walker and Ridgway, and saw most of the high-ranking officers in Korea from close up, recalled that one of the great myths of the war was,

... MacArthur's claimed knowledge of the Oriental mind. We may have known the rich businessman in Manila, and the cowardly and corrupt Chinese leaders in Chiang's army, and the condescending Japanese in Tokyo. But we knew nothing about the battle-hardened North Koreans or the dedicated Chinese who had whipped Chiang. It was a classic failure to apply the most basic tenet for military commanders: know your enemy.

Since the September authorization of operations above the 38th Parallel had stipulated that "no non-Korean ground forces will be used in the northeast provinces ... or ... along the Manchurian border," MacArthur's act caused a stir in Washington. He replied to a query from the Joint Chiefs, stating the decision was based on "military necessity," and further that "tactical hazards might even result from other action," though none of these possible negatives were identified. Once again, MacArthur's supposed superiors gave way to his view. In retrospect, the plan to use the forces then available to push through to the Yalu makes sense only with reference to the official assumption that no serious resistance was anticipated. In the entire geographic region for which X Corps was now responsible, only three routes led north to the border: the coastal route by which ROK I Corps was advancing, and two roads through the inland mountains. The eastern route, from Sinchang north through Kapsan to Hyesanjin, was assigned to the 7th Division. The other, 50 miles to the west, ran from the port of Hungnam into the mountains, through Funchilin Pass up to the Taebaek plateau, then down the Changjin Valley to the Yalu. This route was assigned to the Marines.

Suddenly, at the end of October, signs of increased enemy activity became apparent. Air Force reconnaissance flights along the Yalu spotted large concentrations of fighter planes at Antung airfield on the Manchurian side of the lower Yalu. Air Force and Navy pilots reported coming under fire from antiaircraft batteries located in Manchuria. The APS-6 radars used by the aircraft of VMF(N)-513 and VMF(AW)-542 enabled a pilot to map the terrain ahead for nearly 80 miles, allowing operations over the cruggy mountains at night in conditions in which other units would be grounded. First Lieutenant W. P. Garton from VMF(AW)-542 reported seeing the Chinese buildup on his first night mission to the Yalu:

> For one hour, I orbited the Korean side of the river and counted the trucks coming across the bridge between Antung and Sinuiju. The trucks left brightly lit Antung with their lights on; halfway across the bridge, they would switch to black-out lights and grope their way through dimly lit Sinuiju. The traffic appeared to be almost entirely one-way, and in the hour I observed them, I counted over 150 trucks crossing the bridge.

On a mission later in the month, Garton reported seeing more than 200 trucks cross in the hour he observed them. Despite these and numerous other reports made by the night-flying Marines and their Air Force counterparts, higher headquarters continued to maintain that any intervention by Chinese forces would be limited in its scope and operations.

On the night of October 25, the ROK 15th Regiment of General Paek's division came to a complete halt under a hail of mortar fire, then the ROK 12th Regiment and then the 11th Regiment were hit on their flanks and attacked from the rear. General Paek saved his men by pulling the division back to Unsan. The South Koreans had been mauled by the 116th Division of the People's Volunteer Army, while the rest of ROK II Corps broke and retreated. Paek took a captured enemy soldier, who he had identified as Chinese, to the headquarters of Major General Frank Milburn, Army

II Corps commander, where he repeated his interview with the prisoner in front of Milburn. The man identified himself as a member of the PVA 39th Division and confirmed he was Chinese. Milburn immediately reported what he had seen and heard to the Eighth Army headquarters, where it was passed on to General Willoughby in Tokyo, who decided the prisoner must be a Korean resident of China who had volunteered to fight. It was a judgment that would have pleased the prisoner's commanders, because it was exactly what they wanted the Americans to think, that the way north was open as they drew them forward into the greatest military ambush ever planned.

None of the doubt and confusion in the upper ranks of the front-line American forces over the nature of their enemy filtered down to the troops, who still expected to finish the war in a matter of weeks. On the same day the Chinese struck the ROK 1st Division, Major General Laurence "Dutch" Keiser, commander of the 2nd Infantry Division, summoned his officers for a special staff meeting. Forward artillery observer First Lieutenant Ralph Hockley of the 37th Field Artillery Battalion remembered after the war that "The general was in a wonderful mood, telling us 'We're all going home and we're going home soon, before Christmas. We have our orders.'"

The air war also suddenly changed. On October 31, F-80 pilots of the 51st Fighter Interceptor Wing reported seeing "silver, arrow-shaped jets" in the sky over Antung across the Yalu. These were tentatively identified as MiG-15s. On November 1, the first combat took place when eight MiG-15s of the 29th IAP (Fighter Aviation Regiment) intercepted 15 F-51D Mustangs of the 8th Fighter Bomber Wing attacking the Yalu bridges. The Soviet unit had been specially organized, the majority of its pilots World War II aces. The Russian-flown MiGs scored when Senior Lieutenant Fyodor V. Chizh shot down the Mustang flown by First Lieutenant Aaron Abercrombie. Later that morning, the first jet-versus-jet combat in history took place over the Yalu when pilots of the 51st Wing were attacked by three MiG-15s that used their altitude advantage to dive on the American formation. First blood went to the Soviets when Senior Lieutenant Semyon Fyodorovich Jominich shot down an F-80C, killing the pilot, First Lieutenant Frank Van Sickle. The USAF officially listed these November 1 losses as being the result of North Korean antiaircraft fire until Russian records were opened following the end of the Cold War.

In the afternoon of October 31, the men of the 8th Cavalry reached Unsan without experiencing any difficulty. Shortly after arrival, Sergeant "Pappy" Miller of 3/8 Battalion took his squad out on a patrol 5 miles north of the town, during which they came across an old Korean farmer who informed them there were thousands of Chinese soldiers in the area, many of whom had arrived on horseback. When he returned to his battalion headquarters and reported the conversation, he was met with disbelief by the intelligence officers, who completely discounted the possibility of Chinese in the area, let alone on horseback.

Lieutenant Colonel Harold "Johnny" Johnson, former commander of 3/8 Cavalry and now commander of the 5th Cavalry Regiment, arrived at 3/8 headquarters shortly after Miller made his report. Johnson, a survivor of the Bataan Death March and three years as a POW, was one of the pessimistic officers in the division. Like Paek, the emptiness of the countryside made him uneasy. He wasn't happy when he observed his former troopers spread out in flat paddy land and not dug in. When he voiced his concern to his replacement, Lieutenant Colonel Robert Ormond, who had come from duty as a staff officer in Tokyo and had never held a combat command, Ormond responded that there was no likelihood of an attack. Johnson responded "You've got to get these men out of this valley and up on the high ground! They're much too vulnerable where they are! You have no defense if you're hit!" Ormond refused the experienced officer's advice. The night went quietly, but the men awoke the next day to forest fires throughout the surrounding mountains, which had been set by the Chinese to block any chance of their movements being spotted from the air.

At the 1st Cavalry Headquarters on the morning of November 1, Colonel Edson, who had now agreed with Colonel Thompson regarding the likelihood of a Chinese attack, requested permission to pull back his three battalions from Unsan because he believed they were too exposed, with no other American units on their flanks. The 1st Cavalry commander, Major General Hap Gay, who had been Patton's chief of staff in World War II, agreed with Edson's assessment. Gay believed Tokyo had little feel for the enemy or the terrain, and no curiosity about either, and that MacArthur's failure to respect the ability of the enemy was creating the opportunity for a great American disaster. As for the talk about being home for Christmas, Gay had said "That's stupid talk. All it does is get the troops excited about going home, and they get careless." Unfortunately, corps commander Major General Milburn did not want to be the officer who approved a "retrograde movement," the Army term for "withdrawal," in the face of all the optimism coming from Tokyo. Despite having witnessed Paek's interview with the captured Chinese soldier, Milburn ordered Gay to maintain his present positions.

That afternoon, Gay received a report from an observer in a spotter plane that two columns of enemy troops were moving in the vicinity of the villages of Myongdang-dong and Yonghung-dong, 5 miles from Unsan. Gay ordered the artillery into action and again requested authority to pull back the 8th Cavalry, which was again refused.

As dusk fell, the 5th Cavalry, which had been moving north to link up with the 8th Cavalry, ran into a major Chinese roadblock. Soon after darkness fell the regiment was in a fight for its life against well-trained, experienced troops.

By nightfall on November 1, the 8th Cavalry was surrounded on three sides by the 115th and 116th Divisions of the People's Volunteer Army. The Chinese struck the three battalions of the ROK 15th Regiment, 2 miles away, at 2200 hours with two battalions. The ROK troops broke and ran as they retreated across the Kuryong River, after which they were left alone.

Twenty minutes later, 1/8 Battalion, the northernmost of the three battalions, was hit. The first warning was the sound of what was thought at first to be bagpipes. In reality, the sound came from the bugles and flutes that the two regiments from the PVA 115th Division were using to signal each other, which had the added effect of unnerving those Americans who heard it. Nearly half the men in the foremost platoon were barely trained Korean troops who could not communicate with their American compatriots. At 2230 hours, the Chinese swept through the battalion. The KATUSAs (Koreans Attached To US Army) melted away with the first bugle blasts. The rest of the battalion was positioned so thinly the Chinese swept through them "as if they were in a footrace," as one survivor remembered. Troops broke and ran, and the unit seemed to melt away. The battalion command post quickly disintegrated. Men tried to organize secondary lines of resistance but were overwhelmed. There were wounded men everywhere. A convoy of ten trucks was organized by the 1st Battalion commander Lieutenant Colonel Jack Millikin Jr. to take out the wounded, escorted by two tanks. A mile south of Unsan, the road split, one branch heading southwest toward the position of the 3rd Battalion, and the other southeast. Millikin chose to turn southeast, away from possible help. Six hundred yards down the road, the Chinese waiting in ambush opened up with heavy fire. The convoy, with so many wounded, had no way of fighting back as enemy soldiers swarmed over the trucks and killed the wounded men. Second Lieutenant Ben Boyd, leader of the

2nd Platoon, Baker Company, survived by feigning death as a Chinese soldier went through his pockets.

At 2300 hours, the 2nd Battalion on the western side of the position was hit by two regiments of the PVA 115th Division. It was penetrated as easily as the 1st had been, with a similar result. Twenty minutes later, two Chinese regiments that had crossed the Nammyon River hit the 3rd Battalion to the south. Battalion commander Ormond was killed as he ran to regimental headquarters, then the executive officer deserted. As the Chinese came through the perimeter at several places, the surprised Americans pulled back. Within ten minutes, Chinese troops were outside the battalion command post. The survivors formed a new perimeter, centered around three tanks, and managed to hold through the night.

C Battery, 99th Field Artillery Battalion was badly hit at about the same time. By the time they managed to organize for withdrawal, it was almost too late. A mile south of their original position, they were hit by a Chinese ambush of troops armed with the Thompson sub-machine guns inherited from the Guomintang after the Chinese civil war. Of 180 men in the company, only a handful managed to retreat north and make it into the 3rd Battalion perimeter shortly after dawn.

During the day of November 2, a helicopter tried to land at the improvised perimeter, but was driven off by Chinese fire. A few more stragglers managed to find their way in, but the troopers were cut off and surrounded by an overwhelming number of Chinese. An air strike by a pair of B-26 Invaders failed to hit the main enemy force. The number of wounded grew and ammunition ran out. A spotter plane dropped supplies, but there was no medicine or ammunition. That afternoon, the wounded officers decided that the wounded would remain behind, while the able-bodied would attempt to make their way in small groups to the American lines when the opportunity presented itself. Shortly after this decision was announced, the Chinese were heard digging a trench toward the perimeter. A sergeant took several hand grenades and moved out to stop them. Grenade blasts were followed by a burst of fire. The sergeant didn't return, but the Chinese stopped digging.

General Gay had ordered the 5th Cavalry forward to rescue the 8th Cavalry, but they were stopped again by Chinese forces that had picked near-perfect ambush positions. Taking 250 casualties in one battalion, the 5th Cavalry was forced to pull back. At Unsan, a spotter plane dropped a message telling the survivors to get out as best they could.

When night fell, the Chinese attacked in force. The surviving Americans fired the last of their bazookas at their own vehicles; the resulting fires and explosions provided light to fight by and the Americans were able to hold off the enemy with a machine gun and with Thompsons taken from the enemy dead. By the morning of November 4, there were fewer than 50 unwounded troopers left in the perimeter. The last tank took off on its own, leaving them without radio communication. The Chinese had withdrawn from close contact at daybreak. Sergeant Bill Richardson led a four-man patrol to find an escape route. To the east, they came across hundreds of wounded Chinese in a riverbed, who begged them for water. Richardson realized they could perhaps escape down the riverbed, and they returned to the perimeter. The 150 wounded were desperate not to be left behind for the Chinese, despite the order of their senior officer who was one of them. Richardson followed orders and at 1700 hours, he led the 60 survivors who could move out of the perimeter and down to the riverbank.

Captain Chaplain Emil Kapaun, a Roman Catholic priest who had served as a chaplain during World War II, was among the less badly wounded, and could have left with Sergeant Richardson. He refused to leave the position despite being given a direct order to do so, and remained behind to care for the other wounded. Shortly after the departure of Sergeant

Richardson's group, the Chinese occupied the position. That night, the men were forced to begin what would become a 16-day march north into captivity. During this, Chaplain Kapaun became the *de facto* leader of the survivors and was able to keep them organized enough to support each other when they arrived in the POW camp at Pyoktong. Over the next seven months Chaplain Kapaun dug latrines, mediated disputes, gave away his own food, and did all he could to raise morale among the prisoners, being noted for stealing coffee from the Communist guards and tea and a pot in which to heat them, and also leading prisoners in acts of defiance while he smuggled stolen dysentery drugs to the camp doctor. Despite suffering dysentery himself, he led an Easter sunrise service on March 25, 1951. He died from malnutrition and pneumonia on May 23, 1951. After the war, he was posthumously awarded the Legion of Merit for his service as a POW. In 1993, Pope John Paul II declared Chaplain Kapaun a Servant of God, the first stage on the path to Catholic sainthood. On April 11, 2013, President Barack Obama presented the Medal of Honor posthumously to Captain Chaplain Kapaun.

Only some twenty of the survivors who left managed to escape Chinese patrols and regain the American lines. Sergeant Richardson was among those captured, and would spend the next two-and-a-half years as a POW. Of the 2,400 men in the 8th Cavalry, 800 were casualties and more than a thousand were wounded. The unit had been routed on the first night. Only some 200 men of the 800 in the 3rd Battalion survived. Unsan was the worst American defeat of the Korean War to date. The Chinese had seemingly appeared out of nowhere and inflicted a crushing defeat on an elite unit of an elite division. A spokesman for the division compared the event with that of Custer's battle at the Little Big Horn.

In reporting the appearance of Chinese troops on the battlefield, General Willoughby deliberately minimized their numbers and intentions, stating there were no more than

34,000 Chinese in North Korea, though the truth was that over 20,000 had attacked at Unsan alone.

The Chinese did not just attack the Eighth Army at this time. Also on October 31, 30 miles above Hamhung, north of Sudong, a village only a few miles south of the Chosin Reservoir, the ROK I Corps troops of the 26th Regiment were hit by a Chinese infantry attack and the unit was forced to retreat on November 1 to positions south of Sudong.

The Marines had been ordered to begin the movement north, with the departure of the 7th Marines from Hamhung set for November 1. This was the first step in the advance to what the Marines' Japanese maps identified as the Chosin Reservoir. Following the Chinese attack the day before, the 7th Marines were ordered to relieve the ROK 26th Regiment in the vicinity of Sudong on November 2.

Hamhung and Hungnam are frequently confused. Hungnam, the port, lies on the north shore of the Songchon River where it meets the Sea of Japan. The town of Yonpo is on the south side of the estuary; the airfield at Yonpo, where MAG-33 would relocate to from Kunsan, would prove to be of critical importance in the coming weeks. Hamhung is the inland rail and highway center, located 8 miles from the port on the main rail line coming north from Wonsan.

What the Marines would come to know as the Main Supply Route (MSR) to the Chosin Reservoir began at Hungnam. A narrow-gauge rail line ran from Hamhung to Chinhung-ni, from where a now-inoperative cable car then climbed through Funchilin Pass to the high Taebaek plateau. A road paralleled this rail line. The Marine Corps official history of the Chosin campaign describes the route to Chosin thus:

> The road – if an oxcart path can be called such – began at Hungnam, where the Songchan River flows into the Sea of Japan. From Hungnam to Hamhung is eight miles; from Hamhung to Sudong is twenty-nine miles; from Sudong

to Chinhung-ni, six miles; from Chinhung-ni to Koto-ri in the high country, ten miles through Funchilin Pass – which rises to thirty-five hundred feet in eight miles; from Koto-ri across the plateau to Hagaru-ri, eleven miles; from Hagaru-ri through Toktong Pass at an elevation of four thousand feet to Yudam-ni – on the west side of the north end of the Chosin Reservoir – fourteen miles. Not a mile was easy. The road was narrow and winding. Of dirt and gravel, oxcarts had a hard time passing, let alone tanks, trucks and artillery.

In fact, the tanks, trucks and artillery would only be able to advance to the Taebaek plateau due to the Herculean efforts of the Marine engineers, who widened the MSR from an oxcart path to a (mostly) two-way dirt road by mid-November.

The most difficult section, Funchilin Pass, was a slow, steady climb of 10 miles to the high country; the zigzagging single-lane road was described as "a cliff on one side and a chasm on the other" in the official history. North of Koto-ri, the road ran across the high plateau to Hagaru-ri at the southern tip of the reservoir, where the road divided, with the western branch climbing and winding through Toktong Pass before descending into the Yudam-ni Valley on the western side of the reservoir, while the eastern branch wound along the eastern shore of the reservoir to Sinhung-ni. The Taebaek Mountains that surrounded the route had jagged peaks as high as 8,000 feet. The Marines were moving into very forbidding country indeed.

On October 31, reconnaissance patrols from 1/7 Battalion under the command of Captain Myron E. Wilcox Jr. reached the ROK 26th Regiment command post south of Sudong, where the South Koreans showed them a Chinese prisoner, one of 16 they had identified as members of the 124th Division of the "Chinese Communist Forces," the UN term for the People's Volunteer Army. The prisoner confirmed he and the others had crossed the Yalu several weeks earlier in mid-October, and that they were in the 370th Regiment of the 124th Division. He also stated that the 125th and 126th Divisions were part of the 42nd Army, the Chinese equivalent of a US corps. They learned from the prisoner that the 124th Division was deployed to defend the Chosin Reservoir, with the 126th at the Fusen Reservoir and the 125th in the the Taebaek Mountains on the western flank of the 124th.

Litzenberg received Wilcox's report with foreboding. At that point, the Marines had encountered no enemy anywhere from Wonsan north to Hamhung, but Litzenberg was certain that the Marines would face Chinese adversaries soon, and passed on his concerns regarding the possibility of meeting them to his senior officers, telling them "We can expect to meet Chinese Communist troops and it is important that we win the first battle. The result of that action will reverberate around the world, and we want to make certain the outcome has an adverse effect in Moscow as well as Peking." Litzenberg was so concerned about the possible outcome of such a battle that he told the men the regiment "might well be taking part in the opening engagement of World War III."

On November 1 a stronger patrol from the Division Reconnaissance Company, mounted in 21 jeeps under the command of First Lieutenant Ralph B. Crossman, reconnoitered the Huksu-ri area 45 miles northwest of Hungnam. They ran into a small North Korean guerrilla force about 3 miles short of their objective and dug in for the night without encountering more enemy forces. While this patrol moved forward on November 1, the rest of the regiment was trucked from Hungnam to an assembly area halfway between the villages of Oro-ri and Majon-dong, without encountering any opposition. Just before departure, Litzenberg learned of the battle fought the night before between the 8th Cavalry and the unidentified but likely Chinese forces at Unsan.

That afternoon, General Smith and Fleet Marine Force Pacific commander General Lemuel Shepherd flew up to Hamhung to confer with Litzenberg, who informed them of the report he had received from the Marine patrol who had seen the Chinese prisoner and the report of the South Koreans' interrogation of the others. The two Marine generals agreed with Litzenberg's assessment that the Koreans had correctly identified their prisoners. General Smith stated that General Almond was insistent they advance to the reservoir, regardless of any difficulties suffered by the army to the west and despite the fact that doing so would open an 80-mile gap between the Marines on the left of X Corps' advance and the Eighth Army on the other side of the Taebaek Mountains.

Lieutenant Colonel Ray Davis was ordered late on November 1 to make a reconnaissance-in-force to the ROK positions north of Majon-dong the following morning. That night at 0100 hours, a Chinese patrol estimated to consist of two platoons probed the ROK positions. 1/7 Battalion moved out and headed for the ROK positions, shortly after dawn on 2 November, covered by pilots from VMF-312. The aircraft made 12 attacks against enemy troops spotted in the surrounding hills before the Marines arrived at Majon-dong at 1030 hours, where they reported the South Koreans were very happy to be relieved.

Through the day, the main body of the regiment advanced just short of a mile from their previous position, utilizing what Litzenberg called a "walking perimeter." With shadows lengthening in the wooded hills, a halt was called at 1600 hours south of the village of Sudong. 1/7's Ray Davis and Randolph S. D. Lockwood, commanding 2/7 Battalion, set up command posts in the valley while they positioned their rifle companies atop the surrounding hills.

Captain David W. Banks' Able 1/7 was on the right side of the road on what the Japanese maps identified as Hill 532, with Captain Wilcox's Baker 1/7 in position along the ridge between Hills 532 and 698, where Captain William C. Shea's Charlie 1/7 occupied the front side, less than a mile from the village. South of the 1st Battalion positions, 2/7 Battalion's rifle companies took position with Captain Milt Hull's Dog 2/7 on the lower side of Hill 698, not too far from the road, with Captain Walter D. Phillips' Easy 2/7 higher on 698, a few hundred yards from the crest, while Captain Elmer J. Zorn's Fox 2/7 was high on Hill 727 on the right side of the road. Several hundred yards to their rear, around a bend in the road near the regimental command post, the artillerymen of Major Maurice Roach's 3/11 Battalion deployed what was in effect a separate perimeter protecting the regimental train, with George Battery 3/11 astride the road, How Battery 3/11 on the hill to the left flank and Item Battery 3/11 on the hill to the right, near 1st Battalion's flank. Each company of the regiment was essentially on its own, too far from the others for support, particularly due to the problems being experienced with radio communication in the mountains. The halt had been called too late in the day for the big 81mm mortars to be set up and sighted in from positions near the battalion command posts, and it was not possible for 3/11's 105mm field howitzers to provide close support in the hills without effective communication from forward observers, which was not available.

As the light faded, Marines in foxholes recently pickaxed out of the hard ground smothered the tiny fires they had set to heat their meals and buttoned up their summer jackets against the chill that rapidly spread with the setting of the sun while they huddled in their sleeping bags to fight off the cold. No orders were given to maintain a 50 percent watch during the night, because there was no sign of the enemy and no reason to expect an attack since the Marines had only seen straggling North Korean units which had turned and ran.

The Sudong Valley was silent as night approached.

On the ridge occupied by Baker 1/7, Second Lieutenant Joseph Owen tried to find a way to distribute his mortars so they could provide support for the company, which was ranged around the ridge crest in thinly held positions. The poor radio communications meant the individual rifle platoons would be on their own if anything happened, connected only by field telephones with wires that could be easily cut in an attack. Owen worried that the position he had been ordered to site his mortars from, which put them 500 yards from the most extended foxholes held by the 1st Platoon and prevented the mortars reaching out beyond the Marine lines more than 200 yards at maximum range, should they be attacked that night. Not only that, but one mortar section was unaccounted for and out of radio communication, leaving him with only two 60mm mortars to provide defense for the company.

What the Marines didn't know as night fell was that the 371st Regiment, PVA 124th Division was massed to the north and west of them, while the 370th Regiment occupied the high ground east of the road. The 372nd Regiment stood as a ready reserve in a hidden encampment several miles to the rear, near Chinhung-ni. When the Marines were spotted moving north from Wonsan, the PVA 124th Division had moved south of Funchilin Pass to block them, in the process running into the Korean 24th Regiment.

In the brush below the Marine lines, the Chinese assault squads waited in disciplined silence for the bugles and whistles that would signal their attack. Their quilted cotton uniforms kept them warm in the cold, while their tennis shoes would allow them to move through the brush with a silent tread when the time came. Their scouts had gathered detailed information during the day while the Marines dug into their positions, and they knew the location of the machine guns along the lines they faced. After dark, they had crawled within grenade range of their opponents. The soldiers felt honored to have been chosen to attack the Marines, whom they were taught were selected from the dregs of capitalist society, vile men chosen for their depravity and given license to rape and plunder. Their officers had ordered them to exterminate the Marines the way they would kill snakes in their homes. They were confident because they knew how quickly the Americans at Unsan and the ROK units at the Yalu had broken and run in the face of determined attack. These American Marines were bullies to be taught a lesson.

First Lieutenant Harrol "Chuck" Kiser's 3rd Platoon was stretched thin for a hundred yards along the front of the ridge the company held. Kiser's platoon sergeant, Archie Van Winkle – a combat veteran of Guadalcanal, Peleliu, and Okinawa – crawled from hole to hole, calming some men, reassuring others. His task completed, he moved up the 35-degree slope to where Navy Corpsman Ed Toppel and three other men occupied a hole at the crest of the position.

Five hundred yards away from Kiser, Lieutenant Owen awoke with a start at the whoosh of a green rocket that exploded out of the darkness below, followed by a red rocket from a different direction. His watch read 0030 hours. Bugles blared and whistles shrilled in the surrounding darkness. This was followed by the whine of incoming mortar rounds, exploding throughout the Marine lines, while chattering machine guns opened up, followed by the thumping bursts of the Thompson submachine guns the Chinese troops carried.

Within moments, Owen heard the deeper sound of Browning automatic rifles (BARs), American .30 caliber machine guns, and the crack of M-1 rifles as the Marines responded. The screams and cries of wounded men and profanities in two languages soon echoed in the darkness.

The fact that the attackers were indeed Chinese was confirmed by First Lieutenant Kurt Chew-Een Lee, the Baker 1/7 machine-gun platoon commander. He called out into the darkness in Mandarin on hearing shouted commands he identified as being in Chinese. There was a momentary pause from the attackers, before a curse was hurled back in what Lee identified as Cantonese.

Van Winkle heard movement below and worked the phone to notify Kiser when the first grenades exploded and the phone went dead. "The whole area seemed to explode. There were flares, tracers, grenades. It sounded like a symphony with me in the middle of the orchestra." The Chinese spotted the outpost where Van Winkle and the others crouched and a group moved toward them. Van Winkle decided on a fighting retreat, telling the men they would go down the hill to the platoon CP. Flares burst overhead from Owen's mortars, lighting the entire area. Van Winkle shot at five different figures in quick succession as he made his way back to Kiser. Dropping to the ground when he saw an incoming grenade, he collided with Toppel, who had tried to give aid to a wounded Marine. Toppel rose and fired his pistol at the Chinese while Van Winkle put his carbine on full-auto and sprayed the enemy. Arriving at Kiser's position, Van Winkle threw a grenade at the next wave of attackers, then rallied the Marines nearby and they charged down the hill toward the enemy, who pulled back and faded into the night. Van Winkle didn't realize he had been shot in the arm until Toppel saw the wound in the light of a flare, but Van Winkle shrugged it off and continued.

Kiser was firing as fast as he could. "Once they struck, there was no doubt they were going through. You can only shoot what you can see. It was dark and they were just forms gliding by in the darkness. They had the advantage since they had Thompsons and could just spray the area. We had rifles and had to aim them." He managed to rally the surviving Marines of the platoon to make a stand. The push against Kiser's central position on the saddle of the ridge was the enemy's main effort. The first wave of Chinese stormed forward, but were stopped by a hail of rifle and BAR fire from Kiser's hastily organized resistance. More charged through, climbing over the bodies of their dead comrades, to be checked by a volley of Marine grenades, before another group of Chinese poured in. While the Americans termed these "human wave" attacks, they were in reality small units of 30–50 soldiers, operating the way German shock troops had in the close combat trench fighting of 1918. One Marine foxhole went silent, then another as the Marines who gave way crawled up the hill, away from the relentless enemy. Kiser moved from man to man in his position, building a base of aimed fire.

Van Winkle moved to the left side of the platoon position and leaped into the hole where one of Lee's machine guns was sited. "I started shouting orders, but there were more Chinese than there were Marines. Every time I turned around to try and find someone I knew, I saw another Chinaman." Van Winkle lost his carbine and picked up a 1903 Springfield bolt-action rifle that had been issued for sniping. After firing one shot, he began swinging the rifle like a club, dropping it when it smashed in two over the head of an enemy soldier. "It got very exciting about this time, and somewhere along the line I lost my cool." The Marines were fighting hand-to-hand and losing when a Chinese potato-masher grenade flew out of the darkness and exploded in front of Van Winkle's face, knocking him down and showering him with shrapnel. The other Marines grabbed grenades and threw them at the Chinese, stopping the attack at that point. A bloody Van Winkle got up and launched his own attack into the flank of the Chinese moving toward Kiser's position, firing a Thompson he had taken from a dead enemy.

To the right of Kiser, Chew-Een Lee rallied Marine survivors and moved down the hill to hit the other flank of the attacking Chinese. Lee spread his impromptu squad into a firing line. On his signal they threw grenades, then poured fire into the Chinese exposed by the light from more of Owen's flares.

A survivor from the crew of Owen's lost mortar showed up in his position at 0100 hours to report they had been routed from the position they had been in, and had abandoned their weapon. Owen turned to his platoon sergeant and announced he was going to recover the mortar. He took his runner, Corporal John Kelley and two other volunteers, Corporal Winget and Private Bifulk, and headed toward the position the survivor had described. Halfway down the slope, they encountered a Chinese soldier who was quickly dispatched. "We encountered no more Chinese on our way to finding the abandoned gear. There were no enemy soldiers in sight, but we heard them stirring somewhere below us. In the darkness, I almost fell into a waist-deep pit. Inside was my missing mortar, all three parts still strapped together, still in transport carry. One of the others found the still-unpacked mortar shells." Suddenly grenades exploded and Owen spotted three Chinese coming toward them. The four Marines opened fire with their carbines on auto and the Chinese withdrew. "I looked down the hill and could see the battalion command post under heavy fire. The Chinese had emerged from a railroad tunnel across the river from the CP and were pouring fire into the perimeter." Owen had a mortarman's dream target. He and the others quickly unlimbered the recovered mortar as they heard nearby Chinese approach their position. Owen set the tube for a 600-yard range and the first shot was fired. It was a misfire, the worst of all possibilities. Winget turned the mortar upside down and slid the round out of the barrel; Owen caught it and threw it out of the hole, discovering in the process that it was a dud. Winget cleared the obstruction in the tube and they fired a second time as Kelley and Bifulk opened fire on the approaching Chinese. The round fell short of the target. Owen changed the range and the third round hit on the right end of the Chinese line. They quickly fired two more, then changed the sight and fired two again. The effect on the Chinese across the river was devastating as the Marines fired off all the rounds they had. Out of ammo, the four Marines grabbed the mortar and made their way up the hill, pursued by Chinese soldiers firing on full-auto until they made it back to their position where other members of the mortar platoon drove off the pursuers. The 1st Battalion command post was saved.

As the Chinese continued their attempt to break through Kiser's position, Baker Company Gunnery Sergeant George Foster grabbed two machine-gun crews from where they were positioned with the 1st Platoon, and moved the men and weapons up behind Kiser's line where they commenced firing. Chew-Een Lee's impromptu squad advanced on the Chinese left flank, while the force Archie Van Winkle had gathered fired into the right flank. The withering fire from in front and to their flanks stymied the Chinese attack. Soon Marines heard a series of whistles, then the attackers fell back, crawling over their dead but pulling their wounded with them as they retreated down the mountain and back into the woods.

While this attack was in full force, another group of Chinese moved around Baker 1/7's left flank, and discovered a squad of Marines who had taken position in deep holes previously dug by ROK troops. The men were asleep in their sleeping bags, and the 30 attackers made quick work, killing three Marines in their bags with gunfire and bayonets. Then the Chinese attack faltered when they found the Marines' food. While the Chinese soldiers dug through the cans, the surviving squad members were able to kick free of their bags and crawl away. One man went for help and ran across Chew-Een Lee, who grabbed two BAR men and was able to set up in time to catch the attackers as they finished scavenging the dead. Those not killed in the blast of fire pulled back.

Confused fighting reigned across the Baker 1/7 position. Corporal James Jones and Private John Martz made a stand behind a boulder as Jones held off the Chinese with his BAR while Martz fed him ammo. They were surrounded by Chinese when they ran out of ammo and dropped to the ground, hoping the Chinese would think them dead. The attackers moved on; the next morning, 22 dead Chinese were counted on the slope around the boulder.

Able 1/7 on nearby Hill 532 was surrounded by attacking Chinese who came down the slope of the higher Hill 727 at 0045 hours. Sergeant Robert Olson remembered that "The Chinese just ran by us. We got a lot of them but they didn't seem to care. They just wanted to get down to the valley."

Baker 1/7's 2nd Platoon was atop Hill 727. Platoon commander First Lieutenant William Graeber recalled that a matter of minutes after the Chinese went through their position, they were ordered to abandon the hill and rejoin the rest of Baker Company. Once out of their holes, the men were spotted by other Chinese who opened fire. "Chinese were all over the place, we couldn't get through the crossfire and we sure couldn't go back where we'd been, so we just stayed where we were and began shooting Chinese." The platoon fought for the next two hours before the Chinese enemy moved back and they were able to cross the road and rejoin the rest of the company.

In the valley, the Chinese threatened the battalion command posts, and were able to occupy the ground between the 1/7 and 2/7 command posts and the 3rd Battalion's perimeter. Chinese atop the hills poured fire down at the Marines.

Second Lieutenant Robert Wilson had one of the strangest individual experiences of the night. Wilson, a pilot with VMF-312, had reported to the 7th Marines as an air liaison officer, responsible for coordinating air support with the Corsairs of MAG-33, just before the regiment had left Hamhung. When the order came to stop for the night, Wilson found a position that was perfect for air control work, just at the leading edge of the Baker 1/7 command post, on a hill with a slope too steep for an enemy to climb. In daylight, he would have an unobstructed view up the valley. He was awakened when Chinese mortar shells started dropping around the command post. As he crawled from his sleeping bag, a round struck nearby. The concussion lifted him into the air and deposited him halfway down the slope from his position. His only chance lay in moving down into the valley, with mortar shells landing on the slope above. He moved and lost his footing, sliding down the hill into bushes at the base of the hill. He tried to move toward the road but heard Chinese moving all around and burrowed beneath a heavy bush. This was the young aviator's first experience of ground combat. After a night spent in hiding, he was able to find a gully in the dawn light and make his way back up the hill without being shot.

Bill Graeber's 3rd Platoon was surprised when a Soviet T-34 tank appeared out of the darkness and roared past their position, the Marines manning the roadblock on the MSR having mistaken the enemy tank for a friendly bulldozer. Marines ducked in their holes as the armored monster sought targets with its searchlight. The men fixed bayonets and prepared to meet the infantry they expected to follow the tank. Fortunately, the supporting troops had become separated from the tank and there was time to spot them and set up a hot reception before they closed on the platoon's position. The Chinese and Americans exchanged fire within ten yards of each other before the surviving Chinese fell back and faded into the darkness just as the Marines began to run short of ammunition. In the meantime, the T-34 ran through the Marine supply point at the bottom of the hill, scattering stacked rations. As the Marines holding the position retreated up the hill, the Chinese troops who had assaulted the 3rd Platoon swarmed into the supply point. Spotting the ration cans, the soldiers stopped to loot. The tank advanced through the company headquarters area and then through the 1/7 81mm mortar position, reaching Davis' command post. The defenders engaged the tank with recoilless rifles and the T-34 took one or two hits that damaged it. The North Korean tank commander realized he had lost his support and turned around, guns blazing as he managed to get clear of the Marine positions.

By dawn of November 3, 1/7 Battalion still held their positions, but only barely. All three 1/7 rifle companies had taken heavy casualties.

During the battle, the Chinese got down to the road and took a position between 2/7 and 3/11 Battalions, overrunning the regiment's 4.2-inch mortar company as they did so and taking one of the tubes. Dawn found the Marines facing a confusing situation, with the Chinese still in position holding the bend in the road that separated 1/7 and 2/7 Battalions from 3/11. The battle to clear the road took all day.

The fight to clear Hill 698 was the bloodiest action of the day. Atop Hill 698, Baker 1/7's 3rd Platoon held the ridge. Bodies were all around them, and the Marines estimated they had been attacked by at least two companies of infantry. A hundred yards away on the other side of the hill, Charlie 1/7 had been bypassed by the Chinese, who had seemed anxious to get down to the road. Second Lieutenant Ty Hill experienced an extraordinary battlefield moment when he spotted Chinese below in the valley, firing at the 1/7 command post. Hill hastened to get one of the machine guns moved into position to take on the Chinese. He focused his binoculars on the group of Chinese, and saw one soldier raise his rifle to his shoulder. "He looked right at me, at our position, then he fired. I felt a bullet hit me in my leg like I had been kicked in my shin." Hill went down with a bullet in his knee, but was patched up by a corpsman and managed to get the gun firing. "The best thing I can figure is I saw the guy who shot me."

Easy 2/7 was on an outcrop 150 feet down from the crest of Hill 698. The Chinese came at them out of the fog that covered the valley at dawn. The 2nd Platoon was hardest hit, fighting through the morning before they were able to dislodge the enemy. That afternoon, the platoon was ordered to clear the hillside to the top and make contact with the companies of 1/7. Private James Gallagher, who had been thrown out of the Marines when he tried to enlist at age 16

Marines advance past a burned out American half-track on the outskirts of a Korean town, September 3.

US Marines of a forward element pursue the enemy, passing a total of five knocked-out Communist tanks in a few miles, September 17.

Major General O. P. Smith of the Marine Corps and Vice Admiral J. H. Doyle of the Navy aboard USS *Rochester*, prior to the Inchon invasion.

Private First Class Thomas A. Martell of the 1st Cavalry Division looks at the body of a dead North Korean soldier, killed by advancing US troops near Kaesong. An immobilized Russian T-34 tank is in the background. October 13.

LCVPs, amtracs, and DUKWs arrive at the invasion beach on October 26 as other tractors and vehicles reassemble on the beach at Wonsan.

Lieutenant General L. C. Shepherd in Wonsan. As soon as he arrived at the airport on October 31, he met with local army and USMC commanders. Left to right these are: Major General W. J. Wallace, Lieutenant General Shepherd, Major General O. P. Smith, Major General E. M. Almond, and Major General Field Harris.

F4U Corsairs at Wonsan Airfield preparing to take off, November 2.

F4U Corsairs in a line for refueling and rearming, November 2.

The first Chinese Communists captured by 1st ROK Corps (November 3), 19 miles outside of Hamhung.

H Battery, 11th Marines, run their guns forward in support of the 7th Marines as they drive Communists into the mountains of North Korea on November 5.

Captured Russian self-propelled SU-76 tanks in a railroad yard at Hamhung on November 5.

A tank of B Company fords a stream on the road to Hamhung, November 10.

Technical Sergeant Patrick J. Duggan of the 7th Marines fills a 5-gallon can with water from a frozen river leading to the Chosin Reservoir, November 17.

A tank convoy of 1st Tank Battalion crosses the mountains on the way to Chosin from Hamhung, November 19.

Crewmen arm F4U-4 Corsair fighters with rockets on the snow-covered flight deck of the USS *Badoeng Straits* (CVE-116), November 21.

Leaders of the drive to the Yalu look out over the river separating their forces from Manchuria on November 21. Left to right these are: Brigadier General Homer Kiefer, Brigadier General Henry I. Hodes, Major General Edward M. Almond, Major General David G. Barr, and Colonel Herbert B. Powell.

General Douglas MacArthur, Commander-in-Chief of the UN Command, aboard a jeep on November 24 with General Walton H. Walker at Sinanju Airfield, on their way to discuss the huge UN offensive against North Korea.

Marines of the 5th and 7th Regiments. In five days and nights of below-zero winds and icy roads, from November 28 to December 3, they fought back 15 miles through Chinese ambushes to Hagaru-ri, on the southern tip of the Chosin Reservoir, where they reorganized for the epic, 40-mile fight down mountain trails to the sea.

Marines man an observation point on the 7th Marines' front near the Chosin Reservoir.

The 1st Marine Regiment at Koto-ri, on the supply and withdrawal route of the 5th and 7th Marines in the Chosin Reservoir area, on November 28. Chinese attacks on the vital lifeline were kept at bay with close air support, bombs and napalm.

21st Troop Carrier Squadron loads ammunition cases onto C-47s at FEAF Combat Cargo Command, ready to be airdropped to the 31st Infantry Regiment, who had been cut off by advancing North Korean troops. November 29.

Taking their wounded and equipment, the 5th and 7th Marines reorganize at Yudam-ni, after fighting off three Chinese divisions on November 29, before beginning a five-day battle over the 15 icy miles back to Hagaru-ri.

Men of the 1st Marine Division take a break from their drive to Hagaru-ri and eat their C-ration meal, November 30.

During the drive to Hagaru-ri, the 1st Marine Division waits for mortar crews to eliminate a strong enemy position, November 30.

(Opposite) Ammunition and supplies for the embattled 1st Marine Division in the Chosin area are dropped from a C-119 Flying Boxcar of the Far East Air Forces Combat Cargo Command, November 30.

A tank offers support to Fox Company, which held a flanking position in Toktong Pass, protecting the withdrawing 5th and 7th Marine Regiments from Chinese attacks.

After four days of bitter attacks by Chinese forces, on November 30 Fox Company was reached by the rest of 2nd Battalion, who arrived to find layers of enemy dead surrounding their fellow Marines.

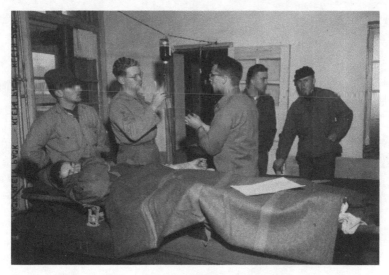

Navy Medical Corps staff at the 1st Marine Division Hospital, Hamhung, administer a blood transfusion to Private First Class Ralph Stephens, who was wounded at Koto-Ri, December 1.

Exhausted Marines take advantage of a lull in the fighting from Yudam-ni to Hargaru-ri and catch a moment's rest, December 1.

A Marine F4U Corsair takes off from Yonpo Airfield for a strike in support of the 1st Marine Division in the Chosin area, December 2.

Crewmen rearm a Marine Corsair for an early December strike against the Chinese. In the background are Marine R5I Skymasters ready to take wounded marines back to Japan, and onward to the USA.

A Marine Corsair offers close contact with the enemy as it zooms through the smoke after dropping napalm on an enemy area, December 6.

Marines move forward after effective close air support flushes the enemy from their hillside entrenchments, December 7.

Marines arrange a tank and a captured Russian-type tank destroyer in defensive positions at Koto-ri, December 8.

The tank crews in this picture struggle with the problems caused by icy roads.

The 1st Marine Division takes to the road on withdrawal from Koto-ri, December 8.

Bodies of US Marines, British Royal Marines, and soldiers of the Republic of Korea are gathered for mass burial at Koto-ri on December 8.

Marine tanks at Majon-dong guard the supply route to Koto-ri, December 9.

On December 9, Sergeant First Class Grant J. Miller of the 3rd Infantry Division (on Task Force Dog) halts his patrol on the way to meet elements of the 1st Marine Division and the 31st Infantry Regiment, 7th Infantry Division.

Marine tanks clear a path for the 1st Division on the road back from the Chosin Reservoir, December 9.

Mountain gales lash the Marines in sub-zero weather on December 9 as they move out from Koto-ri to return to the sea.

The Marines maintain brave faces as they march south from Koto-ri, December 9.

The 7th Marines descend from Chosin to arrive at a blown-out bridge at a power station south of Koto-ri.

Chinese troops wearing tennis sneakers, rags and American footgear surrender to Charley Company, 7th Marines, south of Koto-ri, December 9.

Colonel H. L. Litzenberg Jr. takes a unit of C Company, 7th Marines, to repair a bridge south of Koto-ri, December 9.

A small-scale war within a war as Marines with a light machine gun outflank a Chinese roadblock in the far distant center. The Marines firing the gun were cut off from their regiment during the withdrawal from Koto-ri.

Marines of the 7th Regiment leave the icy shores of Hungnam on December 11 after their 13-day flight from Chosin, heading toward transport ships for redeployment.

Leathernecks of the 7th Marines advance through a Chinese roadblock near Hagaru-ri, December 26.

Passing through icy mountain passes, Chinese attacks, and roadblocks, the 1st Marine Division and fleeing Koreans come down from Koto-ri, December 10.

Soldiers of the 1st Marine Division check the baggage of refugees as they pass through the southern perimeter of the Chosin Reservoir on December 10.

(Opposite) Men of the 5th Regiment, 1st Marine Division, board a transport from the LCM that brought them out from the beach during the evacuation of Hungnam, December 13.

Koreans awaiting evacuation from the beach at Hungnam during the withdrawal of UN forces on December 19.

USS *Begor* (APD-127) at Hungnam, ready to load the last UN landing craft as US Army explosives teams destroy the harbor facilities during the withdrawal on December 28.

in 1947, then succeeded in joining in 1950 in time to join Easy 2/7 just before they shipped out from Camp Pendleton, assigned as a machine gunner.

> Lieutenant Yancey, our platoon commander, was the kind of guy who didn't say "we'll take that hill," he said "follow me up that hill." We did. My assistant gunner was hit, so I had the gun and two cans of ammo I was carrying on my own. When Yancey charged up that hill I grabbed my gun and followed him. There were about ten of us made it to the top. Yancey grabbed a BAR and fired it so fast at the gooks that it caught fire in his hands. I was able to set up my gun and give fire support that broke their attack.

The ten Marines, survivors of two squads, held off a second Chinese counterattack. "We were using gook bodies for sandbags. I'll never forget the sound of a bullet when it hits a frozen body."

First Lieutenant Leonard Clements led 17 Marines of the 1st Platoon up the hill to reinforce the 2nd Platoon. The men made it up the hill through furious fire without a single injury, arriving just in time to help hold against a third Chinese counterattack, with Clements personally shooting the Chinese officer leading the attackers. The Marines were able to hold until late afternoon, when their enemy retreated.

Ground Controller Wilson regained his original position and found all his gear still intact. At first light his comrades in VMF-312 arrived overhead in their Corsairs and Wilson was able to call in several effective strikes against the exposed Chinese. In mid-morning, VMF-312 was joined by VMF(N)-513's Tigercats, which pounded the enemy with rockets, fragmentation bombs, and cannon fire. VMF-312 expended 1,500 rounds of 20mm in strafing attacks.

At 1130 hours, Ray Davis and a platoon of Marines defending the 1/7 command post spotted a company of

Chinese troops moving down the railroad tracks that ran through the valley. "They didn't know we were there, until we opened fire. There were few survivors." Though the Marines didn't know it at the time, this was the turning point at Sudong. The Chinese commanders began ordering their men to break off contact and move north up the valley.

In daylight, Lieutenant Colonel Francis E. Perry's 105mm howitzers were finally able to provide the yeoman service light howitzers were known for. By darkness on November 2, the 18 guns had fired 49 missions delivering 1,431 105mm rounds, while Marine infantry were able to flush out the Chinese, now fragmented into individuals and small groups.

Marine trucks were able to come up with resupply in the afternoon, carrying 100 wounded Marines back to Hungnam after making their deliveries. Total Marine casualties for the two days of battle were 61 dead, 1 missing, and 283 wounded, most from 1/7 Marines. Among the wounded was Sergeant Archie Van Winkle. He would be evacuated to Japan and spend a year in hospital, during which time he would become the first Marine to receive one of the 14 Medals of Honor awarded for action in the Chosin campaign.

When the fighting was finished, 662 enemy dead were counted in 1/7's area of operation. In total, the PVA 371st Regiment lost the equivalent of five companies in its 1st and 3rd Battalions, while the 370th had two companies destroyed in its 3rd Battalion. Many of the Chinese wounded who had been pulled back would later freeze to death in their mountain camps. One Marine commented, "They were a helluva lot better than the North Koreans – better trained, better equipped, and better led." Platoon sergeant Richard Danforth of Fox 2/7 said "If these are the goddamn stragglers, don't even show me the diehards."

While the battle at Sudong was over, the advance to the Chosin Reservoir was just beginning. When the PVA 124th Division withdrew from the valley on the night of

November 3/4, they left the remnants of the NKPA 344th Tank Regiment to fend for themselves in the village of Sudong as the 370th and 371st Regiments withdrew to the defense line that had been established by the 372nd Regiment north of Chinhung-ni at the foot of Funchilin Pass. The NKPA 344th Tank Regiment had suffered losses in the battle for Seoul that reduced it from its original three armored and three infantry companies to just five tanks. One of those five had been the T-34 that attacked 1/7 Battalion the first night. Damaged in the attack, it was abandoned the next day. The 344th Tank Regiment had retreated as far as they could. The road through Funchilin Pass was too narrow for a tank, and would remain so until the Marine engineers widened the road to allow Marine armor and trucks to make the climb.

The Marines increased their patrols to the north, beginning at dawn on November 4; 1/7 Battalion moved out to the edge of Sudong and met no resistance. The Division Reconnaissance Company moved out in jeeps at 0800 hours. First Lieutenant Ernest C. Hargett's jeep took point into Sudong, where they ran across a group of Chinese soldiers in the middle of the town. Three were killed with 20 more taken as willing prisoners. Second Lieutenant Donald W. Sharon's 2nd Platoon moved into the point while the rest of 1/7 Battalion followed them into Sudong. At the highway entrance to the town, the Marines unknowingly passed the first T-34, which was hidden under brush on the right of the road. Shortly thereafter, Sharon's patrol bumped into the second T-34 hidden in a grove of trees and bushes, which Sharon and two of his Marines managed to damage with hand grenades. Marines from Charlie 1/7, armed with 3.5-inch "bazookas," moved into position while a section from George Battery 3/11 equipped with 75mm recoilless rifles provided cover. The Marines opened fire but the tank continued to move until Forward Observer Wilson called in a flight of Corsairs that attacked with 5-inch rockets, stopping the tank and setting it afire. The Marines then spotted the bypassed first tank. Two Marines climbed onto it, smashing the periscope and dropping two grenades down the hatch. Smoke and fire belched from the gun ports.

The third T-34 was hidden in a thatched hut 75 yards farther down the road. As the Marines advanced, the tank smashed through its camouflage and drove toward them, traversing its 85mm cannon. Before it could fire, Wilson called in the target and a Corsair blew the tank open with two 5-inch rockets. The crew quickly abandoned their burning steed and surrendered without further fight. The fourth tank was then spotted just beyond the hut where the third had been hiding, tight against the hillside. After seeing the fate of the first three T-34s, the crew of the fourth surrendered without a fight; the NKPA 344th Tank Regiment was no more.

At 0900 hours, the 7th Marines moved out in regimental strength from Sudong, headed for Funchilin Pass. Progress was relatively rapid over the first 43 miles out of Hungnam, where the NSR was a two-land highway over flat terrain. However, three miles beyond Sudong at Chinhung-ni, the road lost the second lane as it wound up steep Funchilin Pass. The regiment moved like a fort, using Litzenberg's "walking perimeter," with 1/7 Battalion in the lead, followed by 3/11, with 2/7 bringing up the rear. Perimeters were maintained to right and left, front and rear, with artillery closed up. Company-size patrols preceded the rest of the unit as the Marines moved cautiously. The sky was now overcast and the air was numbing as Siberian winds whipped down the pass, freezing bodies, weapons, plasma and morphine as the Marines suffered in their summer dungarees.

The regiment reached Chinhung-ni at 1600 hours and dug in for the night. A further reconnaissance into Funchilin Pass was ordered. Six jeeps, manned by four Marines each armed with a .50 caliber machine gun, passed through the forward perimeter and headed up the road. A mile into the pass, they moved past the surviving troops of the PVA 370th and 371st Regiments, now dug in on the slopes of the two massive Hills 987 and 891, flanking the road. The jeeps rounded a hairpin turn and came within range of the Chinese, who opened up with machine guns. Two jeeps were destroyed and the others shot up, while two Marines were killed and several others wounded. The Marines were driven to cover until dusk, when three Corsairs of VMF-312 strafed the Chinese positions. The patrol managed to drive out of the pass and regain the safety of the perimeter.

The next day, 5 November, 3/7 Battalion moved through the positions held by 1/7 Battalion and attacked Chinese positions on Hills 891 and 987. The advance up Funchilin Pass could not resume until these positions were neutralized. First Lieutenant Ernest C. Hargett led the way with the jeeps of his 1st Reconaissance Platoon. The platoon ran into Chinese fire as they rounded a hairpin turn, with four Marines wounded. 3/7 Battalion's Item Company, commanded by First Lieutenant William E. Johnson was assigned to take Hill 987 while George Company, led by Captain Thomas E. Cooney attacked Hill 891. Despite their losses, the soldiers of the PVA 370th and 371st Regiments put up a stiff resistance. Both Marine companies were stopped by mid-morning, with the Marines hanging on to their positions under heavy small arms and machine-gun fire.

As the day wore on, the battle consisted of more and more dueling artillery, with the 105mm howitzers of the 11th Marines opposed by Chinese 122mm mortars. The Marines fired 982 shells at the two hills, while VMF-312's Corsairs flew 37 close air support missions.

At dusk, the Chinese still held their positions atop the hills.

On Monday, November 6, Corsairs hit the two hills with rockets and bombs in support of a barrage from the 11th Marines' howitzers throughout the morning. By mid-afternoon, How Company, led by First Lieutenant

Howard H. Harris, moved up the southwestern slope of Hill 891 at the same time that Item company resumed its assault on Hill 987. Both assaults were slowed by the terrain, particularly the powdery soil which provided poor footing for the attackers.

How Company Marines persevered in their attack. As they neared the crest, a Chinese hand grenade landed in the middle of the Second Platoon. Platoon commander, Second Lieutenant Robert D. Reem threw himself onto the grenade and was killed, though he saved his men. Company commander Harris contacted the battalion commander and informed him How Company was exhausted. Major Roach passed this information on to Colonel Liztenberg, who ordered How to disengage and withdraw.

When the Marines resumed their attacks the next morning, they found the enemy had disappeared overnight. With the road now clear, a patrol of 15 Marines led by First Lieutenant William F. Goggin of 2/7 Battalion left Chinhung-ni at 1200 hours on November 8. The men reached Koto-ri at the top of the pass by dusk and remained overnight, returning unscathed to the lines of 3/7 Battalion by 1600 hours on November 9.

November 10, 1950 was the 174th birthday of the Marine Corps. At 0800 hours, the "deuce and a half" trucks carrying 1/7 Battalion passed through 3/7 Battalion and 90 minutes later entered Koto-ri, having gone up the "road" in four-wheel drive all the way. The rest of the regiment struggled up the steep pass and took control of Koto-ri, where a traditional Marine Corps birthday party was held. Winter had arrived on the high plateau now, with nighttime temperatures falling to zero degrees Fahrenheit.

November 11 was Armistice Day, and marked the final battle between Chinese units and Marines during the advance to the high country when Charlie 1/7 ran across a Chinese unit while patrolling north of Koto-ri.

In the ensuing firefight, four Marines were killed and four wounded, while the Marines claimed 40 of their opponents. Over the next three weeks, traffic was able to move north through the pass and across the Taebaek Plateau unimpeded by the Chinese.

The 7th Marines had given the Chinese the "bloody nose" that Colonel Litzenberg had hoped for. It was later learned that the PVA 124th Division was rendered useless for a year. In the aftermath of Sudong, the Marines gained valuable insight into how the Chinese military fought. Chinese leadership at the small unit level was surprisingly good, but their communications were extremely poor. Troops cannot be effectively maneuvered in night combat using bugles and whistles. Perhaps most important, the Marines learned a central rule that would hold throughout the war: no matter how large the attacking Chinese force and no matter how deep their penetration, if the defenders could hold out until daybreak, overwhelming American artillery and air power would drive them to cover.

The Chinese leadership had hoped to achieve a monumental military and political coup by being the first military force to utterly destroy a division of Marines, America's elite fighting force. They had also learned from their encounter with the Marines. Unlike the Army units that had broken and run when pressed at Unsan, the Marines had held their ground and inflicted serious damage to their opponents. If they were to prevail against this enemy in the fight to come in the reservoir, the commanders of the People's Volunteer Army understood they would have to employ overwhelming force and hit all Marine positions simultaneously. Rather than continue with sporadic piecemeal attacks, they allowed the Marines to advance unopposed to the Chosin Reservoir. The 40,000 men of the PVA 58th, 60th, 76th and 77th Divisions waited in the hills to either side of the MSR, observing the Marine advance.

While the Marines were fighting at Sudong, the leadership of the Eighth Army finally decided that a "retrograde" movement was necessary. American units were withdrawn south of the Chongchon River, where they awaited the next attack. However, the Chinese had disappeared as mysteriously as they had first appeared, quietly departing the battlefield to return to their positions in the forbidding mountains and moving north. There they would wait for the Americans to resume their advance and move into an even bigger trap, even farther from their bases. What had happened at Unsan was only the beginning.

While the men on the front lines in Korea on both sides had taken each other's measure, the men in Tokyo were engaged in creating a smokescreen over the entire event and doing their best to ignore the facts before them. The political leadership in Washington was concerned that the appearance of the Chinese troops was perhaps the signal that a major war was breaking out between the United States and China. The Joint Chiefs cabled MacArthur on November 3, asking for a response to "what appears to be overt intervention in Korea by Chinese Communist forces."

The question of Chinese intentions became the central issue between Washington and MacArthur. Temporarily shaken by the Chinese attacks, MacArthur regained his confidence once it appeared the Chinese had pulled back. The Eighth Army commander Major General Walton Walker had cabled after the Unsan attack, "An ambush and surprise attack by fresh well-organized and well-trained units, some of which were Chinese Communist Forces." The candor of the message did not please the supreme commander. Despite this news, MacArthur's reply to the Joint Chiefs continued to try to downplay the event. The Chinese, he stated, were in Korea to help the North Koreans "keep a nominal foothold in North Korea" that would allow them to "salvage something from the wreckage." He advocated that the advance to the

Yalu resume. At the same time, Walker was advising him to hold the present positions in Korea until the spring, due to the increasing force of the North Korean winter.

On November 6, MacArthur issued a communiqué in Tokyo stating that the Korean War had been brought to a practical end by the way a "trap had been sprung" north of Pyongyang. Never mind that the trap had been sprung by the enemy. In his communications with Washington, MacArthur called for an end to the limitations on bombing the bridges over the Yalu, saying that the ability of the Chinese to use the bridges "threatens the ultimate destruction of the forces under my command."

In Washington, Dean Acheson lamented that control of the war had passed to the Chinese, and then to MacArthur, and that it now appeared the administration "had no influence at all on the former and marginal influence on the latter."

The battles at Unsan and Sudong were the last chance to break off the drive into North Korea and avoid a larger war with China. But as Acheson later wrote, "We sat around like paralyzed rabbits while MacArthur carried out this nightmare."

CHAPTER SIX

WHERE IS THE ENEMY?

As quickly as they had first appeared on the battlefields of North Korea, the forces of the People's Volunteer Army disappeared over the three weeks following the battle at Sudong. Even after this clear demonstration of Chinese fighting ability, and the lack of ability among the ROK divisions and even US Army divisions, MacArthur persisted in his plans for a drive to the Yalu. The conduct of the campaign demonstrated contempt on the part of the UN commander for intelligence and military prudence unmatched in previous American military history. The fact that no more Chinese forces were encountered only strengthened this continued denial of reality.

The leadership of the American forces – despite the drubbing the 1st Cavalry had received, despite the way in which the ROK units had been routed, and despite the fact that the Marines had hung on at Sudong by their fingernails – refused to recognize the fighting ability of the new enemy. The term of disrespect used by both General Walker of the Eighth Army and General Almond of X Corps was "laundrymen," with both generals berating their respective lower commanders for "being worried about a bunch of Chinese laundrymen," as General Almond so memorably stated. The innate racism of Americans toward non-whites they have been in conflict with, which has been obvious in the Indian Wars stretching from King Philip's War in the 17th century over the next 200 years of transcontinental expansion, the Philippine Insurrection, the Central American Banana Wars, and the Pacific Theater of World War II, allowed these leaders to ignore what was there to be learned on the battlefield, with little or no dissent in the ranks. Historically, every army that has refused to treat its enemy seriously in planning for confrontation has found itself outmatched and surprised by the enemy's actions when battle finally erupted. Events in the next 30 days would clearly demonstrate the US military was not immune to this rule.

In Washington, Army Chief of Staff Omar Bradley speculated that the Chinese had merely intended to make a face-saving gesture demonstrating support for the defeated North Koreans. The CIA estimated on November 8 that there were 30,000–40,000 Chinese already in North Korea with 700,000 poised in Manchuria to enter Korea. Official opinion in Washington, however, remained convinced that the Communist world acted only in concert from a pre-arranged plan, a plan directed solely by the Soviet Union, and that thus the Chinese could not operate independently of the Soviet leadership, who were unwilling to see the war extended now that their North Korean proxy had been defeated. On November 9, CIA Director Walter Bedell Smith, formerly Eisenhower's chief of staff in World War II, urged the National Security Council to give MacArthur an even freer hand in North Korea, arguing that "the Kremlin's basic decision for or against war would hardly be influenced by this local provocation in this area." On November 21, Air Force Chief of Staff General Hoyt S. Vandenberg stated that if the Chinese attempted to block MacArthur's advance to the Yalu, they should be told to quit or "... we would have to hit them in Manchuria." The official wisdom in Washington was that the Chinese warnings in October and probes in early November were evidence of weakness and reluctance to fight, and that the bluff should be called.

In truth, the Chinese did enter the war reluctantly, committing themselves to all-out war only after they saw from the events of early November that the UN forces in North Korea were not such formidable foes as had been assumed, and that unless the American-led forces were defeated on the battlefield, they were committed to advance to the Yalu. Even after their successes against the ROK and US Army forces in early November, the Chinese leadership was willing to stop further operations to see if their message was heeded. The response in Tokyo and Washington finally convinced them that only an all-out offensive would end the threat of American forces on the Manchurian border.

On November 4, General O. P. Smith moved his headquarters from Wonsan to Hungnam in preparation for the full movement of the 1st Marine Division to the Chosin Reservoir and on to the Yalu. The Marines began shipping supplies by rail from Wonsan to Hamhung. North Korean guerillas were still active in the area, as was shown on November 6 when a supply train that was forced to halt at Kowan due to torn-up rails was attacked by a guerrilla unit. Taken by surprise, the Marines from Charlie Company, 1st Amphibian Tractor Battalion who guarded the train were hard hit with eight dead and two wounded in the firefight. Following this attack, troops rode in open gondola cars whose sides provided protection from mortar fragments and small arms fire, though there were no more attacks.

Despite the reports being sent back to Tokyo by the Marines, General MacArthur informed the Joint Chiefs on November 6 that he believed complete victory was still possible, since the Chinese could not cross the Yalu in decisive numbers in the face of US airpower.

After the determined stand the Marines had made at Sudong, the Chinese leadership had decided that the PVA 42nd Army's three divisions in eastern North Korea were insufficient to achieve the goal and would need major reinforcement. On November 4, the Ninth Army Group, commanded by General Song Shilun, composed of 150,000 men in the PVA 20th Army, PVA 26th Army and PVA 27th Army with four divisions in each army, a total of 12 divisions, was ordered to enter Korea, cross the mountains and "seek opportunities to destroy the four divisions on the east." The first units of the Ninth Army Group crossed the Yalu on November 5. The three component armies then separated to meet the UN threat. The four divisions of the PVA 20th Army would take position outside Yudam-ni, to cover the routes leading west across the Taebaek Mountains. The PVA 27th Army was positioned to cover the route north from Changjin. The PVA 26th Army crossed last at Linjiang to take up positions between Linjiang and Huchang as the army group reserve.

The American leadership in Tokyo and Washington would have been amazed had they seen the Chinese report assessing the situation in North Korea made at about the same time as MacArthur's report to the Joint Chiefs belittling the likelihood of major Chinese military intervention. Written by People's Volunteer Army commander Marshal Peng Dehuai's chief of staff, Xie Fang, it stated:

> Our Ninth Army Group main forces have successively entered Korea from J'ian and Linjiang to assume eastern front operations. We have over 150,000 men on the eastern front, the enemy over 90,000, giving us a 1.66 advantage over him. We have 250,000 men on the western front, the enemy 130,000, giving us a 1.75 advantage over him. Our forces are superior on the eastern and western fronts.

On November 12, General Song submitted a plan to Mao Zedong, proposing to attack and destroy the two leading units of the 1st Marine Division, the 5th and 7th Marines. He believed that with such a defeat, the rest of X Corps could then be annihilated, unit by unit. Mao replied: "The American Marine First Division has the highest combat effectiveness in the American armed forces. It seems not enough for our four divisions to surround and annihilate its two regiments. You should have one to two more divisions as a reserve force. The 26th Army should be stationed closer to the front."

Xie Fang reported on November 16:

> Our forces on the eastern front abandoned Hwangch'o [Funchilin] Pass on the 7th. On the 10th the enemy on the eastern front continued advancing northward along three separate routes. From Hwangch'o Pass, P'unsan [Pungsan], and Myongchon, still far from our pre-selected killing zones.

As the American Marine and Army units continued their movement north, the Chinese troops remained hidden in the mountains, where they could observe American movements without being discovered unless they chose to expose themselves. The 1st Marine Division was now strung out along the MSR from Wonsan, where the 1st Marines were still based, to Hamhung where the 5th Marines were beginning to move north, to Koto-ri, where the 7th Marines were beginning to experience an enemy even more relentless than the Chinese as the icy winds blew out of the Gobi Desert over Manchuria and Siberia, across the Taebaek plateau: the North Korean winter. Suddenly, on November 11, the weather turned miserable. 1/7 commander Ray Davis recalled, "I had taken a bath in the river on the 9th, it was that warm. And two nights later it went down to 16 below with the wind blowing. When we got up in the morning, none of the vehicles would start. Men had their noses turn white with big spots on them. It was just an absolutely unbelievable change in the temperature in 24 hours."

Throughout Europe and Asia, winter has traditionally been the time when wars slow down or even stop. The Marines had spent the majority of their time in combat since the Spanish-American War in warm, tropical climates, with only the Marine involvement in the American Expeditionary Force in France in 1918 intervening. Other than service in smaller units in Beijing during the Boxer Rebellion and continued Legation service in company-size formations there before World War II, deployment to Iceland in 1941–42, and the limited service of III Amphibious Corps in North China in the postwar period of 1945–49 during the Chinese civil war, few members of the Marine Corps had any personal experience of the requirements of fighting in the cold. The division staff knew that Hagaru-ri, which was to be the main jump-off position for the advance to the Yalu, was reputed to be the coldest place in North Korea, with recorded winter temperatures of minus 35 degrees Fahrenheit, though these extreme temperatures were not recorded until the depths of winter in January and February. The winter climate on the Taebaek plateau approximated that of Minnesota or North Dakota. While the winter of 1950 would be a cold one, it was not unusually so. Fortunately, the Marines had adequate warning that it was coming and considerable preparations were made.

During the Chosin campaign, some units claimed nighttime temperatures of minus 35 and even minus 40 degrees Fahrenheit. The best-documented temperatures experienced are the records kept by the 11th Marines, who had to factor in temperature as an element of gunnery for their artillery. They routinely recorded temperatures of 20–25 below zero. Snow showers were frequent but not much snow accumulated, since winds blowing at 35–40 miles per hour scoured the rocks and frozen earth free of snow, while adding in a wind-chill factor that likely accounted for the belief that the weather was far colder than it was. Men would later remember that, when morning came in the reservoir, ice crystals in the air glinted in the dawn like "diamond dust."

General O. P. Smith was among those Marines with personal experience of cold weather, having commanded the 1st Battalion, 6th Marines, 1st Marine Provisional Brigade that arrived in Iceland in August 1941 to relieve the British forces there. Lieutenant Colonel Raymond L. Murray, the 5th Marines commander, had served with Smith in Iceland as commander of a machine-gun company, and had also served as a "China Marine" at the American Legation in Beijing and Tientsin before World War II and so had experience of the north China winter. Other senior Marines, including Chief of Staff Colonel Gregory A. Williams, G-2 Colonel Bankson T. Holcomb, Jr., and Colonel Lewis "Chesty" Puller, commander of the 1st Marines, had also seen substantial service in pre-World War II China, including an opportunity for Puller to observe operations by the Chinese Communist Eighth Route Army in Hunan during winter. Puller, who was much better read and more a student of military history than his flamboyant reputation suggested, had also studied Japanese winter operations in northern Korea and Manchuria during the Russo-Japanese War of 1904–05. Perhaps most importantly, Major General William P. T. Hill, Quartermaster General of the Marine Corps, was an "Old China Hand" who had explored the Gobi Desert in the 1920s and well understood the weather conditions the Marines were moving into. General Hill began shipping out cold-weather clothing, including Navy parkas, to Korea in early October 1950. Replacements that arrived during November to fill out battlefield losses had been given training back in California in the use of cold weather gear.

Both Army and Marines practiced the "layer principle" with winter clothing, which simply meant one would pile on as much clothing as could be obtained. A man wore cotton underpants and shirt, known to the Marines as "skivvies," pulling on heavy cotton or wool "long johns" over, with outer wear consisting of a flannel shirt, utility pants or green wool trousers, all topped by green sateen winter pants, a sweater under an alpaca vest, followed by a utility coat and woolen muffler, and an M1943 field jacket if available. Over all this was a long, pile-lined, hooded Navy parka that was warm, but also heavy and clumsy. Where possible, Marines got hold of the Army parka. This shorter, anorak-type of parka was considered superior to the Navy type. The Army "trooper" pile lined winter hats with ear flaps were popular with Marines when they could obtain one. The most common glove combined a leather and fabric outer shell with a knitted wool inner mitten.

Perhaps the worst piece of winter gear was the "shoe-pac," boots with waterproof rubber lower sections and laced leather uppers. These consisted of felt innersoles and heavy woolen boot socks. Men were given two sets each and ordered to keep one set inside their clothes next to their body, and to change frequently. The instructions were good in theory and difficult in practice, since the extra pairs were often soaked through by perspiration caused by marching or other work, and then froze when they were exposed to cold air. The innersoles worn in the shoe-pacs also absorbed perspiration moisture, which was then held close to the skin, creating prime conditions for the onset of frostbite. Some Marines were fortunate to obtain rubber galoshes, which they wore over their standard boots, which were thus kept dry. Ernie Gonzales in Fox 2/7 remembered taking both boots and galoshes from a dead comrade during the campaign since "he sure didn't need them anymore," an act he credited with saving him from the frostbite experienced by many who wore the shoe-pacs.

The sleeping bags the Marines carried now had a heavier lining and were indispensable. They were easily carried rolled up and tied to the bottom of a haversack. While they provided warmth for sleeping, warming feet and preventing the wounded freezing to death, they could also be a deathtrap for the Marine standing night watch who might pull the bag around his knees to warm his feet, then pull it up further and nod off. Many Marines died when caught by the enemy inside their sleeping bags.

All the functions of life were affected by the cold. A Marine also had to carry his daily C-ration, which came in a shoebox-sized cardboard box containing six tin cans – three "heavy" and three "light" – along with a day's supply of toilet paper and a packet of four cigarettes. The "heavy" cans contained meat-based meals and had a wider variety of items than the hated C-ration of World War II. Hamburgers were prized, along with chicken and vegetables, ham and lima beans, and meat and beans; the least favorite were sausage patties. The "light" cans contained at least one variety of fruit, the item liked best, along with biscuits that were descended from the hardtack of the Civil War and "pound cake." Salt, pepper, packets of instant coffee and candy were also included. After ripping open his box, a man stuffed his pockets with what he liked or thought he could trade, and threw the rest away.

The biggest problem for those on the line was heating the meat. The best method involved heating the can in a GI can or bucket of boiling water, though neither utensil was usually available and a wood fire burned more than it cooked. Marines also used unused mortar increments or C-3 plastic explosive, both of which burned with a hot, quick heat. Improvised stoves could be fashioned by placing dirt in a large can and dousing it with gasoline, though such open fires were more likely to scorch that part of the meat closest to the heat while leaving the rest frozen; once cooked the food froze as soon as it was removed from the source of heat. Drinking coffee from an aluminum mess cup was dangerous since lips or tongue could freeze to the metal cup. Since it was impossible to heat meat while on the march, bread and fruit were the first items consumed. Drivers of jeeps and trucks learned to wire their food can to the engine; once the run was finished, they could enjoy a hot meal. Efforts were made inside the defensive perimeters to establish consolidated field messes serving hot chow, but this seldom benefited those men in the front line. An exception was the flapjacks or pancakes that were made around the clock by a battalion mess at Hagaru-ri, and served to thousands of Marines and soldiers.

The B-ration included large square cans of ground coffee. Those who could find space in a jeep trailer would hoard these until there was an opportunity to boil up a batch of real coffee. The ration also contained oatmeal, which could be boiled and flavored with sugar and powdered milk. Canned peanut butter was prized, since it could be passed from man to man to dig out a mouthful. Candy was passed out for quick energy, with the disks of chocolate most popular along with hard candies; the most popular were Tootsie Rolls and Charms.

Obtaining sufficient water was problematic. Water in "Jerry" cans or individual canteens quickly turned to ice. Marines had carried two canteens since the Second World War and many carried one inside their overcoat to keep it from freezing. Some officers and noncoms filled one canteen with whiskey, which they would dole out on an as-needed basis. The medical reams also had two-ounce bottles of medicinal brandy, which was highly prized for thawing out canned peaches, known as "brandied peaches" and considered a delicacy.

Elimination of bodily waste was a continual problem. In the settled bases, the four-hole collapsible "heads" that had been used since the Banana Wars were installed in warming tents, while artillery and mortar packing tubes were used as urinals. Those on the line or on the move lacked access to such facilities, which led to some frontline infantrymen simply ceasing bowel movements, which led to impacted colons and created difficulties if wounded.

The troops quickly learned to stop oiling their weapons, since the lubricant would freeze the weapon's action. Many men refused to bring their weapons into a warm space or keep them in their sleeping bags, so that they would function properly when needed. Marine weapons worked well in the cold, other than the M-1 and M-2 carbines, which were universally despised for their designs in which the safety and clip release were so close both could be operated accidentally by a mittened hand. Most men armed with carbines exchanged them for the ever-reliable M-1 Garands taken from the dead whenever possible. The water-cooled M1917A1 .30 caliber machine gun worked well with anti-freeze in the water jacket, while the air-cooled light machine guns had a tendency to burn out barrels.

The availability of tents gave the Marines an enormous advantage over their enemy. They could be quickly erected and retained sufficient heat from the M1941 stove, though the sidewalls were generally rimed with frost. Warming tents were utilized throughout the campaign, with one tent per platoon the standard. Men cycled through in relays as the situation allowed for around 20 minutes at a time, though such were not available other than at way stations for those on the move. Generally, a communal pot was constantly simmering on the stove with "slum." Upon entering, a man would take a bowlful and donate one of his meat cans to the pot; tabasco sauce was the favored condiment.

Army survivors of the 31st Regimental Combat Team (RCT-31) told a different story about how they lived in the cold. Private First Class Ed Reeves of King Company, 31st Infantry, recalled:

Aboard ship at Pusan, we were issued our winter gear: wool long-johns, pile liner vest to go under the field jacket, shoe-pacs, two pair of wool socks, dress leather gloves with wool inserts, cotton reversible green/white camouflage parka – an unlined windbreaker used by the 10th Mountain Division in World War II – and water-resistant (until you slid down or crawled across a few ridges) field pants. To help keep our ears warm, we turned down the ear flap in the fatigue cap we wore under our helmets. The men in my company who received winter gloves were on crew-served heavy weapons. At the temperatures we experienced at Fusen and Chosin, the leather gloves most of us had would become as stiff as cardboard and you could not load, fire or service your weapon. Riflemen wore their second pair of socks as mittens so they wouldn't freeze to their weapon. Some men who were issued the winter gloves and extra insoles for shoe-pacs thought everyone got the same issue and had lost them or traded them off. We never knew what a warming tent was.

One good thing about the extreme cold was that a Marine who was badly wounded didn't die immediately, since the cold coagulated the bleeding quickly. The Navy corpsmen that provided immediate battlefield care learned to carry their morphine syringes in their mouths to keep them warm enough to use, while blood packs were stuffed inside their clothing next to their bodies. The Marine tradition of never leaving the wounded or the dead behind provided a morale boost for those wounded who knew they would get the best treatment their buddies were capable of providing. Each battalion had a Navy medical staff of surgeons and corpsmen that could provide immediate care for wounds. For those more severely wounded, evacuation back to Hungnam and on to Japan was possible. VMO-6 pilot Ed McMahon found that his most worthwhile employment was evacuating two stretcher cases per flight in his OY-2. "I could fly casualties from Hagaru to Hungnam in about an hour. Carrying two guys on stretchers in our little planes was stretching it performance-wise in that cold air at that altitude, but once you flew past Koto-ri, it was all downhill from there." Before the division was surrounded, those whose wounds didn't require immediate attention were regularly transported to the rear in returning convoys once the road through Funchilin Pass was widened enough for trucks. Later, when the division was surrounded, casualties were flown out of the recently finished Hagaru-ri airfield in C-47s.

While the Marines were as well-equipped for winter warfare as the US military was capable of in 1950, the Marines who would be the last ones to receive such equipment were the ones most in need of it. The 7th Marines were the first to advance to the Taebaek plateau the week after the battle of Sudong. The unit received a partial supply of cold-weather gear following the battle, but Joe Owen recalled that "our lightweight dungarees were the same ones we had worn while fighting in the steamy humidity of South Korea." When they first arrived in the Chosin region, the Marines slept in the open, and frequently found when they awoke in the morning that there were several inches of snow on the ponchos they wrapped around their sleeping bags. Owen reported to his commanding officer that nearly everyone in his mortar platoon had pneumonia, which was widespread throughout the regiment, and for which the corpsmen could only give a man on morning sick call an APC for treatment. The situation on the plateau did not change until after November 18, when trucks were able to bring supplies up through Funchilin Pass and all Marines were finally re-equipped for cold weather. By that time, Owen wrote that "it was colder than hell."

As bad as the cold was for the Marines, it was worse for the Chinese, who were not nearly as well prepared to withstand the sub-zero temperatures. Throughout the battle, the People's Volunteer Army had only the supplies its soldiers and porters could carry on their backs when they crossed the Yalu, and their quilted cotton-padded winter uniforms. There were no mittens or gloves in their equipment; a man warmed his hands by slipping them into the sleeve of the opposite arm and warming them with his own body heat. Items such as tents and stoves were far beyond such a transportation capacity, as was sufficient food. Chinese troops did not receive a single known resupply of food or ammunition during the Chosin campaign after they crossed the Yalu. This meant that on numerous occasions Chinese troops would pause after overrunning an American position to loot the food supplies, which gave Marines the chance to get away and fight again, or to organize a quick and bloody charge to throw the enemy back. During the campaign, the Chinese starved and lost strength, and developed crippling stomach ailments. Their medical care was either primitive or nonexistent. Only a small minority received immediate battlefield treatment for critical wounds, and even for these lucky few there was only slow evacuation – when there was any at all – to hospitals in China. The majority of frostbite cases received no treatment at all. Most of those wounded in battle or the victims of frostbite eventually froze to death, since the best they could hope for was to be treated inside a cold mountain cave.

Additionally, the Marines were resupplied with food and ammunition throughout the battle, first by trucks through Funchilin Pass, and later by air with Marine R4Ds and R5Ds bringing supplies in to Hagaru-ri as well as making airdrops with Air Force C-47s and C-119s to Yudam-ni, Koto-ri, and Toktong Pass. Because the Chinese divisions had only the weapons and ammunition they originally carried, this meant that in terms of fighting ability a Chinese division was capable of all-out combat once, being then forced to withdraw from the fight until they could hand-carry more ammunition from China.

The American "ace in the hole" was air power. Even with the withdrawal of half of Task Force 77's carrier striking force from its position off the coast in the Sea of Japan in late October, there was still substantial air power available to cover the eastern front in the form of the six fighter-bomber squadrons of MAG-33 that had now moved up to Yonpo, 20 minutes' flying time from the Taebaek plateau, with the "Death Rattlers" of VMF-323 aboard the escort carrier *Badoeng Strait* offshore and the two Navy air groups aboard the fleet carriers *Philippine Sea* and *Leyte*. In early November, 77 Squadron of the Royal Australian Air Force, which had been committed to the Korean War in late June, transferred from operating with the Fifth Air Force in support of the Eighth Army and arrived at Yonpo with their F-51 Mustangs under the command of Squadron Leader Dick Cresswell, one of the leading RAAF fighter leaders in the fighting over New Guinea during World War II. By November, the Australian pilots were highly experienced in providing close air support.

While air power gave the outnumbered UN forces the decisive edge in most situations, winter flying was dangerous for all concerned. At times the weather was more hazardous to pilots than flying against the enemy. Snowstorms could develop quickly that could prevent pilots successfully attacking their target, or having difficulty when they returned to their base to find a blowing snowstorm, and there was no reliable weather forecasting since the storm tracks all originated in Manchuria and Siberia. Takeoff could be difficult ashore or afloat, since thick ice and snow had to be removed each morning from the aircraft and the flight decks or cleared from the runways. Sergeant Paul Ritter of VMF-214 recalled that failure to clean the wings completely of ice could leave an aircraft unable to remain airborne after takeoff, which meant crashing while carrying a heavy supply of explosive ordnance. For the pilots aboard the carriers, should they have to bail out or ditch at sea, their immersion suits gave them less than 15 minutes in which to be rescued before the freezing water would kill them. A man who bailed out over the forbidding countryside could be in even greater danger, since the mountains were now snow-covered and flying gear did not provide the same level of protection as the clothing worn by the ground troops. While the UN air forces had developed an efficient air rescue system to pluck a man from behind the lines by helicopter and many hundreds would be saved that way during the war, in the mountains there was always the chance that the enemy might capture or kill a pilot first.

The two Marine night fighter squadrons flew an increasing number of missions after November 10, in an attempt to interdict the movement of the enemy into their attack positions. By the middle of the month, adverse weather and extremely icy conditions began to have serious effects on air operations for all the units, but most especially the night fighters who operated during the coldest hours. The F7F-3N Tigercat had no de-icers, and the cockpit heating system left a lot to be desired. Captain Ray Stewart remembered that the heating system "...would cook the lower part of your legs while your upper extremities froze." Chinese antiaircraft defenses became more intense, particularly at night when the gunners were defending the supply trucks. By the end of the month, VMF(AW)-542 would have only 14 Tigercats left; ten of the original 24 the squadron had brought to Korea having fallen victim to enemy fire over the rugged mountains. The worst event however, was a "blue on blue," when a B-29 damaged by flak on a mission against the Yalu bridges attempted to land at the MAG-33 base at Yonpo and the big bomber careened off the icy runway into VMF(AW)-542's parking area, clipping off the vertical fins of four of the F7Fs, which put the valuable fighter-bombers permanently out of commission.

During November, the 7th Marines were joined on the plateau first by the 5th Marines and later by the 1st Marines as plans for the Yalu offensive were changed and modified throughout the month, with the 5th Marines deployed and redeployed as plans changed. 1/5 Battalion was left at Chingyong on November 4, detached to division control, while 3/5 Battalion, the oldest unit in the Corps, commanded by Lieutenant Colonel Robert D. "Tap" Taplett, took position near Oro-ri. Lieutenant Colonel Harold S. Roise's 2/5 Battalion was sent into the Sinhung valley 5 miles north and 15 miles east of Koto-ri in an attempt to find a northern route to the Chosin Reservoir or the Fusen Reservoir to the east, which was ultimately unsuccessful. Patrols soon found evidence that Chinese and some North Korean units were in the Sinhung Valley, though they kept their distance. A Dog Company patrol captured a Chinese soldier they found asleep in a ruined house, who readily told them he belonged to the PVA 126th Division and that six PVAS armies were in North Korea from the east to west coasts and that 24 divisions in total were committed to the battle. When asked how he was so well-informed, he stated that unit commissars had provided the information after his regiment crossed the Yalu.

On November 8, contact was established with the Army 7th Infantry Division when a Marine patrol from 2/5 met up with an Army patrol from the 31st Infantry Regiment. That same day, a patrol composed of Able 1/5 and Baker 1/5 Companies, led by 1/5 Battalion's executive officer, Major Merlin R. Olson, reconnoitered in force west of Oro-ri to Huksu-ri. They ran into a substantial North Korean force just before reaching Huksu-ri, and were recalled. The next day, Colonel Murray was ordered to concentrate the 5th Marines on the MSR south of the Chosin Reservoir. Two days later, 1/5 Battalion's move to Majon-dong was delayed when a patrol was ambushed and had to be rescued by the rest of the battalion before they could get to the village. Three days after that on November 13, 2/5 Battalion retired from the Sinhung Valley to relieve the 7th Marines at Koto-ri so they could advance to Hagaru-ri. An airstrip capable of handling light aircraft became operational at Koto-ri; engineers worked to expand it so that TBM-3R Avenger aircraft now used as light transports could operate from the field.

On November 10, General Smith received orders from X Corps commander General Almond that the Marines were to split their attack to the Yalu at the Chosin Reservoir, with one regiment moving north along the eastern side of the reservoir and another heading north along the western side. Smith was concerned when he received this order, since it meant that neither regiment would be able to provide support to the other in case of trouble, with the reservoir between them.

General Smith now ordered the 1st Marines, still at Hamhung, to take Huksu-ri. The 7th Marines were to prepare to advance on to Yudam-ni in the reservoir upon being ordered, in order to advance up the western side of the reservoir to the Yalu. The 5th Marines were assigned to protect the MSR at Majon-dong, Chinhung-ni, and Koto-ri, and to prepare to pass through the 7th Marines at Hagaru-ri and advance on to Changjin 40 miles to the north along the eastern side of the reservoir.

As the 7th Marines moved on to Hagaru-ri, 11 miles north of Koto-ri, the leading element spotted parties of Chinese troops in the distance that fell back into the hills as the Marines approached.

Immediately after receiving Almond's order, and alarmed by the prospect of making a simultaneous attack in two different directions, General Smith sidestepped the chain-of-command with a personal letter written to General Cates, commandant of the Marine Corps, in which he stated:

> Someone in high authority will have to make up his mind as to what is our goal. My mission is still to advance to the border. The Eighth Army, 80 miles to the southwest, will not attack until the 20th. Manifestly, we should not push on without regard to the Eighth Army. We would simply get further out on a limb. If the Eighth Army push does not go, then the decision will have to be made as to what to do next. I believe a winter campaign in the mountains of North Korea is too much to ask of the American soldier or marine, and I doubt the feasibility of supplying troops in this area during the winter or providing for the evacuation of sick and wounded.

In conclusion, Smith underscored his concern over "the prospects of stringing out a Marine division along a single mountain road for 120 air miles from Hamhung to the border." On November 15, Rear Admiral Albert K. Morehouse, chief of staff for US Naval Forces, Far East, visited Smith. Believing he was speaking within the naval family, Smith outlined his concern over what he considered Almond's unrealistic planning and tendency to ignore enemy capabilities to Morehouse, for him to pass on to Vice Admiral C. Turner Joy, commander of Naval Forces, Far East. When these concerns were later brought up by Admiral Joy in Tokyo and the letter to General Cates became public, the relationship between Almond and Smith soured almost to the point of closure. When he was asked about this event after the war, General Almond said, "My general comment is that General Smith, ever since the beginning of the Inchon landing and the preparation phase, was overly cautious of executing any order that he ever received."

The commander of 1/7 Battalion, Ray Davis, interviewed long after the event, recalled:

> General Almond was something of an apple-polisher, eager to give his superiors what they wanted without overmuch thought being put to whether or not what they wanted was a good idea or not. General Smith was aware that if something bad happened to 1st Marines, it could affect the entire existence of the Corps as a result. Had he been a "good scout" and gone down the road Almond wanted to travel, there is no doubt in my mind that the disaster we would have faced in the event would have been far worse than what in fact happened to the Eighth Army. At best, it would have been the worst surrender in our military history.

The same day Smith met with Admiral Morehouse, the 7th Marines occupied Hagaru-ri. Nighttime temperatures had dropped to minus 4 degrees. Just north of Hagaru-ri there was a sawmill in the hamlet of Sasu-ri with a large supply of fresh-cut lumber which the Marines appropriated. As tents began to spring up, what was left of the town with its mud-and-snow streets, tents, and rough construction with raw lumber reminded one Marine officer of an Alaskan gold camp.

Mid-November saw the air war heat up as Navy aircraft from *Philippine Sea* and *Leyte*, along with the newly arrived USS *Princeton* (CV-37), struck the Yalu crossings. On November 9, Navy Lieutenant Commander William T. Amen, flying an F9F-2 Panther of VF-112 from USS *Philippine Sea*, shot down the MiG-15 flown by Soviet Captain Mijael Grachev. Amen was leading 12 F9F-2 Panthers from VF-111 and VF-112 as escort for a strike by F4U-4 Corsairs and AD Skyraiders against the Yalu bridge at Sinuiju. He later reported,

We could clearly see the big runway at Antung across the river in Manchuria but were too far away to ascertain what type of aircraft were parked along the runway. As the bomb-laden ADs started their dives on the bridge, I radioed the leader to find out if any of them had sighted MiGs. Ten seconds later a voice came on the radio to say there was a fast-moving jet coming up behind our formation. I looked over my shoulder and there it was, a shiny swept-wing aircraft banking toward me from my seven o'clock position. I immediately turned to meet him head-on. The MiG pilot raised his nose and started a steep, almost vertical climb to about 15,000 feet, where he leveled off. Just as he started his climb, my wingman and I got off a burst of 20mm. It was ineffective. We stayed on his tail. If we'd hesitated the MiG pilot would have gained the advantage. He already had a 100-knot speed advantage. If he'd chosen to remain straight and level he could easily have outdistanced us, but every time he turned we closed the gap. We were firing short bursts as we closed in, and the other two Panthers of our division were firing long bursts as they tried to close in. Evidently that scared the MiG pilot into a dive and I got on his tail. We were heading almost straight down and my airspeed hit 500 knots as I was firing all the way. Suddenly my Panther started to buffet as the nose was trying to tuck under and I hit my dive brakes and stopped firing. The MiG's dive angle had increased to about 40 degrees. As we passed through 3,000 feet the MiG flipped over on its back. I thought the pilot was either crazy or had one of the best fighters ever built! A second later I could see mountains coming up fast. Then I saw trees and rocks. Pulling hard, I bottomed out with no more than 200 feet to spare. As I turned the nose up, my wingman called to report I had gotten the MiG, which had gone straight in and exploded.

The next day, MiGs again attacked Amen's Panthers and four of the Soviet jets were engaged by Amen's division in a ten-minute fight that saw him damage a MiG. From November 11 on, the MiGs intercepted nearly every Navy mission flown near the Yalu. On November 18, Panthers from VF-52 aboard *Valley Forge* and VF-31 from *Leyte* engaged in combat with eight MiGs. LCDR William Lamb and Lieutenant Robert Parker of VF-52 shared a MiG-15 while VF-31's Ensign Frederick Weber scored a second MiG-15. Despite the American victories, it was obvious the MiG-15 was technologically superior, with luck and pilot training of the Americans being the deciding factors. The Navy's effort to block the Yalu crossings saw a record number of flight operations. *Leyte* refueled on November 13 and Air Group 3 flew 130 strike flights over the next two days. So much ordnance was expended that the ship had to pull off the line on November 16 to refuel and re-arm. On its return, 145 missions were flown on November 17–18. This pace was about average for the three carrier air groups operating in Task Force 77 at the time. Commander Harlan Foote remembered that "At that time, we were operating in heavy seas in winter conditions. There were gale-force winds often, and it frequently happened that the ship would take green seas over the bow, which would freeze on the flight deck. Takeoffs were adventurous to say the least, and landing could be a nightmare with the deck pitching through 20–30 feet at times, and rolling constantly."

On November 16, General Smith again visited the Chosin plateau, this time driving up in a heated station wagon. By coincidence, he met Major General Field Harris, commander of the 1st Marine Aircraft Wing, in Chinhung-ni. Harris had flown to Chinhung-ni in a helicopter, where he discovered, as General Smith had on November 10, that helicopters could not operate at the altitude of the plateau in the cold, and thus planned to go the rest of the way to Hagaru-ri by open jeep. Smith offered a ride in his heated station wagon. As they drove comfortably to Hagaru-ri, in a rare burst of humor Smith promised Harris a station wagon of his own, in exchange for continued close air support. Harris came to Hagaru-ri at Almond's request to find a location for an airstrip large enough to operate C-47s. The two generals walked the round and discovered a stretch south of the town that seemed suitable. The soil consisted of thick, black loams, but they both agreed that after the ground froze it would work as a landing strip.

Lieutenant Colonel John Partridge's 1st Engineer Battalion had been working since November 10 to widen the road through Funchilin Pass, to allow truck, armor and artillery traffic to move up to the reservoir. After this was completed on November 18, construction of the Hagaru-ri airfield began. Smith had requested X Corps Army engineers but could get none, so the job was given to the Marine engineers. Hagaru-ri was at an elevation of almost 4,000 feet. The operating manuals prescribed a minimum runway of 3,900 feet at that altitude for C-47 operations, but there was only 3,000 feet available. The engineers crossed their fingers that it might do. Once begun, construction of the airstrip proceeded 24 hours a day, with work at night under floodlights. In the end, it would be completed under fire and not a moment too soon.

A new addition to the 1st Marine Division arrived in Hungnam on November 20 in the form of the Royal Marines' 41 Independent Commando, 14 officers and 221 enlisted Marines commanded by Lieutenant Colonel Douglas B. Drysdale, RM, which had undertaken commando missions in North Korea prior to the Inchon invasion, landing from submarines. Smith had replied he would be glad to get them, planning that 41 Commando would operate with the Division Reconnaissance Company to screen the flanks of the Marine advance.

On November 21, the 1st Marine Division's southern boundary was adjusted, giving responsibility for Huksu-ri to the US Army 3rd Infantry Division, which had finally completed its landing at Wonsan on November 15, freeing Puller's regiment to fill in behind Murray's and Litzenberg's regiments.

The same day saw a battalion of the 7th US Division's 17th Regiment reach the Yalu without encountering opposition. General Almond flew up to join them and remembered the triumphal moment years later:

> And on the 21st of November, the leading battalion of the 17th Infantry reached the Yalu River and I was present when they did so. I accompanied General Barr, the division commander; General Hodes, the assistant division commander; and General Kieffer, the artilleryman; with the regimental commander, Colonel Powell. We all walked behind the lead company down the road to the river bank. This was the first element of the American forces to reach the Korean–Manchurian border, although earlier elements of 6th ROK Division with I American Corps on the west

flank, the Eighth Army front, got to the river but did not succeed in remaining there.

Almond and his commanders paused on the banks of the Yalu for a ceremonial urination into the river waters.

On November 23, General Smith confirmed the plan for the 1st Marine Division's advance to the Yalu. The 7th Marines would move out from Yudam-ni to advance up the western side of the reservoir while the 5th Marines would advance up the eastern side from Hagaru-ri. The 1st Marines would protect the MSR from positions at Hagaru-ri, Koto-ri, and Chinhung-ni. The advance was now set to begin on November 27, three days after the scheduled commencement of the Eighth Army's advance. Smith wrote in his log:

> I did not want to push Murray too far or get Litzenberg out on a limb at Yudam-ni until I could close up Puller in rear of them... I had hoped there might be some change in the orders on the conservative side. This change did not materialize and I had to direct Litzenberg to move on to Yudam-ni.

Thursday, November 23, 1950, was Thanksgiving. General MacArthur had promised "Thanksgiving dinner with all the trimmings" for every American soldier and Marine in Korea. At Hungnam, the Royal Marines of 41 Commando stared in shock as trucks arrived, loaded with shrimp cocktail, stuffed olives, roast young tom turkey with cranberry sauce, candied sweet potatoes, fruit salad, fruit cake, mincemeat pie, and coffee. They were amazed at the waste involved in such an effort, and at the same time were impressed by a country that could afford such an event.

The American Marines further north remembered the event a little differently than General MacArthur had intended. The extreme cold of the high plateau effectively ruined the meal.

Most of the 7th Marines had their Thanksgiving dinner at Hagaru-ri below the heights of the ridge soon to be known as "East Hill." By the time most men got their hunks of turkey and spoonfuls of the rest of the meal dropped into their mess kits, after standing in line for several hours in the cold, the food was frozen. Ernie Gonzales of Fox Company recalled it as "the most disappointing Thanksgiving of my life," and vowed that if he returned home safely, he would never allow anything to mar a Thanksgiving dinner so long as he lived.

On November 24, General Smith drove with Colonel Litzenberg from Hagaru-ri to Yudamn-ni, to see the village the regiment had occupied earlier that day. The road crossed the crest of Toktong Pass, 4 miles to the northwest of Hagaru-ri and 4,000 feet in elevation, then descended into a narrow valley before reaching Yudam-ni. The pass controlled entry and exit to the reservoir. Smith personally ordered Litzenberg to position a company on a commanding hill at the crest. He later wrote that he was concerned about his ability to extract the 5th and 7th Marines from the reservoir "if my concerns about the intentions of the Chinese were confirmed."

The next day, November 24, General MacArthur made a personal visit to Korea to see the Eighth Army's commencement of the "Victory offensive" that would end the war. He announced to the correspondents gathered to meet him that the war would be over in two weeks and that "the boys will be home for Christmas," as it was later reported in the press. Following the press conference, he approved General Almond's plan to advance to the Yalu.

On November 25, General Almond decided to modify that plan. A regiment from the Army's 7th Division would relieve the Marines on the east side of the reservoir so that the 5th and 7th Marines could join together at Yudam-ni for the western advance. He ordered the 7th Division to send a regimental combat team for this purpose by November 27, when the Marines would jump off from Yudam-ni. Major

General David G. Barr, commander of the 7th Division, was now aware of local intelligence that Chinese troops in massive numbers had crossed the Yalu at Linchiang and were moving into the gap between his division and the Marines, and had already begun pulling together his scattered battalions. He sent the 1st Battalion of 32nd Infantry, commanded by Lieutenant Colonel Don Carlos Faith, which was bivouacked northeast of Hamhung and was thus the Army battalion closest to the reservoir, to reinforce Colonel Allan MacLean's 31st Infantry Regiment, which was composed of 31st Infantry's Headquarters and Service Company, the regiment's 2nd and 3rd Battalions, 31st Tank Company, and 57th Field Artillery Battalion, to undertake Almond's orders in the reservoir. Historically, Regimental Combat Team 31 has come to be known as "Task Force MacLean" and later "Task Force Faith." However, neither name existed during the Chosin operation. The unit was known as the 31st Regimental Combat Team, or RCT-31. During the Korean War, a "task force" was an organization of disparate units pulled together for a single task and dispersed once that task was completed. The task force names were the later inventions of historians. Significantly, RCT-31 was also augmented with a platoon from D Battery, 15th Antiaircraft Artillery Automatic Weapons Battalion, which was equipped with four M16 Multiple Gun Motor Carriage "Halftracks" armed with the "quad-50" Maxson M45D Quadmount firing four M2 .50-caliber machine guns, and four M19 Gun Motor Carriage "twin-40" self-propelled guns armed with two 40mm Bofors AA cannon. These high-powered rapid-fire weapons would prove excellent for providing close-in infantry fire support in the coming battles, a purpose for which they had heretofore never been used. RCT-31 arrived at Sinhung-ni on the east side of the reservoir to relieve the 5th Marines at midday, November 26 and the Marines fell back to Yudam-ni by the end of the day to take up positions with the 7th Marines.

Colonel Charles E. Beauchamp's 32nd Infantry had advanced to the northwest of the 17th Infantry with orders to reach Singalpajin on the Yalu, which had originally been a Marine objective. On November 22, a 34-man patrol commanded by future four-star general Second Lieutenant Robert C. Kingston was sent out from the 3rd Battalion, 32nd Infantry, to reconnoiter the area toward Singalpajin. They arrived in Samsu, 23 miles south of the Yalu on November 24. Between then and November 27, the patrol was reinforced by tanks, artillery, engineers and infantry. Still under the command of Second Lieutenant Kingston, "Task Force Kingston" moved on to Singalpajin where they arrived the next day and fought a brief house-to-house fight with a North Korean unit. As the second and last group of Americans to stand at the Yalu border, they took their turns urinating in the river. In all its adventures, "Task Force Kingston" suffered only one casualty: a soldier killed by a Siberian tiger.

While the Americans had been finalizing their plans to move forward, People's Volunteer Army commander Marshal Peng Dehuai had other plans. General Song's Ninth Army Group in the Taebaek Mountains would attack X Corps in coordination with the attack on the Eighth Army that the Chinese forces in the west planned to commence on November 25. The attack was eventually pushed back two days as a result of delays in getting units into position. The biggest problem the Chinese faced was poor communications. Lacking radios at unit levels below regimental command, the only reliable form of communication they possessed were messengers, who could bring new information from forward units about changes in enemy dispositions to higher commanders, who might be able to communicate further by the one radio each regimental command unit possessed, though the cold weather substantially reduced the viability of radios by draining their batteries, not to mention the difficulty of radio use in the mountains. Thus, as the Marines unexpectedly changed their positions in response to changes in their plan of attack, the Chinese observing them attempted to provide this new information to their commanders. Getting the information from the front to General Song's headquarters could take as long as three days. The difficult communication system would ultimately determine the outcome of the battle.

General Song had deployed his army group to surround and destroy the Marines with overwhelming force. At Yudam-ni, the four battalions of the PVA 89th Division would hold the road against the Marine advance on the western side of the reservoir. At the same time, the PVA 79th Division would attack the 7th Marines in Yudam-ni from the north on the night of November 27, while the PVA 80th Division and a regiment of the PVA 81st Division would attack and destroy what the Chinese expected would be the 5th Marines moving up the east side of the reservoir. The PVA 59th Division would cut the road south of Yudam-ni and hold Toktong Pass to prevent a withdrawal, with the two Marine regiments then being destroyed in detail. At the same time, the PVA 58th Division would attack Hagaru-ri from the southwest and take the town and the PVA 60th Division would cut the road between Hagaru-ri and Koto-ri and take Koto-ri.

As the North Korean winter became fierce, the offensive that Douglas MacArthur and the "Bataan Gang," and all senior American leaders in Washington, believed would be a "victory parade to the Yalu," was about to begin. MacArthur's official communiqué issued the morning of November 24, 1950, announcing the offensive perfectly illustrates the attitude of the senior commanders:

> The United Nations massive compression envelopment in North Korea against the new Red Armies operating there is now approaching its decisive effort. The isolating

component of the pincer, our air forces of all types, have for the past three weeks, in a sustained attack of model coordination and effectiveness, successfully interdicted enemy lines of support from the north so that further reinforcement therefrom has been sharply curtailed and essential supplies markedly limited. The eastern sector of the pincer, with noteworthy and effective naval support, has now reached commanding enveloping position, cutting in two the enemy's geographical potential. This morning the western sector of the pincer moves forward in general assault in an effort to complete the compression and close the vise. If successful, this should for all practical purposes end the war, restore peace and unity to Korea, enable the prompt withdrawal of United Nations military forces, and permit the complete assumption by the Korean people of full sovereignty and international equality. It is that for which we fight.

The Eighth Army's offensive began more like a walk in the park, as the troops experienced no opposition. By the end of the day, UN forces were advancing at the rate of 16,000 yards per day and were fast outrunning their supply lines. Many of the advancing GIs tossed away extra equipment in the belief it had no further use.

CHAPTER SEVEN

THE CHINESE ATTACK

O n November 24, 1950, the Eighth Army Yalu Offensive began with UN forces attacking north from the Chongchon River. On the left, II Corps advanced through the coastal plain while IX Corps, with the 2nd Infantry Division on its right, moved through the valleys of the Kuryong and Chongchon rivers. On the right flank at Tokchon, ROK II Corps was ordered to establish contact with X Corps, 70 miles to the northeast. The weather by now was so cold that tank engines had to be run throughout the night; when they were ordered to move out in the morning many tankers found their tracks frozen to the ground and could only move after being pushed by another tank. Ice floes were seen in the rivers.

The Eighth Army's advance only lasted a day. On November 25, units of the PVA Thirteenth Army Group of 18 divisions, which were in position in the mountains above the Chongchon River, met the advance and stopped it cold. B Company, 1/9 Infantry, 2nd Infantry Division, advanced on Hill 219 on the east bank of the Chongchon, when they were suddenly under grenade and small arms attack. By evening, the entire 9th Infantry was engaged with Chinese forces. At 2200 hours, the 2nd Infantry Division soldiers in bivouacs and vehicle parks all along the Chongchon Valley were awakened by a cacophony of bugles, whistles, drums and rattles, followed by gunfire, as Chinese assault units smashed through unprepared perimeters and overran position after position. By dawn on November 26, the 2nd Infantry Division had been driven 2 miles back down the valley. On the 2nd Infantry Division's left, the 25th Division was also under attack. Throughout the Eighth Army, troops found themselves overwhelmed by the surprise attack and fell back in retreat.

What was happening along the Chongchon was nothing compared to the disaster that befell ROK II Corps on the night of November 25. The three Korean divisions were hit by five Chinese divisions and collapsed overnight as they fell back in chaos, abandoning guns, vehicles and equipment. By the morning of November 26, a chasm 80 miles wide existed between the Eighth Army and X Corps. When the Turkish Brigade attempted to advance to support the Koreans that day, they were stopped at Wawon, well south of what was considered to be the front line. The Eighth Army was now in danger of being cut off from the south and surrounded. General Walker ordered an immediate retreat.

After hard fighting, the 2nd Infantry Division was finally able on November 28 to organize its units and commence a retreat to Kunu-ri where they expected to hold. By the next day, Chinese units were already attacking positions south of the line of retreat. The division was ordered to continue directly south to Sunchon. To this point, the Chinese had allowed American units to escape once overrun. Colonel Paul Freeman, commander of the 23rd Regimental Combat Team, which became the rearguard of the retreat, later saw the initial attacks as having been a test of American strength and will. "They came tongue in cheek at first, to see what we would do. Then they

The Chinese Attack, November 25, 1950

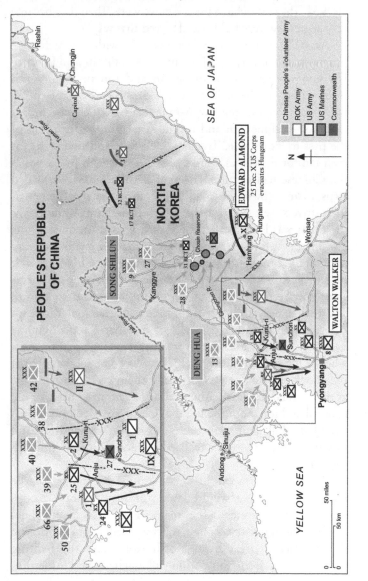

found what a thin line we had, how easily the South Koreans cracked. They saw what a pushover we were. Then they became very aggressive, very bold – and stayed that way."

At 0130 hours on November 30, with the defensive perimeter at Kunu-ri shrinking under assault, the 2nd Infantry Division was ordered to move out and run the road south to Sunchon. The vehicle convoy soon became a nose-to-tail traffic jam on the narrow 6-mile road as they ran into a storm of machine-gun and mortar fire from the high hills of the pass to either side. Trucks keeled over and caught fire as men ran for their lives. Tanks blew up when hit by bazookas the Chinese had captured from the Americans. Overloaded jeeps roared down the road, careening into the ditches as their drivers were killed. "The Death Ride From Kunu-ri," as the event was later recalled by the survivors, was among the grimmest events in the history of the US Army, with Secretary of State Dean Acheson later stating that "The Chinese assault in North Korea was the greatest defeat of American Arms since the Second Battle of Bull Run." Vehicles sought to smash their way through the blazing wreckage of those hit before while a deathly paralysis of command and discipline overtook the division. Survivors later reported passing men who sat motionless in their vehicles, overcome by the force of the attack and unable even to rouse themselves to return fire as they waited for death. The mortaring and machine-gun fire continued throughout the night as Chinese troops came down out of the hills and soon there was desperate hand-to-hand fighting as the Americans realized the enemy intended to kill them all.

Some men escaped in small groups by taking to the hills, though many would later run into Chinese troops and become prisoners. The majority of UN POWs held by the Communists through the war were captured during the American retreat from North Korea and the fighting that followed. Even the coming of daylight and American fighter-bombers did not save things as the survivors crawled out of the pass. In the afternoon and evening of November 29 and the night of November 30, the 2nd Infantry Division lost 3,000 men and nearly all its equipment on the road between Kunu-ri and Sunchon. The division fell apart almost completely during the following days as the retreat became a rout, and it would be six months before the 2nd Infantry Division was considered capable of re-entering combat.

On the road south from Sunchon to Pyongyang, panic spread throughout the Eighth Army. Major John Willoughby of the 1st Middlesex Regiment, British 27 Brigade, was shocked to attend a briefing at which his American counterpart warned, "Remember, if you see a red Verey light, just get everybody you can together and head south." The vast supply dumps at Pyongyang were set afire to prevent their capture by the enemy. Between November 25 and December 2 1950, the Eighth Army took 11,000 casualties, dead, wounded and missing. The events of late November and early December in western North Korea would later be called by historian Martin Gilbert "... the most thorough defeat of a previously victorious army in recorded history."

Amazingly enough, word of the disaster enveloping the Eighth Army failed to get through to the Marines on the other side of the Taebaek Mountains. On November 26, the 1st Marines finally arrived on the plateau. Regimental headquarters and 1/2 Battalion arrived in Koto-ri and relieved 2/5 Battalion, which moved on up to Hagaru-ri and then to Yudam-ni. Early that evening, How and Item Companies of 1/3 Battalion arrived in Hagaru-ri, while George Company remained in Koto-ri. Chinese scouts in the hills around both locations noted the late arrivals. Crucially, they had no way of informing their superiors of these reinforcements.

The Chinese probed Lieutenant Colonel Donald M. "Buck" Schmuck's 1/1 Battalion's position around Chinhung-ni, the entrance to Funchilin Pass, on the night of November 26 with a series of light attacks. The next morning, patrols were sent out that failed to make contact with the enemy, and the Chinese again attacked the perimeter that night. The attack was easily repulsed. On November 28 and 29, patrols were sent out and found that their Chinese adversaries were hiding in the houses to the west of the battalion's position. Unfortunately, Colonel Schmuck's reports did not change the plans being made in Hagaru-ri.

Hagaru-ri was the most important Marine position in the campaign, since it contained both the soon-to-be-operational airfield and divisional headquarters. Given its importance and Smith's fears about the coming offensive, it is surprising how lightly defended the town was. On the morning of November 27, the two companies of 1/3 Battalion relieved 2/7 Battalion after moving up from Koto-ri the previous day. 2/7's Dog and Easy Companies had already arrived at Yudam-ni.

The task of defending Hagaru-ri that confronted 1/3 Battalion commander Lieutenant Colonel Thomas L. Ridge was difficult, since he had only two companies of his battalion to hold the defensive line. Major Joseph D. Trompeter, the battalion S-3, and Weapons Company commander Major Edward H. Simmons concluded after touring the village and surrounding territory that enclosing all of the village would require a four-mile perimeter, which was impossible for a single battalion with only two rifle companies. Ridge himself thought that two complete regiments were needed to hold the position successfully.

How Battery, 11th Marines, was in place in the northeast corner of the sketchy perimeter with their 105mm howitzers. They were supported by the recently arrived Dog Battery, which positioned their guns just southeast of the village on the flats. In the cold, the guns had a range of 9,000–9,500 yards, only about two-thirds of their normal 12,200 yards. The two rifle companies, How and Item, were positioned in a salient southwest of the all-important airfield. The greatest threat to the defense was the hill to the east which would come to be known as "East Hill." Weapons Company was placed in position covering the road running south to Koto-ri, while the Marine Service Battalion was placed as a roadblock on the road running east to Sinhun-ni. Dog Battery, 11th Marines, had arrived at Hagaru-ri along with 1/3 Battalion. Dog Battery commander Captain Andrew J. Strohmenger positioned his guns on the flats just southeast of the village.

The rest of the perimeter was manned with units created from the Service Battalion, Division Headquarters Battalion, and that part of 2/7 Weapons Company that had not gone on to Yudam-ni. How Battery, like Dog Battery, was used as a front-line unit.

General Smith's plan for the eastern advance was to have the 5th Marines pass through the 7th Marines at Yudam-ni and attack to the west on the morning of November 27. The distance from Yudam-ni west to Mupyong-ni, following the road over another mountain pass and then through a narrow valley, was estimated at 55 miles. After taking Mupyong-ni, where it was expected they would meet ROK II Corps, the Marines would then advance north to the Yalu. The three X Corps columns – the 1st Marine Division's two regiments, the 7th Infantry Division's RCT-31, and the ROK I Corps – would spread from the Chosin Reservoir to the Yalu like an opened fan.

The village of Yudam-ni lay in the center of a broad valley dominated by the reservoir, surrounded by five prominent ridgelines. Counter-clockwise from the north, the Marines had given them the prosaic but useful designations North, Northwest, Southwest, South, and Southeast. The 7th Marines' perimeter commanded all the ridges except the Northwest Ridge. The village of Yudam-ni was a sorry collection of peasant houses that were largely wrecked by air attack and long abandoned. The MSR that was the Marines' lifeline forked at Yudam-ni, with one road continuing north up the eastern side of the reservoir, while the other headed west to Mupyong-ni, where it turned north to Kanggye.

According to Smith's plan, all elements of the 5th Marines were to be relieved by 1200 hours on November 26, and would take their positions at Yudam-ni preparatory to passing through the 7th Marines' positions to lead the advance to Mupyong-ni. At 1200 hours, 3/5 Battalion arrived after a hard five-hour motor march from Sinhung-ni on the east side of the reservoir, and was assigned an assembly area west of the village where the road forked to the north and west. 1/5 Battalion did not arrive until dusk and was given an assembly area east of the village.

Dog and Easy Companies of 2/7 Battalion had made it through the pass by dusk. Lieutenant Colonel Randolph Lockwood, the battalion's new commander, was still in Hagaru-ri with Fox Company, H&S Company, and Weapons Company. Dog and Easy were attached to Davis' 1/7 Battalion pending the arrival of the rest of 2/7 Battalion.

Switching the 5th Marines with the RCT-31 involved some confusion. The RCT-31's newly assigned 1st Battalion, 32nd Infantry, composed of 731 American and 300 Korean troops, had performed well during the invasion of Inchon and battle for Seoul, under the leadership of Lieutenant Colonel Don Faith, for which action Faith had been awarded the Distinguished Service Cross and added to the reputation he had developed during World War II in Europe as a "comer," serving on the staff of General Matthew B. Ridgway of 101st Airborne. This was his first combat command. Faith's officers were well trained and many had gained combat experience in Europe or the Pacific, while there was a core of combat-experienced non-coms. However, the mix of Americans and KATUSAs in the rank and file was a problem, since most Americans didn't speak Korean and few of the barely trained Koreans could speak English. The battalion had moved up to Hagaru-ri on November 25, where they took the right-hand fork to meet the 5th Marines several miles up the eastern side of the reservoir near Sinhung-ni. Murray had explained to Faith that his 3/5 Battalion held a good defensive position four road miles north of the Pungnyuri-gang Inlet. He suggested to Faith that he assemble his battalion near the village of Twiggae and cautioned Faith not to move further north unless he received orders to do so since there were "a lot of Chinamen out there." Following Murray's suggestion, Faith established his battalion command post in a hut in Twiggae on the lower slope of Hill 1221.

That afternoon, the Marines moved out of their positions and departed for Yudam-ni, leaving Faith in communication with the 1st Marine Division through the four- man Marine tactical air control party commanded by Captain Edward P. Stamford that had accompanied the battalion since Seoul. He was later visited by the 7th Division's assistant commander, Brigadier General Henry I. Hodes, who informed him the rest of RCT-31 would arrive by dusk. In the surrounding hills, Chinese observers noted the replacement of the Marine regiment with an Army unit and the departure of the Marines to the west, but were unable to provide this crucial information in a timely manner to their commanders in the PVA 80th Division.

Unfortunately, Colonel Litzenberg's report of the capture of three Chinese soldiers from the PVA 60th Division and their subsequent interrogation – during which the prisoners stated that the 58th, 59th, and 60th Divisions of 20th Army were now in the vicinity of Yudam-ni – had been passed on to the Army. Crucially, the prisoners had made no mention of Chinese forces on the eastern side of the reservoir. Colonel MacLean and the rest of RCT-31 had arrived shortly after Hodes' departure, where he learned of the intelligence regarding the enemy that Faith had received from Murray.

MacLean concentrated on preparations for the advance to the Yalu. Like Faith, MacLean's previous experience during World War II was entirely as a staff officer. Command of RCT-31 was his first combat assignment.

Ignoring Murray's warning about moving further north, Faith asked MacLean for permission to move his battalion forward on November 27 to take the positions formerly occupied by 3/5 Battalion. MacLean gave his assent to Faith's request, and set up his regimental command post in a schoolhouse in Hudong-ni, a village a mile south of Hill 1221. The Chinese scouts who observed all this noted that the positions previously occupied by the Marines were now empty, but they could only send off messengers to their regimental headquarters with the news.

Ray Murray briefed his officers that night at 2200 hours: 2/5 Battalion would move out as the lead element at 0800 hours the next morning; close air support would be provided by Corsairs from VMF-312 on station in relays throughout the day, with a VMO-6 OY-2 on station for aerial reconnaissance; the 7th Marines would support 2/5's attack with patrols and a secondary attack to the southwest; the 11th Marines would deploy 30 105mm howitzers in Yudam-ni to support the advance while the single M-26 Pershing heavy tank to have made it to Yudam-ni would take the lead. The first objective would be the road junction at Yongnim-dong, 27 road miles west. Interviewed after the war regarding the 1st Marine Division's planned attack, Murray said: "It was unbelievable. The more you think about it, the more unreal it becomes ... those were the orders and that's what we started to do." That night, the temperature at Yudam-ni went down to zero degrees Fahrenheit.

While Murray held his briefing, Colonel Litzenberg met with his commanders. As a result of the prisoner interrogation, he was concerned with the question of where exactly the Chinese divisions were. He ordered a company-size patrol to move down the MSR toward Hagaru-ri the next day and find out if the Chinese had cut the road. He ordered 3/7 Battalion to extend its position on Northwest Ridge, and How Company to occupy Hill 1403, which overlooked the road to the west.

At dawn on November 27, General Smith visited Yudam-ni. During the night, he had learned that ROK II Corps had been attacked and thrown back in the vicinity of Tokchon the previous night. As yet, Smith had no notion of the fact that even before the Marine advance from Yudam-ni was scheduled to begin, the Eighth Army's offensive had been stopped in its tracks, with disaster soon following. Smith had come after receiving Colonel Litzenberg's report about the capture of three Chinese soldiers from the PVA 60th Division on November 25 and their subsequent interrogation.

At 0500 hours on November 27, the Marine artillery barrage opened up, pounding the hills to either side of the road leading out from Yudam-ni. The attack began at 0800 hours, led by Fox 2/5 Company. As they advanced toward their first objective between Hills 1403 on the right and 1426 on the left, they came under long-range small arms fire. The VMO-6 spotter plane reported there were Chinese positions all across the front. The Marines halted and waited for support. At 1150 hours, six VMF-312 Corsairs hit the enemy positions and immediately after Fox Company renewed the advance, spotted Chinese troops fleeing to the west.

Dog Company joined Fox at 1200 hours, and by 1430 hours they had advanced about a mile to the west of Yudam-ni. They were ordered to stop the advance and take up defensive positions. 3/7 Battalion had advanced approximately the same distance southwest before they ran into stiffer opposition and dug in for the night.

At 1100 hours, General Almond and his aide, Captain Alexander Haig, accompanied by a staff operations officer, walked into the 7th Marines command post unexpectedly after driving up from Hamhung. Litzenberg was not present, but Executive Officer Lieutenant Colonel Frederick R. Dowsett briefed the visitors on the situation. Following MacArthur's example, Almond passed out three Silver Stars to an officer and two enlisted men to "encourage enthusiasm." After learning that the advance had stopped, Almond returned to Hamhung down the MSR, which was jammed with traffic in both directions. The trip took nearly five hours, and upon his arrival at HQ, Almond reported to MacArthur who was now back in Tokyo that enemy strength in the reservoir was stronger than expected and suggested that the disposition of the Marine Division be re-examined.

The Chinese goal on November 27 was to stop the Marine advance, which was accomplished by mid-afternoon when the leading Marine units dug in for the night pending further support. The two Marine regiments were facing the PVA 20th Army, commanded by Zhang Yixiang and composed of the PVA 58th Division under the command of Huang Chaotian with the 172nd, 173rd and 174th Regiments; the PVA 59th Division commanded by Dai Kelen with the 175th, 176th, and 177th Regiments; the PVA 60th Division under the command of Chen Ting with the 178th, 179th and 180th Regiments; and the PVA 89th Division commanded by Yu Guangmao with the 265th, 266th, and 270th Regiments. All were now in the mountains west of Yudam-ni. The Chinese strategy throughout the previous month had been to "suck us in and isolate us," as First Lieutenant Jim Eaton would later explain the battle. The decision to block the Marine advance while the 5th Marines were still close enough to Yudam-ni to get support from the 7th Marines and the artillery of the 11th Marines was the first crucial mistake made by the Chinese commanders. This was most likely due to the fact that the commanders above the regimental level had no way of knowing that the Marine strategy had changed in the previous 36 hours and that there were now two regiments in

Yudam-ni rather than the expected one. Had the PVA 89th Division allowed the Marines to move on up the road out of range of supporting artillery, the outcome of the fighting at Yudam-ni could have been radically different.

Across the reservoir, early in the afternoon of November 27, Don Faith completed the move of his battalion into the positions vacated by the Marines. It was a typical Marine Corps perimeter, horseshoe shaped and occupying the high ground. Faith put a rifle company on each of the exposed sides, with the battalion command post in the center, while the open side to the rear was covered by elements of his Headquarters and Service Company and Weapons Company. Since he lacked the strength in men and weapons of a Marine battalion, Faith could not fill all the foxholes.

Colonel MacLean had returned to Hudong-ni, where he was told that several hundred Chinese had been sighted east of Pungnyuri-gang inlet. MacLean sent out his Intelligence and Reconnaissance Platoon to investigate. The men in their machine-gun armed jeeps roared out of the compound and were never seen again. Lieutenant Colonel William E. Reilly's 3/31 Battalion arrived at Hudong that afternoon. The unit was followed by the 57th Field Artillery Battalion under the command of Lieutenant Colonel Raymond Embree. MacLean ordered Embree to set up bivouac near the hamlet of Sinhung-ni just south of Pungnyuri-gang Inlet, with the two batteries of 195mm howitzers situated on the south side of the inlet, on low ground surrounded on three sides by high ridges. D Battery, 15th Anti-Aircraft Automatic Weapons Battlion, set up its weapons carriers near Embree's HQ on the slope of Hill 1456, a mile south of the artillery positions.

The 31st Heavy Mortar Company set up its 4.2-inch mortars close to Maclean's CP halfway between Faith's and Reilly's battalions, while the 31st Tank Company's 20 M4A4 Sherman tanks and two M4A5 Shermans armed with 105mm howitzers reached Hudong-ni by dusk. The evening of

November 27 found the units of RCT-31 stretched 10 miles along the road in seven separate positions. Shortly after registering his artillery and mortar defensive fire, Don Faith received orders from MacLean to attack the next morning toward Kalchon-ni. MacLean arrived a few hours later to spend the night at Faith's CP.

While MacLean and Faith remained confident, RCT-31 already faced serious problems. In addition to the disappearance of the Intelligence and Reconnaissance Platoon, communications between the units scattered along the road were poor at best. There had been no time to lay landlines, and radio communications were virtually nonexistent due to the effect of the cold on the radio batteries. Furthermore, RCT-31 was not in contact with the 7th Infantry Division headquarters at Pungsan or with the Marines in Hagaru-ri. The scattered units were dangerously isolated, not only from the rest of the 7th Infantry Division and the Marines, but also from each other.

In Yudam-ni that afternoon, it was obvious to the Marine commanders that the next move by the Chinese would be an attempt to cut off communication between Yudam-ni and Hagaru-ri, trapping the two Marine regiments and RCT-31 in the Changjin Valley around the reservoir. It was crucial that the "back door" remain open. Colonel Litzenberg ordered 2/7 Battalion commander Lieutenant Colonel Ralph Lockwood to provide a force to hold crucial Toktong Pass, the key to the Marines' escape from Yudam-ni if it became necessary. Lockwood ordered Fox Company 2/7 to move up from Hagaru-ri into Toktong Pass and establish a defensive position there to protect the MSR.

Fox 2/7 had taken heavy casualties in the campaign to capture Oijongbu north of Seoul after the Inchon invasion, and more casualties in the advance into the high country from Hamhung over the past month, though the company had not been in the thick of the fighting at Sudong. By early

November, over half the company was composed of "boots" fresh from training at Camp Pendleton, and most of the company officers were also new to the war. A week after Sudong, their company commander had been transferred to the division staff. On November 7, 1950, they met their new commander.

Captain William E. Barber, Jr., was a "mustang" who had been promoted from sergeant to second lieutenant in time to land on Iwo Jima as the junior platoon commander in Easy Company 2/26 Marines. Fighting on the island was so intense that within two weeks, Barber had become company commander as all the officers above him were dead or had been evacuated as casualties. His leadership in the last two weeks of the campaign had been exemplary, and he had been awarded the Silver Star for the rescue of two of his Marines under fire; he remained company commander after the battle as the 26th Marines trained for the invasion of Kyushu. When the Korean War broke out in June 1950, Barber was a recently promoted captain, training reservists of Company D, 6th Infantry Battalion, at the Marine barracks in Altoona, Pennsylvania. He received orders to join the 7th Marines on September 15.

Private Bob Ezell remembered his first look at Barber: "His dungarees were starched, and he was all dressed up like a well-kept grave." A believer that a Marine's appearance should reflect combat-readiness, Barber told the company officers that they reminded him of Pancho Villa's bandit gang. He did not endear himself to his new command when he ordered the men to field-shave with cold water, clean their filthy uniforms and weapons, and be ready for a conditioning hike at 0600 hours the next morning. Before heading off on the hike, newly arrived reservist Ernie Gonzales remembered Barber informing the company that it was his belief "there was a helluva lot more war to fight, nobody was going home for Christmas, and we were going to damn well be prepared for what was coming." Barber concluded his remarks by informing the men, "I may not know much about strategy, but I know a lot about tactics. And frankly I'm a helluva good infantry officer."

Before taking command, Barber had read a translated copy of *Military Lessons*, a document the Chinese command had given out to their troops, which had been found on the body of a Chinese NCO after Sudong and distributed throughout the 1st Marine Division. The document described the American enemy thus: "Their infantry is weak. These men are afraid to die, and will neither press home a bold attack nor defend to the death. If their source of supply is cut, their fighting suffers, and if you interdict their rear, they will withdraw." Barber was determined that his new command would stand up to the coming challenge. During the march from Koto-ri to Hagaru-ri, he had been aghast when an entire squad failed to take out three fleeing North Korean soldiers a few hundred yards away. Following that incident, Barber instituted a daily session of rifle practice, using cans begged from the mess tents for targets. The men disliked the time spent in the cold and snow while their compatriots were inside warming tents, but even the most reluctant had to admit they had become better shots as a result. On November 27, Barber was satisfied that his "training on the run" as he later described it, had transformed Fox 2/7 into a company of "genuine Marine riflemen."

The 192 officers and enlisted men of Fox Company were reinforced by a ten-man team with two 81mm mortars and two water-cooled .30-caliber machine gun teams from Weapons Company, while the 105mm howitzers of How Battery 6 miles south in Hagaru-ri were registered on the pass, which was just in range. A pilot from VMF-312, attached as forward air controller, could call in air support. A total force of 240 Marines and Navy corpsmen were ready to move out when they received their orders at 1400 hours on November 27.

Fox Company began to move out from Hagaru-ri at 1500 hours. Because of a shortage of motor transport, it was only through the efforts of the forward artillery observer to obtain the loan of artillery trucks from How Battery that the company was able to avoid a road march up into the steep pass in the freezing weather that would have had them arrive in the middle of the night. Instead, the men arrived at the crest of the pass at 1700 hours as the sun was setting, having been delayed when they came up by the trailing vehicles in the convoy of three 155mm howitzer batteries with 18 big cannons in tow from 4/11 Marines, commanded by Major William McReynolds, which would turn out to be the last Marine unit to make it through the pass to Yudam-ni from Hagaru-ri.

Toktong-san, the commanding height in the pass that would become part of Marine legend as "Fox Hill," topped out at 4,850 feet in an 80-yard-wide crest on the promontory about 50 feet below the top of the mountain. The wind, which howled out of Siberia down the pass, was the coldest anyone had experienced and seemed to scour the hill. Minutes after their arrival, the first snowflakes began to fall. Within 30 minutes, the cold had almost completely drained the batteries that powered the radios and field telephones keeping Fox Company in touch with their support and with each other.

On the northwest quadrant, the ground extended out to form a narrow saddle, humped like a whale over its 75-yard length which ended at a rocky knoll with steep drop-offs to either side. Toktong-san was separated from the surrounding heights in all directions by snow-covered valleys. Neat rows of fir trees with trunks 4–5 inches thick and around 40 feet tall, standing 10 feet apart, had been planted some 20 years earlier by the Japanese for reforestation and climbed two-thirds of the way up the slope from the MSR at the foot of the hill. Above the tree line, the crest sported patches of gnarled brush that pushed through the knee-deep snow. A shallow gully, 60 feet wide, ran straight up the middle of the hill from the road.

As he studied the position, Barber had a premonition that he needed to get his men protected in fighting positions before worrying about setting up warming tents. Ernie Gonzales, assigned as assistant to BAR gunner Private First Class Warren McClure, remembered that the ground was frozen so hard "we couldn't blast fighting holes for our positions with dynamite." Shallow holes were pickaxed out of the frozen ground by men whose sweat froze on their bodies.

"We arrived in the late afternoon after which we unloaded and were positioned for the night," remembered Corporal Howard W. Koone. "Our position was off to the right of the road up on a saddle-like hill. The ground was like a sheet of concrete and very barren." The position Captain Barber selected on the hill commanded the road and had all-around fields of fire. In the fading light, the 62 Marines of First Lieutenant Elmo Peterson's 2nd Platoon dug in across the steeper western slope, while the 54 Marines of First Lieutenant Robert McCarthy's 3rd Platoon dug in across the crest, linking up with 62 Marines of First Lieutenant John Dunne's 1st Platoon, who took positions down the gentler eastern slope, leaving the perimeter in the general shape of an inverted horseshoe with the piers 75 yards apart at the MSR. The stretch along the road was defended by the 69 Marines of the heavy weapons teams, the mortar platoon, and the headquarters and staff platoon. Barber ordered the crews of the three 60mm and two 81mm mortars to use what daylight was left to register their weapons on the rocky knoll and ridge where he expected the major attack would come from.

Atop the surrounding hills, Chinese observers could count the number of Marines on Toktong-san as they dug in for the night, but they could not inform their superiors about these new reinforcements which had suddenly arrived at the most vital position on the battlefield. As the last of the sun faded behind the western hills, the men of Fox Company pulled up their sleeping bags and began the evening routine of half the men taking watch, relieved by the others at two-hour intervals. The snow continued to fall.

As darkness fell at Yudam-ni, Baker 1/7 Company, which had been patrolling South Ridge, came under heavy attack near Hill 1419. 1/7 Battalion commander Ray Davis received permission to take another company to extricate Baker. Davis led Charlie Company, less one rifle platoon, commanded by Captain John F. Morris, down the MSR to a position across the road from Hill 1419. Baker 1/7 pulled back from its engagement and Davis took it back into Yudam-ni, leaving Morris' Charlie Company on Hill 1419, 2 miles south of the incomplete perimeter at Yudam-ni and 3 miles north of Fox 2/7's position, guarding the entrance to Toktong Pass from the reservoir. With only two of his three platoons, Morris organized a crescent-shaped defense on an eastern spur of Hill 1419, well below the crest.

Artillery support at Yudam-ni was provided initially by Major Parry's 3/11 Battalion with three batteries of 105mm howitzers, 18 tubes in all, which was enough to support a regiment in a narrow zone of attack, but not enough to provide adequate 360-degree support for a sprawling two-regiment defensive perimeter. Fortunately, 4/11 Battalion, with three batteries of heavier 155mm howitzers, was the last unit to make it into Yudam-ni during that busy November 27.

That night, the temperature dropped to minus 20 degrees. Northwest Ridge, the last to be occupied, had a front line of foxholes chipped out of the frozen ground which was occupied by tired and cold-numbed Marines. Captain Leroy M. Cooke's How Company, 3/5 Battalion, held the high point on Northwest Ridge, Hill 1403. Easy and Fox Companies of 2/5 Battalion were on How's left flank, occupying the rest of the ridge until it dropped down to the defile where the road to the west passed through. 2/5 Battalion commander Lieutenant Colonel Roise had positioned his command post behind Easy and Fox, while a roadblock manned by Weapons Company 2/5 covered the road to the west. Across the road, Dog Company 2/5 manned a line that curled back toward Southwest Ridge.

3/5 Battalion's assembly area had been turned into a defensive perimeter with a platoon from Item Company holding an outpost on a spur of Hill 1384 about 500 yards forward of the battalion position. Chinese harassing fire commenced against the position at 2045 hours.

At 2200 hours, the 266th and 267th Regiments of PVA 89th Division attacked the ridges on the north and northwest of Yudam-ni with the goal of annihilating the Marines in one stroke. Close-range fighting developed as the attackers infiltrated the Marine positions. Marshal Peng Dehuai had repeatedly told his senior officers of his belief that the Americans were afraid of close combat, in which the Chinese troops excelled. Peng himself was a specialist in what the Chinese called a "short attack," in which units of 50–60 men hammered away at enemy defenses with successive compact assaults, until a breakthrough or puncture of the enemy line was achieved. This was a very similar tactic to that used by German storm troops during the fighting on the Western Front in 1918.

The Chinese hit suddenly all along the line, firing submachine guns and throwing grenades, supported by machine-gun fire and an intense mortar barrage. The attack aimed to fix the Marines in position while a dense column of Chinese troops assaulted them on a narrow front against the boundary between Easy and Fox 2/5 Companies. The Chinese assault succeeded in penetrating the Marine position, where they overran Fox Company's right-flank platoon. Captain Samuel Jaskilka, commander of Easy Company, turned back his left flank to cover this penetration while the battalion's 81mm mortar team opened up on the attackers to cover a platoon from Dog Company which was sent to reinforce Fox Company's ruptured right flank. By dawn, the break in the line had been repaired and Chinese bodies littered the hillside around the Marine positions.

Things did not go as well for How Company in the fight for possession of Hill 1403. Captain Cooke had situated his three rifle platoons in a semi-circle on the forward edge of the crest of the hill. When the right flank crumbled under assault by the 266th Regiment, Cooke bravely led a counterattack and was cut down by Chinese machine-gun fire. Second Lieutenant James M. Mitchell took temporary command of the company until First Lieutenant Howard H. Harris, How's previous commander, arrived at midnight, when he could find only one officer, Second Lieutenant Minard P. Newton, Jr., still on his feet. The Chinese staged a second assault at about 0300 hours. After an hour of being pounded by the Chinese, 3/5 Battalion commander Lieutenant Colonel Fred Harris (no relation to Lieutenant Harris) ordered How Company to pull back behind 2/5 Battalion, leaving Hill 1403 in Chinese hands.

At the same time, the PVA 89th Division attacked Northwest Ridge, while the three regiments of the PVA 79th Division attacked North Ridge, which was held by two widely separated companies of 2/7 Battalion – Dog Company on Hill 1240 and Easy Company on Hill 1282. A long saddle separated the two hilltops. The PVA 235th Regiment attacked in a column of battalions against Hill 1282 at midnight. Easy Company held its ground while the PVA 236th Regiment moved against Dog Company's position on Hill 1240. Murray, the 5th Marines commander, had anticipated such an attack against North Ridge and had moved 1/5 Battalion out of its assembly area, over to the reverse slope of Hill 1282. The first units of Able 1/5 Company reached a spur on Hill 1282 just in time to reinforce Easy 2/7 Company, which had been hit by the PVA 235th Regiment. Easy Company's commander was killed and the executive officer, First Lieutenant Raymond O. Ball, took command. Then Ball was hit and died in the battalion aid station. Command now devolved on the senior platoon leader, First Lieutenant Robert E. Snyder. In the desperate battle, Easy Company was cut down to the size of a single platoon. By daylight, the Chinese held the crest of Hill 1282.

Chinese troops of the PVA 236th Regiment attacked and overran the command post of Dog Company commander Captain Milton Hull, wounding him. Hull counterattacked at 0300 hours with the few squads that were still organized and won back a foothold but was wounded again. By dawn, Hull had only 16 Marines left, surrounded by the enemy who were now on the crest of Hill 1240.

During the fight, some Chinese troops crossed the saddle separating Dog and Easy Company's positions and took the 5th and 7th Marines command posts under fire. At midnight, a few half-dressed How Company mortar men who had survived the attack on Hill 1403 managed to find their way into the 3/5 Battalion perimeter with a warning that the Chinese were flanking the position. At 0145 hours, the outpost platoon on Hill 1384 started to receive increasingly heavy fire. In short order, two Chinese companies overran the outpost and brought the 3/5 Battalion command post under direct attack, killing the battalion executive officer, Major John J. Canney, a World War II aviator turned infantryman.

Across the reservoir at Sinhung-ni, the PVA 80th Division moved out of the surrounding mountains after sunset and surrounded the unsuspecting units of RCT-31. Just after dark, the 31st Medical Company, pushing north from RCT-31 headquarters at Hudong-ni to join Faith's battalion, was ambushed and badly shot up in the vicinity of Hill 1221. The few survivors who made it back to Hudong-ni gave the first indication that the road had been cut, but it was impossible to pass the word to the other units due to the failure of the radios since the cold had drained their batteries.

The Chinese attacked all RCT-31 positions at 2200 hours while their comrades assaulted Yudam-ni, waking the unready Americans with the sound of bugles and screams. Cut off and unable to communicate with each other, the isolated units fought for their lives. Faith's 1/32 Infantry was hit along the north side of its perimeter and a firefight developed on A Company's front on the forward edge of Faith's position, during which the company commander was killed. Captain Edward P. Stamford, the Marine forward air controller, assumed temporary command of A Company and also called in air strikes by the night fighters of VMF(AW)-513 and VMF(N)-542. Even though the air strikes inflicted heavy casualties on the attacking Chinese troops, the attack spread until it encompassed the rest of the battalion perimeter. Faith's battalion suffered over 100 casualties before the Chinese pulled back at dawn.

South of Pungnyuri-gang inlet, the two batteries of the 57th Field Artillery Battalion, and 3/31st Infantry came under heavy attack. The Chinese overran the battalion command post and both artillery batteries, severely wounding both American commanders. The battle raged throughout the night, with the Chinese finally withdrawing at dawn for fear of American air attacks. The eight antiaircraft vehicles proved their worth in ground combat, as the twin 40mm cannons of the four M19 weapons carriers and the quad .50 caliber machine guns mounted on the four M16 half-tracks decimated the attackers, who were, however, still able to destroy one of the M19s.

While the attacks on Yudam-ni and Sinhung-ni savaged the American units, the PVA 59th Division completed a wide sweeping movement to the southeast and moved into position to cut the MSR between Yudam-ni and Hagaru-ri. Until around midnight, truck traffic on the MSR was still active and unimpeded, composed mostly of empty trucks from the 1st Motor Transport Battalion heading back to Hagaru-ri after delivering the last Marine reinforcements to Yudam-ni. By midnight, the snow had let up, allowing the full moon to cast deep shadows through the clear, cold skies in the silence of the freezing night, etching the ruts of the MSR.

At approximately 0130 hours, Captain Barber was roused by a call from the 2nd Platoon commander Elmo Peterson, reporting his men could hear noises in the dark in front of their position. Barber told Peterson to remain alert, that he would come to check things out. "I looked down the hill at the road and there were still trucks moving south, so I didn't think that we were under attack," he later recalled. Just as he pulled his boots on to crawl to the 2nd Platoon's position, gunfire rattled along the line. "We popped flares and I saw a mass of Chinese coming down from that high rocky knoll. They were probably about a hundred yards from us when we got our first inkling they were on their way."

The attackers from the PVA 59th Division hit the 3rd Platoon, stretched across the crest of the hill, the hardest. The two squads positioned forward on the crest and one machine-gun position were quickly overrun, with 15 killed and nine wounded of the 35 Marines in the two squads. Among the Marines in the forward-most squad was Private First Class Hector Cafferata, who had already acquired the nickname "Moose" due to his 6-foot 3-inch 220-pound size since his arrival in Fox Company as a replacement on November 15. Assigned with his friend Private First Class Kenneth Benson and two other Marines to a listening post positioned 25 yards in front of the rest of the platoon, he had immediately fallen asleep after being relieved on watch, just after pulling off his boots and changing socks, stuffing his wet boots in the sleeping bag to warm them.

> It must have been around 0130, I was zipped up in my sleeping bag lying out on the frozen ground behind some rocks and pine trees we'd cut and put up as a wind break. Kenny Benson was next to me in his sleeping bag. We heard some rifle fire and then a machine gun opened up. I realized this was for real. I unzipped my bag and grabbed my M-1 rifle. There were Chinese all around us. I shot five or six right in front of me immediately.

Cafferata grabbed his BAR, but it was frozen. "I checked to see how the other two guys were, but they were dead. There were Chinese all around us, so I knew we had to get the hell out of there. Benson and I started crawling back toward our lines. I wasn't sure where we were." A Chinese potato-masher grenade fell in front of Benson. Cafferata threw himself to the left to get away as Benson picked up the grenade and threw it just as it exploded. The explosion broke Benson's glasses, blinding him, and burning his face. Cafferata told Benson to grab his foot and the two young Marines crawled up the gully till they found a deep spot where three other members of the platoon had taken cover after being wounded. "I looked up, and the Chinese were right there on top of us again." Cafferata clubbed two with a shovel, grabbed the Thompson submachine gun one dropped, and emptied it into the mass of advancing enemies. "Since Benson couldn't see because his glasses were broken, he loaded rifles and passed them to me. They were running everywhere. You couldn't miss hitting something if you just kept shooting." Another potato-masher landed near the three wounded Marines. Cafferata grabbed the grenade and threw it as it exploded, blowing the flesh off one of his fingers on his right hand and severely injuring his arm. He picked up his rifle and fought on. "For the rest of the night I was batting hand grenades away with my entrenching tool while firing my rifle at them. I must have whacked a dozen grenades that night with my tool. I was the world's worst baseball player. I couldn't hit a bull in the ass with a baseball bat, but I didn't miss any that night." Benson later recalled that "Hector was standing up and firing at anything that moved. He wasn't touched. It was unbelievable." The two Marines finally took cover behind the pile of Chinese bodies.

The first wave of Chinese troops that charged the Marines carried Thompson sub-machine guns with 50-shot magazines. They were followed by a second wave, who threw hand grenades. Over and over, they repeated that attack procedure and were repulsed each time by the Fox Company Marines. The 2nd Platoon was soon in trouble. Lieutenant Peterson was hit as he rallied the men in the face of the onrushing Chinese. A corpsman bandaged the wound, which stopped bleeding due to the freezing temperatures, and Peterson continued to fight. Barber arrived in time to rally the men, shift some positions, and re-establish the line. He was busy throughout the night as he moved from platoon to platoon, losing two runners killed during the fight as the perimeter shrank. At one point, Barber shot three enemy soldiers less than 10 feet from him with his pistol. The 1st Platoon had been the last to arrive and dig in. Private First Class James Kanouse remembered:

We arrived after dark and were told to dig in shallow, that we would improve our positions in the morning. Fortunately, when the attack came, it didn't come at our positions. If it had, I'm sure we would have been very unprepared. We were rapidly surrounded, and gunfire seemed to be coming into our positions through the other platoons. The third platoon was pushed off the crest of the hill and bent backward into our position.

Fox Company's position was almost cut in half, but the two wing platoons managed to hold their ground. One party of Chinese penetrated as far as the company command post and the 81mm mortar position. Marines and Chinese soldiers fought hand-to-hand under the cold light of the moon.

By dawn, Cafferata was the only Marine still offering resistance in the 3rd Platoon position; most of the rest had been killed or wounded. As the grey light of dawn rose from the bloody night, bugles recalled the Chinese attackers. McCarthy, the wounded commander of the 3rd Platoon, looked downhill to see the Chinese massing at the foot of the hill for one final assault. Just at that moment, the roar of aircraft engines echoed through the hills, and two four-plane flights of F-51s from 77 Squadron RAAF swept over the crest of the hill, machine guns chattering as they strafed the Chinese, who broke and ran in the face of the aerial assault. The Australians had taken off from Yonpo before dawn to get in position to provide support at first light. The Marines on the hill cheered as the Mustangs disappeared in the distance.

McCarthy found Cafferata and Benson. There were 125 Chinese bodies on the slope in front of their position. As the adrenaline faded, Cafferata suddenly realized that he had fought the entire night in his stocking feet, which were now completely frostbitten. Unable to stand, he fell to the ground. McCarthy called for corpsmen, who carried the young Marine to the improvised aid station where he would remain through the next three days, unable to move. He would lose all his toes.

South of Yudam-ni, at 0230 hours, while the assaults against North and Northwest Ridges were at their height, the Chinese also struck Charlie 1/7 Company on the spur of Hill 1419. The Marines held on grimly until dawn when artillery fire finally made the Chinese break off their attack. With a third of the men killed or wounded, Charlie Company was effectively pinned into position by Chinese fire continuing to rain down from the heights. The Marines could do nothing more than hold their position and hope that help would come from Yudam-ni.

The PVA 59th Division had cut the MSR through Toktong Pass a mile north and 2 miles south of Fox Company's position, cutting off Yudam-ni from further reinforcement and supply from Hagaru-ri, but the Marines of Fox Company still held the key to the crucial escape route. In the first night of battle for control of Fox Hill, the company had lost 20 killed, three missing and 54 wounded, one in five of the survivors. The Chinese left 450 dead on the rocky slopes with the two assault battalions so battered they would take no further part in the battle.

Across the reservoir at dawn, General Hodes, the assistant commander of the 7th Division, directed Captain Richard E. Drake, commander of the 31st Tank Company, to move out from Hudong-ni and attempt to break through to Pungnyuri-gang inlet. Hodes rode with Drake as a passenger as 16 Shermans headed north, though he did not take tactical command. Lacking infantry support, the tanks were unable to break the Chinese position on Hill 1221, which blocked the route north. During the fight, several tanks skidded out of control on the icy road. The relief column was then attacked by Chinese troops using captured American bazookas, knocking out two of the tanks. A wild fight ensued as Chinese troops swarmed the tanks and attempted to open the hatches. Two more tanks become mired in the mud and had to be abandoned. Drake ordered his 12 surviving tanks back to Hudong-ni. Hodes returned to Hudong-ni in a jeep, intent on getting to Hagaru-ri for help. At Drake's insistence, he took a tank for transport and arrived at Hagaru-ri, 5 miles away, without further incident. He never returned to Hudong-ni.

At Yudam-ni, the tactical situation on Northwest Ridge was still unresolved as dawn broke. Hill 1403 had been lost to the enemy, while elsewhere Marines and Chinese clung to the high ground; 2/5 Battalion had managed to keep a firm grip on its section of the line, as the Marines kept position to resume the offensive from the day before; 3/5 Battalion was to come up on 2/5's right flank to reinforce the assault. Murray and Litzenberg met at the 7th Marines command post, where both agreed the situation dictated they change from offense to defense. Murray canceled the attacks to be made by 2/5 and 3/5. Later, Murray would remember that,

> [Litzenberg] had a reputation of being sort of a fussbudget, a stickler ... he seemed to be a studious type of person, knew his business, and as far as I could tell from talking

with people in the 7th Marines, it seemed everyone respected him and his abilities... Many people have asked why he didn't just assume command up there. I can't answer that question definitively. After all, there was a division headquarters over the hill from us, and we were still part of that division, so we had a common head. But in any case, we decided to operate very closely together, and we did.

At 0300 hours, 2/5 Battalion had commenced a counterattack against the spur of Hill 1384 with two George Company platoons commanded by First Lieutenants John J. "Blackie" Cahill and Dana B. Cashion. Shortly after dawn, they reached the crest of Hill 1384, just as the order canceling the offensive was given. Cahill and Cashion were ordered to hold where they were. With the two platoons now atop the hill, How 3/7 Company, reduced to 80 officers and men, completed its withdrawal from Hill 1403. On Hill 1240, 1/5 Battalion consolidated its position. Charlie 1/5 Company moved on to Hill 1282, where a company from the PVA 235th Regiment had taken the hilltop. A hand-to-hand assault won back the hill by mid-afternoon.

At 0800 hours, 1/7 Battalion commander Ray Davis assembled Able and Baker Companies and set out to move south into Toktong Pass and relieve both Charlie 1/7 and Fox 2/7 Companies. Able Company, commanded by First Lieutenant Eugenous M. Hovatter, moved into a gorge separating South from Southeast Ridge. Three hundred yards south of the Yudam-ni perimeter, they came under fire from the Chinese. By 1300 hours, five hours of fighting found Able Company still a mile short of Charlie Company's position at Hill 1475. Baker then joined the attack and the two companies managed to reach Charlie 1/7 at 1500 hours. With Charlie Company relieved and the wounded evacuated, Litzenberg ordered Davis to pull back to the

Yudam-ni perimeter, not wanting the battalion trapped in the gorge at night.

At about the same time that Davis set out from Yudam-ni to relieve Charlie and Fox Companies, 2/7 Battalion commander Lieutenant Colonel Lockwood was ordered by Colonel Litzenberg to move out of Hagaru-ri up to Toktong Pass to assist Fox Company. Lockwood borrowed a platoon from 1/3 Battalion as an escort, but the effort was unsuccessful, with the Marines returning to Hagaru-ri by mid-morning.

At 1100 hours, Murray ordered 2/5 Battalion to move back to Southwest Ridge from the road and establish contact with 3/7 and 3/5 Battalions on the ridge. At 1300 hours, 2/5 began the withdrawal a company at a time. Shortly thereafter, Davis and his two companies returned to the perimeter. Other than some harassing fire, the Chinese did not interfere with any of this.

Also on the morning of November 28, General Smith ordered Chesty Puller to send a force up the MSR from Koto-ri to meet a tank patrol coming down from Hagaru-ri. Dog Company under Captain Welby W. Cronk moved out, but they were stopped a mile north of the Koto-ri perimeter by a strong Chinese force which was entrenched on both sides of the road. Dog Company withdrew under cover of air strikes made by the busy Corsairs of VMF-312. The fighting cost the Marines four killed and 34 wounded. Three prisoners were taken and they identified their unit as the 179th Regiment, PVA 60th Division.

CHAPTER EIGHT

HOLDING ON

After the PVA 79th Division had taken heavy losses at Yudam-ni on November 27–28, the Chinese command realized the bulk of the 1st Marine Division was stationed at Yudam-ni in a garrison strength double their initial estimate. Concluding that any further assaults would be futile, Song Shilun ordered the Ninth Army Group to switch the main attacks to Sinhung-ni and Hagaru-ri. Yudam-ni was left alone November 28–30, while Chinese attention was paid to cutting them off from the rest of the division by defeating Fox Company and taking full control of the MSR. All Marine eyes were on the struggle in Toktong Pass.

At about 1300 hours on November 28, Major General Almond flew into the 1/32 perimeter at Sinhung-ni to meet and confer with MacLean and Faith. Almond seemed unaware of the crisis at hand, and announced that Task Force MacLean would press on with the planned attack the next day, once the 2nd Battalion, 31st Infantry, joined the regiment. Unfortunately, 2/31 and C Battery of 57th

Field Artillery were far south of Koto-ri, marooned on the traffic-clogged MSR below Funchilin Pass. Almond went on to say that the Chinese units facing them were nothing more than the remnants of retreating units. He finished by saying, "We're going all the way to the Yalu. Don't let a bunch of Chinese laundrymen stop you." MacLean did not object, despite the fact he knew that RCT-31 was in no position to attack anyone. As further encouragement, Almond then informed Faith that he wanted to present three Silver Stars, one for Faith himself and the other two for whomever Faith designated. Faith called a wounded Platoon leader and a mess sergeant to come over. Captain Alexander Haig recorded their names while Almond pinned the three Silver Stars to the men's parkas. The general and his aide then got back aboard their helicopter. As it flew off, Faith and the lieutenant tore the awards from their parkas and threw them in the snow. Almond and MacLean would both be criticized later for their failure of command in the events east of Chosin. Almond failed to fully understood or appreciate the enemy's strength, while MacLean failed to clearly explain the situation facing his own task force to Almond.

Following Lockwood's failure to get through Toktong Pass from Hagaru-ri, Litzenberg ordered Barber to break contact with the enemy and fight his way to Charlie 1/7's position at Hill 1475 to meet up with Ray Davis' rescue column. However, Fox Company, with 54 wounded, was unable to leave their position to reach the rescuers. That morning, How Battery in Hagaru-ri registered in on the area surrounding "Fox Hill" and conducted harassing fire throughout the day. At 1300 hours, Marine R5D (C-54) transports dropped medical supplies and ammunition which landed right on target on top of the hill. Around 1500 hours, 2/7 commander Lockwood radioed Barber with the news of the failure of Davis' rescue attempt, and Barber replied that he believed they could hold a second night. Two tents were set up as an aid station and warming position. Throughout the day, the Marines of Fox Company began to reinforce their positions with the frozen corpses of their enemies to provide cover for the attack they knew would come. As evening fell, Barber told his platoon leaders there was no prospect of immediate relief

At Yudam-ni by the evening of November 28, 1/5 Battalion had relieved the shattered remnants of Dog 2/7 Company. With the Yudam-ni perimeter tightened and mended, the two regiments faced the night of November 28 with quiet confidence. The Chinese, who had not expected to fight two Marine regiments at Yudam-ni, did not attack that night.

At approximately 2230 hours, the PVA 59th Division renewed its attack against Fox Company in Toktong Pass. The attack was a replay of the first night, with the Marines holding against daunting odds. During the battle, Captain Barber was shot in his leg but remained in command with two riflemen dragging him in a stretcher from position to position to rally his men. By dawn, 150 more Chinese bodies littered the hillside, while five Marines had been killed and 29 more wounded.

Across the reservoir, November 28 saw the badly battered 3/31 Battalion and the 57th Field Artillery Battalion painfully reorganize and consolidate their positions. At dusk, the Chinese resumed their attack with the focal point of their effort being the destruction of the M16 and M19 self-propelled guns. The high-volume automatic 40mm and .50-caliber fire did its lethal work against the massed attacks and the perimeter held, with many Chinese killed.

Fighting continued throughout the day north of Pungnyuri-gang Inlet. A dominant hill position was lost to the Chinese despite close air support strikes by Marine Corsairs called in by Captain Stamford. Long columns of Chinese marching south, some of them mounted on Mongolian ponies, were spotted to the east. Stamford called in air strikes against these units and the pilots claimed good results.

The Marines at Hagaru-ri had waited through the night of November 27/28 for the Chinese attack that never came, thanking their lucky stars for such a break. Fortunately, the Chinese did not realize Hagaru-ri's importance to their American enemies, and did not attack the town on the first night of their assault, when such an attack might have carried them to a victory that would have assured the destruction of the 1st Marine Division. However, tank infantry patrols sent out to the north toward Yudam-ni and to the south toward Koto-ri on November 28 were pushed back in by mid-afternoon. Hagaru-ri was surrounded and cut off from the rest of the division.

During the afternoon of November 28, Division G-3 Colonel Bowser telephoned Lieutenant Colonel Ridge to confirm his appointment as defense commander at Hagaru-ri. By then, Ridge was aware that his last unit, George Company, commanded by Captain Carl L. Sitter would not be able to occupy East Hill since the company had only reached Koto-ri that day. That afternoon, Company D, 10th Combat Engineer Battalion, came into Hagaru-ri from the tent camp the engineer soldiers had set up outside the perimeter on the road to Koto-ri after their arrival on November 27. A defense commander at Hagaru-ri, Ridge commanded all units, both Army and Navy. The engineer company commander, Army Captain Philip A. Kulbes, protested that he was at Hagaru-ri to build a new command post for General Almond and that his 77 Americans and 90 South Koreans had no infantry training aside from individual weapons. Ridge asked if Kulbes would accept tactical advice from a Marine officer, pointing out to him that the four .50 caliber heavy machine guns, five .30 caliber light machine guns, and six 3.5 inch "Bazooka" rocket launchers were of vital importance for the defense. Kubes agreed. Captain John C. Shelnutt, executive officer of Weapons Company, was assigned as "liaison" officer, accompanied by a radioman, Marine Private First Class Bruno

The Battle of the Chosin Reservoir, November 27–28, 1950

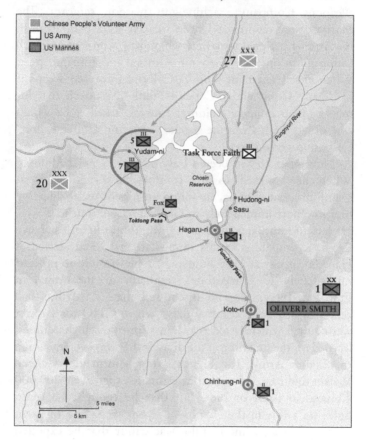

Podolak. Ridge privately advised Shelnutt that, in face of Kulbes' reluctance, he would have to take *de facto* command. Kulbes' reluctant men procrastinated in moving their trucks and construction equipment into a motor pool and were not ready to move up East Hill until dusk.

The roadblock facing south toward Koto-ri was manned by ten Marines led by Gunnery Sergeant Bert E. Elliott, Weapons Company machine-gun platoon sergeant. The Marines were reinforced late in the day by a platoon from the Army 4th Signal Battalion, which had been sent to install communications for General Almond's command post. When First Lieutenant John C. Colborn informed Weapons Company Commander Captain Frank J. Faureck that his men had no infantry training, Faureck asked if he would take orders from a Marine gunnery sergeant. Unlike Kulbes, Colborn eagerly agreed.

November 28 had been a busy day for General Almond. When he returned to his comfortable headquarters at Hamhung that evening, he found an urgent order directing him to report immediately to General MacArthur in Tokyo. He left an hour later for Tokyo from Yonpo in an Air Force C-54, accompanied by his immediate staff, and arrived at Haneda Airport at 2130 hours where he was told to proceed immediately to MacArthur's residence at the American Embassy. There, Almond discovered that MacArthur had called all his senior commanders back to GHQ for a secret war council which lasted two hours, during which Almond learned for the first time of the disaster that was overwhelming the Eighth Army. The Eighth Army commander General Walker told MacArthur that he estimated there were 200,000 Chinese in front of him, but that he thought he could build up a line in the vicinity of Pyongyang. In a moment of braggadocio, Almond told MacArthur that he expected the 1st Marine and 7th Infantry Divisions to continue their attack. In his own mind, however, Almond now realized that X Corps faced a difficult situation due to its dispersion over a 400-mile front. After listening to his field commanders, MacArthur gave his decision: there would be a changeover in Korea from the strategic offensive to a defensive withdrawal to a defendable line.

In Hagaru-ri that night, as MacArthur and his generals conferred about looming defeat in Tokyo, Lieutenant Colonel Charles L. "Gus" Banks, the commanding officer of the 1st Service Battalion, who had seen service in World War II with Edson's Raiders, found himself named sub-sector commander by Ridge. While the Army engineers who had come to build General Almond's new headquarters climbed the south face of East Hill in the setting sunlight, Banks was to send a column of Marines up the north face. The two columns were to meet on the crest. At the same time, the south roadblock was pulled back to a stronger position. Marines led by Gunnery Sergeant Elliott manned the roadblock with the Army signal platoon on the knoll to his left. Elliott, who had been a lieutenant during World War II, was determined to win back his commission. Though tough and battle-wise, he was not well liked, even by his own Marines. Brandishing his .45 pistol, he told the signalmen that if they tried to run, he would shoot them himself.

A light snow fell as the two Army and Marine units struggled up the icy, pockmarked slopes of East Hill and closed in on the crest. At about 2230 hours, three red flares and three blasts of a whistle signaled the Chinese attack. High explosive and white phosphorus mortar shells began falling on the Marine positions in the perimeter's southwest quarter, fortunately the strongest position in the line. How and Item Companies were well dug in, stretched in a thin line along the far side of the airstrip where the engineers continued to labor under lights. The Marines had dug their foxholes by blasting holes through the top 8 or 10 inches of frozen earth, using ration cans filled with C-3 explosive. Some strands of concertina and other barbed wire had been strung out where it could do the most good, with the added embellishment of white phosphorus grenades and gasoline-filled five-gallon cans scattered through the wire. The grenades were controlled by springs and would ignite the gasoline when exploded.

The three gullies that led into the Marine positions had been sown with anti-personnel mines.

Marine supporting arms – some artillery but mostly mortars and machine guns – responded to the Chinese fire, but could not stop the attackers from closing to hand-grenade and burp-gun range. The Chinese attacked in combat groups about 50 strong. While most of the Marine line held, the Chinese were able to penetrate the center of How Company's position. A scratch squad assembled by company commander Captain Clarence Corley was pushed aside when they tried to plug the gap. A few Chinese managed to get as far as the airstrip, where they were killed by the engineers.

The assault continued for an hour. Ridge sent a mixed platoon of Marines and soldiers led by First Lieutenant Grady P. Mitchell, Jr., to reinforce How Company. When Mitchell was killed, First Lieutenant Horace L. Johnson, Jr., took command and was able to deploy them in a ditch behind How Company's broken line. Fortunately for the Marines, the Chinese who penetrated the position were more intent on fighting each other for the food, warm clothes and ammunition they looted from the supply and cook tents than they were in continuing their attack. One wounded Marine survived by feigning death while a Chinese soldier relieved him of his parka. Another scratch platoon formed of men who had been separated from their units, including some who had deserted their positions, was sent in to reinforce Johnson's line. When the situation appeared to be under control by 0130 hours, the engineers turned their floodlights back on and went back to work scraping and grading the crucially-important runway.

While this Chinese attack was stopped, the situation on East Hill was going from bad to worse. The two Army and Marine columns had failed to reach the crest. Marine Captain Shelnutt, leading the Army engineers under heavy fire, informed the Weapons Company commander that the column from Banks' Service Battalion did not seem to be where it was supposed to be. He was ordered to hold for the night while the Chinese continued to oppose any moves he made.

At about the same time, the Marines and soldiers on the south roadblock spotted a company-sized column of Chinese troops marching toward them up the road, who had apparently decided the Marines had abandoned the position in the earlier pullback. The two water-cooled machine guns caught the Chinese in perfect enfilade and few escaped.

Through the night, fighting on East Hill was so intense that the sound of heavy small arms fire and grenades could be heard in Ridge's command post near the airfield. Weapons Company commander Captain Faureck attempted to contact Captain Shelnutt by radio at 0200 hours. Radioman Podolak informed him Shelnutt was dead: "There's nobody up here except me and a couple of doggies." He was sternly ordered to take charge. When Faureck attempted to contact him 15 minutes later, the radio was dead. Through the rest of the night, South Korean and some American stragglers from the Army engineer company streamed back off the hill, taking cover in the ditches and culverts of Hagaru-ri itself. Some few of them, stiffened with a handful of Marines, were rallied into a support line along the road that paralleled the base of East Hill. The soldiers who stayed on East Hill fought bravely and most of them died that night.

At 0430 hours, How Company commander Captain Corley, managed to launch a successful counterattack to restore his main line of resistance. The night's battle cost the company 16 dead and 39 wounded.

The dawn's light revealed how deadly the fight had been. Dead Chinese soldiers covered the ground. Lieutenant Bob Stroemple, who commanded Easy Company's 1st Platoon, later remembered what he saw in a letter written to his wife:

The dead Chinks were actually piled up like wood in front of the machine guns. There were 1,200 within a three-quarter mile area. You couldn't walk five feet in any direction without having to step over them. The mortars just blew them apart during their attack. Our white phosphorus shells burned them to a crisp. The snow was red with blood right up to our positions. They were very well-equipped – every third man had a Thompson submachine gun. Needless to say, I picked up a good submachine gun and carried it through the rest of the battle, as did a lot of the other guys.

The situation on East Hill was the greatest concern. If the Chinese had possession of the crest at dawn, the defenses of Hagaru-ri would be exposed to full view and assault by mortars. At 0530 hours on December 29, Ridge ordered a counterattack. The battalion executive officer, Major Reginald R. Myers, volunteered to lead a force up the hill. There was no organized unit that could be used; some 250 service troops and stragglers found skulking in the village were dragooned into the provisional company. The Marines were joined by a few soldiers when they formed up beside the battalion CP and were assigned to platoons and squads. The first platoon, formed by Marines of the 1st Engineer Battalion and led by First Lieutenant Robert E. Jochums, was in the best shape. Morning mist delayed the attack until 0930 hours when Corsairs appeared overhead to provide close air support. By the time Myers led the attack with supporting fire from How Battery, the company had been depleted during the wait by the loss of stragglers who had deserted again in the confusion. They headed toward East Hill, past the roadblock where the Army signalmen had stood and fought.

East Hill was steep and icy. As the unit came under fire, men stumbled and fell and were carried to the rear by those who were only too willing to save themselves by saving the wounded. The force was soon reduced to about 75, mostly Marines. Lieutenant Jochums was wounded in the foot but continued to lead his platoon of engineers. Myers reached the military crest after an hour of such struggle under fire, but East Hill's topographical crest was still held by the Chinese.

A supporting attack by Able Company, 1st Engineer Battalion, led by Captain George W. King, made it up the south face and passed through Myers' position. As they started up the hill at noon, the orders were changed. The company was pulled back and marched a mile north, where they were ordered to attack up the north face. Like Myers, King was able to reach the military crest on the north side. At dusk, the two units were separated by about 500 yards. The Chinese remained in control of the topographical crest. Major Myers later received the Medal of Honor for his leadership in combat in this action.

While the Marines had fought to hang on to Hagaru-ri by their fingernails, across the reservoir the situation of RCT-31 was becoming desperate. Around midnight, the PVA 80th Division attacked again. The fighting was savage, often hand to hand. By 0100 hours on November 29, the Chinese were attacking in massed formations but were beaten off. An hour later, MacLean ordered Faith to break out to the south in the darkness with the objective of reaching 3/31 Infantry's perimeter. The unit's trucks were unloaded so the wounded could be carried out. Orders were given to disable but not destroy everything left behind, since the move was to be a temporary one to consolidate forces before attacking the following day, as ordered by Almond.

After disabling and abandoning several vehicles and loading the wounded into trucks, 1/32 Infantry began organizing the move south at 0500 hours. The darkness and falling snow made the move difficult, but fortunately, the Chinese did not detect it and attack. MacLean and Faith began their march-out at 0600 hours on November 29.

Rifle companies broke contact, with the noise of their retreat down the hillsides sounding loud in the post-battle silence. The sixty vehicles moved south down the road with Marine Corsairs overhead. Along the way, the convoy gathered up the 31st Heavy Mortar Company, located halfway between the 1/32 and 3/31 positions, which had supported the two battalions during the Chinese attacks.

MacLean and Faith led the way in the command party and the battalion reached the 3/31 perimeter at about 0900 hours, only to find it under heavy enemy attack. Since the units were not in communication, an attempt to enter the perimeter would be an extremely hazardous operation. Furthermore, the Chinese had created a roadblock at the bridge over Pungnyuri-gang inlet, on the road leading into the perimeter. As they approached the bridge, the command party came under fire. Faith gathered and led a party of soldiers who successfully drove the Chinese off the bridge and cleared the block.

MacLean drove forward in his jeep and spotted a formation of troops he believed were the overdue 2/31 Infantry. They were actually Chinese and the soldiers within the 3/31 perimeter began firing on them, much to MacLean's dismay. Still believing they were Americans, he jumped out of the jeep, shouting, "Those are my boys!" He ran out onto the frozen reservoir towards the perimeter, trying to stop what he believed was friendly fire. Suddenly, Chinese soldiers concealed near the bridge opened fire on him. Witnesses saw him hit several times before he fell onto the ice. After a long moment, he pulled himself erect and staggered out of sight. Colonel MacLean was declared missing, but after the war an American POW stated that he died of wounds on his fourth day of captivity and was buried by fellow American prisoners by the side of the road. Colonel MacLean was the second and last American regimental commander to die in Korea.

With the loss of Colonel MacLean, command of RCT-31 devolved to Don Faith as the senior surviving officer. Under his leadership, the unit would enter Korean War mythology as "Task Force Faith," though the name was never official. There was no time to attempt to rescue MacLean, since Faith had to get his men into the 3/31 perimeter before they were surrounded and cut off by the attacking Chinese. With the men crossing the frozen inlet on foot while the vehicles with the wounded dashed over the bridge under harassing fire from the Chinese, most of the column managed to make it inside the perimeter by 1300 hours. Faith surveyed the carnage and destruction. Hundreds of American and Chinese dead littered the position, evidence of the desperate fight that had happened overnight. 3/31 had taken over 300 casualties and its L Company no longer existed.

Faith quickly organized a new perimeter with what was left of the two battalions, bringing some of the high ground to the south inside the defensive line. General Hodes sent a helicopter from Hagaru-ri that took out Reilly and Embree, the two wounded battalion commanders. Captain Stamford called in Marine close air support and requested an airdrop of desperately needed 40mm and .50 caliber ammunition for the M16s and M19s, which were crucial to stopping massed Chinese attacks. The airdrop had mixed results, with much of what was dropped falling outside the new perimeter, where it could not be retrieved. Most importantly, no .50 caliber or 40mm ammunition had been dropped. Faith now sent out search parties to look for MacLean, but it was too late.

That afternoon, the 31st Tank Company made another attempt to reach the 3/31 perimeter, having formed an assault unit with 11 tanks and administrative personnel from regimental headquarters formed into a scratch infantry force. The attack was stopped by Chinese dug in on Hill 1221. After four hours under fire, the tanks retreated to Hudong-ni.

The survivors of RCT-31 remained in position the rest of the day. With almost 500 wounded to care for, they were in no position to carry out the attack that had been ordered by Almond, yet Faith had no authority to order a further withdrawal. The situation was desperate, particularly since Faith had still not been able to establish communication with the Marines or the 7th Infantry Division headquarters.

Brigadier General Hodes had spoken briefly with General Smith when he arrived from Hudong-ni in the evening of November 28. The next day he met with Smith at noon and provided more detail about the condition of RCT-31. Smith had no force he could spare for a rescue mission and told Hodes that the unit would have to keep moving toward the Marine positions as best it could. Smith recorded in his logbook:

> The inference was that they should be rescued by a larger force. I have nothing now with which to lend a hand except the battalion at Hagaru-ri and it has its hands full. I cannot see why the cutoff battalions cannot at least improve the situation by moving toward us.

That afternoon, General Almond, who had returned at noon from his trip to Tokyo, gave his senior staff members a complete briefing on the MacArthur decision to go over to the strategic defensive and informed them that he had also issued orders for ROK I Corps to pull back from Hapsu where the ROK 3rd Division was, and from Chonjin where the Capital Division was holding, and then withdraw to Songjin, 100 miles northeast of Hungnam. He also informed the staff that he planned to turn over operational control of American forces at Chosin to General Smith.

General Barr flew to RCT-31's position following the meeting to inform Faith he was now to operate under Smith's command. He further informed Faith that it was his understanding that the Marines could provide air support, but other than that Faith and his men would be on their own as they continued their withdrawal. To add to the bad news,

Barr also told Faith that the 31st regimental headquarters, 31st Tank Company, and Headquarters Battery of 57th Field Artillery had withdrawn from Hudong to Hagaru-ri that afternoon, further isolating RCT-31. Everything that could go wrong for Faith and his men had gone wrong. Barr then departed to confer with General Smith in Hagaru-ri.

Later that afternoon Almond arrived in Hagaru-ri and met with Smith, Barr, and Hodes at Smith's forward command post. The generals were a few hundred yards from where the Marines were still fighting for possession of East Hill. Almond announced he had abandoned any idea of consolidating positions in the Chosin Reservoir area. A withdrawal would be made as quickly as possible to Hungnam. Almond, who had been so eager to advance against all evidence to the contrary, now authorized Smith to destroy everything that would impede what was a retreat whether the general could call it that or not, promising re-supply by air. Smith refused, telling Almond he planned to bring out everyone he could and could not discard anything they would need for their defense. Almond didn't argue. He then directed Smith and Barr to work out a plan to pull back "Task Force Faith." Further, Almond stated that if Faith failed to execute his orders, he should be relieved. He then informed General Barr that on his flight up to Hagaru-ri, he had passed over the 2nd Battalion, 31st Infantry, whose truck column was stopped south of Koto-ri. He suggested to Barr that he relieve the slow-moving battalion commander, Lieutenant Colonel Richard F. Reidy. Barr refused, stating he did not know the situation confronting the battalion. Almond then telephoned his chief of staff, and ordered him to expedite 2/31's movement, to join Puller's forces at Koto-ri.

While Almond appeared to have finally recognized the situation confronting his forces in the reservoir, he could not help himself from telling Smith and Barr of the "magnificent job" the 3rd Division had accomplished in covering the gap with the Eighth Army. One has to wonder what he was thinking, since at this point the Eighth Army was in headlong retreat out of North Korea and there was no force to the west for anyone to link up with. Following Almond's departure, Smith and Barr agreed that RCT-31 would have to remain on its own at least until the 5th and 7th Marines returned to Hagaru-ri from Yudam-ni.

That evening, X Corps Operation Order Number 8 was signed by General Almond at 2100 hours. The order stated that the attack to the northwest be stopped and that the various units of X Corps were to withdraw into the Hamhung–Hungnam perimeter. All Army units in the Chosin Reservoir area were placed under Smith's command effective as of 0800 hours on November 30. Optimistically, the order also directed that one RCT be redeployed from Yudam-ni to Hagaru-ri and establish contact with RCT-31 while securing the NSR from Hagaru-ri to Koto-ri.

General Smith outlined the situation that faced the 1st Marine Division on the evening of November 29, 1950 in his log:

It was vital to the 1MarDiv to keep open the MSR between Hagaru-ri and Yudam-ni. Two RCTs of the division were in the Yudam-ni area. Stocks of ammunition and supplies had been built up at Hagaru-ri to support these RCTs and the bulk of 1st MT Battalion was at Hagaru-ri available to transport the ammunition and supplies to Yudam-ni. Furthermore, the C-47 air strip at Hagaru-ri was nearing completion, and, when completed, it would be possible to fly in ammunition and supplies to augment the stocks already at Hagaru-ri. We had not yet considered the wholesale airdrop of supplies by the Combat Cargo Command operating from Japan. However, the entire capability of this command (75 tons per day) was not sufficient to sustain two RCTs in heavy combat.

On November 28, we had no information regarding any plans of the Corps for withdrawal. We, ourselves, had stopped the attack but could take no additional steps without sanction of the Corps. It was our responsibility to plan for the continuing support of RCTs 5 and 7 at Yudam-ni. For this purpose we needed to open up the MSR between Hagaru-ri and Yudam-ni and this required infantry.

While the tragedy of RCT-31 was unfolding 8 miles away across the reservoir, the Marines in Hagaru-ri maintained their positions during the daylight hours of December 29, while Corsairs from VMF-312 and VMF-214 flew 31 sorties over the town, most of them strikes against East Hill. VMF-312 pilot First Lieutenant Harry W. Colmery took a bad hit from Chinese fire as he made a strafing attack, but successfully crash-landed inside the perimeter. Between November 28 and December 4, when the withdrawal from Yudam-ni was complete, MAG-33's four Corsair fighter-bomber squadrons and two night fighter squadrons would fly an incredible 1,403 individual sorties in support of the Marines and RCT-31.

During the night of November 29, the PVA 59th Division sent a third assault battalion against Fox Company in Toktong Pass. Marines were awakened at 0200 hours by a voice that called out in accented English: "Fox Company. You are surrounded. I am a lieutenant from the 11th Marines. The Chinese will give you warm clothes and good treatment. Surrender now." The answer was several 81mm illumination shells. Three companies of Chinese troops were exposed by the harsh light and the Marines opened up with accurate rifle and machine gun fire that mowed down many Chinese where they stood, though some managed to close and exchange hand grenades. After this single assault the Chinese withdrew. The Marines had suffered no more killed, but they now had more wounded. When he made his report that morning, Barber intimated to Lockwood that the company might not be able to continue to hold on their own.

Throughout the Chosin campaign, there was a marked difference in the care of wounded by the Chinese and the Marines. For a Chinese soldier, a wound was a death sentence; he was left to die of exposure. Each night of the battle, Marines could hear the cries of the Chinese wounded, which died away as they froze to death. In spite of the cold, Marine wounded were adequately cared for as the Marines maintained their tradition of leaving no wounded behind. The presence of warming tents and medical supplies, blankets, and stretchers at forward positions were crucial to the survival rate.

On the morning of November 30, following Barber's report, Colonel Litzenberg was ordered to mount a second move into Toktong Pass to relieve Fox Company. A composite battalion was put together with Able 1/5 Company, along with Baker 1/7 and George 3/7 Companies, while 3/11 Battalion provided a section of 75mm recoilless rifles and two sections of 81mm mortars. Major Warren Morris, executive officer of 3/11 Battalion, was put in command. He assembled the force in front of 1/7's CP; they marched out at 0800 hours. Morris assembled his force in front of the 1/7 Battalion command post and marched out to the south at 0800 hours. Only 300 yards beyond the Yudam-ni perimeter, heavy machine-gun fire laced into the Marines. Corsairs overhead struck the positions they could spot, and the Marines pushed on. A Corsair pilot dropped a warning that Chinese positions were spotted on both sides of the MSR through the pass.

At Fox Hill, Marine R5Ds again made an accurate supply drop at 1030 hours. Twice-wounded 2nd Platoon commander Peterson took a patrol out into no man's land to recover mortar ammunition which had fallen outside the perimeter. Shortly thereafter a helicopter from VMO-6 landed with fresh batteries for the radios. As it hovered in to land, the helicopter came under enemy small arms fire, with one round passing through the cockpit while several hit the fuselage. Before any wounded could be put aboard for evacuation, the pilot had to take off to avoid further damage.

At 1315 hours, Colonel Litzenberg was warned that Morris' column was in danger of being surrounded, and ordered him to return to the Yudam-ni perimeter, leaving Fox Company alone in Toktong Pass another night.

At 1500 hours, Air Force C-119 "Flying Boxcars" of the Combat Cargo Command arrived over Fox Hill to make an airdrop. They were asked to drop on a large "X" laid out on the saddle of the crest, but the drop was off by 600 yards. How Battery in Hagaru-ri provided covering fire to protect the men who ventured out into no-man's-land to retrieve the bundles. The enemy return fire was so heavy that only part of the drop was recovered, and it was necessary to delay recovery of the rest until nightfall. With the final recovery of this airdrop at dusk, Fox Company had a plentiful supply of ammunition. At dusk, Barber called his officers together and informed them that the rescue attempt had failed and there was no prospect of relief anytime soon.

At Chinhung-ni on November 29, a patrol sent out in the afternoon from Captain Wesley Noren's Baker Company confirmed Lieutenant Colonel Schmuck's conclusion regarding the location of the Chinese force that had been bothering the Marines in the deserted village. The colonel decided to attack the suspected Chinese position the next morning, using Captain Robert H. Barrow's Able Company with a part of Baker Company, reinforced with 81mm and 4.2-inch mortars.

While Hagaru-ri had withstood the Chinese assault the night of December 28/29, it was obvious that if this crucial position was to be held in the face of expected continued attacks, the makeshift defense had to be reinforced.

At dusk on November 28 three very different units – 41 Commando, Royal Marines; the Marines' George 3/1 Company; and Company B, 31st Infantry, 7th Infantry Division – had arrived at Koto-ri following an uneventful motor march up from Hamhung. Chesty Puller pasted the three together into a task force, and put Lieutenant Colonel Douglas B. Drysdale of the Royal Marines in command, with orders to fight his way through to Hagaru-ri the next day.

The Royal Marines were a very different kind of force from their American counterparts. They were a far smaller organization, and had specialized during World War II in commando operations, a strategy they maintained afterwards. The previous summer, 41 Commando had been the first British ground unit to enter combat in Korea. They had been used for commando raids along the northeast coast, operating from the assault transport submarine USS *Perch* (ASSP-313). That September, 41 Commando had made a raid against a train tunnel on the northeast coast of Korea west of Tanchon. The target had been destroyed with the loss of one man who was buried at sea. In mid-October 41 Commando had been attached to X Corps, and remained at Hamhung while various plans were made to utilize them for other commando raids which were planned and then canceled as the campaign went on.

Once placed in command of the Hagaru-ri relief task force, Drysdale and his men barely had time to uncrate their newly issued American 81mm mortars and .30 caliber light machine guns before they moved out at 0945 hours on November 29. The leading truck-borne column carrying the Royal Marines and the American George Company was followed by several trucks carrying non-combatant headquarters troops on their way to the division headquarters at Hagaru-ri. Where before the Chinese attack the trip from Koto-ri to Hagaru-ri had taken less than an hour to drive the 10-odd miles, no one in the task force knew how many Chinese they would encounter on this trip, or how long it would eventually take.

Drysdale's plan had the Royal Marines take the lead by assaulting the Chinese positions on the right side of the road a half mile north of Koto-ri, while Captain Carl Sitter's reinforced George Company Marines would assault Hill 1236, a mile and a half north of Koto-ri, while the GIs of Baker Company, 31st Infantry, remained in reserve.

The Royal Marines routed the Chinese out of their positions without much trouble, but George Company ran into serious resistance before taking Hill 1236 after an hour's solid fighting. The British and American Marines then advanced together a mile farther north on the road, where they were stopped by Chinese machine-gun and mortar fire coming from positions on Hill 1182.

Puller radioed Drysdale at noon that tanks would arrive in an hour. Drysdale then ordered Captain Sitter to break off the action and bring George Company back down to the road to await the tanks' arrival.

1/1 Tank Battalion's two platoons of Dog Company's M-26 Pershing heavy tanks and Anti-Tank Company's platoon of M4A3 Shermans, had only arrived at Koto-ri at noon; they were ordered to immediately head out to support the task force. Dog Company's Captain Clarke refused to cooperate with Colonel Drysdale's plan to distribute the armored vehicles through the length of the column, insisting they must remain together at the head of the column. Drysdale found Dog Company's Captain Clarke to be what he termed "an opinionated young man."

Resigned to the situation after a lengthy argument, Drysdale resumed the advance at 1350 hours, with George Company following 17 tanks that led the way. The advance was a series of short movements followed by pauses while Chinese strongpoints were knocked out with the Pershing's heavy 90mm cannon and machine-gun fire. Even with the tanks present, progress was slow and George Company took heavy losses.

Baker Company of 1/1 Tank Battalion arrived at Koto-ri at 1500 hours. Puller ordered the commander, Captain Bruce F. Williams, to leave two of his platoons in Koto-ri and join the rear of the Drysdale task force with his remaining two platoons. A rifle platoon was sent from Easy 1/2 Company to help evacuate casualties.

Task Force Drysdale halted about 4 miles north of Koto-ri at about 1600 hours. It was clear they would not make it to Hagaru-ri in daylight, and they were too far advanced to turn back, given the need of their force at Hagaru-ri. The two tank commanders advised Drysdale and Sitter that they believed the tanks could get through to Hagaru-ri, but that they were dubious about further movement by trucks in the looming darkness. Drysdale reported the situation to General Smith, who ordered him to continue, The need to refuel the tanks took more time, and when at last the column began its advance again, darkness led to combat troops and headquarters troops becoming intermingled and unit integrity was lost.

Midway between Hagaru-ri and Koto-ri was a mile-long valley. The all-night battle there would embed the place in Marine memory as "Hellfire Valley." As the task force moved into the valley, it came under increased Chinese attack from the high ground to either side, and broke in half. Trucks carrying George Company, three-quarters of 41 Commando, and a few soldiers from B Company, led by the tanks from Dog Company, broke through the attacking Chinese and continued on toward Hagaru-ri. The remainder of 41 Commando, most of Company B and the survivors of the headquarters troops were cut off on the road when the Chinese closed it behind them. In the face of continued Chinese attacks, the men took cover in the shallow ditches to either side of the road. Command fell to Lieutenant Colonel Arthur A. Chidester, assistant division G-4, who attempted to return to Koto-ri; in the attempt to turn the column around, Chidester was wounded and captured, leaving Major James K. Egan in command, but he too was quickly wounded and made prisoner.

The survivors managed to form one large and three smaller perimeters, strung out along the road over nearly a mile; the largest perimeter was farthest north, composed of 140 Royal Marines, Army infantry and some of the headquarters troops and Associated Press photographer Frank "Pappy" Noel, close to the hamlet of Pusong-ni. The senior officer was Major John N. McLaughlin, assistant division G-3 and a veteran who had fought in the 5th Marines at Guadalcanal, Cape Gloucester, and Peleliu during World War II. There was little ammunition, and organizing the men under fire was difficult.

The Baker Company tanks in Koto-ri attempted to move out for a rescue, but were stopped by Chinese who had re-occupied the positions on Hills 1236 and 1182 that had been captured by the Marines that morning. The southernmost group managed to take to the hills and work its way back into the Koto-ri perimeter by 2200 hours without much trouble. The headquarters troops in the middle group, led by Lieutenant Colonel Harvey S. Walseth, the division G-1, managed to return by 0230 hours, though they lost most of their trucks along the way. By dawn all of the Baker Company Pershing tanks had returned to Koto-ri.

The troops in the northern position remained trapped in Hellfire Valley, still hoping to be rescued by the tanks. Once again, the Chinese surrounding them seemed to have greater interest in looting the trucks than annihilating the defenders. Major McLaughlin twice tried to send a patrol back to the south to link up with the others but they were beaten back both times. The wounded were gathered in a ditch and everyone prayed for daylight and the arrival of Marine Corps aircraft. By 0200 hours, they were out of grenades. At 0230 hours, a 75mm recoilless rifle manned by soldiers was hit, with the crew killed and wounded. When AP photographer Noel and two others tried to drive a jeep through the gauntlet, they were captured when the jeep was hit by a bazooka rocket.

At about 0410 hours, several prisoners were sent into the position, carrying a demand that the Americans surrender. Major McLaughlin and a British Marine went out to parley under a white flag. Trying to gain time, McLaughlin attempted an act of bravado by pretending the Chinese were surrendering to him; the enemy was having none of this and gave him ten minutes to surrender or have his force wiped out. McLaughlin had almost no ammunition and only 40 able-bodied men; he agreed to surrender only if the most seriously wounded were evacuated. The Chinese agreed but did not carry out their promise. Following the surrender they permitted some of the wounded to be placed in houses along the road where they might eventually be found.

A few British and American Marines, as well as a number of GIs, were able to slip away from the two southernmost perimeters while McLaughlin negotiated his surrender. Major Henry W. "Pop" Seeley, Jr. led the escapees in a cross-country hike through the snowy hills to return to Koto-ri successfully by dawn.

After the two parts of the column became separated, Drysdale continued the start-and-stop progress with Dog Company's tanks, George Company, and the larger part of 41 Commando. He had no way of knowing what had happened to the others. A tank was knocked out, while Drysdale was hit in the arm by a grenade fragment and forced to pass command to Captain Sitter.

The first Dog Company M-26 Pershing smashed through Hagaru-ri's south roadblock at approximately 2230 hours flattening a Weapons Company jeep; it had taken 13 hours of nearly continuous combat to traverse the ten miles across the plateau. The tanks were followed by the battered trucks carrying George Company's survivors. Following its training, 41 Commando split into small groups. For most of the rest of the night, Marine sentries heard English voices calling out of the darkness that they were coming in. At midnight,

Drysdale saluted Lieutenant Colonel Ridge and reported 41 Commando ready for duty.

Task Force Drysdale had started out with 922 officers and men: 400 reached Hagaru-ri, while another 300 managed to get back to Koto-ri. The unit had lost 162 dead or missing and 159 wounded; of the missing, 44 were taken prisoner, of which only 25 escaped or survived their captivity. Both Chidester and Egan died in prison camps. The column had started out with 141 vehicles and 29 tanks. Of these, 75 vehicles and one tank were lost. For his leadership, Lieutenant Colonel Drysdale would be recognized with the Distinguished Service Order and the US Silver Star.

The defenders of Hagaru-ri welcomed the reinforcements. Fighting throughout the perimeter continued the night of November 29/30. Lieutenant Colonel Ridge and his command group were very well-informed regarding the extent of the enemy forces surrounding Hagaru-ri, as a result of the reports by "line-crossers," Korean agents who moved in and out of the perimeter. The PVA 58th Division's plan to renew the attack against Hagaru-ri was thwarted by air strikes during the day of November 29 and heavy artillery and mortar fire that night. The Marines also experimented with night close air support, in which converging lines of machine-gun tracer fire were used to point out targets to the F4U-5N Corsairs of VMF(N)-513 orbiting overhead.

At 1430 hours, November 29, another helicopter had flown in to Fox Hill with replacement batteries for the radios. Like the helicopter the day before, it too received heavy small arms fire on its approach, and was forced to take off as soon as the batteries were dropped off. With the bitter cold at night, the batteries were crucial to the defense of the position, as the company depended on its radios for artillery and air support.

At 0230 hours on November 29, the Chinese renewed their assault on Fox Company, coming up the hill from the south, across the valley. Machine guns and mortars mowed down many, while those who managed to reach the road were finished off at close range with grenades. After this single assault was beaten off, there were no further attacks that night. The attacking PVA 59th Division was running out of both men and ammunition to sustain the assault.

At Hagaru-ri, 41 Commando was held in reserve. The British officers spent most of December 30 reconnoitering potential counterattack routes and becoming acquainted with fire support plans. Drysdale later recalled that "I felt entirely comfortable fighting alongside the Marines."

At dawn on November 30, Colonel Schmuck ordered his attack on Chinhung-ni. Fox Battery, 11th Marines, under First Lieutenant Howard A. Blancheri, laid down preparatory 105mm howitzer fire, then the infantry swept forward. As Major William L. Bates, Jr., the battalion's Weapons Company commander recalled, the Marines "ran the Chinese right out of the country." The houses the Chinese had used for shelter were burned. There would be no more trouble at Chinhung-ni.

In Hagaru-ri at 0800 hours, after only a scant night's sleep, George Company was ordered to pass through Myers' position on East Hill and continue the attack. George Company commander Sitter sent out the 1st and 2nd Platoons to attack on both sides of the ridge; the 3rd Platoon and two platoons of Army A Company engineers would follow in reserve. Progress was slow as the reserve was used to envelop the Chinese right flank. When the attack became bogged down, Captain Sitter asked permission to set up defensive positions on the ground that had been held by Myers, who had withdrawn his small force. Corsairs attacked the Chinese on the crest of the hill again and again, but George Company could not take the position, though an entire company of Chinese had been killed. Captain Sitter was later awarded the Medal of Honor for his leadership in this fight and his actions with Task Force Drysdale.

After sunset, the PVA 58th Division threw its last remaining 1,500 soldiers into a last-ditch attempt to capture Hagaru-ri. The reinforced defenders mowed down most of the attackers, with only the defenses around East Hill giving way. As the surviving Chinese tried to advance from East Hill, they were cut down by the Shermans of the Army 31st Tank Company.

Both the Marines and their Chinese opponents used the same radio equipment, the Chinese having captured theirs the year before from the defeated Kuomintang forces in China. As a result, both sides could hear the other's calls. Ninth Army Group commander Song Shilun was thus aware from signals intercepts that the Marines would soon make a move to break out of Yudam-ni. He ordered the PVA 59th Division to position itself in Toktong Pass to stop the attempt.

The Chinese commander was not far off in his understanding of what was coming. At 0600 hours on November 30, Litzenberg and Murray received orders from General Smith to expedite the breakout from Yudam-ni and bring the two regiments into Hagaru-ri. The Marines in Yudam-ni spent the rest of the day and that night preparing their move.

At twilight on November 30, another Air Force airdrop was made to Fox Company in Toktong Pass. In the fading light and poor visibility, the C-119s dropped too soon, and some supplies landed as far as 800 yards east of the Marine position. However, since the Chinese had exhausted their combat capability, no difficulty was experienced in retrieving the supplies. As night fell, it began to snow again, with approximately 4 inches of snow falling by midnight.

At 0100 hours on December 1, the Chinese took advantage of the reduced visibility from the storm and moved four machine guns into position on the high hill to the north of Fox Hill. Their fire was not very effective, but Captain Barber decided to bring artillery to bear on these guns, with illumination from the 81mm mortars. In a remarkable coincidence, How Battery scored a "hole in one" as the enemy guns were taken out with the first salvo. Though the Chinese remained visible in large numbers, there was no further attack that night; the Chinese had run out of men and ammunition.

Through the day of December 1, Barber put the men to work cleaning up the company area, burying ration cans and gathering the equipment of Marine casualties and captured Chinese weapons. The positions were now completely "sandbagged" with the frozen bodies of the Chinese dead. Ernie Gonzales remembered that the sight of the fighting hole he shared with his friend and fellow Angeleno, Fred Gonzales, surrounded by these frozen bodies, was enough to give him a lifetime of nightmares. At 1030 hours, Corsairs from VMF-312 attacked the high hill to the north, where the Chinese had set up their machine guns the night before. During the air strike, Air Force C-119s arrived to make another airdrop, and the Corsairs pulled away temporarily. Again, part of the drop was wide. Barber requested the Corsairs give cover to the men he sent out to retrieve the drop, who were able to bring the supplies back without incident thanks to the presence of the dark blue fighters overhead.

Though no one realized it at the time, Friday, December 1, 1950 was the turning point of the Chosin campaign. The First Engineer Battalion had succeeded in fashioning a useable runway in twelve days of dangerous around-the-clock effort that saw the engineers down tools and pick up weapons on several occasions to defend themselves. Heroic though the effort was, the airstrip was only 40 percent complete. The rough runway, 50 feet wide and 2,900 feet long, was considerably short of the length and condition specified by regulations for operation of transport aircraft at such altitudes and temperatures.

An impossible load of casualties overwhelmed the division field hospital, which was nothing more than a collection of tents and half-destroyed Korean houses. Navy Captain Eugene R. Hering, the division surgeon, met with

General Smith that morning to inform him of the situation. Even with the two additional surgical teams that had been flown in by helicopter from Hungnam the previous day, Charlie and Easy Companies of the 1st Medical Battalion had some 600 patients. Hering expected 500 more casualties from Yudam-ni and 400 from the Army battalions east of the reservoir. Grim as his prediction of casualties was, Hering's estimates would prove too low. Until the airstrip was operational, aerial evacuation of the most serious cases had been limited to those that could be flown out by the nine helicopters and 10 light aircraft of Major Gottschalk's VMO-6. From November 27 to December 1, VMO-6, struggling to fly in the cold, thin air, had lifted out 152 casualties – 109 from Yudam-ni, 36 from Hagaru-ri, and seven from Koto-ri. One of the squadron's pilots, First Lieutenant Robert A. Longstaff, was killed on an evacuation mission to Toktong Pass. Smith decided the urgency of the evacuation was such that the uncompleted airfield must be used, ready or not.

At 1430 hours that afternoon, the first Air Force C-47 touched down on the frozen snow-covered runway. Thirty minutes later the plane, loaded with 24 casualties, bumped its way off the rough strip into the air. Three more C-47s came in that afternoon, taking out about 60 more casualties. Smith noted in his log that "It takes about a half hour to load a plane with litter patients. Ambulatory patients go very much faster." The last plane to arrive that day came in heavily loaded with ammunition and collapsed its landing gear; it had to be destroyed.

Smith received a report from Dr. Hering that while 919 casualties had been evacuated on the first day, there had been a large number of malingerers among them. Smith responded with a policy the next day that had MPs guarding the airplanes and allowing no one aboard without a ticket issued by the medical staff. When the planes landed at Yonpo, they were met by a clearing station established by X Corps medical teams, where triage separated the wounded into those who would recover in 30 days or less, who were sent to either the Marine hospital or the 121st Army Evacuation Hosptial, or to the USS *Consolation* in the harbor. Those requiring more extensive recovery were flown on to Japan.

At the end of the day, Lieutenant Colonel William J. McCaffrey, Almond's deputy chief of staff, visited Smith. He outlined the plan to regroup into a perimeter at Hungnam and its subsequent defense. The 3rd Infantry Division was to move units to the foot of Funchilin Pass at Chinhung-ni, to provide a covering force through which the Marine division would withdraw. The Marines would then organize a defensive sector west and southwest of Hungam while the 7th Infantry Division would occupy a sector northeast and north of Hungnam.

The consolidation of X Corps included the evacuation of Wonsan. Major General Field Harris, commanding the First Marine Aircraft Wing, ordered MAG-12's three tactical squadrons and a headquarters squadron to move from Wonsan to join MAG-33 at Yonpo. The movement was completed that same busy December 1, with planes taking off from Wonsan, flying a mission, and landing at Yonpo. As of December 2, the First Air Wing was the sole ground-based air support for the withdrawal, as Air Force units were moved south.

Due to General Smith's foresight, Hagaru-ri was stockpiled with six days' worth of rations and two days' worth of ammunition. The first airdrop from Air Force C-119 "Flying Box Cars" flying from Japan came on the afternoon of December 1. The drops, called "Baldwins," delivered prearranged quantities of ammunition, rations, and medical supplies. Some drops were by parachute, some by freefall. The Combat Cargo Command of the Far East Air Forces at first estimated it could deliver only 70 tons of supply a day, enough for a regimental combat team, but not a division. Over the next four days, with what became a steady stream of transports landing on the strip and airdrops nearby, the Air Force drove its deliveries to 100 tons a day by December 4. Private Stanley Kot of How Battery recalled that during one request the unit made for resupply, the Marines called out for "Tootsie Rolls," which was for them the code word for artillery shells. When the supplies were dropped, the Marines were surprised at the contents. "We were like, 'What the hell is this?' But I survived for two weeks on those boxes of Tootsie Rolls." From that moment on, the men of How battery all called themselves the "Tootsie Roll Marines."

During the fighting at Hagaru-ri between November 28 and December 1, 3/1 Battalion had suffered 43 killed, two missing, and 270 wounded, for a total of 315 casualties, a third of original strength. The other bits and pieces of Marine and Army units which made up the rest of the Hagaru-ri defense force experienced casualties this high if not higher.

In the meantime, the two Marine regiments at Yudam-ni and the Army's RCT-31 were about to experience the bloodiest four days of battle in American military history.

CHAPTER NINE

BREAKOUT

During the daylight hours of November 30, Don Faith worked out plans to deal with a penetration of his perimeter, which was now isolated with no friendly forces between it and Hagaru-ri. Not waiting for nightfall, the Chinese began their attack in the late afternoon. At about 2000 hours, they launched a second mass attack. By midnight, the assault against RCT-31 had built to unprecedented intensity. There were multiple penetrations of the perimeter, but they were sealed off with local counterattacks. During the struggle, the task force suffered another 100 casualties killed and wounded. Medical supplies were completely exhausted. The frozen dead were laid out in rows stacked four bodies high.

The Chinese pulled back with the coming of dawn and Marine fighter-bombers. Faith concluded the survivors of RCT-31 could not survive another major attack and determined the unit must break out to Hagaru-ri. He summoned his surviving officers and ordered them to prepare to move out at 1200 hours. Without a solid radio link to the

Marines, and only a chancy relay through Captain Stamford's tactical air control net, Faith was unable to inform anyone of his decision and ask for support. His own battalion would take the lead, followed by the 57th Field Artillery, with 3/31 Infantry as the rearguard. All remaining trucks were unloaded in order to carry the 600 wounded. The 57th Field Artillery spiked their howitzers, while most of the jeeps and all inoperable trucks were destroyed along with all supplies and equipment. The 30 trucks still in operating condition formed up in column. The overriding mission was now to protect the truck convoy with the wounded.

Under the cover of VF-32 Corsairs from *Leyte*, the last remaining M16 twin 40mm self-propelled gun, followed by the last two M19s with their quad .50s, led the column out of the perimeter at 1300 hours. They immediately came under fire from the Chinese forces in the surrounding hills. Captain Stamford called in strikes and the Navy pilots rocketed and bombed the hillsides, strafing the enemy with their 20mm cannon in repeated runs and dropping napalm. As Lieutenant (jg) Tom Hudner of VF-32 recalled, there was no organized return fire from the Chinese other than from random machine guns. Several casualties resulted from one napalm canister dropped close to the RCT-31 command group. The accident was demoralizing but the survivors welcomed the Navy close air support, without which they would never have made it out of the perimeter.

The situation quickly went from bad to worse. Heavy fire from the hills to either side of the road killed many of the wounded in the trucks. As the convoy reached Hill 1221, the soldiers could see the Chinese in plain sight on the surrounding high ground. Mortar rounds continued to cause more casualties, while Chinese infantry began pressing in. The fighting for the first half-mile was particularly heavy. Officers and NCOs suffered disproportionate losses and overall control broke down. Fair was forced to draw his pistol to stop a fallback by some soldiers, while KATUSAs and other Americans tried to climb onto the trucks with the wounded. Riflemen covering the flanks drifted back to the road, losing cover for the convoy.

At the northern base of Hill 1221, the Chinese blew a bridge, which forced a two-hour delay as the M19 self-propelled gun had to winch the 30 trucks across the stream. The enemy held the high ground on both sides of a roadblock while troops on the hill kept up their heavy fire. The only way to break through was to take Hill 1221. Faith gathered enough men to reduce the roadblock while several hundred others, including many wounded who said they preferred to die fighting than while waiting in the trucks, charged up the hill. Despite suffering heavy casualties in the attack, they drove the Chinese off most of the hill. However, many of the Americans kept going over the crest and down the other side, running out onto the frozen reservoir in a desperate attempt to get to Hagaru-ri. As Major Robert C. Jones, Faith's staff supply officer, remembered, "After Hill 1221, there was no organization left."

By sunset, the survivors were a bit over 4 road miles from Hagaru-ri when they ran into another roadblock at a hairpin turn. Faith again led the assault that cleared the enemy. When he reached a position approximately 30 yards from the roadblock, he was mortally wounded when a grenade fragment penetrated his chest just above his heart, but he continued to direct the attack until the roadblock was overrun. Fearing a complete loss of morale if it became known Faith was dead, his men wrapped his corpse in a blanket and propped it in a truck cab. With Faith's death, the remaining command structure of the task force collapsed. Major Jones remembered that "When Faith was killed, the task force ceased to exist."

Jones and Captain Stamford attempted to provide leadership, but the task force quickly fell apart. Another roadblock, this one composed of disabled tanks from the

31st Tank Company and other vehicles, caused further delay. The Chinese blew another bridge at Twiggae, which forced the surviving trucks to attempt a risky crossing of a railroad trestle under fire. More of the men left the trucks to hide or attempt to escape across the reservoir. Most died from wounds and exposure, or were captured by the Chinese.

Just north of Hudong, the survivors ran into a third Chinese roadblock. Chinese troops threw grenades and fired into the trucks, killing more of the remaining wounded. As the convoy struggled on south, the Chinese continued the destruction, truck by truck.

During the night of December 1/2, groups of RCT-31 survivors straggled into the Marine perimeter at Hagaru-ri. The commander of the Motor Transport Battalion, Lieutenant Colonel Olin L. Beall, personally led rescuers in jeeps out onto the ice, with air cover from Corsairs that flew so low the colonel later recalled he could have scratched a match against their bellies. 319 soldiers suffering from wounds and frostbite, many in a state of shock, were rescued; fortunately the only Chinese opposition was some long-range rifle fire.

Captain Stamford, who had been briefly captured by the Chinese but escaped, made it into the perimeter at 0230 hours on December 2. By the middle of the morning, a total of 670 survivors had made it in to Hagaru-ri.

There are no official casualty figures for RCT-31. Approximately 1,050 survivors reached Hagaru-ri by December 4, of which only 385 were considered mentally or physically fit for further service. These men and other 7th Division soldiers were organized into a provisional battalion attached to RCT-7. Known as 31/7 Battalion and led by Major Jones, they played an active role in the 1st Marine Division's breakout from Hagaru-ri to the coast. All the equipment of RCT-31 was lost in the breakout. The 31st Infantry suffered 90 percent casualties, killed and wounded. The regimental colors were captured and have been held in Beijing, China, since 1950.

For years afterward, the terrible tale of Task Force MacLean/Faith was largely ignored. Many believed the collapse and panic that engulfed the unit had brought great shame on the Army. On closer examination, however, their role in the Chosin battle proved much more noteworthy. Many historians now agree that RCT-31 managed to block the Chinese drive along the eastern side of Chosin for five days, which prevented the PVA 80th and 81st Divisions from attacking Hagaru-ri before the Marines had concentrated enough force to successfully defend it. Loss of Hagaru-ri would have blocked the only escape route for the Marines at Yudam-ni and other Army units, resulting in a very different outcome to the battle of the Chosin Reservoir. The sacrifice of RCT-31 allowed the Marines on the west side of the reservoir to withdraw into Hagaru-ri, while the Army troops' resistance broke the PVA 80th Division, which did not re-enter combat until 1951. In recognition of their bravery, Task Force MacLean/Faith/RCT-31 was finally awarded a Presidential Unit Citation in September 1999. In 2001, the United States Navy awarded RCT-31 the Navy Distinguished Unit Citation in recognition of their decisive role in the breakout from the Chosin Reservoir.

In 2004, a Joint Prisoners of War, Missing in Action Accounting Command (JPAC) team surveyed the area in North Korea where Don Faith was last seen. His remains were located and returned to the US for identification through DNA comparison with his surviving brother. On April 17, 2013, Lieutenant Colonel Don Carlos Faith, Jr., was buried at Arlington National Cemetery with full honors. His Medal of Honor citation concludes:

> ... Throughout the five days of action Lieutenant Col. Faith gave no thought to his own safety and did not spare himself. His presence each time in the position of greatest danger was an inspiration to his men. Also, the damage he

personally inflicted firing from his position at the head of his men was of material assistance on several occasions.

In Yudam-ni on December 1, Litzenberg and Murray finalized the plan for breaking out to Hagaru-ri. The individual units of the two battalions by now were thoroughly intermixed. Casualties had reduced many companies to the strength of a platoon. More than 500 casualties in the aid stations awaited evacuation. The news that the first Air Force C-47 had landed at Hagaru-ri gave both commanders hope that their wounded would be flown out to Japan as soon as they could get down the MSR.

The final plan put Litzenberg's best unit, Ray Davis' 1/7 Battalion, "the Ridgerunners," at the forefront of a cross-country advance through the mountains west of the MSR, while Murray's best battalion, Lieutenant Colonel Robert D. Taplett's 3/5 Battalion would lead the advance down the MSR. The two columns would meet at Fox Company's position in the middle of the pass, with Davis charged to relieve Barber's men.

Air support came from all available Marine aircraft, joined by aircraft from *Valley Forge* and *Leyte*. With great reluctance, the decision had been made to abandon Marine tradition and bury the dead at Yudam-ni, a field burial for 85 Marines being held on the evening of November 30.

"The big parade," as First Lieutenant Jim Eaton would later call it, left Yudam-ni on December 1 at 0800 hours. 3/5 Battalion took the lead when they came out of their positions north of the village, followed by 1/5 Battalion 90 minutes later. Baker 1/5 Company formed the rearguard while 3/7 proceeded to clear the road on both sides with How Company taking Hill 1419 while the rest assaulted Hill 1542.

Davis' 1/7 Battalion was relieved by 2/5 Battalion on Hill 1276, freeing Davis' "Ridgerunners" to pursue their overland mission to relieve Fox Company at Toktong Pass.

With How company now his responsibility, Davis sent Able Company to add its weight to How Company's effort. How Company's commander, First Lieutenant Harris was wounded and Second Lieutenant Minard P. Newton, Jr., assumed command as they attacked Hill 1419. 1/7's Able Company, led by Captain David W. Banks, passed through How Company's position and took the hill at about 1930 hours. 3/5 Battalion advanced down the MSR even as fighting continued on the flanks. There would be no stopping for darkness as the Marines continued their do-or-die advance, pushing on through snow that reached the men's knees.

Davis stripped his battalion of every piece of gear that could not be hand-carried for the cross-country trek. He took only two 81mm mortars and six heavy machine guns with double crews for support. The battalion vehicles were left behind with the sick and walking wounded, with frostbite cases as drivers, ordered to join the regimental train on the MSR. Baker 1/7 Company, now commanded by First Lieutenant Joseph R. Kurcaba, led off the advance, followed by Davis and his command group, then Able Company, Charlie Company, battalion headquarters, and How Company, which had been detached from 3/5 Battalion and assigned to Davis' command.

The snow on the hillsides ranged from knee-deep to waist-deep as the Marines struggled forward. The night was very dark and the guide stars soon disappeared behind overcast skies. In the lead as trail-breaker was First Lieutenant Chew-Een Lee, who now led the Second Platoon of Baker Company despite the fact his right arm was in a sling, the result of a sniper wound that had seen him sent back to Hamhung for further transfer to Japan, which he foiled by stealing a jeep and driving back to the unit just before the Chinese attacks. The 8-mile cross-country move through unmapped mountains, occupied by unknown numbers of Chinese troops overlooking the service road, was nearly impossible in the reduced visibility of night in a snowstorm, and normal land navigation techniques were unworkable. The rocky snow-covered hillsides all looked alike and those on point had to break trail, plowing through the snow. Once beaten down, the path across the hillside became icy and treacherous. Marines stumbled and fell and staggered to their feet to continue the advance as Lee navigated by compass. "If I had followed the instructions, we pretty much would have ended up in disaster. To me, it was an exhilarating experience. Everything was simplified. My mind was clear. I experienced no fear whatsoever."

All effort was made more difficult by the cold. During the four days of the breakout, the temperature varied between 20 degrees above zero during the days to minus 20 degrees at night; the wind chill factor caused by the Siberian winds blowing down from the north brought skin temperature down even more. Davis found himself almost unable to carry on in the cold. He recalled the night of December 1/2, when he had to orient himself,

> I got down in one of these abandoned Chinese pits to recheck my map orientation with a compass. I remember crawling down, poncho over me, with my flashlight, getting my map oriented, to check out the direction. Then I fixed my hand for a marker, turned the light out and lifted off the poncho and got up to check the direction, and I couldn't remember what had happened down there under that poncho. I got up and just stood there in a daze. Two or three people would say something and when they were done, I had forgotten what it was I was trying to do. I had to do it all over again. Everybody had to repeat orders back to you two or three times to be sure of what was supposed to happen.

Baker and Charlie Companies converged on Hill 1520, where there was a platoon of Chinese, and took them by surprise. Davis stopped on the eastern slope of Hill 1520 to reorganize the exhausted battalion. Enemy resistance had slackened off to only small arms fire from ridges across the valley, but the men were numb with cold and exhausted. Davis recalled that at one point, "Among Able Company, I found men already completely exhausted and in a state of collapse. I asked them what outfit they were from and they could not even answer. I'd shake them bodily to try and arouse them and I got my command group to do the same thing." At 0300 hours, he again halted the advance to give the men a rest, sending out small patrols for security. For the first time since pushing off, he gained radio contact with Litzenberg.

Meanwhile, on the MSR, Taplett's 3/5 Battalion moved south, led by the solitary Pershing tank, which was followed by a platoon from How Company and a platoon of engineers. Taplett's radio call sign was "Darkhorse," which suited his dark visage. After advancing for about a mile, the battalion was halted by heavy fire from both sides of the road. How and Item Companies moved out and cleared the opposition by 1930 hours.

The battalion took a brief rest, then resumed their advance. Item Company ran into stiff resistance on the reverse slope of Hill 1520 east of the road. Company Commander Captain Schrier obtained permission to fall back to his jump-off position in order to better protect the MSR. The Chinese then hit Item Company with mortars and an infantry attack, during which Schrier was wounded a second time and Second Lieutenant Willard S. Peterson assumed command. George Company and the attached engineers moved into defensive positions behind Item Company as the Marines engaged in what would become an all-night fight.

Elsewhere on the MSR that night, 1/5 Battalion got into a night-long fight east of the road when they were hit by a Chinese force that had apparently crossed the ice of the reservoir. More than 200 Chinese were killed, at least 50 of them cut down in front of Charlie Company's machine guns.

At dawn, December 2, Item Company counted 342 enemy dead in front of their position. Only 20 Marines were still on their feet when George Company passed through their position to continue the attack. By this point, George and How Company were both down to two platoon strength.

The combined Dog-Easy Company from 2/7 Battalion had been held in reserve. Dog-Easy moved onto the road between How and George Companies. By noon, George Company had taken Hill 1520 and Dog-Easy had run into its own fight on the MSR. Second Lieutenant Edward H. Seeburger, the last surviving officer of Dog Company, was severely wounded while giving a fire command to the solitary Pershing tank. He refused evacuation and continued to lead the fight. He would be evacuated by air from Hagaru-ri and after a year's hospitalization would retire due to his wounds. In 1995, he received a belated Navy Cross for his actions in the fight.

Corsairs were finally called in and they quickly reduced the roadblock holding up Dog-Easy Company. 3/5 Battalion trudged on, with the remains of How and George Companies on both sides of the MSR and Dog-Easy on the road, followed by the engineers and the solitary tank.

At dawn on the hillside east of the MSR, Ray Davis reoriented the direction of the march. 1/7 Battalion advanced over the east slope of Hill 1520 and attacked toward Hill 1653, which was 1.5 miles north of Toktong Pass. His radio batteries depleted by the cold, Davis could not reach Barber on Fox Hill or directly talk to the Corsairs circling overhead. As they moved out from a small stand of trees, the lead elements came under heavy fire and were pinned down. Seeing that the fire came from enemy positions located under some big boulders near the crest of a steep rocky hill, Lieutenant Lee quickly deployed his Second Platoon on line, including his sole remaining machine gun. At his signal everyone opened fire at the same time to establish fire superiority and his men swept up the steep hill to overrun the enemy positions, killing about ten in their foxholes, of whom Lee personally shot and wounded two himself. He was astounded to see the reverse slope pockmarked with enemy foxholes. A staggered line of about 20 enemy soldiers were floundering in the snow about 400 yards distant, fleeing in panic from the Marines. In such a situation, the Marines were lucky that the rest of the Chinese opposition was light except for scattered rifle fire from isolated positions against the rear of the column where How Company struggled through the snow as they brought up the wounded on litters. Able, Baker and Charlie companies converged on Hill 1653.

Finally, at 0630 hours on December 2, Davis made radio contact with Fox Company. Such was the spirit of his men that Barber offered to send out a patrol to bring Davis' battalion onto the hill. Davis and his men finally reached Fox Company's position at 1125 hours. He recalled the moment of the rescue:

> As we approached Fox Company's position at Toktong Pass, I first contacted Captain Barber on radio when I was about 600 yards away and we discussed the situation. He told me that he would send a patrol out to bring me in. I thought this was rather remarkable, because I was coming in to relieve him and here he was offering to come out and save me, though I had a battalion. When I saw him, he was hobbling about and could just barely walk. I think we just shook hands and looked at one another for a few minutes until we got unchoked, and then I told him he had done a wonderful job.

During five days of fighting at Toktong Pass, Fox Company had suffered 118 casualties: 26 dead, three missing, and 89 wounded, almost half of the original complement of 240. Six of the seven company officers, including Barber, were wounded. They had destroyed three assault battalions of the

PVA 59th Division, killing or wounding over 1,500 of their enemies, with most of the enemy wounded subsequently freezing to death. The battle on Fox Hill was the bloodiest small-unit action in the history of the United States Marine Corps. Both Private First Class Hector Cafferata and Captain William E. Barber were awarded the Medal of Honor for their actions during the fighting.

Twenty-two wounded Marines were carried to safety on the hill; Navy Lieutenant Peter Arioli, the battalion surgeon, was killed by a Chinese sniper during this. Two Marines who had cracked and were restrained in makeshift strait jackets, died of exposure before they could be evacuated. That afternoon, the Marines of Baker Company took the high ground which dominated the loop in the road where the MSR passed through Toktong Pass. Able Company followed them and the two units set up a perimeter for the night. Meanwhile the balance of Davis' battalion joined Barber on Fox Hill. The way was now open to continue the advance to Hagaru-ri.

At the rear of the column on the MSR, 2/5 Battalion, the designated rearguard, had trouble on Hill 1276 during the pre-dawn hours of December 2, when Fox 2/5 Company came under a Chinese attack that was thwarted by F7F-3N night fighters of VMF(AW)-542 that were vectored to the enemy by white phosphorus mortar rounds. Even with the air support, the fight continued until 1000 hours, when it was time to give up the position and continue the march south.

Meanwhile, 3/7 Battalion continued to experience trouble on Hill 1542. Litzenberg sent "Jig Company," a composite unit made up of artillerymen, headquarters troops, and other individual Marines, under the command of First Lieutenant Alfred I. Thomas for reinforcement. At the end of the fight, Marine casualties amounted to 35 killed and wounded.

That morning, 3/5 Battalion had to fight every foot of the way to sustain the advance down the MSR. George Company still had to cross Hill 1520 while Dog-Easy moved along the road itself. At a sharp bend in the road south of Hill 1520, a bridge over a ravine had been blown, and Dog-Easy was stopped by Chinese machine-gun fire. Twelve Corsairs overhead were called in by the Marines and the aircraft ripped the Chinese in the ravine with cannon fire and rockets. Dog-Easy Company was reinforced by How Company, and resumed the advance; Technical Sergeant Edwin L. Knox and his engineers managed to patch up the bridge sufficiently to allow vehicles to cross. The unit was now down to 17 men of the 48 who had begun the trek a day earlier. The Marines continued to advance through the pass during the second night. By 0200 hours on December 3, the Marines were only 1,000 yards short of Fox Hill. With the radios so badly affected by the cold, the two Marine columns were out of contact and battalion commander Taplett could only guess where Davis might be.

In the rear of the column, the Chinese continued to harass the Marine rearguard as they withdrew from Hills 1276 and 1542. The Marine Corsairs were able to hold off much of the harassment, but the vehicles on the road moved slowly with the result that the jeep and truck drivers were targets for Chinese snipers. Lieutenant Colonel Feehan's artillerymen were only able to stop a Chinese breakthrough on the night of December 2/3 by firing their howitzers point-blank at the enemy.

Six inches of new snow fell that night. The Marines advancing south on the MSR faced the same problems Davis' men had confronted on their cross-country advance. Dawn found Dog-Easy and George Companies so reduced from all-night combat that the remnants of Dog-Easy were combined with George Company, with First Lieutenant Charles D. Mize, who had led George Company until November 17, resuming command.

Shortly after dawn, Davis' Battalion attacked the Chinese who still held a spur blocking the way to Hagaru-ri and pushed them into the machine guns of 3/5 Battalion. Over

500 Chinese troops were slaughtered. At 1300, Davis' "Ridgerunners" replaced Taplett's "Darkhorses" as the lead unit on the MSR with the single M-26 still in the lead. When the truck column reached Fox Hill, the critically wounded of Fox Company and 1/7 Battalion were loaded into the already over-burdened vehicles, while those less severely wounded had to walk. 1/5 Battalion moved up to take the position behind 1/7, while 3/5 Battalion remained in Toktong Pass until after midnight; 2/5 and 3/7 Battalions maintained the rearguard.

Several months later, Sergeant Robert B. Gault NCOIC of the 7th Marines Graves Registration Section recalled of the unit's work in picking up the dead, "That was the time when there was no outfit, you was with nobody, you was a Marine, you were fighting with everybody. There was no more 5th or 7th; you were just one outfit, just fighting to get the hell out of there, if you could."

The six fighter-bomber squadrons of Brigadier General Field Harris' 1st Marine Aircraft Wing flew 145 sorties on Sunday, December 3, most of them in close support of the Marines advancing down the MSR. Additional interdiction missions were flown over the Taebaek Mountains by Navy squadrons searching for Chinese troops. Commander Foote remembered that the weather was so bad at sea that the frozen spray had to be chipped from the flight decks to allow takeoffs. "We were immediately in the clouds after takeoff, and climbed on instruments till we came out at maybe 20,000 feet. We'd go 'feet dry' and start looking for a hole to get back down where we could do some good." With this aerial umbrella, Davis' 1/7 Battalion marched south almost unimpeded. As the sun began to set, Lieutenant Colonel Ridge sent out 41 Commando, supported by tanks from the Army's 31st Tank Company, to open the door to the Hagaru-ri perimeter.

At 1900 hours, a few hundred yards outside the perimeter, Davis formed his battalion into a route column. As he later recalled,

I was thinking of everything these men had done, from that ill-trained mob back at Camp Pendleton in July and August, to what they had just accomplished, and I was so proud of them, so proud we were all Marines together, that I started to sing the Marine Hymn to myself. The guys next to me heard me and joined in, and by the end of the stanza, the whole battalion was singing it at the top of their lungs. It sounds corny as hell, but I cried. I was never so proud to be a Marine in my life as I was right then, to be there with those men.

Hagaru-ri's defenders gave the marchers a tumultuous welcome. A field mess offered an unending supply of hot cakes, syrup, and coffee. Litzenberg's command group arrived shortly after Davis' battalion and was welcomed into the motor transport area by his old friend, Olin Beall.

As the singing Marines marched into Hagaru-ri, in Tokyo Douglas MacArthur informed the Joint Chiefs of Staff that X Corps was being withdrawn to Hungnam as rapidly as possible. He informed them there was no possibility of uniting X Corps with the Eighth Army in a line across the peninsula, stating that such a line would have to be 150 miles long and held alone by the seven American divisions, the combat effectiveness of the South Korean army having now been spent.

While the Chinese had made no serious attempt to oppose the final leg of the march, that changed at 0200 hours on December 4, when the prime movers pulling the heavy 155mm howitzers ran out of gas. The column was forced to halt, which brought on a Chinese attack. 3/5 Battalion, unaware of the break in the line, continued their advance. The artillerymen, assisted by platoons from 1/5 and 2/5 Battalions that were on the high ground to the flanks defended themselves. It was a bad moment. The eight heavy howitzers had been pushed off the road, and would have to be destroyed the next day by air strikes. After an hour's combat, the artillerymen were rescued by 3/5 Battalion after they learned of the problem and managed to turn around. Ironically, half a mile farther down the MSR was a cache of air-delivered diesel fuel that could have fueled the prime movers if they could have gotten that far. By 0830 hours on December 4, the road was again open. Chinese losses were estimated at 150 dead.

At 1400 hours on Monday, December 4, the 3/7 Battalion rearguard marched into Hagaru-ri. The four-day, 14-mile breakout from Yudam-ni was over, at a cost of 1,500 casualties, some 1,000 caused by the Chinese, the rest by the cold. The two regiments had been in continuous combat over the entire period of the breakout. Smith observed in his log: "The men of the regiments are pretty well beaten down. We made room for them in tents where they could get warm. Also they were given hot chow. However, in view of their condition, the day after tomorrow [December 6] appears to be the earliest date we can start out for Koto-ri."

While the PVA 80th and 81st Divisions east of the Chosin Reservoir had shattered RCT-31, the units themselves were reduced to a state of ineffectiveness and were unable to participate further in the campaign. At Yudam-ni and Toktong Pass, the PVA 79th and 59th Divisions were out of action. The PVA 60th Division had been sufficiently weakened that it was unable to attack Koto-ri, and the PVA 89th Division had taken serious losses. The heavy casualties suffered through ground and air action were compounded by the cold. The terrible cold was at once the Marines' worst enemy and their greatest ally. Chinese combat capability was greatly weakened by the awful losses the poorly clothed troops suffered because of frostbite and exposure. Compounding the weakening of the Chinese units by combat and cold was the failure of their logistics system. Over two or three days of fighting, most units used up the meager allotment of ammunition they had brought with them when they crossed the Yalu. In addition to running out of ammunition, they suffered shortages of food so severe that several opportunities to inflict real damage on Marine units were lost when the victorious Chinese troops broke their advance to loot the riches of the American supplies they came across, which allowed the Marines to regroup and hold their positions.

On December 2, Song Shilun ordered the PVA 26th Army to move south from the Huchang River and take over the assault on Hagaru-ri. The 26th Army's movement was slowed by air attacks from carrier-based Navy and land-based Marine squadrons. On the night of December 2/3, several elements of the 26th Army got lost in the snowstorm that had slowed the Marines in Toktong Pass. The 26th Army was unable to reach Hagaru-ri and launch an attack before December 5, when they were up against a defending force that included all the Marine units. An advanced element of the PVA 76th Division did reach East Hill and held that until they were pushed off on December 6 by two battalions of the 5th Marines holding Hagaru-ri as the rearguard, following the commencement of the final Marine withdrawal through Funchilin Pass that day.

Since the war, the Chinese have admitted that non-combat losses from cold during the battle were extraordinarily heavy. One Chinese source claims a total loss of 40,000 for the Ninth Army Group, which came primarily during the period of November 27 to December 4, 1950. The Marines estimated Chinese losses at 25,000 killed by air and ground action during the battle, with 12,500 others wounded. This is nearly the exact reverse of the normal ratio of killed to wounded in combat, but in the vicious cold, with almost no access to medical help for the Chinese, even a minor wound could be fatal. Total losses in the Ninth Army Group may have been as much as half the entire force.

CHAPTER TEN

"RETREAT, HELL, WE'RE JUST ATTACKING IN A NEW DIRECTION!"

Across western North Korea, what came to be called "The Big Bugout" was in full rout, following the catastrophe that had befallen the 2nd Infantry Division in the pass north of Kunu-ri. The Army's retreat covered some 120 miles in the ten days following the initial Chinese attack, with wounded left behind to become prisoners, and equipment left in the field. The rush south became what Sir Martin Gilbert would later term "the greatest defeat of a previously victorious army in recorded history," and Sir Max Hastings would compare it with the French collapse in 1940. Secretary of State Dean Acheson later called it "the greatest defeat of American arms since the Second Battle of Bull Run." As the survivors of the 2nd Infantry Division headed south, they passed huge fires visible for miles, as the vast stores that had been coming into the country since Inchon were destroyed lest they fall into Chinese hands. Men who were still wearing summer-weight uniforms in the midst of blizzards learned that the winter uniforms that had finally arrived in-country were among the stores being burned. When they tried to get near these supplies, they were turned away by military police at gunpoint. As infantryman Sam Mace later explained, "It was during the chaos after we broke contact and moved south, unable to put it all back together, that I was ashamed of my Army, not the men in my unit, or the men in my division, not after the hell they had been in, but of the men who were in charge of us. That was a moment of complete disgrace and shame."

At the same time, it was known in Washington that the Chinese forces had broken off contact when the Eighth Army retreated south of Pyongyang, mostly due to their own difficulty in obtaining supplies. General Omar Bradley was concerned that General MacArthur had not gone to the front in Korea in the face of the disaster to rally his men. Assistant Secretary of State Dean Rusk asked "Why couldn't we muster our best effort and spirit to put up our best fight? The British had done that time and again early in World War II – why couldn't we?" To Bradley, it seemed "MacArthur was throwing in the towel without the slightest effort to put up a fight."

On November 30, President Truman came close to creating an international crisis during a press conference when he was asked what the United States was going to do in Korea, replying "They will do whatever was necessary to meet the challenge." Another reporter asked "Will that include the atomic bomb?" Truman, now badly rattled, replied "That includes every weapon we have." A following questioner asked if that meant there was active consideration to use the atomic bomb. Truman responded "There has always been active consideration of its use." He proceeded to make things worse by stating it was something the military commanders would decide, adding that the military commander in the field would be "in charge of the use of all these weapons." The reaction around the world – especially among allies – was shock, given that Truman was the man who had ordered the combat use of the atomic bomb in 1945. The administration worked over the following days to walk back the president's statement, but support for the war, already waning, dropped further, as did the president's approval ratings. Even Henry Luce, who looked on the war as the great opportunity to begin the crusade to roll back Communism became concerned over the proximity of the Time-Life Building to Manhattan's Union Square; there was serious talk of moving the corporate headquarters to Chicago.

At MacArthur's headquarters in Tokyo on the morning of December 4, intelligence chief Major General Charles Willoughby held the first "in depth" press conference since the disaster at Kunu-ri. The general was as full of certitude as he had been two weeks earlier when he had briefed the press about the coming "victory offensive," during which he had gone out of his way to belittle the potential danger of Chinese attacks. This time, however, his briefing was an attempt to prove that the intelligence section had been right about the Chinese all along, and had in fact been tracking them from the time they left south China in September. Willoughby went so far as to say that at the time MacArthur had made the famous "home by Christmas" pledge, the command had known that there were 30 Chinese divisions on both sides of the Yalu capable of striking UN forces. When asked by one reporter why the offensive had gone ahead when the commander knew his forces were outnumbered three to one, Willoughby replied that "We couldn't just passively sit by. We had to attack and find out the enemy's profile." He also presented the new political line about how the UN command had been harmed by the failure of the civilian leadership in Washington to allow UN forces to attack the Chinese forces across the Yalu, stopping any "hot pursuit" of the Chinese by bombing their Manchurian bases, which had "placed an enormous military handicap, without precedent in history." *US News and World Report* reporter Joe Fromm, who attended Willoughby's performance, recalled later that,

> I went back to my office, and I thought to myself, 'Now they say they always knew because they're never wrong, and now they say they were never surprised because they can never be surprised, and yet if you checked with the kids who fought there, someone fucked up, because the kids who fought there didn't know about all the Chinese the way MacArthur and Willoughby knew about them.' It was madness. Pure madness. Someone was crazy.

At Hagaru-ri that same day, the defenders breathed much more easily after the arrival in their perimeter of the 5th and 7th Marines. However, they were still in a difficult situation, surrounded and outnumbered by an enemy determined to destroy them.

In Washington, the Joint Chiefs wanted MacArthur to consolidate his forces by folding X Corps back into the Eighth Army to create a unified command and take advantage of the superior mobility of UN forces in comparison to the limited logistical capability of the Chinese, which would allow UN forces to pull back 40 or 50 miles, regroup, and then present a more formidable defensive line backed by air and artillery. As they saw it, the only difficulty in such a plan was the extraction of the Marines up in the Chosin Reservoir. MacArthur had turned down this suggestion immediately, cabling that "There is no practicality nor would any accrue thereby to unite the forces of Eighth Army and X Corps." When General Almond visited General Smith at Hagaru-ri on December 4, he suggested that the Marines abandon all vehicles and make their way down Funchilin Pass as rapidly as possible. Smith summarily rejected the suggestion on the grounds it would leave his men even more exposed to the enemy than they would be dragging their equipment with them.

General Smith's plan for the withdrawal to Hamhung involved using Murray's 5th Marines, with Ridge's 3/1 Battalion and 41 Commando taking over the defense of Hagaru-ri while the 7th Marines would march south to Koto-ri, beginning at first light on Wednesday, December 6. Puller's 1st Marines were to continue holding Koto-ri and Chinhung-ni. All personnel except drivers, radio operators, and casualties would move on foot. Specially detailed units would provide close security to the road-bound vehicles, with any that broke down pushed to the side of the road and destroyed. Troops would carry two days of C-rations and full cartridge belts with an extra bandolier of ammunition for their M-1 rifles.

The vehicles would be divided into two division trains. Lieutenant Colonel Banks, commander of the 1st Service Battalion, was placed in command of Train No. 1, supporting the 7th Marines. Lieutenant Colonel Harry T. Milne, commander of the 1st Tank Battalion, would lead Train No. 2, supporting the 5th Marines.

While Smith had declared the 1st Marine Division would bring out all supplies and equipment, a more realistic plan was established for the disposal of excess material. Commencing on December 4, bonfires were lit and the excess supplies were consigned to the flames. Ironically, loose rounds and canned food that were thrown in the fires exploded, causing casualties among Marines who crowded close for warmth.

By Saturday, December 2, Air Force and Marine aircraft had flown out more than 900 casualties from Hagaru-ri since the field had opened for operations on Friday, with more than 700 following the next day. On Sunday, December 3, 47 casualties were flown out of Koto-ri by the OY-2 Grasshoppers and HO3S-1 helicopters of VMO-6. But on the morning of Tuesday, December 5, nearly 1,400 casualties still remained at Hagaru-ri. Air Force C-47s and Marine R4Ds flew continuously throughout the day, and all casualties were evacuated by nightfall. Between December 1, when the airfield opened, and December 5, 3,150 Marines, 1,137 soldiers, and 25 Royal Marines, a total of 4,312 men, were evacuated. A four-engine Navy R5D managed to land, but takeoff from such a small strip with a load of wounded in such a large aircraft was so hairy it was not attempted again. One Marine R4D wiped out its landing gear on landing and had to be shoved aside by bulldozers, while an Air Force C-47 lost power on takeoff and crash-landed outside the perimeter. Though there were no personnel casualties when Marines rushed to the rescue, the C-47 had to be abandoned and destroyed.

The inbound flights during those five days brought in 537 replacements, the majority of them recovering wounded from hospitals in Japan. Hagaru-ri was suddenly "the place to be" for war correspondents, and those who could wangle spaces aboard the incoming flights. Marguerite "Maggie" Higgins of the *New York Herald-Tribune*, who had covered the Marines during the fighting in the Pusan Perimeter and in the Inchon–Seoul campaign, was one of a group of reporters who arrived on December 5, along with Keyes Beech of the *New York Times* and famed *Life Magazine* war photographer David Douglas Duncan. Higgins announced her intention to march out with the Marines, but General Smith ordered her flown out of the perimeter by nightfall. When a British reporter referred to the withdrawal as a "retreat," Smith pointed out that when surrounded there was no retreat, only an attack in a new direction. The press improved the remark into: "Retreat, hell, we're just attacking in a new direction," despite the fact that Oliver P. Smith was widely known to have never used a swear word in his life. In a show of things to come, a television team from CBS News photographed the evacuation of the casualties and interviewed General Smith and Lieutenant Colonel Murray. The footage was broadcast in the United States four days later.

Another visitor was Major General William H. Tunner, USAF, commander of the Combat Cargo Command. Tunner was a veteran of flying "The Hump" from India to China during World War II and had commanded much of the Berlin Airlift. He arrived with an offer to evacuate the rest of the troops now in Hagaru-ri. Smith turned him down with the reply that no man who was able-bodied would be evacuated.

That same day, Almond ordered Major General Soule, commander of the 3rd Infantry Division, to form a task force "to prepare the route of withdrawal of the 1st Marine Division if obstructed by explosives or whatnot, especially at the bridge site." The bridge in question was in Funchilin Pass. It had been destroyed shortly after the commencement of the Chinese attack and threatened to block the Marines' withdrawal if it could not be repaired. Soule put his assistant division commander, Brigadier General Armistead D. "Red" Mead in command of what was designated "Task Force Dog."

General Smith wanted to march out with his men, but was ordered by General Shepherd to fly to Koto-ri since the death or wounding of Smith (or worse, his capture) was a risk that could not be taken. The presence of seven Chinese divisions had been identified through prisoner interrogations: the PVA 58th, 59th, 60th, 76th, 79th, 80th, and 89th. The 77th and 78th Divisions were reported in the area, but were not yet confirmed. It was later confirmed after the battle that the PVA 26th Army, consisting of the 76th, 77th, and 78th Divisions, reinforced by the 88th Division from the PVA 30th Army, had moved down from the region between the Chosin Reservoir and the Yalu into positions on the east side of the MSR between Hagaru-ri and Koto-ri. Fortunately, the move had been delayed by the snowstorm that hit during the breakout from Yudam-ni, with the result that the Chinese reinforcements had not arrived in time to attack before the main breakout by the Marines began. The PVA 60th Division of the Ninth Army had also moved into positions south of Koto-ri and was preparing to defend Funchilin Pass, basing the defense on the dominant terrain feature, Hill 1081. Farther south, the PVA 89th Division was moving into position to attack Chinhung-ni.

At noon on December 5, Ray Murray assumed responsibility for the defense of Hagaru-ri, and sent his regiment to reinforce the thin lines held by 3/1 Battalion. The Chinese did not choose to test the strengthened defense, but at 2000 hours that evening an Air Force B-26 mistakenly dropped a stick of six 500-pound bombs close to Ridge's command tent. While the forward air controller could not communicate with the Air Force pilot due to crystal differences in their radios, a Marine F7F-3N night fighter from VMF(AW)-542 arrived overhead and promised to shoot down any Air Force bomber that might return.

The plan called for the 7th Marines to clean up East Hill on December 6 while the 7th Marines headed south along the MSR to Koto-ri. Close air support for the attack against the Chinese positions on East Hill would commence with an air strike at 0700 hours. Murray later described the regiment's attack against East Hill:

> I had been ordered to take a little hill, and I had Hal Roise do that job. When he got over there, he found about 200 Chinese in a mass, and he captured the whole crowd of them. So we had about 200 prisoners we had to take care of. A lot of them were in such bad shape that we left them there with some medical supplies, for the Chinese to come along and take care of them after we left.

Heavy air, artillery, and mortar preparation began at 0700 hours on December 6. Dog Company, led by Captain Samuel S. Smith, was first off at 0900 hours, starting a fight that would last until daylight on December 7. All three rifle companies of 2/5 Battalion and Charlie Company of 1/5 Battalion were involved. Estimates of enemy dead in the fighting ran as high as 800–1,000. While East Hill was never completely taken, the Chinese were pushed far enough back to keep them from interfering with the departure of the Marines from Hagaru-ri.

While fighting went on at Hagaru-ri, General Almond was occupied for most of the day with the visit of General J. Lawton Collins, the Army chief of staff. Collins and Almond dropped in at the command posts of the 7th and 3rd Infantry Divisions, but weather prevented them flying to Hagaru-ri or Koto-ri to visit with Smith. Collins left Almond's headquarters in Hamhung at nightfall for Tokyo while Almond noted happily in his diary: "Gen. Collins seemed completely satisfied with the operation of X Corps and apparently was much relieved in finding the situation well in hand."

While the Marines formed the overwhelming majority of the fighting troops involved in the withdrawal from Hagaru-ri, the survivors of Task Force Faith, along with other Army units that had been at Hagaru-ri and Hudong-ni, were formed into a provisional battalion of 490 men under the command of Army Lieutenant Colonel Anderson. As organized, the "battalion" actually was two very small battalions: the 3rd Battalion, 31st Infantry, under Major Carl Witte, and the 1st Battalion, 32nd Infantry, under Major Robert E. Jones, each composed of three very small rifle companies that were little more than platoons. Anderson's unit was attached to the 7th Marines, where it was called "31/7."

The 7th Marines had about 2,200 men on hand for the breakout to Koto-ri on December 6, which was approximately half the original strength that had come ashore at Wonsan in October: 2/7 Battalion, supported by tanks, was on the MSR as the advance guard; while Ray Davis' 1/7 Battalion was on the right between the Changjin River and the MSR; with Anderson's provisional Army battalion to the left; 3/7 Battalion was on the road as the rearguard.

At 0630 hours, the M-26 Pershing tanks of Company D, 1st Tank Battalion, led the shrunken 2/7 Battalion out of the perimeter through the south roadblock. The Marines ran into trouble from Chinese on the left side of the road almost immediately. As the morning fog burned off, close air support was called in. An airstrike hit the tent camp south of the perimeter that had been abandoned days earlier by the Army engineers and was now periodically occupied by Chinese seeking warmth and supplies. Barber's Fox Company and Dog-Easy Company pushed through the camp and the advance resumed at noon. On the right, barely a mile out of Hagaru-ri, Charlie 1/7 Company surprised an enemy platoon on the high ground southeast of the hamlet of Tonae-ri and killed nearly all the Chinese troops.

At 1400 hours, Smith received a message from Colonel Litzenberg that the move south was going well and decided it was time to move his command post to Koto-ri. After a 10-minute helicopter ride, Smith and his aide, former Marine Raider Major Martin J. "Stormy" Sexton, arrived at Koto-ri where Puller was waiting.

Meanwhile, 2/7 Battalion had run into more serious trouble a mile further down the road. Up in the hills, the "Ridgerunners" of 1/7 Battalion could see the enemy but 2/7 Battalion, on the road itself, could not. Fox Company with Dog-Easy Company and the two Army provisional battalions pushed through the Chinese roadblock at about 1500 hours. 1/7 Battalion continued their well-practiced tactic of hop-scotching by company from hilltop to hilltop on the right, as the Marines staggered through the snow and dragged themselves up the slope of the next hill. By sundown, the lead elements of the regiment were only 3 miles south of Hagaru-ri, with another 8 miles separating them from Koto-ri. Enemy resistance stiffened while at the same time aerial reconnaissance spotted Chinese columns coming in from the east, but Colonel Litzenberg decided to push on.

After advancing 2 more miles, 2/7 Battalion was stopped in Hellfire Valley by what appeared to be a solitary Chinese machine gun firing from the left. The problem was solved with a 90mm shot from a tank that landed a direct hit. Half a mile further on, the column was halted by a blown bridge. This was quickly repaired and the march resumed, only to be stopped by another blown bridge. Things got better at dawn on December 7, when air support arrived and scattered the Chinese. 2/7 Battalion experienced no more difficulty as the Marines marched the last few miles into Koto-ri.

Through all of this, 2/7 Battalion commander Lieutenant Colonel Lockwood, who was sick with severe bronchitis, sat in his jeep, numb. Early in the move, the battalion executive officer was wounded by a mortar fragment and put out of action. Major James F. Lawrence, Jr., the battalion S-3, became the *de facto* commander of 2/7 and led the advance through Hellfire Valley and on to Koto-ri. First Lieutenant Leo R. Ryan, the battalion adjutant, became alarmed by Lieutenant Colonel Lockwood's apathy and pressed the battalion surgeon and assistant surgeon, Lieutenants (jg) Laverne F. Peiffer and Stanley I. Wolf, to examine Lockwood. Neither was a psychiatrist, but they concluded he was suffering from a neurosis that left him unfit to command. When Colonel Litzenberg was informed of the situation after he arrived in Koto-ri, he confirmed Major Lawrence as the acting battalion commander for the rest of the withdrawal.

Things went even less well on the left flank and rear of the column through the night of December 6/7. The Army provisional battalion had fought itself out by nightfall and was replaced by 3/7 Battalion. At 2100 hours, Chinese troops got to within hand-grenade range of the trucks on the road.

George and Item Companies were deployed to push them back and a serious firefight developed. Sometime before dawn, 3/7 commander Lieutenant Colonel William Harris, son of Marine Air Wing commander Major General Field Harris, disappeared after being last seen walking down the road with two rifles slung over his shoulder. A later search found no body and it was presumed he had been taken prisoner. Major Warren Morris, 1/7 executive officer, took command of 3/7 Battalion and the unit reached Koto-ri at 0700 hours on December 7. Chinese prisoners taken during the fight were identified as being from the 76th and 77th Divisions of the PVA 26th Army.

At 0900 hours on December 7, both 2/7 and 3/7 Battalions were ordered to move north again and set up blocking positions on both sides of the road between Koto-ri and Hill 1182 to ease the passage of the division train. As they made their way up the road, the Marines of 2/7 Battalion picked up 22 Royal Marine survivors who had been hiding in a Korean house since Task Force Drysdale had moved through the valley on November 29. A VMO-6 pilot had spotted them three days earlier when he spotted the letters "H-E-L-P" stamped in the snow and had dropped rations and medical supplies.

Division Train No. 1, which the 7th Marines were to have shepherded, had not gotten out of Hagaru-ri until 1600 hours on December 6. When the train was a bit more than a mile out of Hagaru-ri, the Chinese came down out of the hills and attacked the column, thinking there would be easy pickings. They were wrong. Major Francis "Fox" Parry's artillerymen of 3/11 Battalion fought as infantry and held them off. A mile further down the road, the fight was repeated, though this time 3/11's howitzers were unlimbered. Firing canister at point blank range, the Marines guessed optimistically that they had killed or wounded all but about 50 of the estimated 500–800 attackers.

There was more fighting along the road throughout the night. The members of the division band demonstrated their skill as machine gunners shortly after midnight, when the division headquarters was attacked. The 160 prisoners of war being escorted by the military police company got caught in the crossfire, where most were killed. F4U-5N night hecklers from VMF(N) 513 attacked enemy positions identified with tracer fire. At dawn the Corsairs from VMF-312 arrived on station and resolved the situation, with the Chinese force scattered after several napalm tanks were dropped. The column moved into Hellfire Valley, where they found bodies still lying about and many vehicles from Task Force Drysdale's fight, several of which were started up after a few minutes' attention. At 1000 hours on December 7, Division Train No. 1 entered Koto-ri.

Back in Hagaru-ri, Division Train No. 2, which had been unable to move onto the road until Division Train No. 1 had cleared, did not get moving until well after dark on December 6. At midnight, the head of the train was still only a few hundred yards out of the perimeter. Lieutenant Colonel Milne, the train commander, asked for infantry help and 3/5 Battalion was detailed to the job as two companies moved forward to provide cover. Nothing further happened until dawn on December 7, when the train was able to move on under air cover.

In Hagaru-ri, the Marine engineers had set explosives that destroyed everything that could be blown up while they set fire to the rest. Because of the traffic jam south, 1/5 and 34/1 Battalions and 41 Commando, were unable to leave until the morning of December 7, engaging with Chinese who were more interested in looting what was left while 2/5 Battalion finally came down off East Hill and assumed the rearguard position.

In all, 10,000 Marines and soldiers, with 1,000 vehicles, marched 11 miles from Hagaru-ri to Koto-ri through enemy-controlled country in 38 hours. Losses were 103 dead, 7 missing, and 506 wounded.

The Koto-ri airstrip had been improved so that TBM-3R utility transports could operate. The TBMs could carry nine passengers or wounded. Along with the OY-2 Sentinels and HO3S-1 helicopters of VMO-6, 2,000 casualties were evacuated on December 7, and 225 more the next day.

The march south was set to resume at first light on Friday, December 8. The rifle companies would leap-frog along the high ground on each side of the road while the heavily laden vehicles of the division trains made their way toward Funchilin Pass and then down to Chinhung-ni, where Task Force Dog of the 3rd Infantry Division manned the outer defenses of the Hamhung–Hungnam perimeter.

However, the road was not yet open. The Chinese had blown a 24-foot gap in the critical bridge halfway down the pass, where water from the Chosin Reservoir moved through a tunnel into four giant pipes called "penstocks." The bridge crossed the penstocks at a point where the road clung to an almost sheer cliff. The gap would somehow have to be bridged if the Marines were to get their tanks, artillery, and vehicles down the pass.

Division engineer Lieutenant Colonel Partridge had made an aerial reconnaissance of the situation on December 6 and determined the gap could be spanned by four sections of an M-2 steel "Treadway" bridge. While he had no such bridge sections, fortuitously there was a detachment of the Treadway Bridge Company from the Army's 58th Engineer Battalion at Koto-ri, with two Brockway trucks that could carry the bridge sections if they could be air-delivered.

A Treadway bridge is composed of four sections, each of which weighs 4,000 pounds. There were eight sections of bridge located in Japan; these were trucked to Tachikawa AFB outside Tokyo on December 6. Eight C-119s flew up from Ashiya AFB to pick up the sections and returned to Ashiya, where the Army 2348th Quartermaster Airborne Supply and Packaging Company packed the sections for airdrop with a

48-foot cargo parachute on each end; they were then loaded on the C-119s, one section per plane. The C-119s then flew to Yonpo, where one section was test-dropped successfully, landing dented but useable.

At 0930 hours, December 7, the eight C-119s arrived over the drop zone outside Koto-ri, which was marked with orange panels. Aboard each transport, all the ropes holding each bridge section had been cut but one, which remained in place to prevent a premature drop. It would be cut with an axe as one very small parachute, spring-loaded to throw it into the slipstream, would then deploy a larger parachute that actually pulled the bridge section out. The spring was tripped by the crew chief on the pilot's command while another crew member cut the last rope. The whole operation took five seconds, which was critical if the sections were to land successfully and safely.

The first section was dropped successfully on target. The rest of the C-119s followed, unloading the bridge sections on order from the engineers on the ground. Five sections were dropped successfully, while the sixth fell into Chinese hands. The seventh was damaged when it hit the ground.

The last C-119 was flown by Captain Jim Inks. As he approached the drop zone, he gave the order to his crew chief, who pulled the spring release while the assistant crew chief cut the last rope. "Unfortunately, that pilot chute mechanism failed to work, and we were past the drop zone with our load still aboard," Inks later recalled. The situation inside the plane rapidly went from bad to worse. "We were in a box canyon with a loose load in the cargo compartment, and it was doubtful if I had the power to climb the overloaded aircraft over the mountains to get out of there." The canyon wasn't wide enough for a 180-degree turn. Inks was sure he could dump the load if he climbed steeply, which would allow them to escape the canyon, but this section of the bridge was vital if the entire thing was to be successfully assembled. Without the drag chutes, there was the possibility the bridge section would hang up in the cargo compartment. Inks ordered the cargo crew to stay forward of the bridge section, while he, his co-pilot and the navigator looked for a way out. "The navigator picked a canyon coming in from the east that he thought would continue downgrade, but as soon as we turned into it, we realized it was upgrade and pretty steep." Meanwhile, the cargo crew managed to get a rope across the 2,500-pound section and secure it somewhat. "We were in a hell of a spot."

The C-119 was less than 200 feet above the rapidly rising canyon floor, when suddenly Inks spotted another canyon beyond the ridge to the left. "We skidded into it not ten feet from the rocks and started back toward the main canyon we had just left." Inks managed to bring the C-119 around and was headed toward the drop zone again. "The crew chief managed to hit the bridge with a sledge hammer that started it on its way out, it didn't hang up, and our span of the bridge was delivered fifteen minutes late."

By late afternoon, the spans had been loaded aboard the Brockway trucks. They would be moved down Funchilin Pass the next morning.

According to the plan, the first objective for the 7th Marines would be the high ground on the right of the road for a distance of about 1.5 miles. The 5th Marines would then pass through and take and hold the high ground for the next mile. Puller's 1st Marines were to remain in Koto-ri until the division and regimental trains had cleared and would then relieve the other two regiments on their high ground positions so the two division trains could pass on into Funchilin Pass. The two regiments would then move down the pass toward Chinhung-ni. The artillery would displace continually from one battery firing position to another, though for much of the time the guns would be limbered up and unavailable to provide support. Thus, heavy reliance for fire support would be placed on the Corsairs. Tanks would follow at the end of the vehicle column so there would be no chance of a crippled tank blocking the road.

Task Force Dog, consisting of the 3rd Battalion, 7th Infantry, liberally reinforced with tanks and artillery, started north on December 7, passing through Sudong. By late afternoon the Army unit had reached Chinhung-ni, where the troops relieved 1/1 Battalion, which moved into an assembly area several miles north of Chinhung-ni where they would attack Hill 1081, the major Chinese position in the pass.

The moves from Koto-ri and Chinhung-ni were made in a swirling snowstorm on the morning of December 8. 1/1 Battalion started their 6-mile march up the MSR to the line of departure at 0200 hours. Charlie Company was assigned to take Hill 891, the southwestern nose of Hill 1081, holding it while the other companies continued the attack. Able Company's assignment was to attack east of the road up to the summit of Hill 1081 while Baker Company moved along the slope between Able Company and the road. Charlie Company took their objective by dawn. Marine 81mm mortars and 4.2-inch mortars, with Army M16 and M19 self-propelled antiaircraft guns from Company B, 50th Antiaircraft Artillery (Automatic Weapons) Battalion were positioned on Hill 891 to support the assault on Hill 1081.

Able Company jumped off at 1000 hours, the Marines climbing the snow-covered icy ridge leading to Hill 1081's summit, as Baker Company moved out along the wooded western slope, meeting scattered resistance. They were stopped momentarily by two machine guns that they took out with their own machine guns and mortars to cover a platoon that moved around in a right hook. They then came across a bunker complex and took it in a savage fight that saw three Marines killed and one wounded.

Meeting no enemy, Able Company were impeded only by the narrow icy ridgeline, which forced them to move in dangerous single file. The Marines glimpsed through the storm a strongly bunkered Chinese position situated on a knob between them and the crest. The 2nd Platoon went left while the 1st Platoon went right and Captain Barrow led the 3rd Platoon in a frontal attack up the center. The Marines counted 60 Chinese dead to their own 10 killed and 11 wounded when the fight concluded. The snowstorm finally ended in the last light of day, giving way to a clear night. A midnight counterattack by a Chinese platoon saw the Marines kill 18 attackers.

The 7th Marines came out of Koto-ri on schedule at 0800 hours on December 8. Counting the Army provisional battalion there were four battalions, two to clear each side of the road while one advanced along the MSR, followed by the regimental train and the reserve battalion. Major Morris' 3/7 Battalion was assigned to take Hill 1328 on the right of the road, and going was slow. By mid-morning, an impatient Litzenberg urged him to commit his reserve company. Morris' response reveals just how heavy Marine losses had been: "All three companies are up there – 50 men from George Company, 50 men from How, 30 men from Item. That's it." Shortly after noon the regimental reserve, Lawrence's 2nd Battalion, moved to assist Morris. By nightfall, the two severely understrength battalions had joined, but Hill 1328 was still in enemy hands.

On the left, the provisional Army battalion jumped off on time and, with the help of two Marine tanks, moved along against light resistance. In two jumps, the soldiers reached Hill 1457 where they dug in for the night. Later, the position was raked by Chinese automatic fire; in a brief, nasty action, 12 enemy were killed at a cost of one soldier killed and four wounded.

Lieutenant Colonel Frederick Dowsett, the regimental executive officer, was shot through the ankle on December 7, which resulted in 1/7 Battalion commander Ray Davis replacing him while Major Sawyer assumed command of 1/7, which was ordered to move a mile down the road and wait for 3/7 Battalion to come up on his right flank. 1/7 now had its own fight.

Lieutenant Lee's lead platoon came under fire from Hill 1304 and Lee was again wounded, severely enough that he was carried down off the hill to join the rest of the wounded in the trucks. Baker Company attacked the high ground just left of the MSR while Able and Charlie Companies moved to the right against the hill. Caught in a crossfire, Baker Company's commander, First Lieutenant Joe Kurcaba, was killed and two of the platoon leaders were wounded. First Lieutenant William W. "Woody" Taylor took command under fire and achieved the objective by nightfall. Meanwhile, Able and Charlie Companies took Hill 1304 without much trouble. As night fell, vehicle movement along the MSR halted.

The 5th Marines were unable to move out of Koto-ri until noon on December 8, with 1/5 Battalion in the lead. Baker 1/5 and Charlie 1/5 Companies were ordered to take Hill 1457. With support from the Army provisional battalion, the soldiers and Marines pushed the Chinese off the high ground by 1500 hours. As nightfall closed in, Baker and Charlie Companies, with the Army troops, formed a perimeter for the night.

Meanwhile, the major problem 1/2 and 1/3 Battalions faced was not the Chinese, but the flood of civilian refugees that moved down the road from the north. They could not be allowed inside the perimeter because of the likelihood they had been infiltrated by the Chinese. During the bitterly cold night, Navy doctors and corpsmen delivered two babies. The refugees were forced to wait outside the lines until the Marines had departed from Koto-ri. They then followed behind until they reached Hamhung.

Before he departed Koto-ri, General Smith, always conscious of his dead, attended a mass funeral: 117 bodies, mostly Marines but including some soldiers and Royal Marines, were buried in a mass grave in what had been an artillery command post, scraped more deeply into the frozen ground by a bulldozer. Robert Gault of the Graves Registration Section, remembered:

> We had a chaplain of each faith, and the fellows had made a big hole and laid the fellows out in rows the best we could and put ponchos over them. As soon as each chaplain had said his little bit for the fellows, we would cover them up and close them in. Everyone was given a very fine burial, I think, under the circumstances. It wasn't like the one back at Inchon, where we had crosses for the boys painted white and all the flowers that we could get for them. It wasn't like that, no. It was one where we were just out in a field, but it was one with more true heart.

More snow fell overnight. Saturday, December 9, dawned bright, clear, and cold. South of Funchilin Pass, the Marines of 1/1 Battalion prepared to assault Hill 1081. Able Company attacked in a column of platoons behind a thunderous preparation by close air strikes, artillery, and mortars. The lead 1st Platoon was hard hit as it moved forward by rushes, and stopped 200 yards from the crest. Under cover of air strikes by four Corsairs and the company's 60mm mortars, the 2nd and 3rd Platoons moved forward; by mid-afternoon the Marines held the high ground commanding Funchilin Pass. The cost of the two-day battle was almost half the company. Baker Company had started up the hill with 223 Marines and was now down to 111. Following the battle 530 enemy dead were counted.

The 7th Marines resumed the attack and by midday the rest of Hill 1304 was taken. Charlie Company and a platoon from Baker Company moved down the road and secured the bridge. The rest of Baker Company followed behind and overran an enemy position manned by 50 Chinese who were so frozen they surrendered without resistance.

The Army Brockway trucks with their precious cargo of bridge sections had been held back in Koto-ri until first light on December 9, when Lieutenant Colonel Partridge considered the MSR secure enough to move them forward. At the bridge site, everything worked like a well-practiced jigsaw puzzle as the Army and Marine engineers rebuilt the abutments with sandbags and timbers. By noon, the first Brockway truck laid the steel treadways and plywood deck panels. Installation of the four sections was completed in just over three hours. At 1530 hours, Partridge informed Lieutenant Colonel Banks that Division Train No. 1 could move down the pass and the first vehicles crossed the bridge at 1800 hours. Vehicles continued to pass over the bridge all night long as Marine infantry kept the Chinese at a distance and captured 60 prisoners.

The leading elements of the column reached Chinhung-ni at the bottom of the pass at 0245 hours on Sunday, December 10. The 7th Marines followed Division Train No. 1 down the pass. At the top of the pass, 1/3 Battalion moved out of Koto-ri and relieved 3/7 Battalion on Hill 1328, where a fight broke out with 350 Chinese troops attempting to retake the position. At 1030 hours, General Smith closed his Koto-ri command post and flew to Hungnam.

The remainder of the 1st Marines moved out of Koto-ri that afternoon. Milne's tanks, along with the tank company from 31st Infantry, followed behind. As the last Americans left Koto-ri, the Army 92nd Field Artillery, firing from Chinhung-ni, shelled the town with its long-range 155mm guns. At the tail of the column, there was confusion as Korean refugees pressed close and the tankers fired warning shots to make them keep back. Panic developed among the refugees as the rumor spread that the Marines were shooting at them. The tanks passed on down the road, protected on both sides by Marines in the hills.

Lieutenant Colonel Ridge pulled his companies off Hill 1304 and the high ground on the opposite side of the MSR at about 2100 hours. The battalion was the last major unit to descend the pass, moving behind the provisional Army battalion and the detachment of the 185th Engineers. The tanks were at the rear with no infantry protection except the lightweight Division Reconnaissance Company mounted in jeeps. By then, both division trains, all of the 5th Marines, and most of the 11th Marines had reached Chinhung-ni.

Beyond Chinhung-ni, guerrillas were reported to be active in the vicinity of Sudong, but the division trains and both infantry regiments passed through without interference. Around 0100 hours, when the vehicles of the 1st Marines reached the town, swarms of Chinese suddenly came out of the houses, firing burp guns and throwing grenades. Truck drivers and other support troops, both Army and Marine, fought a wild, shapeless action. Lieutenant Colonel John U. D. Page, an Army artillery officer, took charge and was killed; he would receive a posthumous Medal of Honor for his leadership. Lieutenant Colonel Waldon C. Winston, an Army motor transport officer then took command and led a successful defense through the rest of the night until the Chinese retreated at dawn. The Marines and soldiers lost nine trucks and a personnel carrier, with eight men killed and 21 wounded.

In the meantime, at around midnight, the 40 tanks descending the narrow, icy-slick road of Funchilin Pass ran into trouble. When they were a mile short of the Treadway bridge, the brakes of one of the rear tanks froze. The thirty tanks ahead continued without it, but the immobile tank now blocked the way for eight tanks behind. With the refugees close behind, First Lieutenant Ernest C. Hargett's reconnaissance platoon was ordered to guard the nine tanks. Moments later, five Chinese soldiers stepped out of the crowd of refugees and one called in English for Harget to surrender. Covered by Corporal George A. J. Amyotte's BAR, Hargett, approached cautiously. The English-speaker stepped aside while the others pulled out burp guns and threw grenades, one of which wounded Hargett. While Amyotte cut down the five, others materialized on the road and the hill. Hargett pulled back and the last tank was lost to the Chinese. While all this was happening, the crew of the tank blocking the road had succeeded in freeing the frozen brakes. However, the crews of the remaining seven tanks had departed, leaving the hatches open. A Marine who had never driven a tank managed to bring one out. The night's adventure cost two men killed and 12 wounded.

The engineers at the Treadway bridge thought the two tanks and Hargett's platoon were the last of the force, and blew up the bridge after they passed. Private First Class Robert D. DeMott of Hargett's platoon had been blown off the road by an explosive charge and knocked out. When he regained consciousness, he joined the refugees just as the bridge was blown. DeMott and the refugees made their way on foot through the gatehouse above the penstocks and continued on down the pass.

At 0300 hours, Able Company received orders to withdraw from Hill 1081. At 1300 hours on December 11, the last units passed through Chinhung-ni. By 1730 hours they had passed through Majon-dong. The last unit reached the Hamhung–Hungnam assembly areas at 2100 hours, where a tent camp waited for them. Chow lines were open, with hot meals continuously served. The weather on the coast seemed almost balmy after the unrelieved sub-zero temperatures of the plateau.

As the 1st Marine Division "attacked in a different direction" between December 8 and 11, casualties came to 75 dead, 16 missing, and 256 wounded, for a total of 347.

General Smith had believed the 1st Marine Division would be given a defensive sector to the south and southwest of Hungnam as late as Saturday, December 9. On December 8, Deputy Chief of Staff Colonel Snedeker issued tentative orders for the Marines to set up a defensive line at Chigyong, with the 5th and 7th Marines ordered to defend Yonpo airfield. However, on December 9 General Almond received orders from MacArthur to redeploy X Corps to South Korea. Smith learned the division would load out immediately on arrival at Hungnam, since Almond regarded the Marines as only marginally combat effective after the losses they suffered in the reservoir. The 7th Infantry Division, which had only lost a complete regimental combat team, was thought to be in better condition. The 3rd Infantry Division was considered to be in the best condition of any X Corps unit, and Almond had decided that after the Marines had passed through the Hamhung-Hungnam perimeter, they would be relieved from active combat and evacuated. The Marines were to be followed by the 7th Infantry Division, while the 3rd Infantry Division held the port as rearguard.

CHAPTER ELEVEN

EVACUATION

The Hungnam-Hamhung defensive perimeter consisted of a 20-mile main line of resistance (MLR) arcing in a semicircle from north of Hungnam around to include Yonpo in the south. A lightly held outpost line of resistance was established beyond the MLR. The northern sector was assigned to Major General Kim Pak Ip's ROK I Corps which began moving into the positions on December 8 after a three-day evacuation from Songjin by LSTs, merchant ships, and the attack transport USS *Noble* (APA 218). Next in line was the 7th Infantry Division with its two surviving infantry regiments, with the 3rd Infantry Division holding in front of Hamhung to the south near Yonpo, where the southern anchor was held by the 1st Korean Marine Corps Regiment with the assignment of defending the airfield.

On December 11, General MacArthur finally managed to visit the front for the first time since the Chinese attacks in North Korea had commenced 17 days earlier when he flew in to Yonpo and met with General Almond to approve the X Corps evacuation plan, complimenting Almond for the achievement of having "tied down" six to eight Chinese divisions that would otherwise be attacking the Eighth Army. Protective of his "boys" as always, regardless of their culpability in the disaster, he told Almond he could return to GHQ as chief of staff, or remain in command of X Corps. Almond stated he wished to stay with X Corps even if it became part of the Eighth Army. Almond's retention as commander of X Corps would create problems for General Matthew Ridgway when he assumed command of the Eighth Army and had to deal with a subordinate commander more closely connected to the top command than he was. The problem would continue until MacArthur himself left the Far East permanently.

The survivors of the 7th Marines boarded MSTS *Daniel I. Sultan* during the afternoon and evening of December 11. The next day the 5th Marines boarded ship, followed by the 1st Marines on December 13. The ships of Task Force 90 would have to make a second, even a third turn-around, to lift the entire force of three divisions. The docks at Hungnam could only berth seven ships at a time, so most troops had to board the ships in the harbor via landing craft. The division's 1,400 vehicles that had been brought down from the Chosin plateau would go out in LSTs which could be beached at Green Beaches One and Two in groups of 11 ships simultaneously.

Marine aviators flew more than 1,300 sorties in support of their comrades on the ground between December 1 and 11, with 254 flown by VMF-323 "Death Rattlers," aboard the USS *Badoeng Strait* and 122 by VMF-214 "Black Sheep," after they re-embarked aboard the late-arriving USS *Sicily* on December 7. VMF-214's Sergeant Ritter remembered that the carrier was almost colder than had been the case ashore, due to poor ventilation and heating on the small carrier. The shore-based squadrons, VMF-312 and VMF-311 at Wonsan, and VMF(AW)-542 and VMF(N)-513 at Yonpo flew the remainder of the sorties. VMF-311, the first Marine squadron equipped with Grumman F9F-2 Panthers, arrived at Yonpo on December 10 and was able to fly four days of air support missions before evacuating back to Pusan. The shore-based squadrons of the 1st Marine Aircraft Wing moved back to K-1 airfield near Pusan, which put them close to Pusan's port facilities for resupply, while the carrier-based squadrons remained aboard the CVEs, to strike advancing enemy troops if the UN forces were in fact forced back to the old Pusan Perimeter, as many now believed would happen.

Flight conditions ashore and afloat were difficult in the extreme for the pilots, who had poor charts, few navigational aids, and problematic radios. The primitive conditions and icy runways at Yonpo created danger for aircraft taxiing to and from the runway. Aboard the CVEs, ice-glazed decks and tumultuous seas made operations potentially deadly. Flight deck crews on *Badoeng Strait* scraped off 3 inches of ice and snow from the deck three mornings running to allow aircraft to be launched. VMF-214's Sergeant Ritter remembered the difficulty of loading the Blacksheep Corsairs with ordnance while the ship rolled through a 30-degree arc and took green seas over her bow. *Sicily* had to stop flight operations in the face of heavy seas and 68-knot winds on December 10. Additionally, losses increased dramatically. Three night fighters went down between December 7 and 10, and there were other crashes ashore and afloat. A pilot who ditched at sea in the arctic waters of the Sea of Japan had only 10–15 minutes before hypothermia set in, even wearing the "poopy suit." Two VMF-312 pilots almost out of gas, arrived over Yonpo airfield to find it closed by a snowstorm; they managed to save themselves and their planes by landing on the *Badoeng Strait*. With a strenuous effort by all hands, aircraft availability at Yonpo was 67 percent and a remarkable 90 percent aboard the carriers. Nearly half the missions flown were not for the Marines but for someone else. A total of 3,703 sorties in 1,053 missions controlled by tactical air control parties were flown between October 26 and December 11. 599 were close air support: 468 for the 1st Marine Division, 67 for the ROKs, 56 for the 7th Infantry Division – mostly in support of Task Force Faith – and eight for the 3rd Infantry Division. Eight Marine aviators were killed or died of wounds while three were wounded, with four missing in action.

The twin-engine R4Ds and four-engine R5Ds from VMR-152 had supplemented General Tunner's Combat Cargo Command in the aerial resupply and casualty evacuation from Hagaru-ri, while the squadron that the 1st Marine Division considered its own private air force – Major Gottschalk's VMO-6, with 10 light fixed-wing aircraft and nine helicopters – racked up 1,544 flights between October 28 and December 15. Of these, 457 had been reconnaissance, 220 casualty evacuation, and 11 search and rescue.

On Sunday, December 10, Wonsan ceased operations as a port. Between December 1 and 9, 3,834 Army troops, 7,009 Korean civilians, 1,146 vehicles, and 10,013 tons of bulk cargo were evacuated.

The 1st Division's sorely-missed assistant commander, General Craig, returned on December 11 from emergency leave and was sent south to Pusan to arrange for the division's arrival.

On December 12, General Almond brought his generals together for a conference and a dinner at X Corps headquarters. Smith, Barr, and Soule and Fleet Marines Pacific Commander General Lemuel Shepherd listened silently to Almond's briefing on the evacuation, then learned the real purpose of the dinner was to celebrate Almond's 58th birthday. General Ruffner, Almond's chief of staff, eulogized his commander, stating that never in the US Army's history had a corps accomplished so much in such a short time. Afterwards, General Shepherd added a few complimentary remarks.

Army artillery interdiction and naval gunfire that included 162 16-inch shells fired by the recently-arrived USS *Missouri* (BB-63), in addition to bombing by Air Force, Navy, and Marine aircraft provided cover for the evacuation. On December 13, the Marines were ready to sail. At 1500 hours, General Smith closed his command post ashore and boarded the USS *Bayfield* (APA 33). Before departing Hungnam, he attended a memorial service for the dead at the cemetery officiated by Protestant, Catholic, and Jewish chaplains. It would not be until the turn of the century before an agreement between the US and North Korea allowed disinterment of the dead at Hungnam and the Chosin reservoir.

The 3rd and 7th Infantry Divisions reported only light probing of the perimeter and minor patrol actions. December 14 saw the last of the land-based Marine fighter-bombers depart Yonpo for Pusan.

With General Smith aboard, USS *Bayfield* set sail for Pusan on December 15 at 1030 hours. 22,215 Marines and their equipment were aboard four troop transports, 16 LSTs, an assault cargo ship, and seven merchant ships. It took a day to return to Pusan, where the Marines landed and returned to their old camp at the "bean patch" outside Masan. General Smith moved into a Japanese-style house. "The toilet works, but the radiators are not yet in operation," he noted in his log.

Airlift from Yonpo continued until December 17 when the field was closed and a temporary field, able to handle C-47s, opened in the harbor area. The only Marine units still ashore at Hungnam were an air naval gunfire liaison company, a reinforced shore party company, and one-and-a-half companies of the 1st Amphibian Tractor Battalion, manning 88 LVT amphibious tractors to assist in the final evacuation. General Smith had resisted the detachment of these tractors, since they were irreplaceable. The Navy earmarked several LSDs to lift off the tractor companies and their vehicles.

The last of the ROK Army units sailed away on December 18. General Almond closed his command post in Hungnam on December 19 and joined Admiral Doyle in the TF 90 flagship, USS *Mount McKinley*. By December 20 all of the 7th Infantry Division was embarked. On the morning of December 24, the 3rd Infantry Division was lifted off seven beaches by LCVPs and transported to the landing ships. The final evacuation was marred by the premature explosion of an ammunition dump, set off by an Army captain, which killed a Marine lieutenant and a Navy seaman and wounded 34 others. Three Marine LVTs were lost in the explosion.

Between December 11 and 24, 105,000 US and ROK troops, 91,000 Korean refugees, 17,500 vehicles, and 350,000 tons of supplies were lifted out of Hungnam in 193 shiploads by 109 ships, with some ships making two or even three trips.

The carrier USS *Valley Forge* (CV-45) returned to station on December 23 to join USS *Leyte* and provide coverage for the final movement. By mid-afternoon December 24, all beaches were clear. At 1530 hours, the waterfront at Hungnam exploded as prepared explosive charges went off, destroying ammunition, POL, and other supplies that could not be lifted off. Aboard the *Mount McKinley*, the embarked brass enjoyed the show before the command ship sailed off. More naval shells had been fired at Hungnam than at Inchon. Navy records for the period December 7–24 list 162 16-inch rounds from the battleship *Missouri*, 2,932 8-inch, 18,637 5-inch, and 71 3-inch shells plus 1,462 5-inch rockets.

On December 31, 1950, the commandant of the Marine Corps reported to the Secretary of the Navy that the Marines had incurred 4,418 casualties between October 26 and December 15. 718 were killed in action or died of wounds, 3,508 were wounded, and 192 were missing in action. There were an additional 7,313 non-battle casualties, almost all due to frostbite, which amounted to one-third of the division's strength. The three infantry regiments had arrived at the "bean patch" at approximately half-strength, having taken the lion's share of the casualties. Some rifle companies had lost as much as 70–75% of their authorized personnel.

The Marines fought at least nine and possibly all 12 PVA divisions, which had each entered combat with an effective strength of about 7,500, or approximately 90,000 troops total. Peng's chief of staff said the Ninth Army Group had crossed the Yalu with 150,000 troops; however, not all of these had come against the Marines. The official estimate of Chinese losses at Chosin is 15,000 killed and 7,500 wounded by the ground forces and an additional 10,000 killed and 5,000 wounded by Marine air power.

By the time the Marines evacuated Hungnam, Song Shilun's Ninth Army Group in the hills above Hamhung probably numbered at most no more than 35,000. The Chinese forces occupied Hamhung on December 17. On December 27 they entered Hungnam. Chairman Mao sent the Ninth Army Group a citation: "You completed a great strategic task under extremely difficult conditions." The assaults against Yudam-ni and Hagaru-ri had nearly destroyed the 20th and 27th PVA Armies. Most of the Chinese fighting from Koto-ri on was taken up by the PVA 26th Army.

Zhang Renchu, commander of the PVA 26th Army lamented:

> A shortage of transportation and escort personnel makes it impossible to accomplish the mission of supplying the troops. As a result, our soldiers frequently starve. From now on, the organization of our rear service units should be improved.
>
> The troops were hungry. They ate cold food, and some had only a few potatoes in two days. They were unable to maintain the physical strength for combat; the wounded personnel could not be evacuated. The fire power of our entire army was basically inadequate. When we used our guns sometimes the shells were duds.

Zhang Yixiang, commander of the PVA 20th Army, equally bitter, recognized that communications limitations had caused a tactical rigidity:

> Our signal communication was not up to standard. For example, it took more than two days to receive instructions from higher-level units. Rapid changes of the enemy's situation and the slow motion of our signal communications caused us to lose our opportunities in combat and made the instructions of the high level units ineffective... We succeeded in the separation and encirclement of the enemy, but we failed to annihilate the enemy one by one. For example, the failure to annihilate the enemy at Yudam-ni made it impossible to annihilate the enemy at Hagaru-ri.

Zhang Yixiang reported 100 deaths from tetanus due to poor medical care in the PVA 26th Army. Hundreds more were sick or dead from typhus or malnutrition in addition to losses from frostbite. The 26th Army reported that 90 percent of the command suffered from frostbite. Peng Deqing, commander of the PVA 27th Army, reported 10,000 non-combat casualties in his four divisions:

> The troops did not have enough food. They did not have enough houses to live in. They could not stand the bitter cold, which was the reason for the excessive non-combat reduction in personnel. The weapons were not used effectively. When the fighters bivouacked in snow-covered ground during combat, their feet, socks, and hands were frozen together in one ice ball. They could not unscrew the caps on the hand grenades. The fuses would not ignite. Their hands were not supple. The mortar tubes shrank on account of the cold; 70 percent of the shells failed to detonate. Skin from the hands was stuck on the shells and the mortar tubes.

In the best Chinese Communist tradition of self-criticism, Peng Deqing deplored his heavy casualties as caused by tactical errors:

> We underestimated the enemy so we distributed the strength wrong, and consequently the higher echelons were over-dispersed while the lower echelon units were over-concentrated. During one movement, the distance between the three leading divisions was very long, while the formations of the battalions, companies, and units of lower levels were too close, and the troops were unable to deploy.

Zhang Renchu, commander of the PVA 26th Army, found reason to admire the fire support coordination of the Marines:

> The coordination between the enemy infantry, tanks, artillery, and airplanes is surprisingly close. Besides using heavy weapons for the depth, the enemy carries with him automatic light firearms which, coordinated with rockets, launchers, and recoilless guns are disposed at the front line. The characteristic of their employment is to stay quietly under cover and open fire suddenly when we come to between 70 and 100 meters from them, making it difficult for our troops to deploy and thus inflicting casualties upon us.

In a December 17 message to People's Volunteer Army commander Peng Dehuai, Mao acknowledged that as many as 40,000 men had perished due to cold weather, lack of supplies, and the fierce fighting. "The Central Committee cherishes the memory of those lost."

Peng Dehuai requested 60,000 replacements. The Ninth Army Group was unable to re-enter combat until April 1951. Had these units been able to participate in the heavy fighting during the first five months of 1951, they might have provided the necessary weight of force to break the Eighth Army and win the war in Korea for the Chinese. The Marine stand at Chosin had not only saved the division, but had saved the entire UN position in Korea. As a result, by May 1951 the UN forces in Korea were able to stabilize their position at roughly the 38th Parallel. In June 1951, negotiations began between the UN forces and the Chinese and North Koreans, a process that would result in an armistice being signed two years later in June 1953, with the forces in roughly the positions they had been in since May 1951.

On Christmas Eve, Olin Beall, commander of the 1st Motor Transport Battalion, wrote to his old commanding officer, General Holland M. "Howlin' Mad" Smith, now retired and living in La Jolla, California:

> I just thought that you might like to have a few words on first-hand information from an ole friend and an ole timer. I've seen some brave men along that road and in these hills, men with feet frozen, men with hands frozen still helping their buddies, men riding trucks with frozen feet but fighting from the trucks. I think the fight of our 5th and 7th Regts, from Yudam-ni in to Hagaru-ri was a thing that will never be equaled. Litzenberg and Murray showed real command ability and at no time did any of us doubt their judgment. The night we came out of Koto-ri, the temperature was 27 below zero and still we fought. Men froze to their socks, blood froze in wounds almost instantaneously, one's fingers were numb inside heavy mittens. Still men took them off to give to a wounded buddy. We are now in Masan in South Korea re-outfitting, training and getting some new equipment. I'm very, very proud to be able to say that in all our operation my Battalion has lost only 27 trucks and every one of these was an actual battle casualty, so I think my boys did pretty good. Oliver P. Smith and Craig make a fine team and we'd stand by them thru hell and high water.

An epidemic of flu and bronchitis swept through the Masan

tent camp. The Marines were treated with an early antibiotic, Aureomycin, taken orally in capsules the size of the first joint of a man's finger. The division rebuilt itself rapidly. Replacements arrived. Some units found themselves with an "overage" of vehicles and weapons that had to be returned to the Army.

A refrigerator ship brought in a planned double ration of Christmas turkey. Through some mix-up a second shipment of turkey and accessories arrived, so there were four days of holiday menu for the Marines. Working parties pretending to be patrols went up into the surrounding hills to cut pine trees to line the company streets of the tent camp. C-ration cans and crinkled tinfoil from cigarette packages made do for ornaments. Choirs were formed to sing Christmas carols. Various delegations of South Koreans, civilian and military, arrived at the camp with gifts and musical shows.

On Christmas Day, General Smith was pleased to note that attendance at church services was excellent. Afterward he held open house for his special staff, general staff, and more senior unit commanders. First Lieutenant James B. Soper, serving at Sasebo, Japan, had sent the general's mess a case of Old Grand-Dad bourbon. Mixed with powdered milk, sugar, and Korean eggs it made a passable eggnog.

An open house was also held for officers of the 1st and 5th Marines by Colonel Drysdale's 41 Commando, with a supply of mincemeat pies and Scotch whiskey sent by the British embassy in Tokyo.

On December 27, General Smith reported his division's losses since the Inchon landing on September 15: 969 killed in action; 163 died of wounds; 199 missing in action; 5,517 wounded in action; total 6,848. There were 8,900 non-battle casualties and 7,916 prisoners of war were taken.

Since the battles in Korea in 1950, there has never been any move to abolish the United States Marine Corps. The Marines not only saved their honor and reputation during the first six months of war in Korea, they saved themselves.

CHAPTER TWELVE

AFTERMATH

O n the morning of December 1, 1950, as the 5th and 7th Marines set out on their epic breakout from Yudam-ni, Colonel Paul Freeman, commander of the 23rd Infantry Regiment, 2nd Infantry Division, turned to his executive officer and said bitterly, "Look around here. This is a sight that hasn't been seen for hundreds of years – the men of a whole United States Army fleeing from a battlefield, abandoning their wounded, running for their lives." Of the Eighth Army units fleeing the People's Volunteer Army forces in western North Korea, Freeman's regiment would be the only one in the 2nd Infantry Division considered combat-ready at the end of the month.

In the ten days following "the death ride to Kunu-ri," the men of the Eighth Army retreated south 120 miles. By December 15 they had crossed both the 38th Parallel and the Imjin River, and were still moving south as rapidly as possible. An officer of the 8th Royal Irish Hussars, an armored unit equipped with Centurion tanks, wrote of the retreat from Pyongyang,

The march out of Pyongyang will be remembered mainly for the intense cold, the dust, and the disappointment. Nothing appeared to have been attempted, let alone achieved. Millions of dollars' worth of valuable equipment had been destroyed without a shot being fired or any attempt made to consider its evacuation. Seldom has a more demoralizing picture been witnessed than the abandonment of this, the American forward base, before an unknown threat of Chinese soldiers – as it transpired, ill-armed and on their feet or on horses.

On the road south of the North Korean capital, ROK General Paek Sun Yup, deeply distressed by the loss of his home city, met his friend Colonel John Michaelis, commander of the 27th Infantry. When he asked his American friend what was happening, Michaelis replied, "I don't know, I'm just a regimental commander. But we may not be able to stay in the peninsula."

From the Eighth Army headquarters to the White House, there was deep dismay at the result of the Chinese attack of November 25, and growing fear that all that had been gained in Korea would soon be lost forever. When making public comment on the situation, the sheer surprise and size of the Chinese offensive were emphasized. The leaders of the US Army knew, however, that this was not the truth. How could an army that possessed overwhelming firepower and air support as compared to its enemy now be in headlong rout? The heaviest weapons the Chinese possessed were 81mm mortars. They had achieved psychological dominance not only over the combat units at the front that broke and ran, but over their commanders to the rear, and most particularly in Tokyo. Chinese skills as tacticians, night fighters, cross-country navigators, masters of fieldcraft and camouflage managed to make even senior American commanders forget their advantages. Worse, the American infantry, man for man, did not prove themselves the equal of their Chinese opponents, who outfought them at every engagement.

What kept the Chinese from achieving total victory at this point was their inability to keep their forces supplied. Once a Chinese unit had used up the ammunition its troops carried, it had to retire from the battlefield to await resupply. This had ultimately been the reason for the successful escape of the Marines from Chosin. Hung She Te, the Chinese officer in charge of logistics for the People's Volunteer Army, performed miracles with his legions of porters and oxcarts, but attempts to bring in supplies by truck failed. Trucks could not move in daylight because the drivers could not hear the approach of American F-80 and F9F-2 jet fighter-bombers. Eventually, the PVA stationed soldiers every 200 yards along Chinese supply routes to listen for American aircraft and warn the supply convoys. The most important contribution of American air power at the end of 1950 was the interdiction of enemy supply routes, which prevented the Chinese from converting battlefield superiority into full-scale destruction and defeat of the UN forces. Hu Seng, one of Marshal Peng Duhai's deputies, recalled many years after the war that it was very easy to obtain intelligence about UN military movements because "There was no censorship in the West at that time about troop movements. We gained much valuable information from the Western press and radio." It was only at the end of December that full censorship was established by UN forces in Korea, and even then reporters managed to get word out past the censors of the fall of Seoul on January 4, 1951.

The Chinese advance south was sustained in this period through the vast capture of UN arms supplies as the Eighth Army continued its precipitous retreat. Li Xiu, a regimental commissar for the 27th Corps recalled that,

> We quickly got used to American biscuits and rice, but we never cared for tomato juice. We were particularly glad to find carbines, because rifles were heavy to carry. Without the

American sleeping bags and overcoats we captured, I am not sure we could have gone on. Two thirds of our casualties were from the cold that winter, against one third from combat. Our hardest job was how to catch up with the Americans in their trucks. Always, the problem was how to win the battle with less advanced weapons than the enemy.

Contrary to what might seem logical militarily, the very speed of the American retreat at this time ultimately saved the Eighth Army from complete defeat and annihilation. In their current state, American units simply could not stand toe to toe on the battlefield with their Chinese opponents; whenever they did attempt a stand, the Chinese defeated them. But American mobility allowed thousands of men to escape to fight again another day. Even so, it was impossible to diminish the dismay over the Army's performance. At Eighth Army headquarters at Taegu, officers routinely stated that each unit should have its own "personal bugout route."

The condition of the American Army at this time was clearly delineated by British General Leslie Mansergh, who visited Korea during the retreat and later delivered a devastating secret report to the British military chiefs in London on the situation:

> I doubt whether any British really think that the war in Korea will be brought to a successful conclusion. The reason for this is primarily because of the American lack of determination and their inability, up to the time of my visit, to stand and fight. Most Americans sooner or later bring the conversation around to an expression of the view that the United Nations forces ought to quit Korea. The British troops, although sympathetic to the South Koreans in their adversity, despise them and are not interested in this civil war. I would judge the American morale is low, and in some units thoroughly bad. They appear to think

the terrain is unfavourable for American equipment and methods. It must be remembered that many thousands of the Americans joined the Army for the purpose of getting a cheap education after their service and that they, at no time, expected to fight. Their training is quite unsuited to that type of country or war and, in spite of lessons learnt, they will not get clear of their vehicles. Their rations, supplies, and welfare stores are on such a scale as to be comic if they were not such a serious handicap to battle. Regular American officers have been a high proportion of those lost. As a result, the problem of replacement with men of experience is becoming very difficult.

They have never studied or been taught defence. They appear only to have studied mechanized and mechanical advances at great speed. They do not understand locality in defence in depth or all-round defence. They do not like holding defensive positions. They have been trained for very rapid withdrawals. Americans do not understand infiltration and feel very naked when anybody threatens their flank or rear. They do not understand the importance of reconnoitring ground. Units in action almost invariably overestimate the enemy against them, the casualties inflicted, and the reasons for their rapid withdrawal. At night, main headquarters blazed like gin palaces. Roadblocks, car parks, dumps, etc., were as crowded as Hampstead Heath on a bank holiday.

General Mansergh found the courage and skill of American artillerymen superior to the infantry, and the skill of the Marines highest of all.

The military assistant to the British ambassador in Korea wrote "Standards of discipline in Korea, never very high, are now lower than I have ever known them." He reported American officers telling him their troops would not fight when ordered to do so. The British observers also made note of the fact that, as in World War II, the American predisposition for a technological war, which meant the highest-quality men were diverted to technical functions, resulted again in only the lowest-quality recruits ending up in the infantry, where the greatest burden of battle, and casualities, fell. This was the opposite to European armies where service in the infantry was considered a soldier's highest calling. The British also noted that the condition and position of Marine infantry within the organization was far higher than that of Army infantry units, similar to the European standard.

Mansergh's opinion of what he had seen in Korea was strengthened by his memory of what he had been told before he commenced his tour, in his first meeting with General MacArthur. Continuing in his report, he reported his feelings on meeting the famed general:

> He appeared much older than his seventy years. Signs of nerves and strain were apparent. When he emphasised the combined efforts and successes of all front-line troops in standing shoulder to shoulder, and dying if necessary in their fight against communism, it occurred to me that he could not have been fully in the picture. I cannot believe he would have made these comments in such a way if he had been in full possession of facts which I would inevitably learn later, facts that some Americans had been far from staunch. It occurred to me then, and was emphasised later, that the war in Korea is reproduced in Tokyo with certain omissions of the more unpalatable facts.

Indeed, MacArthur's performance following the Chinese attacks on November 25 had been and would continue to betray his stunning detachment from reality. In the immediate wake of the attack, he requested reinforcements, only to be told that the only unit available was the 82nd Airborne. He again demanded he be allowed to use Chiang's troops, a request which was again refused. His public pronouncements were no better. He first declared that it was his own drive to the Yalu that had forced the Chinese hand, thus interrupting their plans for a gigantic Communist offensive that would have been disastrous for the UN forces. He next utterly rejected the suggestion his forces were engaged in a retreat, castigating "ignorant correspondents" for their inability to distinguish between a planned withdrawal and "full flight." Truman's response later, when he was asked about MacArthur's statements, was "Now no one is blaming General MacArthur, and certainly I never did, for the failure of the November offensive. But I do blame General MacArthur for the manner in which he tried to excuse his failure."

In Washington, everyone from Truman on down knew things had to change, and change fast. The decision had been made in a cabinet meeting on November 28 that all-out war with China must be avoided. This was despite pleas from Joint Chiefs chairman General Bradley and other top commanders that planning should be put in place regarding the possible use of the atomic bomb. While Truman was forced to issue a clarification after his disastrous November 30 press conference that "only the President can authorize the use of the atom bomb, and no such authorization has been given," and had declared in private follow-up conversations with reporters that use of the bomb was most definitely not an option, in fact military planners had considered use of atomic weapons, going so far as to send ten B-29 "Silverplate" atomic bombers of the 509th Bombardment Wing from their base at Roswell, New Mexico, to Andersen AFB on Guam, with all the equipment needed for an atomic attack except the nuclear cores themselves.

Fear of American use of the bomb was palpable among the European allies, most of whom had reluctantly gone along with the Korean intervention in June because of their desire to keep the United States from becoming totally involved in Asia and sinking back into isolationism with regard to the building Cold War in Europe. On December 2, the British fear of such use of the bomb became subject of a parliamentary debate, in which even such an old warhorse as Churchill came out opposing the use of the bomb against China because it would not solve anything in Asia but would harm the situation in Europe. Conservative MP R. A. Butler and Labour Prime Minister Clement Attlee both spoke in favor of limiting the use of the atomic bomb. On December 3, Attlee announced his intention to fly to Washington and meet with President Truman, which he did on December 4. On December 5, Attlee and his aides, and the British Chiefs, met with Truman, Acheson, Marshall, and Joint Chiefs Chairman Bradley. The British made clear their opposition to a wider war with China, and pointed out that the United States could not actually use the bomb with any success against China because there was no one target or group of targets whose destruction would have the desired effect of making them stop. On this point, the British understood China as well as Mao did. The meeting ended on December 7 with the Americans agreeing they would consult Britain on any future plans to use the atomic bomb in the Korean War, though Acheson was careful to ensure the wording of the statement would not make the United States in any way subject to a British veto in the event.

One very important discussion was held on December 7, with Viscount Slim asking George Marshall if he thought that any use of atomic weapons against China might not cause the Communists to invoke the Sino-Soviet Friendship Treaty, with the result of direct Soviet military intervention in the war. Marshall answered that it would and Truman stated his own anxiety over the possibility. Slim replied that if the Soviet Air Force intervened directly in the Korean War, "we shall have to say good-bye." Attlee then brought up the question of MacArthur, voicing British anxiety over the degree of control his superiors had over the general, whose statements on his own when asked by the Tokyo press about the possible use of atomic weapons had added to anxiety. Truman agreed that MacArthur's statement in which he refused to give a direct answer to a reporter's question about the possibility of using the atomic bomb had been "unfortunate."

Through the first half of December, as bad news piled on top of bad news regarding Korea, there was more and more pressure from the senior American military about the use of the bomb. MacArthur himself would later request authorization to use up to 26 atomic bombs when he submitted a list of "retaliation targets" on December 24 in the event UN forces were pushed out of Korea. Four atomic bombs would be dropped in Korea to stop the Chinese advance, with another four directed against supply centers in Manchuria and northern China, with a possible eight more held back for possible use against targets in mainland China if the results were not satisfactory with the use of the first eight and the remainder "held in reserve." MacArthur later claimed in his memoirs that he had made no such request, that his visits to Hiroshima and Nagasaki as Allied Supreme Commander in Japan had convinced him that the use of such weapons was "unconscionable" outside of the most extreme circumstances, and that his discussion of the use of the bomb in Korea had been "merely speculative." This talk of introducing atomic bombs subsided by the end of December as it became increasingly clear the Chinese did not have the ability to run the UN forces completely off the peninsula and that UN forces might indeed hold on. However, had the UN forces been forced out of Korea, public domestic pressure, congressional pressure, and pressure from the upper ranks of the military to use the bomb against China could have become irresistible.

Domestically, the Democrats had lost a net 28 seats in the November elections to the Republicans, though they still maintained control of the House of Representatives with 235 seats to the Republicans' 199, while holding the Senate

54-42. The party leaders felt they had only managed to hold on to their majority by their fingernails, and the Republicans looked forward to renewed political struggle over the two years leading to the next presidential election. Senator McCarthy had already called for the dismissal of Defense Secretary Marshall and the impeachment of President Truman in the wake of the successful Chinese offensive in November. By early December, American families were getting letters from Korea written by their sons in the Army, to the effect of how useless the war was, and urging them to contact their congressional representatives to express opposition to continued involvement in the war. President Truman felt it necessary to declare a state of National Emergency on December 16 to emphasize the seriousness of the situation. A Gallup poll in early January showed approval of President Truman's actions dropping to 49 percent, while 62 percent expressed the belief that getting involved in the Korean War had been a mistake and 66 percent believed the United States should get out of the war. At the same time, there was majority support in the poll for the possible use of atomic weapons if necessary to defend American forces in Korea. The Republicans in Congress vacillated between those calling for a wider war and condemning the Truman administration for "tying the hands" of American military commanders, and those advocating withdrawal from Korea because of the failure of the administration to achieve its goals.

On December 11, the Truman administration stated it agreed with and would support a resolution brought by a group of Asian nations led by India in the United Nations, calling for a ceasefire-in-place. Though the administration actually opposed such an idea, the step was taken in the belief the Chinese would refuse the offer, which they did on December 12 on the grounds that the resolution did not call for the removal of all foreign troops from Korea and the withdrawal of the Seventh Fleet from Taiwan.

Had China accepted this resolution in December 1950 and commenced negotiations from that point, the outcome of the war might have been considerably different. If Mao been willing to negotiate on the basis of a return to the *status quo ante*, the Communist Chinese would have been in a strong position to have their request to take the China seat at the UN approved by a majority vote of the General Assembly, regardless of the US position. This decision would have divided the United States from its allies should Washington have been reluctant to agree to this and negotiate. However, Mao had now fallen victim to a similar hubris to that which MacArthur had fallen victim in September. With the rout of the Eighth Army in North Korea, the Chinese now deluded themselves that the possibility of reuniting all of Korea under Communist rule was within their grasp. As the first Communist power to inflict a grave defeat on the West, their international prestige was at that moment enormous. Had they accepted a negotiated end to the war with their own armies victorious, China's international standing would have been immense in the following years. They failed to take the opportunity, just at the moment when events began to change to create a situation that would reverse their position.

On December 23, General Walton Walker was killed in a traffic accident while traveling from his headquarters to visit 27 Commonwealth Brigade. An hour after the general was declared dead in the hospital, General Matthew Ridgway received a call at his home from Army Chief of Staff General J. Lawton Collins, informing him of Walker's death and that MacArthur had requested him as Walker's replacement in command of the Eighth Army. On Christmas Eve, he departed Washington for Tokyo, where he arrived just before midnight on Christmas Day. He met MacArthur the next morning at 0930 hours in the Dai Ichi, where the general told him, "The Eighth Army is yours, Matt. Do what you think best." At 1600 hours on December 26, Ridgway stepped off his plane at Taegu airfield, where he was met by the Eighth Army Chief of Staff General Leven Allen. After the war, he recalled that within a few hours,

> I had discovered that our forces were simply not mentally and spiritually ready for the kind of action I had been planning. The men I met along the road, those I stopped to talk to and solicit gripes from – they all conveyed to me a conviction that this was a bewildered army, not sure of itself or its leaders, not sure what they were doing there, wondering when they would hear the whistle of that homebound transport.

From the outset of his command, Ridgway demanded change. There would be fresh focus on defense, and attack, in depth, and Army units would stop sticking with their vehicles. They would dig in on the high ground, with mutual support from units to either side. He refused to countenance any discussion of evacuating the peninsula, stating that the only contingency he was willing to prepare for was a withdrawal to a new Pusan Perimeter, this one dug in and prepared on an unprecedented scale. Army engineers and Korean laborers were soon at work. One of the great American battlefield commanders of World War II, Matthew Ridgway would set his reputation in stone in Korea during the next four months.

Ridgway also examined closely the commanders who served under him. On December 28, the 1st Marine Division had been placed once again under the operational control of X Corps, still commanded by Almond who would soon be promoted to Lieutenant General, though X Corps would now become part of the Eighth Army and Almond would maintain his position as MacArthur's chief of staff. Ridgway met with General O. P. Smith to discuss the recent breakout from Chosin. The two men found mutual respect for each other's achievements. Following this meeting, Ridgway's first act in changing the Eighth Army command structure was to remove the Marines from Almond's command. Matthew Ridgway's hand grenade and battle dressing on his combat harness would become as famous as General Patton's pearl-handled revolvers had been during World War II, and as symbolic of his belief in victory. Within weeks his fighting spirit, which had imbued the 101st Airborne Division at Normandy and Eindhoven and Bastogne, would transform the Eighth Army from a beaten force to an army that could stand and fight.

During the month of January, the 1st Marine Division would be reborn. The replacements who came off the ships that docked in Pusan were men who had received the training their predecessors in the summer of 1950 had lacked, imbued with the knowledge gained on the battlefields in the Pusan Perimeter and the Chosin Reservoir. They were ready and able to meet the challenges that would come in the spring and summer of 1951. At the same time, the survivors of Chosin assumed the senior positions that would make the 1st Marine Division an outstanding unit in the battles to come. Junior platoon commanders like Joe Owen would move up to become company commanders and executive officers. Corporals would become platoon sergeants and company gunnery sergeants, passing on to the new men the knowledge they had gained, painfully, at Yudam-ni, Hagaru-ri, Toktong Pass, Hellfire Valley, and Koto-ri. By the end of January, the 1st Marine Division stood rejuvenated.

At the same time, the Chinese were now the victims of extended supply lines. A senior staff member to Marshal Peng Duhai Hu Seng later wrote, "While we wished to continue to push the enemy, we could not open our mouth too wide. China was unprepared for the new military situation created by the deep advance. We were now in a position where we could not continue to reinforce our army in Korea, because we could not supply more men." The Chinese offensive exhausted its momentum by the end of the year, though

Seoul would fall to the Communists a second time just after the New Year before the advance ran completely out of steam.

Over the next few months, beginning in late January 1951 and ending in June, a series of battles between the Eighth Army and the People's Volunteer Army would see the main line of resistance finally stabilize approximately along the old border of the 38th Parallel. The rejuvenated 1st Marine Division would take a leading role in these actions. While this was happening, the last great battle of the Korean War took place between Tokyo and Washington.

American military tradition has always held that the military leadership is apolitical. But this was one tradition that was difficult to uphold in an era that saw American forces employed overseas in large numbers. While the principle of civilian control of the military was ingrained in the history of the American armed forces, the rising complexity of military technology after World War II had led to the creation of a professional military that was different by 1950 from that which had existed before the war, where men with few prospects in civilian life gravitated to a relatively undemanding military life. Thus, civilian control became increasingly problematic, especially when coupled with a cumbersome, slow-moving constitutional division of powers between the President as commander-in-chief, and the Congress with its power to raise armies and wage war. In an era when the possibility of a sudden strike with atomic bombs might give no time for military commanders to consult their civilian superiors, or for the executive to work with the legislative powers, authority was increasingly delegated away from the civilian leadership.

In fact, the tradition of an apolitical American military was of a more recent origin than traditionally thought, dating back only some 80 years to the period following the American Civil War. At that time few officers voted, not so much due to a lack of interest in politics as because they and their families frequently moved from state to state and into territories on the frontier that had no political self-government. Living on federal bases, which were not considered part of the state they might be found in, these men were disenfranchised under the electoral laws of many states. Under General William T. Sherman, who commanded the Army from 1869 to 1883 and hated politics, the custom of an apolitical military became firmly established. The Truman–MacArthur conflict is couched in terms of the maintenance of civilian authority over the military and the tradition that officers are to be apolitical, something Douglas MacArthur had very definitely never been.

In the second volume of his memoirs, *Years of Trial and Hope*, President Truman wrote that he did not relieve MacArthur because of the military reverses in Korea in November and December 1950, stating his belief that MacArthur was no more to blame for this reverse than General of the Army Dwight Eisenhower had been for the military reverses the American Army had suffered during the Battle of the Bulge. In light of the actual facts regarding MacArthur's decision-making following Inchon, this is most likely an attempt to put a political gloss on a situation that was still tender at the time Truman was writing. In any event, this statement did not mean that these events did not factor into his decision. "I considered him a great strategist, until he made the march into North Korea without the knowledge that he should have had of the Chinese coming in."

On December 1, 1950, the day after Truman's brouhaha with the press in Washington, a reporter asked MacArthur if the restrictions the administration had placed on operations against Chinese forces on the far side of the Yalu River were "a handicap to effective military operations." MacArthur replied that they were indeed "an enormous handicap, unprecedented in military history." In the wake of the appearance of this quote in both *The New York Times* and the *Washington Post*, Truman issued a directive on

December 6 that required all military officers and diplomatic officials to clear all but routine statements with the State Department before making them public, "and ... refrain from direct communications on military or foreign policy with newspapers, magazines, and other publicity media." MacArthur's aide, Major General Courtney Whitney, provided a legal opinion that this order applied "solely to formal public statements and not to communiqués, correspondence or personal conversations." Citing this authority, MacArthur made similar remarks in press statements on February 13 and March 7, 1951.

Following the first battle of the Imjin in early February, which stopped further Chinese advance to the south, the tide of war had begun to turn again in February and March 1951, allowing the Eighth Army to drive north. On March 15, the day after Seoul had been liberated a second time, President Truman had responded to a reporter's question about whether UN forces would again be allowed to move north of the 38th Parallel by saying that it would be "a tactical matter for the field commander." The liberation of Seoul raised hopes in Washington that the Chinese and North Koreans might be amenable to a ceasefire agreement, the administration having come to see that finishing the war on the basis of the *status quo ante* as the UN resolution of December 11, 1950 had proposed was likely the best outcome to the war in the current situation. Truman had prepared a statement to this effect, which MacArthur learned of when he was informed by the Joint Chiefs on March 20. Ridgway had prepared an offensive known as Operation *Rugged*, and pressed MacArthur for permission to launch it. In turn, he warned General Ridgway that political constraints from Washington might soon impose limits on his planned operations. MacArthur then gave Ridgway permission to launch his attack, setting an objective line 20 miles north of the 38th Parallel that would secure Seoul's water supply. On March 23, MacArthur issued a communiqué regarding the possibility of offering a ceasefire to the Chinese:

> Of even greater significance than our tactical successes has been the clear revelation that this new enemy, Red China, of such exaggerated and vaunted military power, lacks the industrial capability to provide adequately many critical items necessary to the conduct of modern war. He lacks the manufacturing base and those raw materials needed to produce, maintain and operate even moderate air and naval power, and he cannot provide the essentials for successful ground operations, such as tanks, heavy artillery and other refinements science has introduced into the conduct of military campaigns. Formerly his great numerical potential might well have filled this gap but with the development of existing methods of mass destruction numbers alone do not offset the vulnerability inherent in such deficiencies. Control of the seas and the air, which in turn means control over supplies, communications and transportation, are no less essential and decisive now than in the past. When this control exists, as in our case, and is coupled with an inferiority of ground firepower in the enemy's case, the resulting disparity is such that it cannot be overcome by bravery, however fanatical, or the most gross indifference to human loss.
>
> These military weaknesses have been clearly and definitely revealed since Red China entered upon its undeclared war in Korea. Even under the inhibitions which now restrict the activity of the United Nations forces and the corresponding military advantages which accrue to Red China, it has been shown its complete inability to accomplish by force of arms the conquest of Korea. The enemy, therefore must by now be painfully aware that a decision of the United Nations to depart from its tolerant effort to contain the war to the area of Korea, through an

expansion of our military operations to its coastal areas and interior bases, would doom Red China to the risk of imminent military collapse. These basic facts being established, there should be no insuperable difficulty in arriving at decisions on the Korean problem if the issues are resolved on their own merits, without being burdened by extraneous matters not directly related to Korea, such as Formosa or China's seat in the United Nations.

This was clearly an attempt on the part of MacArthur to influence political and policy decisions being made by his civilian superiors in Washington by preempting the argument in public, a violation of the tradition of an apolitical military leadership, as well as a statement made in defiance of Truman's gag order of December 6, 1950, and was seen as such by the administration when the communiqué was published in the New York and Washington press. Truman later wrote of this event in his memoirs,

> This was a most extraordinary statement for a military commander of the United Nations to issue on his own responsibility. It was an act totally disregarding all directives to abstain from any declarations on foreign policy. It was in open defiance of my orders as President and as Commander-in-Chief. This was a challenge to the authority of the President under the Constitution. It also flouted the policy of the United Nations. By this act MacArthur left me no choice – I could no longer tolerate his insubordination.

MacArthur did not announce the start of Ridgway's Operation *Rugged* until April 5, a day after it had begun. The announcement that Ridgway had been given permission to advance his forces up to 20 miles north of the 38th Parallel without consulting Washington was MacArthur's fatal error.

Truman would later write in his memoirs that "I was ready to kick him into the North China Sea... I was never so put out in my life."

For the moment, however, the president remained silent. Historically, there had been dramatic confrontations between presidents and military leaders over policy before, the most notable being that between President Abraham Lincoln and General George McClellan over the direction of the Army of the Potomac in 1862, and an earlier one when President James Polk recalled Major General Winfield Scott from command of the American Army just before the outbreak of the Mexican War in 1846. Truman realized that with the public political support MacArthur had, and his influence inside the Republican Party, taking such action would have to be very carefully timed. Harry Truman was a self-taught historian of no small ability and he consulted history books on how Lincoln and Polk had dealt with their generals. He later wrote in his memoirs that Polk was his favorite president because "he had the courage to tell Congress to go to Hell on foreign policy matters."

There were in fact very important and very genuine differences of opinion over policy between MacArthur and the Truman administration. Perhaps most important was MacArthur's deep-seated belief that it was impossible to separate the struggle against Communism in Europe from the struggle going on in Asia, which was a position held by many in Washington, both in and out of the administration. However, a second important policy difference did not have such support. This was MacArthur's belief that China was not, as Acheson maintained, "the Soviet Union's largest and most important satellite," but was rather an independent state with its own agenda that, in MacArthur's words, "for its own purposes is [just temporarily] allied with Soviet Russia." If one accepted MacArthur's thesis, it then followed that expanding the war with China would not provoke a conflict with the Soviet Union. In reviewing Soviet documents from this period that have been released since the end of the Cold War, there is some evidence that this was indeed Stalin's position. He disliked the fact that Mao had come to power in China independent of Soviet support and was thus not beholden for his position to the power of the Soviet Union, as were all the other Communist leaders. China was not a Soviet satellite. Additionally, Stalin was very aware that at this time the Soviet Union lacked an effective way of delivering an atomic attack on North America, since the Soviet strategic air forces were equipped with only a few hundred "reverse-engineered" B-29 bombers, known by the Soviets as Tupolev Tu-4s, which did not have the range to attack more than a small area of the northern United States, and that only if the crews flew a one-way mission. The USSR was still in the midst of recovery from the devastation wrought by the Germans in World War II, and was in no position to compete with the power of the United States. This reality of actual Soviet weakness and inability to compete was not perceived by anyone in the upper circles of the American government, military, or intelligence services, but was certainly well-known to the Soviet dictator. This may well be why the Soviet Union did not provide sufficient supplies to the Chinese to prosecute the war in Korea to a successful conclusion, since Stalin saw advantage in tying down Mao in a war he could not win and could not walk away from.

The Joint Chiefs, and everyone else in authority in Washington, emphatically disagreed with the position that a war with China would not involve war with the Soviet Union, although this contradicted their position that it was Europe and not Asia which was the prime concern of the Soviet Union. There was also little support for MacArthur's position even among Republicans in the China Lobby.

On April 5, Congressman Joseph Martin, the Republican Minority Leader in the House of Representatives, read a letter on the floor of the House that he had received from MacArthur, dated March 20, which criticized the administration's priorities. MacArthur had written:

> It seems strangely difficult for some to realize that here in Asia is where the Communist conspirators have elected to make their play for global conquest, and that we have joined the issue thus raised on the battlefield; that here we fight Europe's war with arms while the diplomatic there still fight it with words; that if we lose the war to communism in Asia the fall of Europe is inevitable; win it and Europe most probably would avoid war and yet preserve freedom. As you pointed out, we must win. There is no substitute for victory.

"No substitute for victory" would become the rallying cry of the political right during the war and in the years following, and would have impact in the politics surrounding the subsequent war in Vietnam. MacArthur later wrote that Martin had released the letter "for some unexplained reason and without consulting me." He had not, however, marked it as confidential or off the record.

Truman met with Marshall, Bradley, Acheson and Harriman on the morning of April 6, to discuss what action should be taken with regard to MacArthur. Harriman stated emphatically that the general must be relieved, but was opposed by Bradley, while Marshall needed more time to consider the matter. While Acheson was personally in favor of relieving MacArthur, he did not say so, instead warning Truman that it would be "the biggest fight of your administration."

In the Western Pacific, it was April 7. Hours after the meeting at the White House, the carriers *Boxer* and *Philippine Sea* departed their position off the east coast of Korea at the conclusion of flight operations for the day and headed south through Tsushima Strait which they transited that night, then turned south-southwest for the Formosa Strait. This move was unknown in Washington. As the ships steamed on through the Yellow Sea, a second meeting was held in Washington, with Marshall and Bradley still opposed to MacArthur's relief. Subsequently, the Joint Chiefs met with Marshall in his office. Each in turn expressed his opinion that MacArthur's relief was necessary and desirable from a "military point of view," however they recognized that military considerations were not paramount. Their concern stemmed from their belief that "if MacArthur were not relieved, a large segment of our people would charge that civil authorities no longer controlled the military." Marshall, Bradley, Harriman and Acheson met again with Truman at Blair House on April 9, where Bradley informed the president of the Joint Chiefs' views. Marshall added that he now agreed with them. Truman later wrote in his diary that "it is of unanimous opinion of all that MacArthur be relieved. All four so advise." The question now was one of timing.

On April 11 in the Western Pacific, *Boxer* and *Philippine Sea* arrived on station in the Taiwan Strait off the west coast of Taiwan at 1100 hours and launched aircraft in an "aerial parade" along the east coast of mainland China. At the same time, the destroyer USS *John A. Bole* (DD-755) took station three miles off the Chinese seaport of Shantou. In response, the Chinese surrounded the ship with an armada of 40 armed junks. When word of the event arrived in Washington, it was immediately seen as an attempt to provoke war with China. At 1300 hours local time, the aircraft launched from Task Force 77 appeared over Shantou and made threatening passes at the Chinese vessels surrounding the *Bole*. Two hours later, the *Bole* retired without hostile action being initiated by either side.

President Truman had already drafted the letter of relief to MacArthur. When word of events on the China coast arrived, he knew that the time had come to issue the order. The president's intention was that MacArthur would be personally notified of his relief by Secretary of the Army Frank Pace, who was touring the front in Korea, at 2000 hours on April 11, Washington time, which was 1000 hours on April 12, Tokyo time. However, Pace did not receive the message due to a signals failure in Korea. Meanwhile, in Washington, reporters began asking the White House if rumors circulating of MacArthur's relief were true. Truman later said that "I decided that we could not afford the courtesy of Secretary Pace's personal delivery of the order," and called a press conference at which he issued his statement to the press:

> With deep regret I have concluded that General of the Army Douglas MacArthur is unable to give his wholehearted support to the policies of the United States Government and of the United Nations in matters pertaining to his official duties. In view of the specific responsibilities imposed upon me by the Constitution of the United States and the added responsibility which has been entrusted to me by the United Nations, I have decided that I must make a change of command in the Far East. I have, therefore, relieved General MacArthur of his commands and have designated Lt. Gen. Matthew B. Ridgway as his successor.
>
> Full and vigorous debate on matters of national policy is a vital element in the constitutional system of our free democracy. It is fundamental, however, that military commanders must be governed by the policies and directives issued to them in the manner provided by our laws and Constitution. In time of crisis, this consideration is particularly compelling.
>
> General MacArthur's place in history as one of our greatest commanders is fully established. The Nation owes him a debt of gratitude for the distinguished and exceptional service which he has rendered his country in

posts of great responsibility. For that reason I repeat my regret at the necessity for the action I feel compelled to take in his case.

In Tokyo, it was shortly after 1400 hours. MacArthur and his wife were attending a luncheon at the American embassy for Senator Warren Magnuson and William Stern, Executive Vice President of Northwest Airlines. Colonel Sidney Huff heard about the president's statement from a commercial radio broadcast and promptly went to the embassy, arriving at about 1430 hours. He then informed Mrs. MacArthur of the news and she in turn told the general. The official notice would not arrive until 1500 hours. Truman's letter, over Bradley's signature, read:

> I deeply regret that it becomes my duty as President and Commander-in-Chief of the United States military forces to replace you as Supreme Commander, Allied Powers; Commander-in-Chief, United Nations Command; Commander-in-Chief, Far East; and Commanding General, US Army, Far East.
>
> You will turn over your commands, effective at once, to Lt. Gen. Matthew B. Ridgway. You are authorized to have issued such orders as are necessary to complete desired travel to such place as you select.
>
> My reasons for your replacement, will be made public concurrently with the delivery to you of the foregoing order, and are contained in the next following message.

The news of MacArthur's relief created shock in Japan. The Diet passed a resolution of gratitude for MacArthur, while Emperor Hirohito visited the general at the American embassy in person, the first time in history that a Japanese emperor had ever visited a foreigner. The *Mainichi Shimbun* editorialized:

MacArthur's dismissal is the greatest shock since the end of the war. He dealt with the Japanese people not as a conqueror but a great reformer. He was a noble political missionary. What he gave us was not material aid and democratic reform alone, but a new way of life, the freedom and dignity of the individual. We shall continue to love and trust him as one of the Americans who best understood Japan's position.

In an article in *Time* magazine, published on December 3, 1973, Truman was quoted as saying in the early 1960s: "I fired him because he wouldn't respect the authority of the President. I didn't fire him because he was a dumb son of a bitch, although he was, but that's not against the law for generals. If it was, half to three-quarters of them would be in jail."

Although Truman and Acheson personally accused MacArthur of insubordination, the Joint Chiefs avoided any suggestion of such an act and MacArthur was not, in fact, relieved for insubordination, since such a charge would be a military offense, for which MacArthur could have requested a public court martial as had General Billy Mitchell in 1925. The outcome of such a trial was uncertain. MacArthur could have been found not guilty with his reinstatement ordered. The Joint Chiefs agreed there was "little evidence that General MacArthur had ever failed to carry out a direct order of the Joint Chiefs, or acted in opposition to an order." General Bradley later insisted that "In point of fact, MacArthur had stretched but not legally violated any JCS directives. He had violated the President's December 6 directive, relayed to him by the JCS, but this did not constitute violation of a JCS order."

Writing his memoirs in 1956 Truman said:

If there is one basic element in our Constitution, it is civilian control of the military. Policies are to be made by the elected political officials, not by generals or admirals.

Yet time and again General MacArthur had shown that he was unwilling to accept the policies of the administration. By his repeated public statements he was not only confusing our allies as to the true course of our policies but, in fact, was also setting his policy against the President's. If I allowed him to defy the civil authorities in this manner, I myself would be violating my oath to uphold and defend the Constitution.

The relief of MacArthur provoked a political firestorm in Washington. Most of the avalanche of mail and messages received by the White House from the public supported MacArthur. On the issues of character, integrity, honor and service, MacArthur was rated the better man. What little support President Truman received was largely based on the principle of civilian control of the military.

Ohio Senator Robert A. Taft, leader of the Republican conservatives, called for immediate impeachment proceedings against Truman, stating "President Truman must be impeached and convicted. His hasty and vindictive removal of General MacArthur is the culmination of series of acts which have shown that he is unfit, morally and mentally, for his high office. The American nation has never been in greater danger. It is led by a fool who is surrounded by knaves."

Leading conservative newspapers like the *Chicago Tribune* and the *Los Angeles Times* editorialized that MacArthur's "hasty and vindictive" relief was due to foreign pressure, particularly from the United Kingdom and the British socialists in Attlee's Labour government. The Senate Republican whip, Senator Kenneth S. Wherry, charged on the Senate floor that the general's relief was the result of pressure from "the Socialist Government of Great Britain."

On April 17, 1951, Douglas MacArthur returned to the United States, a country he had not seen since 1935. In San Francisco, he was greeted by the commander of the

Sixth Army, Lieutenant General Albert C. Wedemeyer, and received a parade attended by 500,000 people. On arrival at Washington National Airport on April 19, he was greeted by the Joint Chiefs of Staff and General Jonathan Wainwright, the man he had left in command at Bataan. President Truman sent his military aide, General Harry H. Vaughan, as his representative. This was seen as a slight from the president, since Vaughan was despised by both the public and professional soldiers as a corrupt presidential crony.

Later that day, MacArthur addressed a joint session of Congress where he delivered his famous "Old Soldiers Never Die" speech, in which he declared:

> Efforts have been made to distort my position. It has been said in effect that I was a warmonger. Nothing could be further from the truth. I know war as few other men now living know it, and nothing to me is more revolting. I have long advocated its complete abolition, as its very destructiveness on both friend and foe has rendered it useless as a means of settling international disputes... But once war is forced upon us, there is no other alternative than to apply every available means to bring it to a swift end. War's very object is victory, not prolonged indecision. In war there can be no substitute for victory.

After addressing Congress, MacArthur flew to New York City where he received the largest ticker-tape parade in the city's history to that time. He also addressed large rallies in Chicago and Milwaukee in the following week.

In response to the political controversy, the Senate Armed Services Committee and the Senate Foreign Relations Committee held "an inquiry into the military situation in the Far East and the facts surrounding the relief of General of the Army Douglas MacArthur" in May and June 1951, in an attempt to avoid a constitutional crisis. The Democrats were anxious, as *Time* reported, "to keep General MacArthur's thundering rhetoric out of earshot of the microphones and his dramatic profile off the screens of twelve million television sets," while the Republicans favored open hearings. In the end, the Democrats had their way, mainly by arguing that open hearings would reveal secrets that might threaten national security. The inquiry was held in closed session, and a full transcript was only made public in 1973. The investigation was chaired by Georgia Senator Richard B. Russell. General MacArthur, Secretary of Defense Marshall, former Secretary of Defense Johnson, JCS chairman General Bradley, Army Chief of Staff General Collins, Air Force Chief of Staff Vandenberg, Chief of Naval Operations Admiral Sherman, State Department legal advisor Adrian S. Fisher, Secretary of State Acheson, General Wedemeyer, Admiral Oscar C. Badger II, former ambassador to China Patrick J. Hurley, General David G. Barr and Air Force General O'Donnell were called as witnesses.

The hearings began on May 3, 1951, and MacArthur was the featured witness. He spoke for more than six hours at the opening session and condemned Truman's Cold War foreign policy, arguing that if the president's "inhibitions" about the war in Korea had been removed, the conflict could have been "wound up" without a "very great additional complement of ground troops." Over the next three days of hearings, he went on to suggest that only through a strategy of complete military destruction of the Communist empire could the US hope to win the Cold War. Over the three days of testimony, MacArthur weakened his case through vague and overstated responses to Senators' questions. His persecution complex became public as he observed that his troubles came from the Washington politicians who had introduced "a new concept into military operations – the concept of appeasement." When Senator McMahon asked MacArthur whether he thought his plan for bombing China might trigger another world war, he had replied that this was not his area of responsibility.

In the days that followed, Marshall's testimony and that of the Joint Chiefs rebutted many of MacArthur's arguments. Marshall emphatically declared that there had been no disagreement between himself, the president, and the Joint Chiefs regarding the decision to relieve MacArthur. General Vandenberg questioned whether the air force could be effective against Communist targets in Manchuria, while General Bradley noted that the Communists were also waging limited war in Korea, having not attacked UN airbases or ports in the "privileged sanctuary" in Japan. The judgment of the Joint Chiefs was that it was not worth the risk to expand the war, though they conceded they were prepared to do so if the Communists escalated the conflict, or if there was no willingness to negotiate forthcoming. They also disagreed with MacArthur's assessment of the effectiveness of the South Korean and Chinese Nationalist forces, with Bradley stating: "Red China is not the powerful nation seeking to dominate the world. Frankly, in the opinion of the Joint Chiefs of Staff, this strategy would involve us in the wrong war, at the wrong place, at the wrong time, and with the wrong enemy."

On June 25 the committees concluded that "the removal of General MacArthur was within the constitutional powers of the President but the circumstances were a shock to national pride." The Senators also found that "there was no serious disagreement between General MacArthur and the Joint Chiefs of Staff as to military strategy."

MacArthur's biographer wrote of the hearings, "By the time Marshall and the Joint Chiefs were finished, MacArthur's strategic thinking, for the first time in his career, had been torn to shreds not by liberal correspondents or politicians but by the top four officers of the American military establishment." While the controversy had ignited incredible passions only weeks before, public interest had declined rapidly as the hearings dragged on. The Senate hearings would mark the last time the "old soldier" would hold center stage and the beginning of his long, slow "fade away" till his death in 1964.

The fact that Truman had not requested congressional approval of United States action in Korea finally came to the political fore during the hearings, with Senator Knowland noting that:

> Article I of the Constitution gives the power to declare war to the Congress and not to the Executive. We are apparently now drifting into a twilight constitutional zone where the executive can put us into war, the fourth largest in our history, without a Congressional declaration or a Congressional resolution recognizing that a state of war started by others already exists. When Congress acts under its constitutional power, every statement for or against the resolution is part of the Congressional Record, and the press and the public are fully informed. The roll-call vote shows how each Member voted. This is responsible and accountable government.
>
> If five or seven men can meet in a closed session in the Blair House or the White House, and put this nation into the fourth largest war, from a casualty standpoint, in our history without their statements and recommendations being recorded or available, and without their positions on this matter being known, we have the war-making power transferred from the Congress, operating in the open, to the Executive, operating en camera. That is not, I submit, either responsible or accountable government.

The committee concluded that "the United States should never again become involved in war without the consent of the Congress." This congressional "consent" would be found by future Presidents in wars to come through resolutions that did not constitute declarations of war, such as the Tonkin Gulf Resolution of 1964 and the Authorization to Use Military

Force of 2002 that led to the invasion of Iraq. There has been no formal declaration of war by an American Congress since December 1941.

Polls over the summer of 1951 showed the majority of the public still disapproved of the decision to relieve MacArthur. President Truman's approval rating fell to 23 percent in July, 1951, and finally hit 22 percent in February 1952, lower than Richard Nixon's 25 percent during the Watergate Scandal in 1974, and Lyndon Johnson's of 28 percent following the Tet Offensive in Vietnam in 1968. It remains the lowest Gallup Poll approval rating recorded by any serving president.

While political crisis enveloped Washington, General James Van Fleet took command of the Eighth Army on April 22, 1951. That same day, the People's Volunteer Army launched their fifth offensive of the war. Eighth Army intelligence knew it was coming. The 1st Marine Division, stationed in the "Iron Triangle" east of Seoul received a two-hour tactical warning of the assault, which came most strongly against the 7th Marines that night. The Marine position deteriorated during the night when the ROK 6th Division collapsed into a rout, impeding the advance of supplies and reinforcements. The 7th Marines had to extend their position to make up the gap in the line until the three British, Australian and Canadian battalions of 27 Commonwealth Brigade could be brought into position to fill the gap, but by April 24 the Marines had held, even though they had given up substantial ground while breaking the Chinese advance and inflicting high casualties on the attackers. At the same time, between April 23 and 25, the 27 Brigade, supported by the gunners of the 16th New Zealand Field Regiment, fought a defensive battle against repeated attacks by the PVA 118th Division, with the Canadian Princess Patricia's Light Infantry surrounded for 24 hours and cut off, resupplied by airdrops. The Commonwealth stand broke the Chinese attack north of Chongchon-ni, inflicting heavy casualties on their opponents while losing few men themselves. By April 25, the center of the UN line had stabilized and held while the surviving attackers withdrew.

While this was happening, 25 miles west along the Imjin River, 29 Infantry Brigade, consisting of three British battalions and one Belgian infantry battalion, supported by tanks and artillery, fought a battle that passed into Korean War legend when the Chinese struck on April 22 with two divisions. When the units of 29 Brigade were ultimately forced to fall back in the face of overwhelming enemy force, their actions in the battle of the Imjin River had blunted the impetus of the Chinese offensive and allowed UN forces to retreat to prepared defensive positions where the Chinese were halted. The battle's ferocity caught the imagination of the world as it was reported in the news, especially the fate of the 1st Battalion, The Gloucestershire Regiment, which was outnumbered and eventually surrounded by Chinese forces on Hill 235, which became known as Gloster Hill. During the night of April 24/25, 29 Brigade was ordered to withdraw following the withdrawal of the Belgian battalion which had taken heavy losses. The retreat began at 0800 hours on April 25, with the Chinese surging behind them. The Centurions of the 8th Hussars saved the day when they took the Chinese under fire. When Chinese troops swarmed two tanks, Captains Peter Ormrod and Gavin Murray were forced to resort to machine-gunning each other's tanks to force them off. The survivors of the 1st Gloucesters were forced to leave their wounded behind when they finally attempted to break out. There was no other time in the Korean War after 1951 when the UN command permitted a substantial force to be isolated and destroyed piecemeal. British casualties in 29 Brigade were 1,000 killed, wounded or captured, a quarter of front-line British strength. Only 169 of 850 Gloucesters survived the battle. But the Commonwealth troops had broken one arm of the Chinese

Communist spring offensive by making their stand where they did. The stand of the Gloucesters, together with other actions of 29 Brigade subsequently became an important part of British military history and tradition.

At the outset of Ridgway's advance on April 5, he became concerned that the Chinese might attempt to open the floodgates of the Hwachon Dam, 50 miles northeast of Seoul in North Korea and flood the Han River, which could have a major impact on UN Forces' ability to advance. On April 9, the Chinese did open the spillway gates, which raised the level of the Han River four feet and damaged two UN bridges. On April 10, the 2nd Battalion, 7th Cavalry Regiment attacked toward the dam but was stopped half a mile from the objective. On April 11, I Company and the 4th Ranger Company attacked but were stopped by Chinese resistance and the attack was called off at dark. As the PVA advanced in late April in their spring offensive, UN commanders became concerned they would close the Hwachon Dam and lower the river level which could aid their advance. It became imperative to prevent any use of the dam as the battle raged. The USAF flew an unsuccessful mission against the dam with B-29s on April 20. On April 29, the Navy was ordered to attack the dam; VA-195 aboard USS *Princeton* (CV-37) was given the mission. The first raid on April 30, with eight AD-4 Skyraiders carrying two 2,000lb bombs each to divebomb the spillway gates, was unsuccessful.

Princeton happened to have eight World War II-vintage Mark XIII aerial torpedoes in her magazine. Air group commander CDR Dick Merrick decided to use them against the spillway gates. Only a few pilots aboard *Princeton* had any training in using torpedoes, including Lt (jg) Ed Phillips, who recalled, "We had to modify the airplanes so that the lower dive brake would not deploy, due to the length of the torpedoes we would carry on the centerline rack." On May 1, CDR Merrick led five AD-4 Skyraiders of VA-195 and three AD-4N Skyraiders of VC-35, with 12 F4U-4 Corsairs of VF-194 for flak suppression, against the Hwachon Dam. Phillips remembered, "We couldn't pull any Gs during the attack or we would damage the torpedoes when we dropped them. The Corsairs went in ahead of us and rocketed the flak positions, knocking out some of them, then we attacked from an altitude of 75 feet and a speed of 150 knots, which felt like we were standing still with all the flak bursting around us. At a distance of 1,000 yards, we dropped to 50 feet and released the torpedoes, then executed that well-known naval maneuver, getting the hell out of there." One torpedo was a dud and one sank when dropped. The other six ran straight and true. The spillway gates were jammed partially open by the explosions, which allowed a minor release of water from the dam, but damaged the gates in a way that they could not be opened or closed. The threat the dam posed to the UN forces was removed. The mission marked the last time aerial torpedoes would be used by the US Navy. VA-195 became known ever after as "The Dambusters."

By April 26, it was apparent that the Chinese spring offensive had failed. The UN troops who had retreated in confusion five months previously had stood and held. Despite this, Marshal Peng Duhai continued to reinforce failure. On May 15, a new assault was launched with 29 Chinese and nine North Korean divisions. ROK III Corps collapsed again, and the Communists advanced 30 miles. Despite taking 900 casualties, the US 2nd Division, only recently recovered from its ordeal in North Korea, held firm as the 38th Infantry stemmed repeated attacks on the night of May 16, with one battery firing 12,000 rounds of 105mm shells in 24 hours. Searchlights were turned on to illuminate the battle area. The 3rd Infantry Division and the 187th Airborne Regimental Combat Team filled the gap created by the ROK retreat. By May 20, the Chinese offensive was spent after taking 90,000 casualties.

On May 22, the Eighth Army went on the offensive. The 187th Airborne and 1st Marine Division reached the Hwachon Reservoir in North Korea, while the 2nd and 3rd Divisions regained the line on the Imjin. Had the political will existed to continue, the Communist front was now open, with the morale of the People's Volunteer Army shattered as they faced UN troops that were now well-trained and well-led. However, Washington had no desire to press north and risk what had been gained. The Joint Chiefs had set the objective for the offensive as "an end to the fighting and a return to the status quo; the mission of the Eighth Army was to inflict enough attrition on the foe to induce him to settle on these terms." Over the course of the summer of 1951, the UN forces stabilized the front in a series of small battles across Korea at approximately the 38th Parallel.

On June 1, UN Secretary General Trygve Lie declared that if a cease-fire could be achieved roughly at the 38th Parallel, the resolutions of the Security Council would be fulfilled. On June 7, Secretary of State Acheson told the Senate Armed Services Committee that UN forces would accept an armistice on the 38th Parallel. On June 23, Soviet UN ambassador Jacob Malik proposed a ceasefire in Korea. On July 10, Communist and UN delegations met for the first time in Kaesong to open cease-fire negotiations.

The Korean War settled into a stalemate that would last for the next 24 months, as companies and battalions fought to hold a hill here or retake one there, with place names like Pork Chop Hill and The Punchbowl being written in blood, in attempts to bring success to the stubborn negotiations that had moved to Panmunjom from Kaesong. The West had demonstrated its determination to resist aggression, but at a high political and military cost, with the relations of the United States and its European allies deeply strained by the behavior of MacArthur. In the whole three years of the war, the only action that is remembered today as being "great" was the breakout of the 1st Marine Division from the Chosin Reservoir, an event that has passed into legend, compared in history with the retreat of the Ten Thousand Greeks under Xenophon from Persia two and a half thousand years earlier.

President Truman declined to stand for re-election in 1952 in the face of the almost universal unpopularity of the war and a series of political scandals which had tainted the administration. The Democratic candidate, Adlai Stevenson, attempted to distance himself from the president, and General of the Army Dwight Eisenhower won the presidency on a pledge that "I will go to Korea." Between January 20, 1953 when he took office and June 30, American forces increased their pressure on the Chinese in Korea with more conventional bombing and renewed threats of using nuclear weapons in attacks against China if the negotiations were not resolved. On March 5, 1953, Soviet dictator Josef Stalin died and the negotiations began to make progress thereafter. The Korean Armistice was signed with effect from June 30, 1953. Since the beginning of the war in Korea 33,686 American troops had been killed, with 92,134 wounded.

Officially, the Korean War is not over, 65 years after the desperate battles in the wintry mountains of North Korea in the fall of 1950. The 38th Parallel remains the most heavily fortified international border in the world.

BIBLIOGRAPHY

Books

Appleman, Roy E., *East of Chosin: Entrapment and Breakout in Korea, 1950* (College Station: Texas A&M University Press, 1987)

Bruning, John R., *Crimson Sky: the Air Battle for Korea* (London: Brassey's, 1999)

Cagle, Malcolm W. and Manson, Frank A., *The Sea War in Korea* (Annapolis: Naval Institute Press, 1957)

Chen, Jian, *Mao's China and the Cold War* (Chapel Hill: University of North Carolina Press, 2001)

Drury, Bob and Clavin, Tom, *The Last Stand of Fox Company* (New York: Grove Press, 2009).

Futtrell, Robert F., *The United States Air Force in Korea 1950–53* (USAF Historical Division; New York: Duell, Sloan and Pierce, 1961)

Halberstam, David, *The Coldest Winter: America and the Korean War* (New York: Hyperion, 2007)

Hammel, Eric, *Chosin: Heroic Ordeal of the Korean War* (Pacifica: Pacifica Press, 2007)

Hastings, Sir Max, *The Korean War* (New York: Simon and Schuster, 1987)

Marolda, Edward J. (ed.), *The United States Navy in the Korean War* (Annapolis: Naval Institute Press, 2013)

Montross, Lynn and Canzona, Nicholas A., *U.S. Marine Operations in Korea 1950–53,* Vol. I: *The Pusan Perimeter* (Washington DC: US Marine Corps, 1955)

_____, *U.S. Marine Operations in Korea 1950–53,* Vol. II: *The Inchon-Seoul Operation* (Washington DC: US Marine Corps, 1955)

_____, *U.S. Marine Operations in Korea 1950–53,* Vol. III: *The Chosin Reservoir Campaign* (Washington DC: US Marine Corps, 1955)

Mossman, Billy C., *Ebb and Flow: November 1950–July 1951.* United States Army in the Korean War (Washington DC: Center of Military History, 1990)

Owen, Joseph R., *Colder Than Hell: A Marine Rifle Company at Chosin Reservoir* (Annapolis: Naval Institute Press, 1996)

Ridgway, Matthew B., *The Korean War* (New York: Da Capo Press, 1986)

Russ, Martin, *Breakout: The Chosin Reservoir Campaign, November 1950* (New York: Penguin, 2000)

Salmon, Andrew, *Scorched Earth, Black Snow; Britain and Australia in the Korean War 1950* (London: Aurum Press, 2011)

_____, *To The Last Round: The Epic British Stand on the Imjin River, Korea 1951* (London: Aurum Press, 2009)

Schnabel, James F., *Policy and Direction, The First Year.* United States Army in the Korean War (Washington DC: Center of Military History, 1992)

Sears, David, *Such Men As These: The Story of the Navy Pilots Who Flew the Deadly Skies of Korea* (New York: Da Capo Press, 2010)

Shisler, Gail B., *For Country and Corps: The Life of General Oliver P. Smith* (Annapolis: Naval Institute Press, 2009)

Smith, Charles R. (ed.), *U.S. Marines in the Korean War* (Washington DC: USMC, 2008)

Stewart, Richard W., *The Korean War: The Chinese Intervention 3 November 1950–24 January 1951* (Washington DC: Center of Military History, 2000)

Stueck, William, *Rethinking the Korean War: A New Diplomatic and Strategic History* (Princeton: Princeton University Press: 2004)

Terry, Addison, *The Battle for Pusan* (Novato: Presidio Press, 2000)

Thompson, Warren, *Naval Aviation in the Korean War: Ships, Men and Aircraft* (Edinburgh: Pen and Sword, 2012)

Articles

Kraus, Charles, *Zhou En-Lai and China's Response to the Korean War* (Washington: Woodrow Wilson Center, 2012) https://www.wilsoncenter.org/publication/zhou-enlai-and-chinas-response-to-the-korean-war

O'Toole, Tony, *The Forgotten Cruise of HMS Triumph and the 13th Carrier Air Group: The First Royal Navy Carrier Force in the Korean War, June–September 1950* (Royal Navy Research Archive, 2005) http://www.royalnavyresearcharchive.org.uk/Article_Forgotten_Cruise.htm#.VcZiWLV8oWk

Rasula, George A. (ed.), "The Chosin Campaign," *The Changjin Journal* http://bobrowen.com/nymas/changjinjournalTOC.html

Roe, Patrick C., *The Chinese Failure At Chosin* (Chosen Few Historical Committee, 1996) http://www.koreanwar.org/html/units/frontline/chosin.htm

Websites

(*Chosin Reservoir, November–December 1951*)
    http://www.chosinreservoir.com/
(*Marine Corps Command and Unit Reports: Korean War*) http://
    www.koreanwar.org/html/usmc_korean_war_records.html

Interviews by the author

Colonel William E. Barber, Jr., Fox Company, 2nd Battalion,
    7th Marines, May 1991.
Major General Raymond G. Davis; 1st Battalion, 7th Marines,
    April and May 1990.
Mr Robert "Bob" Ezell, Fox Company, 2nd Battalion,
    7th Marines, May 1990.
Mr Ernesto "Ernie" Gonzales, Fox Company, 2nd Battalion,
    7th Marines, May 1990.
Captain Thomas J. Hudner, Jr., VF-32, April 1990.
Mr James T. McKelvey, assistant to and friend of President
    Harry S. Truman, June 1970.
Mr Ed McMahon, VMO-6, March 1990.
CDR Ed Phillips, VA-195, February 19, 2016.
Captain Reed King, How Company, 3/7 Marines, January 23,
    2016.

INDEX

Acheson, Dean
armistice negotiations 378
    Chiang Kai-Shek's offer 66, 68, 76
    on China and Soviet Union 362
    on Chinese attack in North Korea 234
    Congressional approval issue 73–74, 75
    Indian Peace proposal for Korea 139
    for invasion of North Korea 16, 144,
        150–151
    Kennan's advice to 64–65, 66
    on Korean "damnable" war 57
    Korean War inquiry (1951) 371
    Korean War outbreak 53, 55, 56,
        58, 62
    and Louis Johnson 68
    MacArthur's removal 364–365, 368
    and MacArthur's speech on Taiwan 90
    meeting with Attlee 351–352
    on prestige and power 63
    for reunification of Korea 138
    and Truman 63
    on US "greatest defeat" 309
African-American servicemen 13–14, 27,
    77, 78, 129–130
Allison, John 142–143
Almond, Gen Edward "Ned"
    on Army sent to Korea 77
    career and reputation 129–132
    on "Chinese laundrymen" 202–203
    Chosin Reservoir campaign 163,
        165–166, 182
    on Collins' Hamhung visit 317
    drive to the Yalu 218–219, 220, 224–
        225, 226–227
    evacuation 332–334, 336–338
    MacArthur's war council (Nov. 28,
        1950) 266
    on Oliver P. Smith 220
    Operation *Chromite* 129
    RCT-31 attack order and retreat 271,
        274, 275–276
    removal from Marine Division
        command 355–356
    retreat 312
    second battle of Seoul (Sept. 1950) 137
    Wilkerson on 13–14

    and Willoughby 157
    and X Corps 276
    Yalu Offensive 241–242, 261–262
Amen, Navy Lt Cdr William T. 221–222
Attlee, Clement 351–352, 369
Australian forces 73, 135, 216, 257
Ayres, Lt Col Harold 81, 82

Banks, Lt Col Charles L. 267, 269, 313,
    329
Banks, Cpt David W. 182, 298
Barber, Cpt William E., Jr. 245–246,
    248–249, 254, 256, 262–263,
    277–278, 279, 287–288, 297, 301,
    302–303, 318
Barr, Maj Gen David G. 166–167, 224,
    227, 274–275, 276, 336, 371
Beall, Lt Col Olin L. 295, 306, 342
Beninghoff, H. Merrell 42
Benson, Pte 1st Class Kenneth 254–255,
    257
Bradley, Gen Omar 15, 63, 66, 69, 87, 203,
    310, 350–352, 364–365, 368, 371, 372
Bridges, Styles 67
British forces 375–376
    British ships 73, 102, 105–106, 118–
        119, 133–135, 137
    HMS *Triumph* 72–73, 82–83, 84,
        85–86, 99, 100, 105–106, 117–120,
        133–134, 135, 137
    Royal Marines 133, 224, 225, 279–285,
        286, 305, 313, 320, 321, 328, 343
    Royal Navy 72–73, 118, 137
Brown, Ensign Jesse L. 25–27, 29–30, 164
Bush, George H. W. 16

Cafferata, Pte 1st Class Hector "Moose"
    254–255, 256, 257, 303
Cairo Conference (1943) 39
Cates, Gen Clifton B. 94, 219, 220
Cevoli, Lt Cdr Dick 24, 25, 26
Chiang Kai-Shek 39, 53, 66–69, 87, 89,
    138, 139, 140
China Lobby 67, 140, 143, 149, 363
Chinese forces *see* People's Liberation Army
    (PLA); People's Volunteer Army (PVA)

Chosin Reservoir campaign (1950) 18–22, 28, 155–156, 179–180
  breakout 292–308
  evacuation 288–289
  map 265
  retreat 312–332
Church, Gen John 80
Churchill, Winston 351
Clubb, Edmund O. 149–150
Cold War 20, 32–33, 34, 64, 159, 351
Collins, Gen J. Lawton 76, 126, 317, 354, 371
Commonwealth troops 73, 100, 118, 119, 374–375
Communism 32–35, 48–49
Craig, Brig Gen Edward A. 95–96, 115, 336, 342

Davies, John Paton 149–150
Davis, Lt Col Raymond G. 108–110, 182, 193–194, 206–207, 220, 238, 249, 259–260, 262, 297–306, 318, 326
Dean, Gen William 81
Democratic People's Republic of Korea (DPRK) 31, 35, 51–52, 55–56
Dewey, Thomas E. 62–63, 139
Doyle, Adm James H. 126, 127, 337–338
Drake, Cpt Richard E. 258
Drysdale, Lt Col Douglas B. 224, 280–282, 284–285, 286, 320, 321, 343
Dulles, John Foster 124, 139–140, 142

Eaton, 1st Lt Jim 242, 297
Edson, Col Hal 169, 174
Eisenhower, Gen Dwight 121–122, 358, 379
Elliott, Gunnery Sgt Bert E. 266, 267
Eulsa Treaty (1905) 38
Ezell, Pte Bob 245

Faith, Lt Col Don Carlos 227, 238–240, 243, 244, 252–253, 261–262, 271–275, 292–293, 294, 296–297
Faureck, Cpt Frank J. 266, 269
Fehrenbach, T. R. 77
Foote, Cdr Harlan 223, 305
Freeman, Col Paul 232, 234, 344

Gallagher, Pte James 192–193
Garton, 1st Lt W. P. 171
Gault, Sgt Robert B. 305, 328
Gay, Maj Gen Hap 174, 177
Gonzales, Mne Pte Ernie 21–22, 209, 226, 245, 248, 288
Grachev, Cpt Mijael 221–222

Graeber, 1st Lt William 190, 191

Hargett, 1st Lt Ernest C. 197, 330–331
Harriman, Averill 73, 74, 75, 88, 89, 90–91, 364–365
Harris, 1st Lt Howard H. 197–198, 251, 298
Harris, Maj Gen T. Field 223, 290, 305, 320
Hellfire Valley 282–283, 319, 321
Hering, Cpt Eugene R. 288–289
Hill, 2nd Lt Ty 192
Hill, Maj Gen William P. T. 208
Ho Chi Minh 34
Hodes, Brig Gen Henry I. 224, 239, 258, 273, 274–275
Hodge, Lt Gen John R. 41–42, 47, 49–50
Hu Seng 346, 356
Hudner, Lt (jg) Thomas J., Jr. 25–27, 29–30, 164, 293
Hudson, 1st Lt William G. 65
Hulbert, Homer 50
Hwachon Dam 376–377

Imjin River, battle of (Apr. 22–25, 1951) 375–376
Inchon, invasion of (1871) 36
Inchon, invasion of (1950) see Operation Chromite and aftermath
India, peace proposal for Korea 139–140
Inks, Cpt Jim 323–324

Japan
  First Sino-Japanese War (1893–94) 37
  Greater East Asia Co-Prosperity Sphere 38
  Japan–Korea Annexation Treaty (1910) 38
  Japan–Korea Treaty (1876) 36–37
  reaction to MacArthur's dismissal 367–368
  reformation of by MacArthur 49
  Russo-Japanese War (1904–05) 38
  WWII and conscription of Koreans 39
Johnson, Lt Col Harold "Johnny" 173–174
Johnson, Louis A. 56, 66, 68–69, 70, 71, 76, 90–91, 371
Jones, Maj Robert C. 294, 295
Joy, Adm C. Turner 94, 127, 220

Kanouse, Pte 1st Class James 256
Kapaun, Cpt Chaplain Emil 177–178
KATUSAs 175, 238–239, 294

Kennan, George 64–65, 66, 123, 139–140, 150
Kim, Il-Sung 31, 35, 42, 44–46, 51–52, 54–55, 140, 141, 145, 151
King, 1st Lt Reed 70
Kingston, 2nd Lt Robert C. 228
Kiser, 1st Lt Harrol "Chuck" 185, 186–187, 189
Knowland, William F. 67, 143, 373
Koone, Cpl Howard W. 248
Korea
  China and The Hermit Kingdom 35–36, 37
  General Sherman incident with US (1866–71) 36
  Japan–Korea Annexation Treaty (1910) 38
  Japan–Korea Treaty (1876) 36–37
  Kim Il-Sung and Korean nationalism 35
  Kim Il-Sung and Soviet occupation of North Korea 44–46
  Kim Il-Sung and Soviet-backed Democratic People's Republic of Korea 51–52
  Korea and European powers 37
  Korea–US Treaty (1882) 37
  Korean Empire (1897–1910) 37, 43
  March 1st Movement 38, 44
  nationalist opposition to Japanese rule 38–39
  Syngman Rhee and Korean Provisional Government in exile 42–44
  Syngman Rhee and US-backed republic of Korea 46–49
  Syngman Rhee as President of the Republic of Korea 51
  UN recognition of independence 50–51
  US lack of interest in Korea (1945–50) 49–50
  US occupation and 38th Parallel 41–42
  World War II and aftermath 39–41
Korean Liaison Office (KLO) 53–54
Korean People's Army (KPA) 51, 52
Korean War (1950–53)
  background
    American faulty analysis of Communism 20, 31–35
    North vs. South (1948–50) 52–53
    Soviet- and China-backed invasion of South 54–55, 56
    US denial of risk of war 53–54, 55–56
  first 9 weeks of warfare

MacArthur's meeting with Chiang Kai-Shek 87, 89
MacArthur's proposal for amphibious operation at Inchon 88–89
MacArthur's speech on Taiwan 89–91
Naktong Bulge, first battle of (Aug. 1950) 103–108
Naktong Bulge, second battle of (Sept. 1950) 115–117
North Korean invasion and US unpreparedness 57–58
North Korean invasion (first battle of Seoul, June 1950) 60–62, 65
Truman's decision to commit ground troops 75–76
Truman's failure to seek Congressional support 73–75
UN Security Council resolution and Truman's decision to go to war 69
US and ROK forces' retreat (July 29–Aug. 5) 99–100
US evacuation of American nationals 60, 62, 65–66
US fear of defeat and decline in Truman's popularity 84–85
US government's rejection of Chiang Kai-Shek's help 66–69, 76
US unpreparedness and defense spending reduction 71–72
wages of hubris 120
see also Chosin Reservoir campaign (1950); Operation *Chromite* and aftermath
Krulak, Col Victor 129
Kulbes, Cpt Philip A. 264–265, 266
Kurcaba, 1st Lt Joseph R. 298, 327

Ladd, Capt Fred 81
Lawrence, Maj James F. 319, 326
Lee, 1st Lt Kurt Chew-Een 112–113, 185, 187, 189, 298–299, 301–302, 327
Lei, Yingfu 141–142
Li, Hung-Chang 37
Li, Xiu 346–347
Lie, Trygvie 58, 378
Lin, Marshal Biao 152
Litzenberg, Col Homer L.
  background and role 110
  battle of the Chosin Reservoir (Nov. 27–28, 1950) 262
  beginning of the war 181–182, 196, 198, 199
  breakout to Hagaru-ri 297, 300, 303, 306

drive to the Yalu 224, 225, 226
Hagaru-ri actions 287
Olin Beall on 342
relief of Fox Company 278, 279
retreat 318–319, 326
Yalu Offensive 239, 240–241, 242,
    244, 258–260
Lockwood, Lt Col Randolph S. D. 182,
238, 241, 260, 262, 319
Luce, Henry 311

MacArthur, Gen Douglas
and Almond 130, 131, 132, 334
career and reputation 121–124
communiqué (Nov. 24, 1950) 229–230
communiqué re. possible offer of
    ceasefire to China 360–361
criticism of his performance 349–350
denial of Chinese threat 27–28, 166–
    167, 200–201, 204–205
dismissal of 364–370, 372, 374

establishment of Korean Liaison Office
    (KLO) 53–54
and Franklin Roosevelt 123
on Korea 49–50
Korean War
    1st Marine Division 114
    Chosin Reservoir campaign 163,
        169–170, 333–334
    command of Eighth Army 354
    contingency plans for occupation of
        North Korea 144
    first report of war 57
    "home by Christmas" pledge 28,
        311
    Inchon invasion see Operation
        Chromite and aftermath
    invasion of North Korea 144,
        146–147, 148
    meeting with Chiang Kai-Shek 87,
        89, 138, 139
    Naktong, first battle of (Aug. 1950)
        103
    Operation Bluehearts 125
    personal visit to Korea (Nov. 1950)
        226
    redeployment of X Corps 332
    request for US ground troops 75–76
    Supreme Allied Commander of UN
        Forces 69
    talk of atomic bomb 351–352
    on uniting Eighth Army and X
        Corps 312
    war council (Nov. 28, 1950) 266

X Corps withdrawal 306
Korean War inquiry (1951) 371–373
Lei and Mao on 141–142
"MacArthur's Bataan gang" 53, 88,
    122, 130, 156, 229
Mansergh on 349
meeting with Truman (Wake Island,
    1950) 154–155, 166
New York Times on 76
"Old Soldiers Never Die" speech 370
on "the Oriental mind" 169–170
Panikkar on 160
and reformation of Japan 49
and Syngman Rhee 46
and Truman 122, 123, 124, 350, 351–
    352, 358–359, 361–362, 364–366
and US occupation of Korea 41
and US tradition of apolitical military
    leadership 358–361
Veterans of Foreign Wars speech 89–90,
    138–139, 141
and Walton Walker 88
Wilkerson on 13, 14–15
and Willoughby 156–158, 167
McAuliffe, Gen Anthony 78
McCaffrey, Lt Col William ("Bill") J. 158,
    290
McCarthy, Joseph 54, 67, 125, 149, 154,
    158, 353
McCarthy, 1st Lt Robert 248, 256–257
McCloy, John J. 47–48
Mace, Sam 309
MacLachlen, Lt Cdr Ian 118
McLaughlin, Maj John N. 283–284
MacLean, Col Allan 227, 239–240,
    243–244, 261–262, 271–273
McMahon, Mne Aviator Ed 22, 113–114,
    213
Main Supply Route (MSR) 179
Malone, George 67
Mansergh, Gen Leslie 347–348
Mao Zedong
    Communism and nationalism 34–35
    on fighting 1st Marine Division 206
    involvement with Korean War 140–
        142, 145, 151, 152
    and Kim Il-Sung 45, 51, 54–55
    and Korean Communists 39
    and MacArthur's meeting with Chiang
        Kai-Shek 87
    Ninth Army Group citation 339
    and North-Korean invasion 71
    Panikkar's view of 147
    proclamation of People's Republic of
        China 53

on PVA casualties 341
rejection of UN ceasefire-in-place
    Resolution 353–354
and Stalin 363
Wake Island 153
Marshall, Gen George
    and Almond 129, 130
    and Chiang Kai-Shek's offer 66, 68
    and invasion of North Korea 144, 146,
        148–149
    and Korean War inquiry (1951) 371,
        372
    McCarthy's call for dismissal of 353
    meeting with Attlee 351–352
    and removal of MacArthur 364–365
    return as Defense Secretary 91
    and Truman 63
    Wilkerson on 15, 16
Marshall Plan 64
Martin, Joseph 363–364
Michaelis, Col John 79, 345
Milburn, Maj Gen Frank 171–172, 174
Milne, Lt Col Harry T. 313, 321, 329
Morehouse, R Adm Albert K. 220
Morris, Maj Warren 278–279, 320, 326
Muccio, John J. 58, 60, 75
Murphy, Lt Jack 163
Murray, Col Raymond L. 111, 208, 218,
    224, 225, 239–240, 251, 258–259,
    260, 315, 316, 342
Myers, Maj Reginald R. 270–271, 286

Naktong Bulge, first battle of (Aug. 1950)
    103–108
Naktong Bulge, second battle of (Sept.
    1950) 115–117
Nieh Jung-Chen 149
North Korean Air Force 60, 91, 99
North Korean People's Army (NKPA)
    4th Division 104, 106, 108
    9th Division 116
    advance (July 29–Aug. 5) 99–100
    battle ready 79–80
    camouflaged gunboats 119
    divisions from Chinese People's
        Liberation Army 140
    as guerrilla force 151
    II Corps 162
    loss of air support 99
    T-34 tanks 81–82
    victory over US and UN forces 84–85,
        86–87
Northeast Anti-Japanese United Army 45

Olson, Sgt Robert 190

Operation Black List Forty 42
Operation Bluehearts 125
Operation Chromite and aftermath
    Gen MacArthur's "brilliant gamble"
        88–89, 125–128, 137–138
    military preparation
        Gen Oliver P. Smith 128–129,
            131, 132
        Lt Gen Edward "Ned" Almond
            129–132
        Lt Gen Lemuel C. Shepherd, Jr. 131
    operations
        deception operation 132–133
        Inchon landing (map) 101
        invasion of Inchon 133–135
        second battle of Seoul (Sept. 1950)
            135–138
    post-Inchon
        Chinese involvement 138–142, 145,
            147, 149, 151–152, 153
        Chinese military intervention 156
        Soviet involvement 151, 152–153
        US decision to invade North Korea
            142–144, 146–151, 154–155
        US invasion of North Korea
            155–160
Operation Firedog 73
Operation Plan 114-50; 167–168
Operation Rugged 359, 361–362
Operation Tailboard 164–165
Ormond, Lt Col Robert 173–174, 176
Owen, 2nd Lt Joseph (Joe) R. 93, 94,
    111–112, 113, 164, 165, 183–184,
    185–186, 187–189, 214, 356

Pace, Frank 75, 76, 154, 366
Paek, General Sun Yup 168, 171–172,
    173, 174, 345
Panikkar, K. M. 147, 149, 160
Partridge, Gen Earl "Pat" 58, 60
Partridge, Lt Col John 223, 322, 329
Peng Dehuai, Marshal 24, 152, 153, 205,
    228, 250, 339, 341, 377
Peng Deqing 340–341
People's Liberation Army (PLA) 51, 79,
    140, 141, 152–153
People's Volunteer Army (PVA)
    58th Division 199, 229, 239, 242, 285,
        287, 315
    59th Division 229, 239, 242, 253–254,
        257, 263, 277, 286, 287, 307, 315
    60th Division 199, 229, 239, 241, 242,
        260, 307, 315, 316
    80th Division 229, 239, 252, 271, 296,
        307, 315

89th Division 229, 242, 243, 250, 251–252, 259, 307, 315, 316
115th Division 175, 176
116th Division 171, 175
124th Division 180–181, 184, 194–195, 197, 199
125th Division 181
126th Division 181, 218
casualty figures 339–341
creation 152–153
limited supplies 214–215
Ninth Army Group 28–29, 141, 205, 228–229, 261, 308, 316, 339, 341–342
Thirteenth Army Group 231
US–China battles and stabilization of line of resistance (Jan.– June 1951) 356–357
weaknesses and strengths 345–347
Peterson, 1st Lt Elmo 248, 254, 256, 278
Phillips, Lt (jg) Ed 376–377
Podolak, Mne Pte 1st Class Bruno 264–265, 269
Powell, Gen Colin 10, 13
Puller, Lt Col Lewis B. "Chesty" 110–111, 132, 208, 224, 225, 260, 275, 280–282, 313, 318, 324
The Pusan Perimeter 87, 98

Radford, Adm Arthur W. 70, 94, 126
Reeves, Pte 1st Class Ed 212–213
Rhee, Syngman 38–39, 42–44, 46–49, 51, 52, 167
Richardson, Sgt Bill 177–178
Ridge, Lt Col Thomas L. 236, 264–265, 267, 268, 269, 270, 285, 305, 313, 329–330
Ridgway, Maj Gen Matthew B. 88–89, 146, 163–164, 169, 238, 334, 354–356, 359, 361–362, 367, 376
Ritter, Sgt Paul 96, 216, 334, 335
ROK (Republic of Korea) Army
1st Division 165, 168, 172
3rd Division 105, 165, 166, 274–275
Chosin Reservoir campaign 156–166, 202
collapse 58, 69, 82
evacuation 336, 337, 338
I Corps 166, 170, 179, 237, 274, 333
II Corps 165, 167, 171, 231, 232, 237, 241
III Corps 377
number of troops and equipment 52–53
reputation 80, 81
retreat (July 29–Aug. 5) 99–100

ROK Marines 135, 333
Roosevelt, Franklin D. 40, 44, 49, 62, 123
Roosevelt, Theodore 43
Rusk, Dean 41, 142, 150

Schmuck, Col Donald M. "Buck" 235–236, 279, 286
Scott, Hugh 144
Seoul, first battle of (June 1950) 57–58, 60–62
Seoul, liberation of (March 1951) 359
Seoul, second battle of (Sept. 1950) 135–138
Shelnutt, Cpt John C. 264–265, 268–269
Shepherd, Gen Lemuel C. Jr. 127, 131, 182, 315, 336
Sherman, Adm Forrest 92, 94, 126, 127, 371
Shufeldt, Cdre Robert W. 36, 37
Sitter, Cpt Carl L. 264, 280–282, 284, 286
Smith, Lt Col Brad 80, 81–82
Smith, Gen Holland McTyeire "Howlin' Mad" 128, 342
Smith, Gen Oliver P.
background and role 114, 128–129
cold weather experience 208
drive to the Yalu 204, 218–220, 223, 225, 226
evacuation 336, 337
evacuation of wounded 289–290
Hagaru-ri actions 287, 307
invasion of North Korea 131–132, 168, 182
mass funeral 327–328
Olin Beall on 342
RCT-31 attack order and retreat 274–275, 276–277
and Ridgway 355
withdrawal 312–315, 318, 329, 331–332, 343
Yalu Offensive 236, 237–238, 241, 260
Smith, Walter Bedell 203
Song, Gen Shilun 29, 205, 206, 228–229, 261, 287, 308
Soviet Union
and Communism/anti-colonialism 33–35
and Democratic People's Republic of Korea (DPRK) 51–52
and Kim Il-Sung 46
and Korean War 31–32, 84, 151, 152–153, 172–173, 221–222, 362–363
and Truman 48–49, 53, 55
and US "containment" policy 64–65

and US occupation of Korea 41
Stalin, Josef 33–34, 39, 46, 48, 54–55,
    62–64, 69, 71, 145, 151–152, 363, 379
Stamford, Cpt Edward P. 239, 253, 263,
    273, 293, 295
Stroemple, Lt Bob 269–270
Sudong, battle of (Oct. 1950) 179–194,
    202

Taft, Robert A. 74, 90, 369
Taft, William Howard 123–124
Taiwan 38, 53, 68, 89–90, 138–139, 140
Taplett, Lt Col Robert D. "Tap" 217, 297,
    300, 305
Thompson, Col Percy 169, 174
Toktong Pass, battle of 21–22
"Treadway" bridge 322–324, 329,
    330–331
Truman, Harry S.
    decline in popularity 85
    desegregation of armed forces 77
    Johnson's resignation 91
    Korean War
        approval of NSC 81/1 Memorandum
            144
        beginning of war 56, 58, 62–64,
            69, 76
        Eighth Army command 88
        failure to seek Congressional support
            73–75, 373
        invasion of North Korea and mid-
            term elections (1950) 154, 159
        rejection of Chiang Kai-Shek's offer
            of help 66–69, 76
        talk of atomic bomb 310–311,
            350–353
    limit on defense spending 71
    and MacArthur 122, 124, 350, 351–
        352, 358–359, 361–362, 364–366
    and MacArthur's dismissal 364–367,
        368–370, 372, 374
    and MacArthur's speech on Taiwan
        90–91
    McCarthy's call for impeachment of
        353
    meeting with Attlee 351–352
    meeting with MacArthur (Wake Island,
        1950) 154–155, 166
    radio broadcast for "free united Korea"
        138
    and Soviet Communism/Truman
        Doctrine 48–49, 53, 55
    and Stalin 64
    on Taiwan 138
    Wilkerson on 15, 16

on Zhou En-Lai's "attempt to blackmail
    the UN" 140

United Nations 16, 50, 140
    Korea-related Resolutions 62, 69,
        73–74, 147–148, 149, 353–354,
        359, 378
    Participation Act 74
United States
    "containment" policy re. Soviet
        expansion 64–65
    denial of risk of war and unpreparedness
        53–54, 55–56
    faulty analysis of Communism 20,
        32–35
    General Sherman incident with Korea
        (1866–71) 36
    Korea–US Treaty (1882) 37
    National Security Council
        Memorandum NSC 81/1 144
    occupation of Korea and 38th Parallel
        41–42
    post-WWII analysis of situation in Far
        East 40–41
    and republic of Korea (South) 52–53
Unsan, battle of (Oct.–Nov. 1950)
    174–179
US Air Force
    3rd Bombardment Wing 59, 133
    8th Fighter Bomber Wing 59, 60,
        65, 172
    13th Air Force 59, 117–118
    51st Fighter Interceptor Wing 59, 153,
        172–173
    68th Squadron 59, 62, 65–66
    339th Squadron 59, 62, 65
    Fifth Air Force 58–59, 60, 216
    Hwachon Dam mission 376
    inter-service battles 69–71
    Operation Chromite 135
US Army 77–78, 347–349, 357
    2nd Infantry Division 117, 125, 155,
        172, 231–232, 234–235, 309–310,
        344, 377
    3rd Infantry Division 224, 290, 317,
        332, 333, 337, 377
    5th Cavalry Regiment 173, 174, 177
    7th Infantry Division 89, 127–128,
        137, 163, 166, 170, 218, 224, 226–
        227, 237–239, 244, 258, 279–280,
        290, 332–333, 336–338
    8th Cavalry Regiment 169, 173,
        174–178
    24th Infantry Division 76–77, 78–79,
        81, 86, 99, 100, 107

25th Infantry Division 86–87, 99, 232

32nd Infantry Division 227, 228, 238–239, 253, 271–272

34th Infantry Regiment 77, 80–81, 82

92nd Infantry Division 14, 129–130

Eighth Army 13, 28, 78, 87–88, 103, 108, 130, 148, 162–163, 166–168, 172, 179, 182, 200, 219 220, 225–226, 230–235, 266, 276, 310, 344–347, 354–357, 374, 378
racism 78–79, 81, 129–130, 202–203
RCT-31 212–213, 227, 237, 238, 239–240, 243–244, 252–253, 262, 292–297
split command 163–164
Task Force Smith 80, 81–82

X Corps 13–14, 130–131, 148, 162–163, 166, 170, 182, 206, 218–219, 231–232, 237, 266, 276, 280, 290, 306, 310, 332, 333–335

XXIV Corps 41

US Marine Corps 69, 70–71, 92–97, 107–108, 342–343
1st Marine Division 24, 27, 89, 92–96, 103, 108–114, 125, 127–128, 131, 161–163, 204, 206, 224–225, 237, 239–240, 261, 263, 276–277, 315, 331–332, 336, 355–356, 374, 378
5th Marine Regiment 21, 24–25, 95, 97, 100, 103–104, 108–109, 111, 125, 134–135, 162, 206, 217–219, 225–227, 237–243, 249–252, 258–260, 263, 278–279, 308, 312–313, 324, 330, 334, 342–343
7th Marine Regiment 24–25, 108–110, 114, 133, 162, 165, 179–199, 206, 217–221, 225–226, 237, 240–242, 251–252, 258–260, 278, 312–313, 316–317, 324, 328, 334, 342, 374
3/7 Battalion 197–198, 241, 259, 260, 278, 297, 303, 305, 307, 318, 319–320, 326–327, 329
casualty figures 338–339
Charlie Company 183, 192, 195, 198–199, 204, 249, 257, 259–260, 262, 298–299, 301–302, 318, 325, 327–328
Dog-Easy Company 301, 303–304, 318
Fox Company 21–22, 183, 194, 241, 244–250, 254–257, 259–261, 262–263, 277–279, 285–288, 297, 302–303, 305, 318
George Company 197, 264, 278,

280–282, 284, 286, 301, 303–304, 320, 326
How Company 197–198, 241, 267, 268, 269, 301, 302, 303–304, 326
Item Company 197–198, 267, 300–301, 320, 326
Marine Air Group-33; 95, 97, 161, 165, 179, 190, 215–216, 217, 277, 290

US Navy 69, 70–72, 84

US ships 36–37, 65, 72, 82–86, 91–92, 97, 99–100, 104–105, 129, 134–135, 164–165, 221–222, 280, 290, 333–338, 364–365, 376
Badoeng Strait 91, 92, 97, 99, 102, 104, 115, 161, 168, 216, 335
Boxer 72, 91, 92, 168, 364–365
Leyte 27–28, 29, 164, 168, 216, 221, 222, 293, 297, 338
Philippine Sea 91–92, 100, 102, 108, 116, 119, 120, 168, 216, 221, 364–365
Sicily 91, 92, 99, 102, 115, 161, 168, 334, 335
Valley Forge 72, 82–84, 85, 99, 102, 116, 119, 168, 222, 297, 338

Van Winkle, Sgt Archie 185, 186, 187, 189, 194

Vandenberg, Gen Hoyt S. 203–204, 371, 372

Vietnam War 20, 32, 34, 150, 364

Walker, Lt Gen Walton 87–88, 103, 163, 169, 200–201, 202–203, 232, 266, 354

Wilcox, Cpt Myron E. 180–181, 182–183

Wilkerson, Col Lawrence B. 10–17

Willoughby, Gen Charles A. 53, 130, 156–159, 166–167, 169, 172, 178–179, 311–312

Wilson, Woodrow 34, 44

Winston, LT Col Waldon C. 330

winter conditions 206–217

Xie Fang 205, 206

Yalta Conference (1945) 39–40

Yudam-ni, battle of (1950) 24–25

Zhang Renchu 339, 341

Zhang Yixiang 242, 340

Zhou En-Lai 87, 140, 147, 150, 151, 152, 153

ABOUT THE AUTHOR

Thomas McKelvey Cleaver has been a published writer for the past 40 years. He is a regular contributor to *Flight Journal* magazine. He has had a lifelong interest in the Korean War and this work is the product of 25 years of research. He is the author of *Aces of the 78th Fighter Group* and *F4F Wildcat and F6F Hellcat Aces of VF-2*, as well as *Fabled Fifteen: The Pacific War Saga of Carrier Air Group 15* and *The Bridgebusters: The True Story of the Catch-22 Bomb Group*. During his 30 years as a screenwriter in Hollywood, he wrote the cult classic *The Terror Within* and worked as a supervising producer on a number of TV and cable series. He served in the US Navy in Vietnam.